Trade, plunder and settlement

Trade, plunder and settlement

Maritime enterprise and the genesis of the British Empire, 1480–1630

KENNETH R. ANDREWS
Professor of History, University of Hull

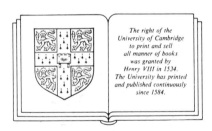

The right of the
University of Cambridge
to print and sell
all manner of books
was granted by
Henry VIII in 1534.
The University has printed
and published continuously
since 1584.

CAMBRIDGE UNIVERSITY PRESS

Cambridge

London New York New Rochelle

Melbourne Sydney

Published by the Press Syndicate of the University of Cambridge
The Pitt Building, Trumpington Street, Cambridge CB2 1RP
32 East 57th Street, New York, NY 10022, USA
10 Stamford Road, Oakleigh, Melbourne 3166, Australia

First published 1984
Reprinted 1986

Printed in the United States of America

Library of Congress catalogue card number: 84–5044

British Library cataloguing in publication data
Andrews, Kenneth R.
Trade, plunder and settlement.
1. Discoveries (in geography) - English
2. Voyages and travels
I. Title
910'.942 G242
ISBN 0 521 25760 3 hard covers
ISBN 0 521 27698 5 paperback

Contents

List of figures

Preface

To the best of my knowledge the last reasonably full account of this subject appeared in the third, revised edition of James Williamson's *Short History of British Expansion, Vol. 1: the Old Colonial Empire*, which was published in 1945. Since then the world has changed and history has changed with it. Professional historians have turned decisively away from the Eurocentric or Anglocentric approach characteristic of Williamson, Sir William Foster, V. T. Harlow, A. P. Newton and all that generation of imperial historians and have applied their industry and imagination to early-modern West Africa, India, North America and so forth perceived in their particular regional or national contexts. Conversely the study of Little England has become so intensive and specialized that political and economic historians are separate tribes, largely ignorant of each other's labours and equally indifferent to the perverse and peripheral efforts of those few who still regard the maritime, commercial and colonial expansion of England as an important historical phenomenon. Thus the disintegration of the British Empire has been accompanied by a disintegration of its history and we are left with a sadly out-dated account of a movement which in the long run deeply affected both this country and various other parts of the world. It is outdated not only because historical scholarship since has greatly enlarged our knowledge and understanding of the period, but also because we ourselves have changed. It is true that in various quarters a nostalgia for the glories of empire lingers on, but I believe that thoughtful people now expect a historian to take a more detached and critical view of the expansion. Personally I have been anti-imperialist since 1939, when I shocked my school-mates and masters by forecasting (without much argument or evidence) the downfall of the Empire, and some sense of commitment to the subject has helped me to persist in and carry through what proved to be a difficult task, involving the re-interpretation of the subject both in detail and in general from a modern viewpoint. Nevertheless I wish to stress that I have not been motivated by any political or philosophical concern: I ceased to subscribe to any sort of marxism nearly twenty years ago and to any sort of political movement ten years before that. I have no more desire to decry the expansion than to glorify it. Nor do I intend to denigrate the work of the historians whom I have mentioned: it will be obvious to the attentive reader that I owe an enormous debt to them and that without their researches and especially their editions of the sources this present undertaking would have been unthinkable. As first-rate scholars, they would have been among the first to recognize that a mere synthesis of received opinion would in present circumstances be worse than useless and that a systematic revision of the subject in the light primarily of the basic sources had to be attempted notwithstanding the probability of mistakes in the handling of so large a body of material.

I thank all those who over the years have taken an interest in my work: they are too many to mention individually. David Quinn, my mentor of old, encouraged me to undertake this project and commented helpfully on several chapters; Howell Lloyd read the introduction with his usual critical power. I am grateful to both of them for their support. I thank also the two anonymous readers whose most valuable advice came to me through the Cambridge University Press when I submitted part of the book in draft. Throughout the writing of it I have, moreover, much appreciated the lively interest taken in its composition by my friend L. V. Hebblewhite.

Cottingham
Yorks

K.R.A.

Abbreviations

BL	British Library
Cal. Salis. MSS	*Calendar of the Manuscripts of the Marquis of Salisbury*
Cal. SPD	*Calendar of State Papers Domestic*
Cal. SP Span.	*Calendar of State Papers Spanish*
EconHR	*Economic History Review*
EHR	*English Historical Review*
HAHR	*Hispanic American Historical Review*
HCA	High Court of Admiralty
PN	R. Hakluyt (ed.), *The Principal Navigations, Voiages, Traffiques and Discoveries of the English Nation* (12 vols., Glasgow, 1903–5)
PN (1589)	R. Hakluyt (ed.), *The Principall Navigations, Voiages and Discoveries of the English Nation* (London, 1589: facsimile edition, Cambridge, 1965)
PRO	Public Record Office
Purchas	S. Purchas (ed.), *Hakluytus Posthumus or Purchas his Pilgrimes* (20 vols., Glasgow, 1905–7)

Introduction

J. A. Froude, the Victorian prophet of empire, looked back for inspiration to the exploits of the Elizabethans. Those heroic endeavours, he claimed, had inaugurated a new era in English history, and Richard Hakluyt in recording them for posterity had compiled 'the Prose Epic of the modern English nation'.[1] Through Froude, through later imperial historians and through the patriotic nostalgia of post-imperial England Hakluyt's rhetoric still echoes:

> so in this most famous and peerlesse governement of her most excellent Majesty, her subjects through the speciall assistance, and blessing of God, in searching the most opposite corners and quarters of the world, and to speake plainly, in compassing the vaste globe of the earth more than once, have excelled all the nations and people of the earth.[2]

When Hakluyt wrote these words in 1589, Englishmen had indeed made some considerable contributions to European exploration of the world, but they had hardly done enough to justify that boast, nor had they much to show as yet for some forty years of effort to expand overseas. More years still were to pass before English ships began to trade in eastern seas and Englishmen began lasting plantations in the New World. Behind the glory of Elizabethan legend and nationalist propaganda lay a long and painful series of failures and disasters, only occasionally relieved by some brilliant feat such as Drake's voyage round the world, or some modest success like the opening of trade with Muscovy. By the end of the reign moreover the Russia trade had disappointed the bright hopes of its founders, and the merchants who had worked so hard to develop trade through Russia into Persia were defeated. The brave and increasingly skilful efforts of English

---

[1] J. A. Froude, *Short Studies in Great Subjects* (4 vols., London, 1891), I, 446.
[2] R. Hakluyt, *The Principall Navigations, Voiages and Discoveries of the English Nation* (1589), sig. *2v.

1

explorers in the search for a northern passage came to nothing and most of the expeditions which attempted to follow Drake's route to the South Sea came to grief. The Elizabethans tried and failed to break into the Guinea trade; they tried and failed to break into the Caribbean slave trade; they tried and failed to establish a colony in North America. They reconnoitred the shores of the Americas from Arauco and the River Plate to California and Baffin Island seeking whatever they might yield – trade, booty, fish, train-oil or the chance to settle. They ventured in hope, often with no fixity of purpose, sometimes because the leaders could not agree, sometimes because they or their backers were too easily distracted from their original aim. Again and again attention shifted from one prospect to another: from the northeast passage to the northwest, back and forth; from Guinea gold to African slaves; from Panama to Magellan's Strait as approaches to the wealth of Peru. The quest for eastern trade was a saga of trial and error on different routes until the final breakthrough in 1600.

Looking back with knowledge of the success which ensued, one can see that between 1550 and 1630 the path of English history did turn in the direction of seaborne empire, but to contemporaries this was by no means an obvious fact even at the close of the period. The nascent empire was struggling for survival in the 1620s. Routed by the Dutch in Indonesia, the East India Company had great difficulty in continuing its operations elsewhere. The sporadic and ill-fated attempts of Englishmen to settle in Guiana since Ralegh's first 'discovery' thereof now approached extinction, and of the three tiny Caribbean colonies founded in this decade one was destroyed by a Spanish expedition in 1629. Virginia, having endured fifteen years of hardship and heavy loss of life as well as capital in maintaining a precarious existence, was severely mauled by the Indians in 1622. The settlement of Newfoundland, which had begun promisingly in 1610, had failed by 1630, leaving only a few tough remnants. In New England the Plymouth colony took root in the years from 1620, but it was small and isolated. Substantial migration to Massachusetts began only in 1630. Nova Scotia, where a colony was started after many delays in 1629, was immediately thereafter sold back to the French.

The gap between the rhetoric and the reality is plain to see, and it provokes certain questions. What caused this movement? How did it arise? What conditions and circumstances shaped its nature and kept it in being? Some attempt to define the historical context and content of the phenomenon as a whole along such lines must come first, since it is fundamental to our analysis. What interest did the monarchs and their ministers take in these enterprises? How deeply was the state involved? The relationship between the crown and its subjects in the promotion and control of overseas ventures was by no means simple, but therein lies the key to many of the peculiar features of the movement. The parts played by various social groups in the direction, financing and conduct of different kinds of enterprise require investigation too. Yet these approaches cannot fully explain why the English found the going so hard. What means could those concerned dispose of, what physical resources of money, shipping, manpower, what mental resources of knowledge and skill? What distance lay between ambition and capability? How far did advancing realism, practical experience or technological progress narrow that gap in the three generations between the last years of Henry VIII and the first years of Charles I? Finally, what motivation sustained this persistence in the face of adversity? What conceptions, hopes, ideals, loyalties or discontents fired all this effort, continually restoring the energy and momentum required to overcome the repeated setbacks? How did those engaged in this work see themselves? What attitudes did they take into the outer world to confront their rivals or to deal with the unknown?

To attempt to discuss these matters without reference to a wider context would imply acceptance of the participants' own narrowly national view of the process of expansion and its historical derivation. England was a part of Europe, and its overseas expansion was part of the much larger process of European expansion. The English learned their geography from Continental masters and apprenticed themselves to the Iberians in the art of navigation. The commercial life of Europe, like its intellectual life, embraced England. The Channel and the North Sea were not barriers, but linked this island to a great network of markets. English exports reached all parts of Europe and were carried beyond its bounds long before England became directly engaged in the oceanic movement. At the same time her imports came from every quarter of the world accessible to European merchants. When the English at last came to take a considerable direct interest in extra-European enterprise they were chiefly reacting to developments on the Continent and more specifically to change in the economic and political relations between England and the Continent.

The age of the 'great discoveries' and of the creation of the Portuguese and Spanish empires was also an age of remarkable prosperity and economic expansion for Europe as a whole, dating from the last quarter of the fifteenth century to the middle of the sixteenth. The rapid growth of population, agriculture and towns stimulated external trade and overseas expansion by increasing demand. In respect of food the growing need was met largely by the extension and development of farming for the market within Europe, but it also had a marked effect upon the fishing industry. Not only did the fishermen exploit their customary grounds more intensively, but they moved further into the Atlantic to exploit new fisheries, especially southwards from Portugal and across the Atlantic to the Newfoundland Banks, and to the Labrador coast for whale. This drive to harvest the sea played an important part in discovery, in the mastering of the ocean and in the initial phase of colonization, both then and later. More important still was the effect of intensified commercial activity upon the demand for precious metals. The revival of the European economy in the later fifteenth century was associated with the promotion of mining in Austria, Bohemia and Hungary and with the swelling stream of African gold. The boom encouraged vigorous exploitation of these sources until they were superseded by the influx of silver from America, which grew large in the middle of the sixteenth century and continued to grow thereafter in response to the further acceleration of European business in the following decades, more especially providing the necessary specie for that most spectacular growth-area of European commerce, oriental trade.

An important feature of this economic expansion was the growth of luxury consumption. The luxury trades boomed, feeding the appetites of the rich with silks, satins, linens and other fine cloths, with wines, sugars and spices, gold and silver ware, jewellery, perfumes and medicaments. Specialized industries like the Nuremberg metal crafts or the silk manufacture of Lucca commanded an international market, and the richest trades interested bankers and princes alike. Such were the exotic trades in Asiatic produce, the 'spices' of the Indies: pepper, cloves, nutmegs, mace, cinnamon, ginger; Chinese and Persian silk, and calicoes and indigo from India, as well as drugs and gems; the cotton, damasks, mohairs, carpets, galls and other precious dyes of the Middle East. Great profit, too, lay in commodities of the Portuguese Atlantic: the ivory, pepper and slaves of Western Africa, the sugar, wines and dyestuffs of the Atlantic islands; and in the lengthening list of Spain's American products – cochineal, cacao, sugar, tobacco and other 'spices' of the West. It was in pursuit of the rich trades that the Portuguese invaded the Indian ocean at the end of the fifteenth century and swiftly deployed their power to create a commercial network reaching to the Moluccas, Macao and Japan, achieving a large share of Euro-Asiatic trade. Those same decades saw the rapid development of the Guinea gold trade and of the sugar plantations of São Thomé, while other islands in the Atlantic were converted from conventional farming to intensive production for the luxury market, which was already extending its tentacles to Brazil before 1550. It was a Spanish attempt to break into oriental trade that led to the discovery of America and the same desire promoted the further exploration of the New World, Magellan's conquest of the Pacific and the eventual linking of China and Peru by way of Mexico and Manila, a silk-for-silver trade. Meanwhile the resources of America were increasingly tapped to satisfy European demand and the transatlantic slave trade developed in response to the demand for labour in Spain's colonies.

The economic dynamo of Europe was thus generating a world-wide trading system. This, however, it did not achieve by seeking export markets for its manufactures or other products – such a misconception of the process could only have arisen in the nineteenth century. On the contrary it strove for imports to feed its various wants, applying force as far as possible to get them cheap, while merchants and governments competed with every available means to gain and protect a share of the richest trades. European overseas expansion in this epoch was fundamentally a commercial movement, an extension of the European trading system, powered by the same forces – ultimately rooted in agrarian growth – which were multiplying mercantile capitalism within Europe. It was not a pacific movement, but an acquisitive and predatory drive for commodities and for the profits to be made on the rich products of the outer world.[3]

The Iberian pursuit of empire often assumed the form of campaigns by soldiers and other adventurers for booty, conquest, tribute and land – for example in Morocco, the Canary Islands and America. The exercise of power to exact a kind of tribute from long-established trades was an important feature of the Portuguese Estado da India.[4] These non-commercial elements in the expansion cannot be ignored, for the corsair and the *conquistador* were its pioneers, looming large in the histories. Generally, however, their enterprise was quickly overtaken by the demands of commerce and the economic power of the merchants. Many of these fighting founders were themselves entrepreneurs, interested in conquering islands or territories to be exploited along business lines within the orbit of the European commercial system: Alonso de Lugo, for example, who undertook the

[3] The overseas expansion was in my view essentially a function of economic expansion within Europe. This does not necessarily contradict Marx's view that the great discoveries, leading to the creation of a world market, greatly stimulated the growth of capitalism. As for the religious aspect of European expansion, it was obviously of great importance, but I make no attempt to deal with it because I am not here concerned to describe the movement but merely to indicate its prime cause.

[4] N. Steensgaard, *The Asian Trade Revolution of the Seventeenth Century* (Chicago, 1974).

conquest and exploitation of Tenerife, La Palma and Gomera in the
Canary Islands in conjunction with Genoese capitalists. In America
those *conquistadores* who could not adapt themselves and their property to the requirements of the European market were speedily
replaced by more businesslike colonists who could. At the other end of
Europe the same pressure of demand caused the Stroganov invasion of
Siberia, extending an already thriving fur empire.[5] Thus the main
driving force of the movement was commercial, even though the types
of people interested and their particular aims, methods and attitudes
varied considerably. For the most part the expansion into and across
the Atlantic was a conquering and colonizing process, which naturally
attracted adventurers with a mind to loot, tribute and land, whereas
the eastward expansion was essentially a trading enterprise. The
empires that resulted differed from each other in important respects,
but the chief source of this difference lay in the differing characters of
the western and eastern worlds. Europe's world-wide empire was a
single system with two main branches which had much in common
and were intertwined and interdependent. This ambivalence was in
due course reproduced in the English overseas movement and in the
peculiar doubleness of the emergent seaborne empire.

Early Tudor England shared the general prosperity of contemporary
Europe. The population, especially that of London, grew, farming for
the market advanced, and above all the woollen cloth industry
expanded in response to rising demand on the Continent. English
cloth exports doubled in quantity between the 1470s and about 1550,
approaching in the peak years a value of nearly a million pounds
sterling.[6] The heavy, unfinished broadcloth of the West Country went
mainly to Antwerp, there to be dressed and dyed for markets all over
northern and central Europe. The lighter, cheaper cloths called kerseys
found their way through Antwerp over the Alps to Italy and many
were dispatched thence to Turkey, the Balkans, Persia. More English
cloths were sold in the Baltic and in the Iberian Peninsula, whence
some were shipped to America. London, already the chief port,
swallowed up more and more of this trade in the reigns of the two
Henries. There members of the Merchants Adventurers Company and
foreign merchants – Italians, Flemings and Germans chiefly – bought
up cloth for export to Antwerp and elsewhere. From Antwerp, too,
England obtained most of her imports, consisting chiefly of luxury
wares. French wines, the produce of Spain and raw materials such as

[5] T. Armstrong, *Yermak's Campaign in Siberia* (London, 1975).
[6] G. D. Ramsay, *The City of London in International Politics at the Accession of Elizabeth Tudor*
(Manchester, 1975), pp. 26–7.

alum, dyestuffs, hemp and iron were notable imports also, and almost the entire bill was in effect paid in cloth.

England's overseas trade was thus already valuable and far-reaching, but her native merchants managed only a minor part of it and their share may well have declined in this period. Aliens exported nearly half the cloth sent to Antwerp, where the remainder passed into foreign hands. Hanseatic merchants controlled most of the Baltic trade and around 1540 the English finally lost their dwindling stake in Anglo-Italian trade. Foreigners were especially dominant in the lucrative import trades. Nor did the growth of exports and imports promote the nation's shipping, which by the mid-century had ceased to operate in the Mediterranean and was rarely to be seen in the Baltic. Even in the thriving London–Antwerp sea link English shipping took second place to Dutch. During Henry VIII's reign many of the outports, unable to compete with London, suffered depression. Only in the southward trades to the Bay of Biscay and the Peninsula did English ships and English merchants hold the lion's share.

Then, in the reign of Edward VI, a wind of change began to blow. Violent trade fluctuations ushered in a prolonged depression in England's commercial mainstay, the so-called Old Drapery, principal feeder of the Antwerp market. Already past its zenith as the commercial nerve-centre of Europe, Antwerp now declined, damaged by financial crisis in the fifties, faced with political troubles and loss of trade in the sixties, largely ruined in the next two decades by the struggle between the Dutch rebels and the Habsburg armies. Severe crisis shook the international economy in the 1550s. England's cloth exports fell well below the levels of the previous period, agricultural prices rose rapidly, dearth and epidemic disease between 1555 and 1560 temporarily reversed the growth of population. This depression marked a transition from the relatively healthy prosperity of early Tudor times to a less spacious age. Population soon began to rise again faster than ever, producing acute population pressure, inflation and a widening gap between rich and poor. In the half century after 1570, though exports gradually recovered, they no longer played their former dynamic rôle in promoting the wealth of the nation. But as the land market boomed and rents soared a minority of the nation profited substantially. Affluence among the nobility, the gentry, the merchants and some others in town and country promoted home demand. A building boom gave rise to new industries – brick-making and glass manufacture, for example. Output of coal and iron increased greatly. Paper manufacture, sugar refining, the silk industry of Spitalfields and a whole range of new textiles – the so-called New Draperies – developed to provide prosperous consumers with luxuries.

These circumstances at home and abroad had a profound effect upon England's overseas enterprise, causing a gradual, cumulative change in its orientation. In the decades from the crisis of the fifties to that of the 1620s it remained difficult to sell English cloth in the main, Continental market. On the other hand the failure of Antwerp and the associated disruption of international trade routes opened up new opportunities and encouraged merchants to develop direct contact with more distant markets where they might not only sell cloth but acquire more cheaply the luxury imports so much in demand at home. Thus the underlying economic pressures upon exports and imports combined to promote a significant change in the composition and geography of the nation's overseas trade and in the ambitions and enterprise of those concerned with it. This was no sudden shift, nor was it achieved easily, since the English had to find their way in competition with entrenched interests and against the fierce hostility of the Iberian powers in their spheres of interest. Nevertheless this was the first phase of a commercial revolution which in the course of the seventeeth century made England into an entrepôt of world trade and the centre of a commercial empire based on the rich trades of the East and West Indies, the Mediterranean and the Levant, Africa and America.

Although the export of cloth through the northwest ports of the Continent remained England's commercial anchor throughout our period, cloth exports played a subordinate rôle in the new trading developments of the Elizabethan-Jacobean era. In some cases – the abortive Guinea and Caribbean enterprises and the East India trade, for example – they played little or no part and in others they were essentially a means to what was almost always the main end: the acquisition of commodities which, if bought at or near their country of origin, would yield great profit either at home or in Europe. The result was that imports of silk, sugar, wines, pepper, currants, tobacco and other exotic goods rose remarkably in this period and brought wealth to the realm because English merchants at the same time secured control of nearly all the country's foreign trade.[7] The tonnage of native shipping doubled between 1570 and 1630 and provincial ports now managed a vigorous and growing share of overseas business. By the end of the period English merchants and ships handled a complex

[7] A. M. Millard, 'The import trade of London, 1600–1640' (unpublished London University Ph.D. thesis, 1956). In general see R. Davis, *English Overseas Trade, 1500–1700* (London, 1973).

network of trade, involving products of many lands. They had exchanged their passive, dependent rôle in Europe's trading system for an active, independent rôle in the world. The East and America were not yet major spheres of the country's overseas trade, but the importance of the Turkey, Mediterranean, Baltic, Muscovy, Morocco, American and East India trades together signalled a decisive change in England's overseas orientation.

The main context and content of Elizabethan-Jacobean expansion were thus commercial. Even so the difference between the eastern and the western wings of the expansion movement was striking. On the one hand a colonial empire of the West was coming into being, the result of Atlantic enterprise in which the men of the West Country – gentry of the western shires as well as merchants of the western ports – played a prominent part. From the first this was an aggressive drive by armed traders bent on breaking into the Portuguese and Spanish Atlantic trades, an unofficial war of trade and reprisals in the course of which emerged ambitions to colonize. This drive was not the main cause of the Anglo-Spanish war (1585–1603), which arose from the political and religious conflict in Europe, but the hostility between the powers transformed the sporadic and ineffectual venturing of the early phase into an Atlantic war. Typical exponents of the bellicose imperialism nourished by this course of events were the Hawkinses of Plymouth, from the pioneering William of Henrician days to his grandson Richard, who wanted to continue the war in 1604 and patronized piracy in the years which followed. Ralegh's vision of empire may well have expressed the ideas and attitudes prevailing among such westward-looking sea-dogs and gentlemen-adventurers, for he saw naval strength as the key to empire, the necessary means of waging oceanic war with Spain, challenging her Atlantic trade and colonial dominion in America. Sea power, trade and overseas empire went together:

This was Themistocles opinion long since, and it is true, That hee that commaunds the sea, commaunds the trade, and hee that is Lord of the Trade of the world is lord of the wealth of the worlde.[8]

The kind of trade he valued most was 'forcible trade' and the kind of expansion he called for and attempted was militant and acquisitively imperialistic. He admired Spain's colonial achievement and urged his countrymen to emulate the courage and endurance of the *conquistadores*.[9]

[8] Cited in P. Lefranc, *Sir Walter Ralegh, Écrivain: l'Oeuvre et les Idées* (Paris, 1968), p. 600. See also p. 189.
[9] *Ibid*. p. 194.

On the other hand the Londoners who led the quest for eastern trade seem to have taken a different view of England's oceanic rôle. The Muscovy Company was not interested in confronting the Iberian powers, but in finding an alternative route to the East in order to avoid conflict. Richard Staper, leader of the Levant Company, sincerely abhorred the activities of English marauders in the Mediterranean, for they invariably injured, he alleged, the merchants' interests.[10] The aims of the East India Company were undoubtedly mercantile in a restricted sense: it eschewed territorial acquisitions and used the substantial force of its shipping only to serve the needs of trade.[11] John Dee, who worked with and for the merchant sponsors of northern discovery and nautical science, expressed ideas they may well have shared in his *General and Rare Memorials pertayning to the Perfect Arte of Navigation* (1577), advocating the establishment of a 'Pety Navy Royal'. This force was to protect 'the skyrts and Purlewes (as it were) of our Brytish, naturall, and appropriate Sea Limits' and to exercise sovereignty in neighbouring seas 'in the most decent, peaceable, and freindly manner', without invading other countries or seeking to monopolize the world in the Iberian fashion. He proposed that some of the funds raised should go 'toward New Forreyn Discoveries making: for Gods glory, the Wealth-Publik and the Honorable Renown of this Ilandish Impire'. It was a peaceful empire of maritime commerce that he envisaged.

But it is easy to overstate the distinction between the two faces of the seaborne expansion. In fact leading Muscovy men backed the commercial assaults on Portuguese Guinea and the Spanish Caribbean, while commercial success in the East always depended on political influence and sea power. Power, whether concealed or overt, was an integral factor in the struggle for the rich trades of East and West alike. On the other hand the Atlantic and the oriental drives had in the long term the same general purpose in view – commercial gain. Though London and the West Country found somewhat different rôles to play, they were not responsible for this fork in the path of expansion, which arose from the broad difference between Asia and America and between Europe's relations with each.

The attitude of the crown towards overseas enterprise and its handling of these matters must be examined primarily in the light of its external policy as a whole. This was concerned chiefly with the security of the realm and with the traditional power-game of western Europe. Queen

[10] K. R. Andrews, 'Sir Robert Cecil and Mediterranean plunder', *EHR*, 87 (1972), 516.
[11] Acts of plunder, reprisal and Anglo-Dutch hostilities notwithstanding – see Ch. 12.

Elizabeth's aims were defensive: to strengthen royal authority within the kingdom, to provide for its defence against invasion and to frustrate the ambitions of foreign powers in Ireland, Scotland and the Netherlands.[12] This does not mean that nothing else mattered. The government did care about English trading interests abroad, which it took pains to protect and expand. It favoured the great merchants of London especially, creating a whole series of chartered companies with monopoly rights over branches of foreign trade: part of the City's reward for its political loyalty and financial help. For the most part the crown supported English traders in their challenge to the Iberian monopolies in West Africa, the Americas and the East and snubbed Portuguese and Spanish protests. It gave its official blessing, in the form of letters patent, to Gilbert's and Ralegh's colonial projects and encouraged their efforts. It organized the great expeditions of the Atlantic war and led the forces of the nation in the plunder of Iberian shipping. But it did not share the notions of overseas empire or oceanic power floated by men like Hawkins, Ralegh, Hakluyt and Dee. It is wrong to assume that the crown subscribed to any such idea. Queen Elizabeth was not an imperialist.

In the very crisis of her reign, the year of the Armada, she demonstrated her attitude in unmistakeable terms by forbidding Grenville to sail with reinforcements for Ralegh's Virginia. This decision sealed the fate of the colony and effectively put an end to any prospect of English western planting until the seventeeth century. It was the decision of a realist. The struggle for the future of western Europe and the Atlantic centred upon the English Channel. To that battle Roanoke was practically irrelevant. Its sacrifice expressed not only the needs of the moment, but the real dynamics of national strategy throughout the age of Hakluyt. The crown welcomed the efforts of its subjects to develop oceanic enterprise, but it always treated them as secondary to the main issues of European power politics, leaving the initiative – especially the financial initiative – to others. The continual dangers and pressures to which the realm was subject made it unthinkable for ministers to translate the dreams of ambitious courtiers and irresponsible sea-dogs into official policy.

Ireland was of course a different matter. Here the crown faced intractable problems in its efforts to subdue an increasingly restless population. Colonial settlement was one of the policies it tried in order to effect its general purpose of Anglicizing Ireland, but Elizabeth was cautious in her use of this method, resisting state involvement in the

[12] R. B. Wernham, 'Elizabethan war aims and strategy', in S. T. Bindoff, J. Hurstfield and C. H. Williams (eds.), *Elizabethan Government and Society* (London, 1961), pp. 340–68.

plantation experiments espoused by Sir Henry Sidney, Sir Thomas Smith, the earl of Essex, Grenville, Gilbert and others in the years before the Munster rebellion of 1579–83. After that her government positively directed and encouraged the plantation of Munster, and finally after the nine years war and the effective conquest of Ireland colonization went ahead with the full support of the crown in Ulster, Munster and elsewhere. Thus settlement became royal policy and private enterprise was put to work for purposes of state, but only under pressure and by stages, as strategic necessity overrode the crown's caution, which in this case derived not only from financial considerations but also from a sense of the divisive effect plantation would and did have in that unhappy country.[13]

Normally the crown was glad to make use of expansionist energy if it could be exploited for political ends without embarrassing the state. This was a question of convenience. For example, when Richard Grenville put forward his aggressive South American scheme in 1574 the queen rejected it because she did not wish to annoy the king of Spain just then. Three years later Drake and the Hawkinses won her secret backing for much the same project. It is unlikely that Drake would have sailed in 1577 had not Elizabeth's relations with King Philip taken a turn for the worse in the summer of that year. Indeed it is reasonable to assume that had the crown remained on good terms with Spain in the later sixteenth century, the overseas expansion movement would have been muted and restricted in important respects. When the Anglo-Iberian rapprochement of the early 1570s caused Grenville's project to be suppressed, English poaching in the Portuguese sphere of influence south of Atlantic Morocco was also curbed. The political climate had a strong influence upon the fortunes of oceanic enterprise, as upon its character, which in the reign of Elizabeth was inclined to aggression and violence. In James's reign the political climate was quite different, and it no longer seemed to the crown desirable to encourage overseas ventures which directly challenged Spanish power in ways likely to arouse hostility. In thus asserting the priority of the crown's European interests over English oceanic ambitions James was following his predecessor's example. Had it suited her to do so Elizabeth herself would have blocked Ralegh's aggressive plans, though perhaps not quite with James's pathetic eagerness to placate the Spaniard. But her political interests did not for the most part seriously conflict with the commercial, maritime and colonial aspira-

[13] D. B. Quinn, *The Elizabethans and the Irish* (Ithaca, N.Y., 1966), pp. 106–22; N. Canny, *The Elizabethan Conquest of Ireland: a Pattern Established, 1565–1576* (London, 1976), *passim*.

tions of her merchant and gentlemen adventurers. Ralegh, it is true, deplored her half-hearted prosecution of the war against Spain, and some others found the queen a timid strategist. But in the main the crown and the promoters of expansion could co-operate. The result was to strengthen the expansion movement, to identify it with patriotism, to publicize and popularize it, and so to make James's application of the bit and bridle hard to bear.

Even so, it was the reign of James that saw the effective beginnings of the British Empire: the establishment of colonies in North America, the development of direct trade with the East, and even the first annexation of territory in a recognized Spanish sphere of influence – the West Indies. James during most of his reign deferred to Spain's pre-emptive claims in the Caribbean, but supported trade and settlement in areas Spain claimed and manifestly did not possess: North America and the East Indies. This was the position Elizabeth and her ministers had maintained in their diplomatic dealings with Spain and Portugal. Guiana in the early seventeenth century was a doubtful case. Despite the difference between the foreign policies of the two monarchs, the crown's attitude to overseas enterprise underwent no radical change in 1603: such matters continued to have low priority. It was only tardily and reluctantly, as its subjects became more deeply involved in the wider world, that the state took responsibility for distant trades and colonies. The East India Company's quarrel with the Dutch in Indonesia was an embarrassment to James and it was for that reason that he took the matter up with the United Provinces as a 'business of state'.[14] The result was by no means satisfactory for the East India Company. In 1624 the king, on the advice of his ministers and after a full inquiry by the Privy Council, revoked the Virginia Company's charter, placing the colony under the direct rule of the crown. This belated and forced decision did not, however, signify any change in the crown's *laissez faire* approach to colonial questions generally.

In fact neither Elizabeth nor James would readily give active support to overseas enterprise unless it seemed likely to yield – and that quickly – some tangible dividend of money or power. The notion of some historians that the crown pursued an expansionist policy based on a set of assumptions and intentions later to be called 'mercantilist' is quite mistaken.[15] Tudor and early Stuart governments habitually larded

[14] K. N. Chaudhuri, *The English East India Company: a Study of an Early Joint-Stock Company, 1600–1640* (London, 1965), p. 31.
[15] The *locus classicus* of this interpretation is G. L. Beer, *The Origins of the British Colonial System, 1578–1660* (New York, 1922), a fundamental study which nevertheless overstates the importance of ideas, especially economic theory, in the making of policy and equally overstates the importance of state policy in the making of that empire.

their statutes, proclamations, charters, and other pronouncements with platitudes about the health and strength of the realm, but the interest of the common weal seldom overrode the needs of the moment. For example, the export of undyed and undressed cloth was officially prohibited, but it was in fact England's main export by virtue of licences which were a source of revenue to the crown. Promoters of new trades or colonies often used *clichés* about unemployment and over-population to recommend their projects to the nation and the state. Whether such professions of concern for the public good were sincere or not is a matter to be considered later, but it is rash to conclude that they indicate the crown's priorities in the sphere of oceanic enterprise. Whatever ministers themselves thought of contemporary economic doctrine, government decisions in practice were dictated largely by far more pressing considerations of revenue and defence, official favour and Court intrigue. Treasure was of course valued above all, but not for mercantilist reasons; it was simply the food of the body politic, which was thin and weak for lack of it.

Hence royal participation is to be found, not in ventures likely to assist exports of cloth or people, but in those expected to yield gold or silver. Royal ships sailed in the Guinea voyages – for gold. Royal ships went with Hawkins to the Caribbean, selling slaves for silver – what little cloth they carried was mainly French. Royal ships took part in Frobisher's northwest enterprise only when it became a mining operation. Further examples can easily be cited. Pioneers like Gilbert, Michael Lok, Ralph Lane and Christopher Newport knew well enough, as they showed by their actions, that treasure found was the best guarantee of royal support. Otherwise the state was disposed to favour the rich trades in order to enhance its customs revenue. The duties on imported silks, currants, tobacco and sweet wines were particularly lucrative. The Turkey Company on its foundation had to agree to import merchandise yielding at least £500 per annum and to maintain an ambassador in Constantinople, since the Anglo-Ottoman entente reinforced Elizabeth's foreign policy. Trades which contributed to defence were of course preferred. The Muscovy Company's supplies of Russian cordage, sold in bulk to the queen's navy at patriotic prices, were highly prized. The Levant and East India trades were valued because they employed heavily armed merchantmen and thus contributed to the nation's sea power. The Privy Council is said to have summoned Thomas Cordell, shipping magnate of the Levant trade, to congratulate him for his service to the state in this respect.[16] The elder Cecil particularly took steps to foster the merchant marine.

[16] T. Park (ed.), *The Harleian Miscellany* (10 vols., London, 1808–13), IV, p. 214.

He regarded the deep-sea fisheries as the nation's 'nursery of seamen' and encouraged the reconnaissance of the Newfoundland–Gulf of St Lawrence region to promote English activity there.[17] Thus the state qualified its support and distributed its favour according to hopes of its own, preferably immediate, advantage.

As for its handling of ventures in commercial, maritime and colonial expansion, it is best expressed by the term 'patronage', signifying a variable interplay of state control and individual initiative in which the great men at Court and in the councils of the realm performed an indispensable rôle as intermediaries. Elizabeth's Principal Secretary, Sir Francis Walsingham, was the most active of these. It was to him that Hakluyt dedicated his *Principall Navigations* in 1589, acknowledging the help the Secretary had afforded him in his career and acquiring for the book itself the stamp of authority. Walsingham had a hand in most of the ventures of expansion that occurred during his period of office from 1573 to 1590.[18] His first wife, Anna Carleill, was the daughter of Sir George Barne, a magnate of the Muscovy Company and a leading figure in new enterprise. As a member of the company and one of its 'assistants' (i.e. directors) from 1569, Walsingham was close to those Londoners most concerned with the drive for eastern trade at that stage and it is not surprising to find him identified in modern research as 'the mind behind the whole Turkish enterprise'.[19] He was keenly interested in the search for the northwest passage and in Gilbert's North American schemes. As head of the anti-Spanish and militantly Protestant elements in Court and Council, he cast a benevolent eye on ventures designed to annoy the king of Spain and backed Drake consistently from the 1577 South Sea expedition to the Lisbon voyage of 1589. Sir William Cecil, Lord Burghley and his son Sir Robert, earl of Salisbury, were also personally concerned with various oceanic and colonial initiatives, as were John Dudley, duke of Northumberland, and his son Robert, earl of Leicester. Elizabeth's lord admirals, Edward Fiennes de Clinton, earl of Lincoln, and after him Lord Charles Howard of Effingham, earl of Nottingham, were both great patrons of Atlantic trade and plunder. The earls of Cumberland, Essex and Southampton and some other prominent courtiers, like Ralegh, used their influence to promote their own and their friends' ventures.

In none of these enterprises, even the expeditions of war, did the

[17] D. B. Quinn, *England and the Discovery of America, 1481–1620* (New York, 1974), pp. 235–44, 316–36.
[18] C. Read, *Mr Secretary Walsingham and the Policy of Queen Elizabeth* (3 vols., Oxford, 1925), III, pp. 370–410.
[19] S. Skilliter (ed.), *William Harborne and the Trade with Turkey, 1578–1582* (Oxford, 1977), p. 27.

state take full responsibility. Sometimes it would intervene to stop a project or to push it: the formation of the East India Company, which was first stopped and then pushed, is an interesting case. Sometimes it watched and waited while private promoters took the initiative – Hawkins in 1562, Frobisher in 1577 – taking a share in the project once it promised rich returns. The links between the crown and its subjects were informal, not deliberately contrived, being perhaps too subtle for man's invention, growing naturally out of a society in which clientage ruled all relationships within sight of the Court, and in which a paternal, but weak and parasitic state could only hope to ride the nation with a loose rein. But government patronage was not merely permissive, and the active interest of powerful men in this various enterprise helped it to gain cohesion and self-consciousness as a national movement. Above all the queen and the Court shone upon it, bathing it in that brilliant publicity which dazzled contemporaries and posterity with a false impression of power and glory. It was this magnificent propaganda which was largely responsible for the illusion, which gained strength in later times, that some grand mercantile and imperial strategy was at work, and that the founding of this essentially commercial empire was a royal achievement, inspired by a coherent policy of economic nationalism.

The crown's indirect conduct and remote control of its subjects' oceanic efforts no doubt encouraged the tendency towards self-government in the emergent empire, which can be observed in the activities of the East India Company as well as in the New World colonies. That tendency, however, seems to have had deep roots. The younger Hakluyt envisaged colonial self-government as early as 1579, for in recommending the occupation of Magellan's Strait he concluded:

But admit that we could not enjoye the same long, but that the English there would aspire to governement of themselves, yet were it better that it sholde be soe then that the Spanyard shold with the tresure of that countrey torment all the contries of Europe. . . . But we myght kepe the cuntry as well as the Spanyards doe, and use traffique with them.[20]

Gilbert's plans of 1582 provided for an equally loose link between the homeland and the colony and the concept of self-government was of course implicit in the North American projects of the Catholics and the Brownists alike. The first American colony to survive was organized as a joint-stock company, self-governing under the crown, and the East India Company, also a joint-stock company, was particularly jealous of

[20] E. G. R. Taylor (ed.), *The Original Writings and Correspondence of the Two Richard Hakluyts* (London, 1935), p. 143.

its autonomy and resistant to royal interference. The crown's attitude to overseas expansion may have been responsible in part for the inclination of the adventurers to manage their own affairs, but it was probably conditioned in the first place by the sort of assumption Hakluyt made, which was based on familiarity with the political character of Tudor England, a largely self-governing society – under the crown. In the long run the movement gained strength from this characteristic, but in the short run it was weakened by its dependence on private initiative and resources, and by lack of central organization, strategic direction, even elementary discipline. The price paid for these deficiencies was heavy: casual planning, under-funding, amateur leadership, continual quarrels among the promoters and the leaders, continual disorder among the sailors, soldiers and planters.

It is usual to classify the promoters of this movement into merchants on the one hand and landed gentlemen – varying from dukes to mere gentry – on the other. The social distinction was important at the time and it is hardly possible for the analyst now to avoid these categories, but in considering the social constitution of such enterprise it is easy to draw the line between the merchants and the gentlemen too sharply. Some merchants came from gentry stock, others married into the gentry, acquired estates and coats of arms, or founded noble families. Gentlemen usually had family connections with merchants. In all kinds of business landed gentlemen and merchants are normally found acting in concert, combining their resources and rôles in patterns characteristic of the society. Many gentlemen engaged in trade, notably the shipowning gentry of the southwest who conducted trade with Spain and Portugal especially, exporting corn and fish, including the Newfoundland cod, in increasing quantity. These formed a powerful interest, embracing the West Country ports and their merchants, a large financial and family network deeply concerned in North American matters and well capable of asserting itself in Parliament, where Devon and Cornish gentlemen like Sir George Somers defended the mercantile interests of the region.[21]

Nevertheless the landed aristocracy and gentry played little part in foreign trade, old or new. The Muscovy Company founders included a considerable group of peers and high officials, it is true, and they were no doubt useful in helping to provide the initial capital for what the City probably regarded as a dubious adventure. It also proved advantageous to the company to have these connections with

[21] P. Croft, 'Free trade and the House of Commons, 1605–6', *EconHR*, 2nd ser., 28 (1975), 17–27.

the government. But the gentlemen were sleeping partners and do not appear to have taken any interest in the business of the Russia trade.[22] In the East India trade, also organized on joint-stock lines, merchants were still more dominant. Until 1609 only one gentleman of the Court – the earl of Cumberland – was admitted to membership. Later for political reasons others were allowed to take shares, but the management of the trade remained in merchant hands and merchants supplied nearly all the capital.[23]

To voyages of exploration the gentlemen of the Court evidently made a more significant contribution, but still a minor one in comparison with that of the merchants. The northeast explorations were all financed by the Muscovy Company and the men who did the work were professional seamen, not gentlemen. In the northwest voyages some courtiers took an interest – notably Ambrose Dudley, earl of Warwick, Adrian Gilbert and Sir Dudley Digges, but Frobisher and Davis both relied mainly on merchants for their capital; London merchants of the East India and Russia companies dominated the Northwest Passage Company and most of the other northwest ventures of the early seventeenth century. Gentlemen adventurers were of course prominent in voyages of plunder – piracy, privateering and the semi-official expeditions of the sea war. Investment in war for booty was an honoured tradition, easily transposed from land to sea in Tudor times, but merchants usually supplied most of the capital. Throughout the period plunder was a commercialized business, dominated by merchants.[24]

Courtiers and other landed gentlemen certainly made an important contribution to colonial enterprise. From the beginning they were the main champions of plantation, whether in South or North America or in Ireland. In the early years of the seventeenth century they again led the way, with Southampton, Sir Ferdinando Gorges and Charles Leigh in the forefront. In the pioneering colonial projects of the sixteenth century merchants played a secondary rôle, supplying some of the money, but often only on loan, and showing no eagerness to take part. But in the reign of James they came into the arena in strength. Calculations concerning the capital invested in colonial enterprise by merchants and gentlemen respectively must be taken with a pinch of salt, since suitable data do not exist. The best relevant evidence relates to the Virginia Company and suggests that the merchants supplied the

[22] T. S. Willan, *The Muscovy Merchants of 1555* (Manchester, 1953).
[23] Chaudhuri, *East India Company*, pp. 33–7.
[24] K. R. Andrews, *Elizabethan Privateering: English Privateering during the Spanish War, 1585–1603* (Cambridge, 1964).

greater part of the money in that case, as they probably did in the other Jacobean colonial ventures.[25]

A change of emphasis in the character of English colonizing enterprise is thus discernible – a certain 'commercializing of colonization'.[26] Some early colonial schemes, dominated by people like Gilbert and Ralegh, gave priority to aims concerned with land and men, with the acquisition of estates and their allotment to dependants, with conquest and tribute, with gold and silver mining, with military and naval power, with booty. Here a quasi-feudal bias is evident, but by no means all Elizabethan planting projects were of this type. Christopher Carleill's proposals, for example, were thoroughly commercial, nor did Hakluyt and Thomas Hariot – both associated with Ralegh – forget the importance of marketable commodities. On the other hand the quasi-feudal type of settlement project remained a significant element in Jacobean colonization, and if commercial attitudes became more pronounced and dominant therein, it was not because any radical change had occurred meanwhile in the character of English society, which was only gradually commercializing itself, but rather because the overseas traders were now willing and able, having considerably improved their resources and confidence, to lend colonization their support and so irresistibly to dominate it.

Among the overseas traders a significant shift of interest occurred between the reigns of Henry VIII and Charles I: the development of a substantial body of Londoners and outport men with a primary interest in extra-European trade, whether foreign or colonial. This was no sudden landslide, but a gradual and cumulative movement of trading capital, led by those relatively few men who really deserved the name of merchants adventurers.[27] In the early stages the leading members of the Muscovy Company were particularly prominent. In

[25] T. K. Rabb, *Enterprise and Empire* (Cambridge, Mass., 1967), made an attempt to analyse merchant and gentry investment in the expansion, but with little success because it depended on the conflation of incompatible and in some cases irrelevant data. The conclusion – that 'the merchants were clearly the vital driving force behind England's expansion' – is probably right, but the intention was apparently to stress that 'the whole movement received a tremendous stimulus merely from the participation of the landed classes' (pp. 68–9).

[26] C. Shammas, 'English commercial development and American colonization, 1560–1620', in K. R. Andrews, N. P. Canny and P. E. H. Hair (eds.), *The Westward Enterprise* (Liverpool, 1978), pp. 151–74. But the 'feudal' type of project remained important in the seventeenth century – see for example the Newfoundland schemes described in Ch. 14 below.

[27] R. Brenner, 'The social basis of English commercial expansion, 1550–1650', *Journal of Economic History*, 32 (1972), 361–84. The best account of the merchants of Jacobean London is unfortunately unpublished: R. G. Lang, 'The greater merchants of London in the early seventeenth century' (Oxford University D.Phil. thesis, 1963).

the Russia trade itself they were the 'principall doers': Sir George Barne and his son of the same name, Sir William Garrard, Sir Rowland Heyward, Sir Lionel Ducket. These and a few others did much also to assist with funds and influence new venturing elsewhere as promoters of the Guinea trade, the slave trade, the northwest passage attempts, Brazil trade and Fenton's ill-fated East Indies expedition. In the last quarter of the century a generation of pioneering merchants associated with the Barbary, Mediterranean and Levant trades made their way forward. Thomas Cordell and John Watts are outstanding figures in this phase; they and others like them undertook privateering on a large scale during the war and went on to assume prominent positions in the East India Company from its foundation. Like the Muscovy Company, the East India Company had its principal doers who were much to the fore in other Jacobean ventures – to the Caribbean, Guiana, Virginia and the northwest passage. The greatest promoter of overseas enterprise was certainly Sir Thomas Smythe, whose tomb was inscribed in 1625:

To the glory of God, and to the pious memorie of the honorable Sir Thomas Smith, knt. (late governour of the East Indian, Muscovia, French, and Sommer Island companies; treasurer for the Virginia plantation; prime undertaker (in the year 1612) for that noble designe, the discoverie of the North-West passage; principall commissioner for the London expedition against the pirates, and for a voiage to the ryver Senega, upon the coast of Africa; one of the chief commissioners for the navie-roial, and sometime ambassador from His majestie of Great Britain to the emperour and great duke of Russia and Muscovia.[28]

These and similar Londoners who set the pace in redeploying the overseas commerce of the country were a minority of the City élite. A section of that élite played no part whatever in overseas trade, and among those who did the Merchants Adventurers, chiefly concerned with the Continental cloth trade, seldom adventured outside Europe. The pioneers of the rich trades were remarkably often Anglo-Iberian traders: this applies to most of the 'principall doers' in the Muscovy Company, to the men who opened up the Barbary, Canary Islands and Guinea trades, the first generation of Turkey merchants and some of the leading figures in the East India Company – Humphrey Slany, for example, who had interests in the Barbary, Guinea and Levant trades and in the Virginia and Bermuda companies, and helped to launch the Newfoundland Company in 1610 with an eye to the Spanish cod market.[29] Spain and Portugal were good markets for English cloth, but

[28] A. Brown, *The Genesis of the United States* (Boston, 1891), p. 1017.
[29] J. P. Croft, 'English trade with peninsular Spain, 1558–1625' (unpublished Oxford

as the Company of the Merchants Adventurers remarked acidly of the Spanish traders in 1579, 'their gain lieth rather in the foreign commodities there bought',[30] meaning the produce of the South – Seville oil, sugar, raisins, oranges, lemons, almonds and Falstaff's sherry sack – as well as the rich commodities of the East and West. It makes sense that importers of such goods should have taken the lead in the Moroccan trade for sugar, the Venetian trade for currants and sweet wines, the Turkey trade and the rest, particularly as political and religious troubles mounted to endanger Anglo-Iberian trade, eventually reducing it to an illicit trickle for eighteen years. Furthermore many of the merchants in the Peninsular trade were shipowners and so well suited to undertake the new trades. The combination of shipowning and importing was the hall-mark of the promoters of the rich trades.

Most of the outport men who made a significant contribution to overseas expansion had links with the Peninsula: the Bristol pioneers of the North Atlantic – the Thornes, Hugh Elyot and Sebastian Cabot himself; Robert Reneger of Southampton and the Hawkinses of Plymouth, pioneers of the southward Atlantic trades; the Bristolians who promoted North American enterprise under Elizabeth and James; the Dodderidges of Barnstaple, venturers in African trade; and the West Country men who built up the Newfoundland trade in the early seventeenth century.[31] Provincial merchants had little to do with the main drive for eastern trade, via Muscovy, the Levant and finally the Cape of Good Hope, but much to do with Atlantic enterprise. The West Country merchants bestirred themselves as shipowners in the privateering war, in which Southampton, Weymouth, Plymouth and Bristol were foremost, and as traders in fish and train-oil, the chief objectives of their efforts in the Gulf of St Lawrence, the Newfoundland and New England fishing grounds and even the River Plate.[32] Plymouth, Bristol and Exeter were the main promoters of the New England voyages from 1602 and together formed the western branch of the Virginia Company in 1606. Their colonizing attempt (in Sagadahoc, the modern Kennebec River, Maine) soon failed, but their fishing and fur-trading on this coast prospered, providing a strong background for

University D.Phil. thesis, 1970), and P. Croft (ed.), *The Spanish Company* (London, 1973). On Slany see G. T. Cell, *English Enterprise in Newfoundland, 1577–1660* (Toronto, 1969), pp. 54–5.

[30] R. H. Tawney and E. Power (eds.), *Tudor Economic Documents* (3 vols., London, 1924), II, p. 54.

[31] The Spanish interests of the early Tudor pioneers are detailed in G. Connell-Smith, *Forerunners of Drake* (London, 1954). On the West Country connections with Spain and Newfoundland see Cell, *English Enterprise*.

[32] On Edward Cotton's ventures to the 'River of Canada' and the River Plate see *PN*, VI, 408–10, and Quinn, *England and the Discovery of America*, p. 315.

the colonies that came later. Bristol men shared with Londoners in the early efforts to colonize Newfoundland, though here again settlements sickened and died while the cod trade flourished. But in the 1620s the hey-day of westward venturing from the provincial ports lay in the future. For the time being, whether in privateering, exploration, colonial endeavour or plain trade, London's resources and drive overshadowed outport initiative, except perhaps in the cases of the indomitable Arctic whalers of Kingston-upon-Hull and those Yarmouth masters of the herring whose praises Thomas Nashe sang so uproariously in his *Lenten Stuff*.[33]

The nautical resources of the nation in the mid sixteenth century were poor in quantity and quality, quite insufficient to sustain the oceanic expansion which nevertheless occurred. Only slowly from the 1570s did shipping and seamanship develop in response to need and experience, which was bought with an appalling expenditure of ships and men.

In Elizabeth's reign ships like the *Merchant Royal* and the *Edward Bonaventure*, both rated at about 350 tons burden, were exceptionally large among merchantmen. A government survey in 1582 revealed that even then, after some recent growth, the country possessed no more than about 250 private vessels of 80 tons and over and fewer than twenty of 200 tons or more. The tonnage burden of a vessel was its capacity estimated very roughly in tuns of Bordeaux wine. The *Ascension* of London, 160 tons, was 'in breadth 24 feet, deep from that breadth to the keel 12 feet and by the keel in length 54 feet', which implies somewhat more than 70 feet from stem to stern. That was about the size of Drake's *Golden Hind*, which sailed round the world. The Elizabethan merchant-galleons mentioned above would have measured little more than a hundred feet from stem to stern.[34] Apart from some distinctive types of river and fishing craft, English ships were unspecialized. All the main ports used much the same all-purpose vessels carrying coal, fish, corn, wine, timber or any other cargo available. A so-called bark was simply a small ship of some 30 to 70 tons, having the standard build and rig. Pinnaces were shallow-draught vessels, rarely exceeding 30 tons, often functioning as aux-

[33] T. Nashe, *The Unfortunate Traveller and Other Works*, ed. J. B. Steane (London, 1972), p. 409.
[34] On tonnage see W. Salisbury, 'Early tonnage measurement in England', *Mariner's Mirror*, 52 (1966), 41–51. R. Davis, *The Rise of the English Shipping Industry* (London, 1962), deals briefly with the period before 1630. M. Oppenheim, *A History of the Administration of the Royal Navy and of Merchant Shipping in relation to the Navy* (London, 1896), is still useful, as are his contributions to the *Victoria County Histories* of Cornwall, Dorset, Essex, Kent, Somerset, Sussex and Suffolk, and his posthumous work, *The Maritime History of Devon*, ed. W. E. Minchinton (Exeter, 1968).

iliaries. They would usually be limited to a single deck, two masts and little of the superstructure fore and aft characteristic of ships; they used oars when necessary, but were essentially small sailing ships rather than rowing boats. The only specialized sea-going vessels in regular use were Dutch types: the hoy, a fore-and-aft rigged carrier of some 30 to 50 tons, the flyboat, another carrier of middling burden, and the highly efficient *fluit*, which came in towards the end of the century. Rarely did English owners acquire any of these types, nor did English shipwrights attempt to copy them.

Ships of that era were by later standards very dangerous and difficult to handle, all the more so now that their seaworthiness, performance and crews had to stand the test of long oceanic voyages.[35] With their high-charged hulls, with masts and spars commonly too large and sides too weak, with only a lateen sail on the mizzen to offset the square fore-course and main-course, it is not surprising that most ships went badly to windward and consequently depended heavily on favourable winds. It was not unusual for expeditions to be delayed in port for weeks for want of a suitable wind, or to be obliged to change their destination while at sea for the same reason. The fear of being driven helplessly onto a lee shore was always with them as they approached a coast and for the most part they kept well clear, particularly at night. Most ships, too, were rendered sluggish by the barnacles and weed which fouled their bottoms. Sheathing the hull with extra planking lined with tar and goat hair – the normal if less then adequate defence against the ravages of tropical worms – made vessels still slower and still less responsive to the helm. A typical result of these built-in defects was that the first three East India Company expeditions took respectively seven, four and eight months to reach Table Bay in South Africa, where further weeks had to be spent recovering from scurvy and making the ships fit to face the rest of the voyage, which would take at least three months. The East Indiamen were among the best English ships of their time, but of the eighty-one ships (34,086 tons) sent out in the years 1601 to 1620 only thirty-five (14,945 tons) returned, the rest having been worn out by hard usage, apart from some that remained in eastern waters and some lost at sea.[36]

Serious accidents abounded and ships were peculiarly vulnerable to them. Violent leaks were by no means a rare occurrence, for the caulking was often defective and seams tended to open under the strain of bad weather or bombardment. Sailors were all too familiar with

---

[35] The best account of the practical difficulties and hazards is G. V. Scammell, 'European seamanship in the great age of discovery', *Mariner's Mirror*, 68 (1982), 357–76.
[36] Chaudhuri, *East India Company*, p. 91.

pumping and searching the bilge for a potentially fatal wound. Rudders were especially subject to damage or actual loss, and masts, too often loose or loosened by slack rigging, easily broke in storm conditions. Anchors tended to be too light for the vessel and their cables too weak; in one way and another anchors were lost and many are the pathetic stories of ships unable to save themselves from wreck for lack of an anchor. The ice and fog of the high latitudes of course confronted seamen like Frobisher, Davis, the Borough brothers, Hudson and Baffin with severe hardship and nautical problems, which they were ill-equipped to meet, but the worst cause of disaster was storm. Storms sometimes overwhelmed barks like Drake's *Marigold* (1578) and pinnaces like Gilbert's *Squirrel* (1583); sometimes they began a ship's death agony by opening her timbers or causing the loss of a mast, a rudder or an anchor. Human error was responsible for many wrecks, for example the loss of Gilbert's flagship, the *Delight*, in 1583, and of Edward Cotton's ship in the same year, 'which perished through extreme negligence' on the coast of Guinea,[37] but no doubt in many of these cases sheer physical exhaustion was to blame. Thus six of her original complement of 91 men and boys brought John Chidley's *Robin* back from Magellan's Strait 'in extreme misery', only to be driven onto the rocks near Cherbourg, having failed to anchor.[38] Such tragedies always proceeded from a complex of interacting causes, but the extraordinarily high casualty rate among ships and men was chiefly due to the inadequacy of the ships and their basic equipment.

From the middle of Elizabeth's reign a steady increase began in the number of relatively large ships. By 1629 the country had roughly twice as many private vessels of 100 tons and over as in 1582 and about 150 of 200 tons and over. Until the end of the Spanish war privateering was the main stimulus, but at the same time and afterwards other demands were at work; deep-sea fishing, especially the Newfoundland trade; coal-carrying out of Tyneside; and the longer-distance trades to the Baltic, the Mediterranean and across the oceans. The largest ships were built in James's reign, mostly for the East India Company, which employed several of over 500 tons and finally in 1610 launched the giant *Trades Increase*, rated at 1000 tons. The East Indiamen were far from typical of the Jacobean merchant navy, in which vessels of under 100 tons still predominated, but during this period the prevalence of violence at sea had a noticeable effect on the character of the nation's shipping. Larger merchantmen were built like galleons and lesser traders took on more guns and men to defend themselves or to pursue prize. Towards the end of the war Dunkirk privateers became a

[37] *PN* (1589), pp. 187–8.   [38] *PN*, xi, 381–4.

menace, and after the war Barbary corsairs harassed shipping in the Atlantic as well as the Mediterranean, reinforcing the English preference for strongly armed and strongly manned ships, but the cost of building, arming and operating such vessels made them less and less able to compete with the Dutch. English freight charges, already high, lagged further behind in the decades around 1600 as the Hollanders lengthened their technical lead with economical carriers adapted to the needs of particular trades. Thus the form of private sea power which served the islanders well enough in their struggle with Spain became a handicap in the very different struggle which ensued with the Dutch.

This trend, however was officially encouraged because the crown relied heavily on private shipping both for defence of the realm and for waging war abroad, whether in conjunction with land forces or ranging the seas to plunder enemy trade. The royal navy, it is true, developed in the Tudor period into a permanent force and James did inherit 'by far the finest fleet of men-of-war then afloat'.[39] But it was still a small navy. Its thirty-one ships of 100 tons and upwards may be compared with the twenty-eight left by Henry VIII and the twenty or twenty-five Elizabeth inherited from Mary.[40] Thanks largely to the work of John Hawkins, the ships of 1603 were bigger and better than those of 1558, but as Sir Thomas Wilson shrewdly remarked in 1600:

The whole navy of the Queen consisting of no great number, it may be wondered att that she should be counted so stronge by sea that no other Prince is able to match her, but the reason is plain that though this fleet be of great strength yett it is not the 20 part of the strength of England, for unto the very one Ryver of Thames there belong 2,000 ships, the worst [wherof] is serviseable both for fight and merchandise.[41]

Wilson overstated the details, but he was right in judging that the royal navy did not keep pace with private shipping – nor, we may add, with the expansion of the nation's maritime interests. The Tudor navy was not built to wage an oceanic war for mastery of the rich trades or to win and protect far-flung colonies. It was built to defend the country and conduct war in western Europe and the intervening waters. Outside that sphere the merchant marine was mainly responsible for the challenge to Iberian maritime dominance. Royal ships played a part, both as merchantmen and as warships, but always in conjunction with private shipping in joint-stock syndicates. Royal ships rarely sailed south or west of the Azores.

[39] Oppenheim, *Administration*, p. 184.
[40] *Ibid.* p. 109; J. S. Corbett, *The Successors of Drake* (London, 1900), p. 411.
[41] F. J. Fisher (ed.), 'The State of England Anno Dom. 1600, by Thomas Wilson', in *The Camden Miscellany*, vol. xvi (London, 1936), pp. 36–7.

Because the Iberians were the possessor powers, the English came into the rich trades as interlopers and armed their ships accordingly. Because Iberian merchantmen carried so much wealth across the oceans, the English mode of sea-warfare was privateering. Oceanic expansion and privateering therefore tended to promote each other and fuse. The product was a powerful interest which embodied to a great extent the actual sea power of the nation, vested as that was in the stronger sort of merchant shipping and the relatively small force of royal ships. For the men who managed, supplied or commanded the latter generally belonged to that same shipowning, mercantile, privateering, expansionist interest: the Hawkinses, the Winters, the Gonsons and other naval officials were themselves shipowners, merchants, oceanic venturers and allied themselves in such business with City magnates like Ducket, the Barnes, Cordell, Myddelton and Watts. The royal navy, moreover, was not entirely distinct and separate from the merchant marine. It was by no means uncommon for private vessels to be bought into the royal fleet, nor for royal ships to be sold off to private owners, or chartered to a trading syndicate, or invested as capital in joint-stock expeditions. The royal navy had no regular officers apart from the members of the Navy Board and a few other shore officials. It recruited its commanders and men from the ports for the duration of the operation. Those who had occasion to serve in both found no great difference between royal ships and merchantmen of the same size in respect of build or rig, for the radical divergence between them was a later phenomenon.

Ships as they grew in numbers, size and range demanded more sailors – and yet more because the sea consumed them so fast. As Hakluyt observed, 'of so many, so few grow to gray heires'.[42] But there was evidently no shortage of ordinary seamen, for during the Spanish war large numbers were prepared to go to sea for nothing but board, lodging and shares in hypothetical prizes. The normal basic wage for the unskilled sailor ranged from ten to twenty shillings a month and he might make something extra by taking merchandise to trade on his own account or in return for handling cargo (primage). Windfalls like these and the irregularity of employment make it difficult to assess seamen's earnings, but beyond doubt what they brought home was a poor recompense for the hardship and danger endured at sea. The strain, the victualling and the incidence of deficiency diseases, espe-

[42] *PN*, I, xxxiv. On the sailors of this period see D. B. Quinn, 'Sailors and the sea', in A. Nicoll (ed.), *Shakespeare in his own Age* (Cambridge, 1964), pp. 21–36; G. V. Scammell, 'Manning the English merchant service in the sixteenth century', *Mariner's Mirror*, 56 (1970), 131–54; K. R. Andrews, 'The Elizabethan seaman', *Mariner's Mirror*, 68 (1982), 245–62.

cially scurvy, were worse in the long, oceanic voyages, worst still in the freezing cold of the Arctic or the humid heat of the tropics, above all in the overcrowded ships of war. Cabins were the privilege of the master and one or two other officers – the rest had to lie where they could. They wore baggy breeches, long woollen hose, jerkin and knitted cap, with a coarse serge gown, hooded, against the worst of the cold and wet. 'To endure and suffer; as a hard Cabbin, cold and salt Meate, broken sleepes, mould bread, dead beere, wet Cloathes, want of fire' – all these were 'within board' according to Luke Fox of Hull, the Arctic explorer.[43]

Crews were becoming more troublesome. Traditionally the men who worked the ship expected to be treated with respect and consulted about matters which concerned them, including the course and duration of the voyage. But in oceanic voyaging various factors eroded this relative independence and intensified stress. Heavy manning increased friction, reduced the contact between leaders and men, aggravated victualling problems. The presence of numerous unskilled men upset the balance between command and consultation, especially in warlike expeditions. The increased risk and uncertainty in long voyages put a heavy strain on the confidence of crews in their commanders. 'Mariners', wrote Richard Hawkins, 'are like to a stiffe necked Horse, which taking the bridle betwixt his teeth, forceth his Rider to what him list mauger his will.'[44] In the face of pressure commanders dealt out punishment or made concessions, but when these failed the horse usually bolted for home, carrying the helpless rider with it, or perhaps left him to die in misery, like Henry Hudson. Hudson's men cast him adrift for victuals; the men of the East India Company's pinnace *Good Hope* murdered their master for victuals; victuals were the chief cause of mutiny and often decided the fate of a voyage.

Next to victuals, plunder was the chief root of disorder. Piracy was not merely a professional business, but attracted numerous amateurs. Large numbers of seamen indulged in it when occasion offered to supplement their meagre earnings. Robbery of neutral merchantmen was an everyday occurrence in the war periods, nor were such incidents uncommon in peace time. The reason was partly that war, peace and neutrality were ill-defined quantities, while the international law of prize and spoil was in its infancy, and partly that the crown was powerless to check the disorders of its subjects at sea.

[43] M. Christy (ed.), *The Voyages of Captain Luke Fox . . . and Captain Thomas James* (London, 1894), p. 11.
[44] J. A. Williamson (ed.), *The* Observations *of Sir Richard Hawkins* (London, 1933), p. 12.

Pirates could not have carried on their trade without the support of merchants, gentlemen and officials, especially admiralty officials, and measures taken against such abettors of piracy were for the most part ineffective, since all too frequently those responsible for executing the law were themselves notorious offenders. Even lord admirals – from Sir Thomas Seymour in Edward's time to the earl of Nottingham in James's – were not above conniving at acts of piracy and pocketing what amounted to bribes. Indeed the lord admirals and their staffs were less concerned with keeping law and order at sea than with profiting, directly or indirectly, from lawlessness and disorder.[45] For the attitude of the state to maritime plunder was in any case ambivalent. While deploring it as inimical to commerce and productive of international friction, the government was quite prepared to adopt pirates as a means of waging war by proxy. As Sir Henry Mainwaring, himself a pirate-turned-admiral, put it: 'the State may hereafter want such men, who commonly are the most daring and serviceable in war of all those kind of people'.[46] The careers of Drake, Frobisher and many less famous men bear out the truth of his remark.

But the rising tide of maritime violence in the sixteenth and early seventeenth centuries owed its force mainly to circumstances beyond the control of any English authority. As the volume, value and scope of international trade increased, so did the scale of international sea-warfare, waged for the most part by corsairs and armed merchantmen. The reliance of states on these methods encouraged indiscriminate disorder. Piracy, moreover, grew spontaneously out of poverty and unemployment among seamen, as Hakluyt, John Hawkins, Captain John Smith and Mainwaring all testified.[47] The response of men like Richard Hawkins to the unruly behaviour of the common sailor was to demand stronger discipline, but it is doubtful whether they made any progress towards imposing their will and exacting obedience. Attempts to infringe what sailors regarded as their rights met passive resistance or open defiance and stood small chance of success at this stage.

It can hardly be maintained, therefore, that the ships which experienced and achieved the maritime expansion were generally well manned. The shortage of skilled mariners led Hakluyt to advocate a

---

[45] R. G. Marsden, 'The vice-admirals of the coast', *EHR*, 22 (1907), 468–77, and 23 (1908), 736–57.

[46] G. E. Manwaring and W. G. Perrin (eds.), *The Life and Works of Sir Henry Mainwaring* (2 vols., London, 1922), II, p. 18.

[47] Taylor, *Writings of the Hakluyts*, p. 319; BL, Lansdowne MSS, 43, fos. 20–21; John Smith, *Works*, ed. E. Arber (2 vols., Birmingham, 1884), II, p. 915; Manwaring and Perrin, *Life and Works of Mainwaring*, II, p. 41.

national training scheme, but nothing came of it.[48] The skilled men had for the most part been apprenticed to the sea and many would become masters, often owning or part-owning the ships they sailed. Thus for a comparatively small element in the seafaring population the sea was a career. A master could earn five or six pounds a month or more apart from his income by trade or freight. The East India Company hired Roger Hankin for their first voyage at £10 a month and a gratuity of £50. Hankin belonged to the new breed of master mariner which emerged during this period, men of the high skill, capacity, responsibility and experience needed in the Russian, Baltic, Mediterranean, transatlantic and East India trades. The majority of masters, however, did not belong to that élite, but rather to that class of 'auncient masters of ships' whom William Bourne condemned as mere 'coasters', 'utterlye without skill', all too ready to deride those who actually used charts and observed the altitude of the Pole Star,

saying that they care not for their Sheepes skins, for hee could keepe a better account upon a board. And when they did take the latitude, they would cal them starre shooters and Sunne shooters, and would aske if they had striken it.[49]

Coasting, with its reliance on accumulated knowledge of the lie and appearance of the coast, of tides and of the sea-floor, and on dead reckoning by compass, sand-glass, log-line and traverse board, remained the essential basic skill for all masters. Only slowly and in response to the necessities of ocean sailing did English masters adopt charts and elementary methods of celestial navigation to supplement their traditional technique. A long process of education was required, which began in the 1550s when the search for the northeast passage brought together the talents of Sebastian Cabot, Richard Chancellor, Stephen and William Borough – all seafaring men – with those of Robert Recorde, Richard Eden and John Dee, men of learning. Stephen Borough, whom Chancellor trained, succeeded him as Grand Pilot of the Muscovy Company and in 1558 was invited to the *Casa de la Contratación* in Seville, whence he returned with the standard navigation manual of the day – Martín Cortes's *Arte de Navegar* – and persuaded the company to have it translated by Eden. Although Borough's scheme for regular training of pilots fell through, he did much to promote the art of navigation through the Trinity House of

[48] *PN*, i, xxxiv. On apprenticeship see J. Webb, 'Apprenticeship in the maritime occupations at Ipswich, 1596–1651', *Mariner's Mirror*, 46 (1960), 29–34.
[49] E. G. R. Taylor (ed.), *A Regiment for the Sea by William Bourne* (Cambridge, 1963), p. 294.

Deptford and as one of the four masters of the queen's ships.[50]

Thus a movement for the advance of navigation developed through the collaboration of mathematical practitioners and practical seamen. John Dee, Thomas Hariot, William Gilbert, Edward Wright, Henry Briggs and Edmund Gunter, all men of outstanding intellect, applied their minds to the solution of technical problems and recognized the need to propagate mathematics among mariners. Manuals of navigation by Recorde, Bourne, Robert Norman, John Davis, John Tapp and others circulated in increasing numbers. In 1598 the Corporation of London and the Mercers Company founded Gresham College for popular education with an emphasis on practical subjects connected with commerce. In due course latitude became a regular aid in ocean sailing and the practice of holding a course due east or west on a selected parallel was common enough. Astrolabe, quadrant and cross-staff became familiar. English masters and pilots at last accepted charts and as they did so an English school of cartography emerged. Hakluyt's 'new map, with the augmentation of the Indies' (so described in *Twelfth Night*), marked an important step forward, based as it was on Emery Molyneux's globe and Edward Wright's mathematical elaboration of Mercator's projection. Published in the second edition of the *Principal Navigations*, it carefully avoided the more imaginative sort of speculation and effectively announced the arrival of scientific geography in England. It coincided with the publication of William Gilbert's treatise on electricity and magnetism and the same period saw the development of logarithms by John Napier, Gunter and Briggs, and Hariot's pioneering though unpublished work on the new science of optics. Sir Francis Bacon, though no scientist himself, thought it was part of God's plan that 'the opening of the world by navigation and commerce, and the further discovering of knowledge should meet in one time'.[51] It was certainly no coincidence. Science and seamanship finally came together in the hard school of the northwest passage, where Davis, Hudson, Baffin and other explorers demonstrated the remarkable progress that the art of navigation was making in England.

Dedicating to Sir Walter Ralegh his translation of René de Laudonnière's account of Florida, Hakluyt shrewdly pointed to the diversity of men's intentions in adventuring overseas:

So sondrie men entring into these discoveries propose unto themselves

[50] D. W. Waters, *The Art of Navigation in England in Elizabethan and Early Stuart Times* (London, 1958), pp. 94, 103–11.
[51] C. Hill, *Intellectual Origins of the English Revolution* (Oxford, 1965), p. 87.

severall endes. Some seeke authoritie and places of commandement, others experience by seeing of the worlde, the most part worldly and transitorie gaine, and that often times by dishonest and unlawfull meanes, the fewest number the glorie of God and the saving of the soules of the poore and blinded infidels.[52]

It is hardly necessary to dwell upon the more or less crude pursuit of riches which was obviously the main if not the sole motive of most of the venturers in expeditions of trade or plunder, in many colonizing projects and even in some exploring voyages; nor on that insatiable thirst for fame and honour which undoubtedly drove Gilbert, Ralegh, Cavendish and some less renowned gentlemen as well as members of the aristocracy to undertake actions they deemed noble, however sordid their conduct and foolish their posturings may appear in the eyes of a different generation. Individual motivation was as variable, complex and obscure in this movement as in any other, defying generalization. On the other hand it may be useful to consider the influence of certain common ideas and sentiments that were continually invoked to explain, justify or recommend projects.

The most respectable of these was the missionary idea of converting the heathen to Christianity. As Hakluyt observed, there were few who made this the alpha and omega of their colonizing work. Few indeed were the clergy who actually undertook it, as distinct from those who preached support for the Virginia Company from safe pulpits in England. Their propaganda was for home consumption and was not matched by an equivalent expenditure of funds and energy on the other side of the Atlantic. In principle, however, this was the highest conceivable motive for plantation and pious individuals like Edward Hayes, the narrator of Gilbert's fatal voyage, believed that plantation could not succeed unless devoted to this end and so blessed by God. Hakluyt, himself a clergyman, naturally gave it pride of place in his argument for western planting, but prudently advised establishing a footing in the country before proceeding to evangelize its inhabitants. Hariot, though evidently undeserving of his reputation for scepticism, seems to have regarded conversion as part of a necessary, desirable and feasible process of civilization rather than as an end in itself, a typically Anglo-Saxon attitude shared by many. John Dee, planning a northwest passage search in 1583, informed a spirit called Medicus Dei that 'this Adrian Gilbert shall cary the name of Jesus among the Infidells to the great glory of god'.[53] The main purpose of this enter-

---

[52] *PN*, VIII, 443.
[53] D. B. Quinn (ed.), *The Voyages and Colonising Enterprises of Sir Humphrey Gilbert* (London, 1940), p. 485.

prise was of course to establish a new trading link with the infidels of the Orient, but there is no reason to doubt Dee's sincerity in claiming that he had higher aims in mind as well. In pleading with the powers of heaven to favour one's design it was certainly the best argument known. Likewise it appealed to the Protestant conscience, which Hakluyt and the Virginia Company's hired preachers duly prodded by reminding Englishmen how much the Catholic church had done to bring a falsified Christianity to the heathen, and how little the Protestants had done to spread the true word. Such exhortations, when uttered by well-meaning believers, should not be condemned as hypocritical, but they had little effect. The missionary ideal was not a major stimulus to English colonial endeavour and the nation's record in this field remained poor.[54]

The concept of a colony as a place of refuge for a persecuted minority probably came to England from France, either when the Huguenots were attempting to appropriate Florida for this and other purposes, or earlier still, when Villegaignon with Calvinist backing created the short lived 'France Antarctique' off Río de Janeiro in the fifties. The Roman Catholic gentleman Sir Thomas Gerrard proposed already in 1569 to take Lancashire Catholics to settle in Ireland and after 1580, when penalties for recusancy were much stiffened, he and Sir George Peckham with other Catholics engaged themselves in Gilbert's plans for North America. Their scheme collapsed with Gilbert's failure and it was probably Spanish hostility which prevented its revival, but in James's reign the prospect of a Catholic refugee settlement in America re-emerged, to become a reality in the shape of Lord Baltimore's Maryland in the following reign.[55] The parallel and eventually more powerful movement among dissenting Protestants can also be traced back to the early part of Elizabeth's reign and thence through the Brownists of the nineties down to the Plymouth Pilgrims and the great exodus to New England which began in the late 1620s.[56] Thus dissidence came to play a major part in the formation of the overseas empire, though it was still a minor factor during the prolonged and difficult gestation thereof. Indeed had this force gained momentum more quickly the whole development would doubtless have been easier and shorter. Meanwhile the anti-Catholic edge of English Protestantism was turned against Spain and militant puritanism fused

[54] A fair examination of the home propaganda occurs in J. Parker, 'Religion and the Virginia colony, 1609–1610', in Andrews, Canny and Hair, *Westward Enterprise*, pp. 245–70.
[55] See the essay on 'The English Catholics and America', in Quinn, *England and the Discovery of America*, pp. 364–97.
[56] *Ibid.* pp. 337–63, 'The first pilgrims'.

with aggressive nationalism in that fanatical, psalm-singing, image-breaking 'cause' espoused by Francis Drake and not a few of his piratical companions. It was in this form, as an ingredient of national feeling, that religion made its chief contribution to the movement of overseas expansion in the period under review, as will be seen shortly.

The literature advocating voyages of discovery, new trades or colonies often gives the impression that the promoters were concerned with nothing more nor less than the public good: in contemporary terms, the common weal. It was usual to indicate that such projects would provide 'vent for our commodities', particularly woollen cloth, and so make work for the 'idle poor', viz. the unemployed. If the scheme involved settlement, the country could export the poor themselves, particularly vagabonds, criminals and convicts, the products of overpopulation. The rich commodities returned by the new trades would make England independent of foreign supplies and so save the present expense of treasure on such imports. Furthermore the crown would gain customs revenue as those imports increased in value. Colonies of course might well yield treasure, which was the supreme commodity. New or expanded oceanic fisheries would be nurseries of seamen and oceanic trades would employ large and powerful ships, potential 'walls of the realm'. In Hakluyt's writings, and more especially in those of his lawyer cousin, Richard Hakluyt the elder, these and associated ideas recur frequently enough to suggest that they subscribed to the loose set of economic notions which constituted the orthodoxy of their time, a form of economic nationalism which had yet to mature into the coherent theory expounded by Thomas Mun and others from the 1620s. This body of ideas had a strong influence on economic and social policy in the difficult days of the fifties and sixties and on the thinking of those intellectual statesmen Sir William Cecil, Sir Thomas Smith and Sir Nicholas Bacon. It did not, as we have seen, inspire Elizabethan or Jacobean governments to pursue a positive policy of overseas expansion, but the questionable assumption that they would be disposed to patronize initiatives promising to benefit the public was an accepted convention.

It is not surprising, therefore, that projectors and promoters made frequent reference in their publicity to unemployment and cloth exports, to overcrowded gaols and mass poverty, strong ships, rich commodities, customs duties and treasure. No doubt the sincerity of their invocations of the common weal varied greatly in degree. The Hakluyts as the leading intellectuals of the movement clearly believed their own case, but many others used the concept of the common weal as a moral *cliché*. Suggestions that North America, South America, the

Caribbean or the Far East might provide great markets for English textiles expressed at best a pious hope. The merchants and gentlemen who drew up these appeals seldom had the slightest interest in or knowledge of the cloth industry and if they were concerned at all with selling cloth abroad their normal policy was to restrict the volume of sales in order to hold up prices. The virtue of planting people and so ridding the country of some of its unwanted poor, whether for charitable or uncharitable reasons, was a point not to be neglected in memorializing a Privy Councillor, yet it does not follow that consideration for the poor or even for the ratepayers had high priority with the founders of any particular colony. Those 'offals of our people' proved indeed a most convenient fodder for plantations, which needed cheap labour, but to suppose that plantations existed for the purpose of consuming excess labour is absurd.[57] Granted that some amateurs of colonization, like William Vaughan the Newfoundland promoter, genuinely wished to remedy poverty, even Vaughan had stronger motives than that for stressing reasons of state, since he and others who advocated Newfoundland settlements had to outbid the fishing interest.[58] Gilbert's discourse on the northwest passage, on the other hand, summons so many arguments, good, bad and indifferent, that the general effect is to undermine confidence in his judgement, let alone his sincerity.[59] Grenville in 1574 offered the queen a similarly indiscriminate collection of benefits to induce her to permit his South American venture. Peckham was another who could not bear to omit any of the alleged advantages of plantation for the realm, though what he wrote about shipping, fisheries and the cloth industry suggests a certain ignorance rather than real concern. There is an element of cant in many such pleas for overseas ventures and the part played by economic nationalism in the genesis of the seaborne empire has often been exaggerated. In fact its main rôle was to clothe other motives in respectable dress.

None of this implies any doubt about the patriotism of these men. National sentiment was at this time probably more intense and generally felt than ever before. The sense of national identity and solidarity, sharpened by the conflict with Spain and the naval drama of 1588, was expressed in the successive publication of three great works: Saxton's atlas of England in 1579, Camden's *Britannia* in 1586 and Hakluyt's *Principall Navigations* in 1589. The last of these pointed to a

---

[57] The phrase 'offals of our people' occurs in the instructions drawn up by Richard Hakluyt the elder for the northeast voyage of Pet and Jackman: *PN* (1589), p. 460.
[58] Cell, *English Enterprise*, p. 83.
[59] Quinn, *Gilbert*, pp. 129–64.

significant shift in the orientation of English nationalism. Formerly anti-French and military, looking to Continental conquest, it was now becoming associated with maritime enterprise and ambition. The trend is marked in the 1580s, which saw a surge of interest in new trades, colonial enterprise, exploration and voyages of plunder. In the following decades a perceptible sea-change in the national consciousness may be sensed in Shakespeare, whose work abounds in knowledgeable reference to seafaring matters, and whose last great play explored the magic of a brave new world revealed by shipwreck in the Virginia voyage of 1609.[60] At the same time the edge of nationalism turned against the Dutch and French as well as the Spaniards. In the first third of the seventeeth century Anglo-French rivalry in North America and the West Indies made its appearance and the former alliance of the Dutch and English, especially at sea, changed into jealousy, resentment and conflict in the North Sea fishery, in northern whaling, in the East India trade and elsewhere. National pride and prestige now heavily reinforced economic interest in the outer world. The English insistence upon deference to their flag, which was a major cause of the first Dutch war, was symptomatic of the intensifying nationalism, at times approaching hysteria, which continually fired their efforts to win a share in the rich trades and the vast lands opened up by explorers.

But the idea of a maritime empire did not immediately seize the imagination of the English people, nor did it arise spontaneously. It had to be propagated. John Dee, who invented the phrase 'British Impire', was the most diligent and influential of the first generation of imperialists. He it was who sketched out the English claim to an empire of the North Atlantic, embracing the Arctic to the east and the west, the northern islands, including mythical Frisland, conquered allegedly by King Arthur and King Malgo, and Atlantis (the continent of North America), first discovered by the Welsh prince Owen Madoc in the twelfth century. All this Dee set down in 1578 in a statement for the queen of 'Her Majesty's Title Royal' to the lands in question, depicted in his 1580 map of Atlantis.[61] Thus the necessary underpinning of myth was provided, to be duly repeated by Peckham, Hakluyt and many more. The two editions of Hakluyt's *Principall Navigations*, in 1589 and 1598–1600 respectively, embodied twenty years of concerted effort to build a tradition of maritime enterprise and achievement. This again

---

[60] See A. F. Falconer, *Shakespeare and the Sea* (London, 1964).
[61] E. G. R. Taylor, *Tudor Geography, 1485–1583* (London, 1930), pp. 122–3; E. G. R. Taylor, 'A letter dated 1577 from Mercator to John Dee', *Imago Mundi*, 13 (1956), 56–68, explores the Arthurian derivation of Dee's imperial ideas further.

was based in medieval record and legend and so showed the multiple initiatives of Tudor times in perspective, implying a national destiny. Moreover Hakluyt brought together the minds of those concerned, from ordinary seamen to lord admirals, from tourists in the Middle East to City magnates and royal favourites, and he engaged the support of those most committed to expansion, notably Richard Staper, Anthony Jenkinson and Michael Lok, all merchant pioneers, Sir John Hawkins, Ralegh and, above all, Walsingham. Thus Hakluyt did more than anyone to integrate and organize the disparate personalities, experiences and aspirations into a movement with a common consciousness and harnessed the horses of nationalism to the chariot of empire.

The Spanish war accelerated the fermentation of these ideas in the national psyche by popularizing them. Not only was the nation as a whole identified with the fleet that defended the Channel in 1588; many sailors, merchants and gentlemen took part directly or indirectly in the privateering war, which focused national attention upon the Atlantic as a theatre of operations and itself a potential prize. Envy of the 'wealth of the Spaniards and Portingals', which had long spurred the pioneers,[62] now became an immediate stimulus activating every port from London round to Bristol, multiplying the nation's ships and fanning the flames of aggressive nationalism. From Henry VIII's time Protestant ideas had tended to take root in seaports and to become associated with anti-Spanish sentiments, particularly when English merchants or seamen fell foul of the Spanish Inquisition. In the later sixties radical, popular and militant Protestantism spread like wildfire as Huguenots, Dutch sea-beggars and English pirates joined forces 'against all Papists'. Already then that fire jumped the Atlantic and soon Francis Drake, the personification of holy wrath, emerged as the hero of the nation. His triumphant encompassing of the globe promoted both confidence and ambition in the maritime forces of the country, for it seemed to lay open the western and eastern worlds to English enterprise. Although for the next two decades those hopes and dreams were continually frustrated, the struggle with Spain ceaselessly nourished them. As the war came to an end the unfinished business of North America was resumed almost as a matter of course by various groups, while the London merchants clubbed together to begin the East Indies trade, which had seemed beyond their reach since Drake's return from the Moluccas. It is true that greater resources were now available to launch eastern trade and western planting, but equally if not more important was the existence of a greater will now

[62] *PN*, II, 240: from Clement Adams's account of the first Muscovy voyage.

that expansion was becoming a national movement, not merely the cause of a small minority, as it had been in 1555, when Richard Eden reproached the English for their backwardness – 'ever like sheep to haunt one trade'.[63] This greater will, resulting from the identification of the expansion movement with English nationalism, was essential to the survival of the seaborne empire in both East and West during the trials and tribulations of the Jacobean years.

With few exceptions the English pioneers carried with them a strong sense of national loyalty and took a predictably ethnocentric view of alien cultures. They reacted sometimes with disgust and contempt, sometimes with kindly condescension to people whom they considered barbarians or savages. Russians, Turks, Persians and various other Asiatics generally fell into the first category, Arctic nomads, American Indians and tropical Africans into the second. Most but not all Europeans were civil. But the English were not equipped with a definite set of ethnic stereotypes nor with anything like a racial ideology. To suppose this is to read back into the sixteenth century attitudes and ideas which grew out of colonial experience and were characteristic of later times. The approach of the Elizabethans and Jacobeans to non-Europeans was normally commercial and pragmatic. Business required a realistic, live-and-let-live relationship and merchants visiting or resident in parts of Africa and Asia had to conduct themselves in a manner acceptable to their hosts, though this was not always easy to do. In Moslem countries they tended to keep themselves to themselves, especially in the Ottoman empire, where there was no love lost between Turk and Frank. There the English adopted Turkish dress, but only in order to avoid insult and injury.[64] Even in Russia they often 'remained isolated and aloof in what they regarded as temporary exile in a barbaric country'.[65]

While in Spain and even to some extent in France learned men speculated about a hierarchy of the human race and earnestly debated the character of the American Indian, the English generally took a more matter-of-fact view of the 'naturals'. They began, it is true, with

[63] R. Eden, *The decades of the newe worlde or west India* (London, 1555), in E. Arber (ed.), *The First Three English Books on America* (Westminster, 1895), p. 55. In the next seventy years the number of books relating to the discoveries (especially translations of foreign works) and to English enterprise grew steadily: see J. Parker, *Books to Build an Empire* (Amsterdam, 1965). Parker tends, I think, to underrate the significance of the new literature, for the conservatism of reading habits was such that a relatively small extension of subject matter may represent an important shift of interest among the public.

[64] A. C. Wood, *A History of the Levant Company* (Oxford, 1935), pp. 235–40.

[65] T. S. Willan, *The Early History of the Russia Company, 1553–1603* (Manchester, 1956), p. 281.

the simple and vague idea of Christianizing and civilizing them, but by and large they did not care enough about savages to make much effort to save their souls. The descriptions of the Virginia Indians by colonists from Ralph Lane and Hariot down to Captain John Smith reveal mixed thoughts and feelings. Contempt alternates with respect for their mental, physical and moral qualities. There is admiration as well as revulsion for their culture. The idea that the colonists regarded the Indians as irredeemably savage is not borne out by the documentary evidence which survives. On the contrary, the initial assumption that the Indians would prove apt pupils and would soon learn to behave like industrious, obedient and God-fearing Englishmen remained the wishful belief of many, particularly at home, in spite of bitter experience. Of course others, notably Smith, took a less optimistic view, based upon a profound distrust. There was no agreed picture of the Indian, but a confusion of images, behind which lay, thinly if at all concealed, one constant drive: to acquire and exploit that land, with or without its people.[66] The same utilitarian attitude is to be seen in one Englishman's disappointed comment on the Baffin Island Eskimo – that their possessions were 'more to be wondred at for their strangenesse, then for any other commoditie needefull for our use';[67] and the same hopeful naivety in the teach-yourself-civility kit left behind by Frobisher, consisting of 'divers of our Countrey toyes, as belles, and knives. . . . Also pictures of men and women in lead, men on horsebacke, looking glasses, whistles, and pipes', all contained in a house built for the purpose, with an oven 'and bread left baked therein for them to see and taste'.[68]

Yet here as elsewhere curiosity kept intruding upon the main purpose. The Eskimo themselves were much wondered at for their strangeness and Dionyse Settle's account of them, published in French, German and Latin as well as English, made an original and significant contribution to European knowledge.[69] Much more elabor-

---

[66] J. H. Rowe, 'Ethnography and ethnology in the sixteenth century', *Kroeber Anthropological Society Papers*, 30 (1964), presents a rather over-simplified view. J. H. Elliott, *The Old World and the New, 1492–1650* (Cambridge, 1970), is a good introduction. Modern literature on English attitudes to Indians in North America often over-emphasizes 'ideology' – e.g. F. Jennings, *The Invasion of America* (Chapel Hill, 1975), and B. Sheehan, *Savagism and Civility: Indians and Englishmen in Colonial Virginia* (Cambridge, 1980). K. O. Kupperman, *Settling with the Indians* (London, 1980), represents a more moderate approach. H. C. Porter, 'Reflections on the ethnohistory of early colonial North America', *Journal of American Studies*, 16 (1982), 243–54, attacks prevalent American interpretations.

[67] *PN*, VII, 221.

[68] *PN*, VII, 362.

[69] For details see V. Stefansson and E. McCaskill (eds.), *The Three Voyages of Martin Frobisher* (2 vols., London, 1938), II, pp. 226–7.

ate, extensive, accurate and influential was the combined work of John White the artist and Thomas Hariot the scientist on the geography, natural history and native population of Ralegh's Virginia, a landmark in the European discovery of America. From Russia the successive reports of Richard Chancellor, Anthony Jenkinson and others published by Hakluyt did much, together with Jenkinson's map, to improve and disseminate knowledge of that country. The servants of the early East India Company, who related in their pragmatic way their own experience and observation of the Mogul empire and other parts of the East, produced a rich body of narrative and description, printed for the most part by Samuel Purchas in his *Pilgrimes* in 1625.[70]

Such people, the real pioneers of the seaborne empire, were practical men: Captains Ralph Lane, John Smith and other soldiers of early Virginia, the merchant-commanders of the East Indiamen, the Arctic explorers from the Borough brothers to Baffin and the sea-captains of the Atlantic. Yet for success the movement needed also the moving power of the ideas propagated by such men as Dee, Hakluyt, Ralegh and Drake. For who can doubt the inspiring force of Dee's Faustian genius, which cast a spell on the minds of mariners and intellectuals alike?[71] Hakluyt's influence was already strong and pervasive in his own time.[72] Ralegh, it has been justly said, 'did as much as any other individual of his age to place American colonization in the public mind as a fixed and continuing objective'.[73] A champion in word and deed of the war on Spain, he saw it as a struggle for Atlantic empire and succeeded in demonstrating that concept even though his own imperial schemes collapsed. As for Drake, he too may now be considered an imperialist, but it was as the popular hero of the sea-war that he made a deep and lasting impression upon the nation, animating its aggressive spirit and pointing dramatically to an oceanic future. All these were men of action, deeply engaged in the enterprise from day to day, not mere propagandists or flag-wavers, but far more important than any particular venture of theirs was the mental effect, emotional as well as intellectual, of what they said, wrote and did upon

[70] S. Purchas, *Hakluytus Posthumus or Purchas his Pilgrimes* (20 vols., Glasgow, 1905–7), III and IV.
[71] As A. G. Debus has shown, both E. G. R. Taylor and F. A. Yates went too far in reversing the older view of Dee as magician and alchemist and in claiming him as a prophet of science, but there is no denying his great influence on contemporaries and his close connection with the work of discovery: John Dee, *The Mathematicall Praeface* (1570; ed. A. G. Debus, New York, 1975). P. French, *John Dee, the World of an Elizabeth Magus* (London, 1972), follows both Taylor and Yates. Preferable as a biography is C. F. Smith, *John Dee* (London, 1909).
[72] D. B. Quinn (ed.), *The Hakluyt Handbook* (London, 1974).
[73] D. B. Quinn, *Raleigh and the British Empire* (London, 1947), p. 269.

an important and growing segment of the English people. Though their rhetoric did not fairly represent reality, it was a part of it, expressing the creative power of imagination and the emotive force of nationalism, which together sustained the movement of expansion through this first and hardest phase.

1

Early ventures
1480–1550

In the years from 1480 to 1510 Englishmen made a significant contribution to the European movement of discovery, which in those decades advanced with such strides as to bring about a revolution in geography and eventually in world trade. Yet the connection between English oceanic enterprise and the main European movement, which was centred in the Iberian Peninsula, remains, in spite of much academic inquiry and speculation, obscure. It is possible to trace throughout the fifteenth century the developing interest of the Portuguese in the Atlantic as they explored and began to exploit the African coasts and islands of the east Atlantic – the Cape Verdes, the Canaries, the Madeiras and the Azores – drawing into the orbit of Lisbon an ever-widening sector of the ocean. Attracted not only by the gold of Guinea, but by new fishing grounds and islands to colonize as they probed outwards, mastering progressively the prevailing winds and currents, they were continually inspired by myths of westerly isles. Of these the Island of the Seven Cities, Brasil and Antilia were the most important, figuring with increasing emphasis in later-medieval maps. After the discovery of Corvo, the most westerly of the Azores, in 1453, the Portuguese explored the North Atlantic still more eagerly, though with little to show for it, almost down to 1492, when Columbus, who had acquired his knowledge of the Atlantic in Lisbon and ventures out of Lisbon, carried their quest to its logical conclusion

Columbus was more concerned, however – as most authorities now agree – with that other and grander objective of the Portuguese pioneers, the discovery of a sea-route to the Indies. Since the middle of the century, and more especially since the ending of the Luso-Castilian war in 1479, the Portuguese drive to circumnavigate Africa had gathered impetus and in the eighties the voyages of Diogo Cão and Bartolomeu Dias opened the way to India. Their success may have been the chief reason why the Portuguese authorities finally rejected

41

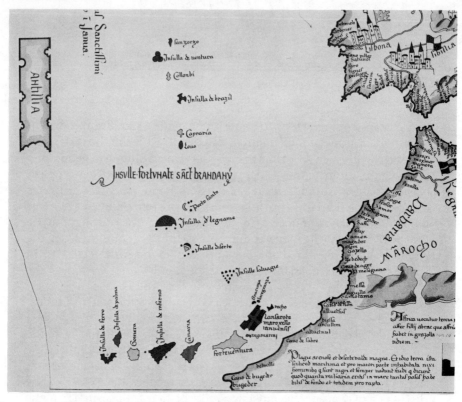

Fig. 1 The Atlantic according to Bartolomeo Pareto, 1455. (From a nineteenth-century copy of a portolan chart in the Biblioteca Nazionale, Rome.)

Columbus's alternative proposal and so turned his steps once more to the Court of the Catholic Kings. However impracticable, his concept of a westward route to the Orient was not so wildly eccentric as to warrant immediate dismissal. Columbus was indeed something of a mystic, possessed by an idea, but that idea was based upon a view of the globe expounded by the Florentine cosmographer Paolo Toscanelli in the 1470s and deriving ultimately from Ptolemy's *Geographia*. That work, which increasingly dominated European geographical thought and cartography in the fifteenth century, encouraged men to envisage the western ocean as a potential link between Europe's farthest West and Asia's farthest East, a notion all but explicit in maps made by the German Henricus Martellus around 1490 and in the celebrated globe designed by Martin Behaim at Nuremberg in 1492, the very year of Columbus's discovery. Moreover, Isabela and Ferdinand backed the Genoese in the knowledge that John II of Portugal might soon launch his invasion of the Indies, and when Columbus returned the two Iberian powers moved into a phase of intense rivalry in pursuit of the great prize – oriental trade – and the lesser goods to be gained by maritime expansion.

The ideas which informed this acceleration of discovery in the late fifteenth century were not the monopoly of any particular group, but circulated quickly in Spain, Portugal, Italy and Germany by normal trade routes, especially because Lisbon and Seville were now becoming important commercial centres. It is not surprising therefore to find that Bristol, having strong links with Lisbon and Seville as well as with the Madeiras, Ireland and Iceland, was an active base of North Atlantic exploration at this time, and it is reasonable to assume, though we have no evidence until the mid nineties, some interchange of ideas between Iberian and Bristolian explorers from about 1480. For it was in the summer of that year that the first recorded Bristol voyage of discovery occurred.[1] A ship of 80 tons under the command of one Thloyde then sailed for 'the island of Brasylle in the western part of Ireland'. After nine weeks she put into an Irish harbour to refit, having failed to find the island.[2] In the following July, 1481, Thomas Croft, one

---

[1] For sources on Bristol–Cabot matters I have used chiefly D. B. Quinn (ed.), *New American World: a Documentary History of North America to 1612* (5 vols., London, 1979), and J. A. Williamson (ed.), *The Cabot Voyages and Bristol Discovery under Henry VII* (Cambridge, 1962). Key secondary works are Quinn, *England and the Discovery of America*, and S. E. Morison, *The European Discovery of America: the Northern Voyages, A.D. 500–1600* (New York and Oxford, 1971), but there is no definitive account.

[2] William Worcestre, 'Itineraria' (Corpus Christi College, Cambridge, MS 210), ed. and trans. J. H. Harvey (Oxford, 1969), cited in Quinn, *New American World*, 1, p. 91. The Latin reads: 'usque ad insulam de Brasylle in occidentali parte Hibernie'.

of the Bristol customs officials, being part-owner of two vessels, the *Trinity* and the *George*, laded them with a quantity of salt which, as he later explained, was 'not by cause of marchandise but to thentent to serch & fynde a certain Isle called the Isle of Brasile'.[3] The evidence concerning these two ventures shows that at that time some people in Bristol were interested in exploring the North Atlantic, specifically for the legendary island of Brasil, which fifteenth-century maps usually located to the west of Ireland. In all probability these explorers were looking for new fishing grounds, for in the 1470s and 1480s German competition in the Iceland trade and fishery became intense and there was good reason for the more enterprising of the English who regularly frequented Iceland to seek alternative fisheries as well as cloth markets elsewhere in the western ocean.[4]

That this Bristolian quest led on to the discovery of North America is quite clear, whether that discovery is attributed to John Cabot and the year 1497 or to Bristol venturers of an earlier date. Cabot, a Venetian, probably came to Bristol in 1494 or 1495. Formerly he had been in Seville and Lisbon seeking assistance for a project similar to that of Columbus: a voyage to the Orient by a westward route.[5] His decision to make Bristol his base must have arisen from knowledge acquired or contacts made in that quarter of the Peninsula, with which the Bristol men had close ties.[6] On 5 March 1496 King Henry VII granted him, in association with his sons Lewis, Sebastian and Sancio, a patent authorizing him to occupy such lands as he might discover in 'the eastern, western and northern sea' and to trade with them through Bristol, acting as the king's subject.[7] It was presumably in the same year that he made his first attempt, of which there is only one brief report, to the effect that he sailed with one ship, but turned back because his crew confused him, he was short of supplies and ran into bad weather. This statement occurs in a letter addressed by one John Day, an English merchant interested in the Iberian trade, to the Spanish 'Almirante Mayor' – almost certainly Christopher Columbus – reporting Cabot's 1497 voyage. Although certain details in Day's account are unclear, he was evidently acquainted with current

---

[3] Williamson, *Cabot Voyages*, pp. 188–9; Quinn, *New American World*, I, p. 92.
[4] E. M. Carus-Wilson, *Medieval Merchant Venturers* (London, 1967), pp. 98–142.
[5] Williamson, *Cabot Voyages*, p. 228, M. Ballesteros-Gabrois, 'Juan Caboto en España', *Revista de Indias*, 4 (1943), 607–27.
[6] Bristol–Portugal links around 1480 are well established (see Quinn, *England and the Discovery of America*, pp. 57–8), but the attempt to link John Jay, the *Trinity* of 1481 and Columbus is unconvincing, though ingenious: T. F. Reddaway and A. A. Ruddock, 'The accounts of John Balsall, purser of the *Trinity* of Bristol, 1480–1', *Camden Miscellany*, 23 (1969), 1–27.
[7] Williamson, *Cabot Voyages*, pp. 203–5.

geographical ideas and well informed about the expedition and its Bristol background, so that his letter, which came to light in 1956, is the most reliable of the various sources.[8]

Taken together with the other evidence, it shows that Cabot sailed from Bristol in May 1497 in the *Mathew*, a Bristol ship of 50 tons with 20 crew, mostly Bristol men. Somewhere west of Ireland he set course due west on a latitude and held it until he made landfall after thirty-five days at sea. The location of this landfall cannot be established because we do not know Cabot's course. Day says that he spent a month exploring the coast, from 'the southernmost part of the Island of the Seven Cities', estimated to be due west of the mouth of the River Gironde, northwards to a certain 'cape of the mainland' reckoned to be 1800 miles due west of Dursey Head in Ireland, from which cape they returned. Cabot may have miscalculated his latitude by anything up to two degrees, which means that the only safe statement of the area discovered is that it lay between 42°N. and 54°N. covering some seven degrees of latitude within those limits.[9]

The return of the *Mathew* to Bristol caused a stir, not only there but in London. The king immediately made an award of £10 'to hym that founde the new Isle' and followed this with a pension of £20 a year to be paid from the Bristol customs revenues. Cabot was fêted, addressed as 'the admiral' and promised royal support for a grand expedition of ten or more vessels to sail the next year.[10] Meanwhile he and others expressed their views of what had happened and what it meant. He believed he had reached Marco Polo's Cathay: 'mainland 700 leagues away, which is the country of the Grand Khan', as a Venetian merchant reported.[11] According to the Milanese ambassador in London, Cabot had been making for the East in quest of the spice trade. Henry intended to back him in a second venture, in which he proposed 'to keep along the coast from the place at which he touched, more and more towards the East', seeking Cipango, which he thought to be the source of spices.[12]

---

[8] L. A. Vigneras, 'New light on the 1497 Cabot voyage to America', *HAHR*, 36 (1956), 503–9. The MS text is in Spanish, which may be a translation from an English original. For English translations see Williamson, *Cabot Voyages*, pp. 211–14, and Quinn, *New American World*, I, pp. 98–9. The author is plausibly identified as Hugh Say, who traded to Spain from Bristol and belonged to a well-connected London family: A. A. Ruddock, 'John Day of Bristol and the English voyages across the Atlantic before 1497', *Geographical Journal*, 132 (1966), 225–33.

[9] There has been much futile argument about Cabot's landfall – see Morison, *Northern Voyages*, pp. 193–5. My interpretation roughly follows Quinn, *England and the Discovery of America*, pp. 93–100.

[10] Williamson, *Cabot Voyages*, pp. 208–17; Quinn, *New American World*, I, pp. 95–102.

[11] Williamson, *Cabot Voyages*, pp. 207–8; Quinn, *New American World*, I, pp. 95–6.

[12] Williamson, *Cabot Voyages*, pp. 209–11; Quinn, *New American World*, I, pp. 97–8.

In the same dispatch, however, the ambassador noted quite a different aspect of the discovery. The sea in that area was swarming with fish, and 'these same English, his companions, say that they could bring so many fish that this kingdom would have no further need of Iceland, from which place there comes a very great quantity of the fish called stockfish. But Messer Zoane [Cabot] has his mind set on even greater things.' Thus the distinction between Bristolian concerns and Cabotian ambitions was clearly drawn. As for the connection between the two enterprises, John Day's letter shows that it was far more important and interesting than used to be realized. As Day put it to Columbus, 'It is considered certain that the cape of the said land was found and discovered in the past [*en otros tiempos*] by the men from Bristol who found Brasil as your lordship well knows. It was called the Island of Brasil, and it is assumed and believed to be the mainland that the men from Bristol found.' That the Bristol explorers had formerly discovered land in the Atlantic is here taken for granted. Day does not quite commit himself to identifying this with Cabot's discovery, but apparently the Bristol men were convinced that their Brasil and Cabot's new isle were one and the same.

It appears to be beyond reasonable doubt that on some occasion before 1497 Bristol sailors had found and reported their 'Brasil'. This in itself is important, since it suggests that the object of the 1497 voyage was in some sense to pursue that earlier discovery. This is also implied by the Spanish diplomat Pedro de Ayala, who wrote to his sovereigns in July 1498: 'For the last seven years the people of Bristol have equipped two, three [and] four caravels to go in search of the island of Brasil and the Seven Cities according to the fancy of this Genoese.'[13] Ayala was obviously confused about the details and unaware of any earlier discovery, but we may accept his main point that the voyage of 1497 was the last of a series, and since it is most unlikely that Cabot led or directed any Bristol ventures before 1496 we may safely assume that the Bristolians were actively engaged in North Atlantic exploration in the years before he joined them. This, added to the fact that Bristol men were already searching for Brasil in 1480 and 1481, indicates a continuing interest if not annual expeditions over a period of at least eighteen years, culminating in Cabot's discovery of North America.

Doubts and debates persist, however, about the Bristolians' Brasil. Was it actually America, and in any case when was it found? Why, moreover, did exploration continue down to 1497 if what was then repeatedly described as 'the new Isle' or 'the new found land' had already been discovered? The first question is unanswerable. Whether

[13] Williamson, *Cabot Voyages*, pp. 228–9; Quinn, *New American World*, i, pp. 101–2.

the Bristolians' identification of Cabot's land with their Brasil was well or ill founded can now only be guessed, though one may wonder why they did not press their claim. As to the rest, two main theories are available. The more obvious explanation is that, having at some stage, possibly even before 1480, found land, the Bristolians had lost track of it. This assumes that the discovery was accidental and that the seamen could only vaguely report its location.[14] Their story was nevertheless convincing enough to induce Bristol men to put money, ships and effort into the search for it over many years, though they searched in vain until 1497. In this case Cabot's was the effective discovery, since he was the first to establish the existence of the new land and to give a reliable account of its geographical position. The alternative view is that the Bristol men made an effective discovery before Cabot, perhaps in the early 1490s, perhaps in or about 1481, but kept the matter secret, presumably because they were exploiting the fishing grounds and did not want competitors to join them.[15]

These and other theories about a supposed pre-Cabotian (or even pre-Columbian) English discovery of America are all highly speculative. More and better evidence is required for a solution of the problem. What is certain is that Cabot's 1497 voyage, itself the outcome of years of Bristol enterprise, was a major event in Atlantic exploration. What followed was an anti-climax. In 1498 he managed to get together only five vessels for a further expedition, one supplied by the king and some London merchants, the remainder by Bristol men. Perhaps the first flush of enthusiasm for a new approach to the Spiceries had already faded. In any case it faded by the end of 1498, for the voyage of that year was a disaster. One ship put into Ireland badly damaged and the rest, with Cabot, were lost at sea. The first known map of America, by Juan de la Cosa, dated 1500, indicates Cabot's 1497 discovery and extends the coast southwards to a point west of Cuba, which has led some authorities to argue that part of Cabot's 1498 expedition reached America, ranged that entire coast and lived to tell the tale. The evidence for this, however, is extremely slight.[16]

14 Ruddock, 'John Day of Bristol'.
15 This is broadly the view taken in Williamson, *Cabot Voyages*, and Quinn, *England and the Discovery of America*, though the two authorities differ as to the probable time of the Bristol discovery. The difficulty I find with it is that the further back in time the discovery is put, the less credible is it that the Bristol men could have kept their secret. If Columbus and Cabot knew it in Spain, it was hardly a secret, but supposing that it was kept, why should the Bristol men have helped Cabot to reveal it to the world? It must in fairness be noted that the authors offer their theories tentatively and that such speculation is necessary and more valuable than Morison's sweeping rejection of any pre-Cabotian English discovery of North America: *Northern Voyages*, p. 208.
16 Williamson, *Cabot Voyages*, pp. 101–11.

Three years later, in March 1501, the grant of a royal patent marked the launching of a new phase of Bristol Atlantic enterprise. Three Portuguese from the Azores and three Bristol merchants were the grantees: João Fernandes, Francisco Fernandes and João Gonsalves, together with Richard Warde, Thomas Asshehurst and John Thomas. They were empowered to explore 'the eastern, western, southern, arctic and northern seas' for lands hitherto unknown to Christians and to occupy, govern and trade with the same.[17] João Fernandes was a farmer (*labrador*) of Terceira, who had obtained a grant for exploration already, in 1499, from the king of Portugal. Although it is not known whether he had before or since then discovered anything, he probably came to England because he found his future as a Portuguese explorer pre-empted by another Azorean, Gaspar Corte Real. The latter set out under Portuguese licence in 1500 and sighted what was probably the southern end of Greenland, which cosmographers concluded to be 'the point of Asia'. It has been argued from later maps that this was the region in which Fernandes was interested, an insular Greenland, the original *Terra Laboratoris* or Labrador associated with his name. The Portuguese – in particular both Corte Real and Fernandes – were thus seeking, it is suggested, a northern route to Asia through the polar region. This interpretation, however, is conjectural: it is not based on any contemporary statement. In fact Corte Real on his next voyage (1501) paid little attention to Greenland, moving west to modern Labrador and coasting south towards New England.[18]

Meanwhile began a series of voyages from Bristol each year from 1501 to 1505. At the beginning of 1502 the king awarded £5 to 'men of bristoll that founde thisle' and in September of that year £20 to 'the merchauntes of bristoll that have bene in the newe founde launde', as well as pensions of £10 each to Francisco Fernandes and João Gonsalves for 'the true service which they have doon unto us, to our singler pleasure, as Capitaignes into the newe founde lande'. In August 1502 three men taken in 'the Newe Found Ile land' were presented to the king: probably Indians rather than Eskimo. Thus we have two voyages, in 1501 and 1502, presumably to roughly the same place, and Henry VII's unwonted generosity suggests that he was considerably impressed by their success or promise of future success. There is

---

[17] Williamson, *Cabot Voyages*, pp. 124–6, 235–47; Quinn, *New American World*, I, pp. 103–9.
[18] On the Corte Real voyages see Morison, *Northern Voyages*, pp. 244–5; Quinn, *England and the Discovery of America*, pp. 111–17; Williamson, *Cabot Voyages*, pp. 116–24, 310–11; H. P. Biggar (ed.), *The Precursors of Jacques Cartier 1497–1534* (Ottawa, 1911), pp. xiv–xx and documents.

nothing in this evidence, however, to indicate that these were north-west passage ventures.[19]

In December 1502 the king issued a new charter for exploration, excluding Warde, Thomas and João Fernandes from the lands discovered or to be discovered, except by permission of Asshehurst, Gonsalves, Francisco Fernandes and one Hugh Elyot, to whom as a group rights and privileges were now granted in new found lands, including lands discovered by Portuguese if they were not 'in possession' – an early formulation of the doctrine of effective occupation. Hugh Elyot's accession broadened the syndicate, for he had important London connections and probably brought in his Bristol partner Robert Thorne. Indeed Thorne's son, also called Robert, later claimed that his father and Elyot were 'the discoverers of the Newfound Landes', though he gave no date and so left us to guess whether they were precursors or successors of John Cabot.[20] Be that as it may, Elyot played a leading part in the affairs of the 1502 group, which became known as 'the Company adventurers in to the new fownde ilondes'. The title itself suggests a trading company, and references to presents received by the king indicate voyages in 1503, 1504 and 1505. In fact the items mentioned – a bow, arrows, parrots, mountain cats – can all be plausibly attributed to eastern North America, and seem to indicate contacts with the Indians there. But the attempt to develop a profitable barter trade must have failed, probably for lack of capital and experience. Lawsuits about money broke out among people connected with the company and there is no further record of its affairs, nor of Bristol venturing to those new found lands.[21]

In spite of the meagreness of our information about this post-Cabotian phase of Bristol's Atlantic pioneering, its general significance is reasonably clear. The voyages of 1501 to 1505 were no more than their promoters consistently avowed them to be: voyages to explore and exploit certain newly found lands to the west, usually thought of as islands. There is no hint that they were trying to reach Asia. No doubt they discussed whether the new lands should be regarded as parts of Asia or as places to be passed on the way thither, but none of the evidence suggests that this was a matter of practical concern to them. Thus Englishmen gained some experience of transatlantic voyaging and some shortlived contact with North America. French and Portuguese fishermen arrived on the Newfoundland Banks in the early

[19] Williamson, *Cabot Voyages*, pp. 215–16, 220–2, 248–9; Quinn, *England and the Discovery of America*, pp. 117–18.
[20] Williamson, *Cabot Voyages*, p. 202.
[21] Williamson, *Cabot Voyages*, pp. 132–4, 216, 250–64; Quinn, *New American World*, I, pp. 111–20; Quinn, *England and the Discovery of America*, pp. 121–7.

years of the century, and although we hear nothing of their English counterparts, it is scarcely credible that Bristol men were not there also at this time. The silence of the records on this point does not imply a negative, for fishing did not normally attract official attention, nor do we have Admiralty Court records from this period. It is not at all unlikely that future research will show Bristol fishermen quietly frequenting those parts from the 1480s to the 1500s, supplying the background without which the Bristol Atlantic story of those decades must remain to some degree enigmatic.

Two motives went into the making of Cabot's discovery: the quest for land in the western ocean, and the quest for a western route to the East. In 1497–8 Cabot fused them, as Columbus had done, but in the years after his death until 1505 there is no evidence that the English were seeking Asia in their western voyages. It is as if the discovery had to be digested before the oriental theme could reassert itself, and when it did so it was inseparable from the problem of the new lands. The exploration of the newly found lands thus at some stage after 1505 became enmeshed with a renewed interest in reaching Asia, taking now the form of a search for some route round or through what was dimly perceived as a distinct region, perhaps a vast continent, perhaps an archipelago. But when did this occur? Specifically, when did the English search for a northwest passage round America to the East begin? And to what extent did English exploration of the western ocean after 1505 remain concerned with the new found lands for their own sake? The evidence available does not permit definitive solutions to these problems, but our object must be to clarify them as far as possible.

The beginnings of England's quest for Arctic routes to Cathay are associated above all with Sebastian, son of John Cabot. Probably born in Venice in the early 1480s, Sebastian grew up in Bristol and stayed there after his father's death, through the 1500s. It has for some time been generally believed that he made a voyage in 1508–9 or thereabouts to the northeast region of North America seeking a passage to the Far East, but our evidence for this is not entirely satisfactory. Nobody connected with the voyage, apart from Cabot himself, ever mentioned it. Those who referred to it wrote well after the event and named Cabot as their source, but contradicted each other wildly with respect to the date and the area explored. Perhaps Cabot contradicted himself, perhaps he was wrongly reported, perhaps both, but even if we suppose that he did make a northwest voyage, we cannot be sure of the details. Peter Martyr, historian of the Spanish

Indies, is our chief informant. He obtained an account from Cabot in 1515 – the earliest available – and added some points in later references in this same work. To him we owe the dating of the voyage at about 1508, which is supported by a later report, though some other authorities refer vaguely to the reign of Henry VII. Apart from the date, Peter Martyr's most important contribution was a clear and consistent definition of the area explored. He called it 'the land of Baccalai', devoted most of his space to the codfish, and put Cabot's furthest north at 55°. Only much later, in 1556, did there appear, in Ramusio's collection of voyages, a quite different story, which Ramusio said he received from Cabot 'many years ago'. It was now revealed that 'our Venetian' had sailed as far as 67° 30′N., aiming for Cathay, and 'would have done it if the ill-will of the master and sailors, who were mutinous, had not compelled him to turn back'.[22]

The disparity between the Peter Martyr and the Ramusio accounts may be explained in three ways. It may be that Cabot did explore far to the northwest of Labrador at the end of Henry VII's reign, but concealed the fact after his emigration to Spain in 1512 and, for fear of offending Charles the king-emperor, modestly described his achievement to Peter Martyr as a mere voyage to the cod-rich Bacallaos; and that only later did he reveal his secret, which appeared in the maps and globes of Gemma Frisius in the 1530s in the form of a strait north of America, and in Cabot's own chart and discourse, no longer extant but mentioned by Richard Willes in 1577, as a passage accessible from the Atlantic between 61°N. and 64°N.[23] Alternatively the first version, related to Peter Martyr, was the closer to reality and Cabot introduced

[22] Williamson, *Cabot Voyages*, pp. 145–72, 265–91; Quinn, *England and the Discovery of America*, pp. 139–44. Fresh circumstantial evidence on the date of this voyage is provided in Quinn, *New American World*, I, pp. 121–3. This suggests that Cabot may have been out of England for about a year (possibly two years) before May 1509, and so supports Peter Martyr's date as well as the likelihood that Cabot did make a voyage at this time. The references to the voyage occur at three different places in Peter Martyr's *Decades*. Ramusio in 1550 published another report, by a certain Mantuan gentleman, giving a very muddled and incredible story allegedly told him by Cabot (Williamson, *Cabot Voyages*, pp. 270–3; Quinn, *New American World*, I, pp. 124–6).

[23] For this theory see Williamson, *Cabot Voyages*, pp. 163–70, 320–4; and pp. 278–9 for Willes. Unresolved questions are: why should Cabot have been afraid that his interest in the northwest passage might offend King Charles? If he was afraid of this, why did he reveal his secret to Frisius and Ramusio? Why should he have given Frisius one latitude and Ramusio another? Why did Philip Jones, a seaman who must have known Cabot, argue that the latter got no further than 52°N. (BL, Harleian MS 167, fo. 107)? And were the members of the London Drapers Company, when asked to subscribe to Cabot's 1521 project, justified in commenting, as they did, that this 'Sebastyan, as we here [hear] say, was never in that land hym self, all if he makes reporte of many thinges as he hath hard his Father and other men speke in tymes past' (Williamson, *Cabot Voyages*, p. 289)? See also Quinn, *New American World*, I, pp. 172–8.

the northwest passage claim later in order to get support for a northwest project which he put to Cardinal Wolsey in 1520–21. That Cabot was quite capable of inventing the Ramusio story is clear from the report of the Venetian ambassador in Spain concerning Cabot's offer to perform the same project for Venice. It would be easy, he said, to convey wares 'from Venice to the harbour, as also spices, gold and other produce from the harbour to Venice, as I know; for I have sailed to all those countries, and am well acquainted with the whole'.[24] A third possibility, which is suggested by recently discovered evidence, is that he made two voyages to the northwest: first a voyage to the new found lands in 1504, serving 'in and aboute' an expedition set forth by Robert Thorne and Hugh Elyot, which would correspond with what he told Peter Martyr;[25] and a few years later the voyage of Ramusio's account, in which he reached a much higher latitude.

Each of the three theories has its weaknesses, for the record is confused not simply by a paucity of evidence typical of the period around 1500, but by Sebastian Cabot himself, who, while not inclined to depreciate his own achievements, failed to produce a definitive account of them. His habit of telling different stories to different people, far from tarnishing his reputation, seems rather to have enhanced it in his own era, and the confusion he created served well as a breeding ground for myth. The next generation gave him credit for his father's discovery and accepted his claim to have found a northwest passage. He succeeded in sowing in Elizabethan minds the ineradicable notion that his secret way to Cathay was theirs by right as an original English invention, theirs also by virtue of the special knowledge they derived from him. Hakluyt and his contemporaries certainly had very muddled ideas about the Cabots, but they adopted Sebastian as their guiding star and followed him northwest.

Other people and events also contributed to the development of a special English interest in the North as a route to the East, the most important episode being the project of Robert Thorne the younger and Roger Barlow. These were Bristol merchants deeply involved in the trade of Seville, where they personally resided during the 1520s. Thorne, who had connections in the Canary Islands and even in Spain's West Indies, inherited from his father a passion for the northern quest, while Barlow himself knew the Canaries, the Azores and Santa Cruz in Morocco and became a notable explorer and geographer. Both were acquainted with Sebastian Cabot. In 1526

---

[24] Williamson, *Cabot Voyages*, pp. 282–91.
[25] A. A. Ruddock, 'The reputation of Sebastian Cabot', *Bulletin of the Institute of Historical Research*, 47 (1974), 95–8.

Thorne combined with Leonardo Cataneo, member of a Genoese banking family, to take a share in an expedition to be led by Cabot to the South Sea and Spiceries by way of the southwest, in which voyage Roger Barlow sailed, along with an English pilot, one Henry Patmer. According to Thorne's plan, these two were:

to bring mee certaine relation of the situation of the countrey, and to bee experte in the Navigation of those seas, and there to have informations of many other things, and advise that I desire to know especially. . . and especially to know what Navigation they have for [from] those Ilandes Northwardes, and Northeastwarde. For if from the sayd Ilandes the Sea do extende, without interposition of lande, to sayle from the North poynt to the Northeast poynt 1700. or 1800 leagues, they should come to the Newe founde Ilandes that wee discovered, and so wee should bee neerer to the sayde spicerie by almost 2000. leagues then the Emperour, or the king of Portingal are.[26]

Thorne wrote this in 1527 to Dr Lee, Henry VIII's ambassador in Spain, in reply to a request for information concerning the rivalry between the Iberian powers for control of the Spice Islands trade. As Thorne explained, each side claimed the islands to fall within its sphere of influence as defined by the treaty of Tordesillas of 1494, and the dispute had become serious since Magellan's voyage. Cabot's venture was only one of a series concerned with establishing a Spanish spice trade, and the emperor seemed to have a good case in longitudinal terms. The English, however, suspected he was weakening and might allow the Portuguese to buy him out (as they did in 1529). Thorne therefore thought it timely to suggest an English alternative: 'Nowe then (if from the sayde newe founde landes the Sea bee Navigable,) there is no doubte, but sayling Northwarde and passing the pole descending to the equinoctiall lyne wee shall hitte these Ilandes, and it shoulde bee muche more shorter way, then eyther the Spaniardes or the Portingales have.'[27]

Thorne's scheme was thus for a voyage over the North Pole into the Pacific, leaving North America on the left. He recognized that such a project invited objections, even ridicule, but after Barlow's return late in 1528 from Cabot's expedition (spent in exploring the River Plate) the two of them drew up an appeal to Henry VIII to promote their polar plan. Thorne bought a ship for the purpose, but in 1532 he died, still a young man, and the plan was shelved. Barlow, however, did not

[26] R. Hakluyt, *Divers voyages touching the discouerie of America* (1582), ed. D. B. Quinn (Amsterdam, 1967), p. 28. On this project see E. G. R. Taylor (ed.), *A Brief Summe of Geographie, by Roger Barlow* (London, 1932); G. Connell-Smith, *Forerunners of Drake*, pp. 67–76.

[27] Hakluyt, *Divers Voyages*, p. 38.

abandon it altogether. In 1540–41 he composed a geographical work, his *Brief Summe of Geographie*, which, though largely based on the book by Martín Fernández de Enciso published in 1519, contained important additions, notably an account of the Plate Basin and, as climax to the whole, a transcript of the key part of the earlier address to the king outlining the northern project. Barlow's book was not published until 1932, but his proposal was considered by the Privy Council in 1541. The Spanish ambassador reported that it was thought English woollen cloth would prove very acceptable in the 'northern regions' and that the idea was dropped only because the king would not agree to the terms of a certain 'pilot from Seville well versed in the affairs of the sea' who was to undertake the venture – Cabot himself presumably. Barlow's plan may have been discussed again in 1546, and in 1551 the Spanish ambassador noted that Cabot and Jean Ribault were working together on a project 'to discover some islands, taking the way of the Arctic Pole'.[28] This is the last we hear of the Thorne–Barlow scheme, which at this point was subsumed in Sebastian Cabot's final triumph, the northeast venture of 1553, the genesis and fortune of which are to be described in the next chapter.

Thus far Henry VIII's record as a patron of westward enterprise must look unimpressive. He did, however, give support to three voyages intended to explore the North American coast. The first of these was promoted and led in 1517 by the lawyer, publisher and writer John Rastell. Rastell married Sir Thomas More's sister and shared More's intellectual interest in the great discoveries and the potentialities of the New World. Having some influence in official circles, he managed to interest people concerned with the king's ships, to borrow money from the crown and to obtain a passport for his venture, which thus took on a semi-official character. Unfortunately he proved himself a remarkably incompetent commander: the expedition disintegrated on its way to Ireland and left him stranded in Waterford. But Rastell's ideas and intentions, which he expressed in a satirical verse play, *A new interlude and a mery of the iiij elementes*, published in 1519, are interesting. Few Englishmen at that time can have been so well informed about the new geography. He recognized the existence of a vast continent, called after 'Americus', including North America, with valuable forests and coastal waters. What is more, he wanted the English to occupy it, and declared that this had been his purpose. Indeed we know from other evidence that he took soldiers and equipment for that purpose. He gave some rough impression of the Indians and advocated converting them. He was not sure whether men could sail from there to Cathay,

[28] Taylor, *Brief Summe*, pp. l–lvi.

but his main concern was with North America, his venture being the first, precocious intimation of English ambition to colonize there.[29]

To Rastell in 1517 the western way to the East was an available concept but not an operational objective. His attention was still fixed upon those lands 'Which the noble kinge of late memory/ The most wyse prynce the vij Herry/ Causyd furst for to be founde.' But the next voyage, led by John Rut in 1527, was intended to seek a passage through or round those lands to Cathay. This was a well-organized expedition, backed by the crown. Rut was the king's man and one of his two ships, the *Mary Guildford*, was the king's. He seems to have sailed first to the coast of Labrador, where he lost contact with his second vessel, the *Samson*, which was never heard of again. Icebergs turned him southwards to Newfoundland and then south again. In November (having left England in June) he reached Santo Domingo, where the Spaniards greeted him with understandable surprise and suspicion. He stayed less than twenty-four hours in the mouth of the river and made off in haste when the warden of the fort sent a lombard ball across his bows. But the Spaniards did learn something about the expedition, particularly that the ship was powerful, in good condition, laden with linens, woollens and other goods for barter, and that it had been sent to explore 'toward the north, between Labrador and New-foundland, in the belief that in that region there was a strait through which to pass to Tartary'. One witness reported the English sailors as saying they had gone as far as 64°N. Why the English had come so far south to the Caribbean remained unclear. Possibly they needed a pilot, as they alleged, possibly they were after provisions and perhaps intelligence of the West Indies. What the Spaniards did not suspect was that Rut was looking for the narrow isthmus between the Atlantic and the Pacific which Giovanni Verrazzano thought he had found in about 34°N. during his recent exploration of the American coast, in 1524. This explanation of Rut's southward course may be the true one, but it is purely conjectural. On the other hand we have good evidence that this was a northwest passage venture: the first well-attested English attempt.[30]

The third voyage, that of Richard Hore to Newfoundland in 1536,

---

[29] J. A. Williamson (ed.), *The Voyages of the Cabots and the English Discovery of North America under Henry VII and Henry VIII* (London, 1929), pp. 85–93; Quinn, *England and the Discovery of America*, pp. 162–9.

[30] Williamson, *Voyages of the Cabots*, pp. 102–11; I. A. Wright (ed.), *Spanish Documents concerning English Voyages to the Caribbean, 1527–1568* (London, 1929), pp. 27–59; Biggar, *Precursors*, pp. 165–77 (giving Spanish texts with translations of Seville documents, including a report from Mona Island); Quinn, *England and the Discovery of America*, pp. 171–82.

likewise had Henry's support. We do not know its purpose, but we do
know it failed rather dismally. The main ship, commanded by Hore
and carrying a number of gentlemen 'desirous to see the strange things
of the world', seems to have got into difficulties on the north side of
Newfoundland or the Labrador coast, where the company took to
eating each other. Finally they seized a French vessel with its stores
and used it to return home. Their consort went to the already well-
known fishery off the southeast of the island and came back to England
with a cargo of fish.[31] After this fiasco neither Henry nor his subjects
ventured to promote exploration in the North Atlantic, so far as we
know.

Indeed the whole record of English North Atlantic enterprise
between 1509 and 1550 contrasts strongly with that of the earlier
period. Whereas from 1480 to 1509 they had led the way in discovery
and reconnaissance of the northeastern shores of North America,
rivalled there only by the Portuguese, after 1509 they achieved nothing
to compare with the work of Fagundes for Portugal, Verrazzano and
Cartier for France, or Gomes for Spain, who then gave Europe some
sketch of the shape and character of that region. Although the English
were participating in the Newfoundland fisheries by 1522, the weight
of the evidence suggests that Portuguese and French fishermen were
dominant there from the early years of the century, which no doubt
has some bearing upon the pre-eminence of those nations in the
second phase of the discovery.[32] In the first period Bristol took the
initiative and maintained the effort throughout, with royal approval
and patronage in the form of patents, pensions and the gracious
reception of presents. London merchants and officials played a small,
secondary rôle. In the second period Bristol faded. If Sebastian Cabot
did make a venture in 1508 or thereabouts, he probably had Bristol
backing, and Bristol entered into his 1520–21 proposals, as into those of
Thorne and Barlow. But the only pioneering expeditions known to
have been launched from England into the northern ocean in this
second phase derived their impetus from official and court circles in
London.

Not, however, from London merchants, who took no considerable
part in these ventures and responded so coldly to Cabot's 1520–21
project that they probably killed it off. This lack of enthusiasm on the
part of the City is understandable. The newly found lands, however
rich in resources, did not offer ready profits comparable in scale to
those available in Continental trade, while heavy, long-term invest-

[31] Quinn, *England and the Discovery of America*, pp. 182–9, and references there.
[32] Biggar, *Precursors*, pp. 142–3.

ment was simply unacceptable to English merchants at that time. Only the fishery was attractive, and that duly became a sphere of business interest, but for Londoners it was a minor one, and in any case required no further initiative. As for attempting to establish direct trade with the East, by way of the west, northwest or north, the idea was far too unlikely and risky to appeal to London merchants so long as their trades with Europe prospered, as they did during the reigns of the first two Tudors. Even later, when the old trades fell upon evil days, northern passage projectors had to offer special inducements (cloth sales, whaling prospects, etc.) and still met resistance.

But this should not surprise us. The pioneering of the oceans never was a business to attract ordinary merchants. The promoters were princes, great Italian merchant houses with capital to spare, and some few seamen, merchants or gentlemen with an eccentric interest in the potential of the unknown parts of the wider world. In England at this time knowledge of the new geography advanced at a snail's pace and men like Rastell or Barlow were exceptional. The impression conveyed by books published in this country before 1550 is that even the educated minority were slow to abandon obsolete concepts such as the tripartite view of the world, a landlocked Indian Ocean and so forth, depending for their geography on Sir John Mandeville or at best Marco Polo and a partly updated Ptolemy atlas. No substantial current of intellectual interest in the discoveries yet existed, and when this is set alongside the absence of any powerful economic incentive to expand the area of the nation's foreign trade, the poverty of the English contribution to the European movement of exploration after 1509, when the special concern of a comparatively small number of Bristol merchants dissolved, is no great mystery.[33] Henry VIII's attitude was by no means negative, as we have seen, but unlike his father he lacked any considerable native movement to patronize.

In these decades the English also began to venture southwards to Africa, the east Atlantic islands and Brazil. These were for the most part Portuguese spheres of interest, the exception being the Canaries, which in 1479, after long dispute, Portugal acknowledged to belong to Castile. By this time the Portuguese had already settled the Madeiras, the Azores and the Cape Verde Islands and were successfully trading in the Atlantic ports of Morocco, in Arguim, in Upper Guinea (Senegal, Gambia, Sierra Leone) and on the Gold Coast. These rich African

---

[33] On the numbers and rôle of the Bristol men see P. McGrath, 'Bristol and America 1480–1631', in K. R. Andrews, N. P. Canny and P. E. H. Hair (eds.), *Westward Enterprise*, pp. 81–94.

trades attracted some foreign adventurers. Castilians had been competing there with the Portuguese for many years and Queen Isabela's withdrawal of her support for these interlopers by the treaty of Alcaçovas (1479) did not entirely end their activities. Flemish ships visited Mina, the focus of the gold trade, in the later 1470s, and in 1481 or 1482 two English merchants, John Tintam and William Fabian, were commissioned by the duke of Medina Sidonia, a Spaniard with ambitions to acquire Santiago Island in the Cape Verdes, to organize an expedition to Guinea. John II of Portugal, however, quickly intervened with a protest to Edward IV, who not only stopped the voyage but forbade all his subjects to venture to Guinea and sent the king of Portugal a written guarantee of this policy. Again in 1488, when a certain Portuguese refugee count tried to find support in England for a Guinea voyage, Henry VII arrested him at the request of John II. Henry, it is true, refused to hand his prisoner over to the Portuguese, but neither this nor any of the evidence about these Guinea projects of the 1480s suggests that English interest in Guinea was anything but weak.[34] Indeed it was not until the 1530s that English ships began to appear on the coasts of West Africa.

Meanwhile the Portuguese developed a flourishing commerce, principally in gold, pepper, ivory, slaves, sugar and wax, and exploited the valuable fisheries off Barbary and Upper Guinea. At the same time they extended their activities to Benin, São Thomé and the neighbouring islands. The fifty years before 1530 were the hey-day of a trading empire of the east Atlantic embraced by a great arc from Lisbon through the Azores and Cape Verdes to the Gulf of Guinea. In this vast region the Portuguese possessed a number of islands and a handful of forts on the mainland coast, which stretched for thousands of miles. The islands, particularly Santiago in the Cape Verdes and São Thomé in the Gulf of Guinea, were important bases for the mainland trades and strategic centres for shipping, but the forts were of local value only. Even the strongest of them – São Jorge da Mina, founded in 1482 – dominated no more than its immediate surroundings. The Portuguese were hostile to foreign interloping, but what enabled them to maintain a virtual monopoly of these trades before 1530 (apart from some Andalusian competition, chiefly in fishing) was evidently lack of initiative on the part of the foreigners rather than the feeble defensive or punitive power at Portugal's disposal.

This situation changed in the 1530s, when French ships penetrated

[34] J. W. Blake (ed.), *Europeans in West Africa, 1450–1560* (London, 1942), pp. 263–8. My account of Portuguese commerce and foreign interloping in West Africa is based on J. W. Blake, *West Africa: Quest for God and Gold, 1454–1578* (London, 1977).

the Guinea trade in considerable numbers, which grew in the following decade, frequenting above all the Malagueta coast for pepper.
Many of these interlopers, moreover, went on from the Cape Verdes,
Sierre Leone or the Malagueta coast to Brazil, where they bartered with
the Indians for brazilwood, a trade the French had pursued alongside
the Portuguese since the early years of the century. From 1530 to 1542
some English merchants joined in the Brazil trade, and the most
important of these, William Hawkins of Plymouth, combined Guinea
and Brazil in the French manner. Hakluyt gives a brief account of three
voyages (1530–32) of Hawkins's 250-ton *Paul*, which brought back
ivory and other goods from the Río de Sestos on the Grain (Malagueta)
Coast and unspecified commodities from Brazil, together with 'one of
the savage kings of the countrey', who created something of a sensa-
tion when presented at court. In 1536 Hawkins asked Thomas Cromwell for royal support to the extent of £2000, four brass guns and a last
of powder for similar 'feats of merchandise', implying that he had just
wound up another such venture, and in 1540 Plymouth customs
records supply details of a further expedition by the *Paul* to Guinea and
Brazil, yielding a hundredweight of ivory and 92 tons of brazilwood.
The signs are that William Hawkins did well out of this enterprise, and
Hakluyt tells us that various wealthy Southampton merchants also
'ordinarily and usually' frequented 'this commodious and gainefull
voyage to Brasil' around 1540, mentioning Robert Reneger and
Thomas Borey by name. One Pudsey of Southampton, 'a man of good
skill and resolution in marine causes', made a voyage in 1542 to Bahia
and erected a fort not far from there, which suggests the existence or
expectation of a regular trade. A London ship, the *Barbara*, went from
Portsmouth to Brazil in 1540 and thence to the Caribbean, where her
crew abandoned her, returning home in a captured Spanish vessel – an
act of piracy for which they were duly arrested. None of these
adventurers apart from Hawkins included Guinea in their circuit so far
as we know, but there is enough material to indicate a considerable
Brazil trade from 1530 to 1542.[35]

Most if not all of the Brazil promoters, including Hawkins, had a
strong interest in Iberian trade, which now, as throughout the century,
proved to be the main source and growing point of English interest in
the ocean trades of Spain and Portugal. In Lisbon and Seville merchants of the West Country particularly dealt in the exotic products of

[35] *PN*, XI, 23–5; J. A. Williamson, *Sir John Hawkins, the Time and the Man* (Oxford, 1927),
pp. 6–19; R. G. Marsden (ed.), 'Voyage of the Barbara to Brazil, A.D. 1540', in *Naval
Miscellany*, 2 (London, 1912), 3–66. The *Barbara* carried a French pilot and twelve
Frenchmen, including interpreters for trading with the Indians, and went to a French
trading station on the north coast of Brazil.

the Iberian empires and picked up valuable intelligence about the routes and conduct of those trades from merchants and seamen with experience of them. This may incidentally explain why the majority of the English involved in the Brazil trade took no part in the more dangerous business of Guinea. The Portuguese in the 1530s began to take stronger measures against the Guinea interlopers, which for those with substantial stakes in trade with Portugal spelt potential ruin, whereas they still had fairly easy and safe access to many parts of Brazil. After 1542, however, we have no record of Brazil voyages by English ships until the late 1570s, nor did the English venture to the Guinea coasts between 1542 and 1553. The French persisted in both regions, but the Portuguese now opposed them still more fiercely, above all at sea. Reprisals and plunder became part of these trades henceforth, and this was probably the reason for the English withdrawal.[36]

The position of English merchants in the Atlantic trades of Spain in the first half of the sixteenth century was quite different from their position in the Portuguese trades. The treaty of Medina del Campo between England and Spain in 1489 gave Englishmen the right to trade in Spain's dominions on the same footing as Spanish subjects. To the Canary Islands, which were part of metropolitan Spain, they could trade directly with their own ships as to other Spanish ports. Business in the Spanish Indies they had to conduct through Seville and in accordance with the regulations of the *Casa de la Contratación* there. Relations between the two countries were good for the greater part of the reigns of Henry VII and VIII, and during the 1520s a strong body of English traders developed in Andalusia. Direct trade between English ports and the Canary Islands probably became considerable in the second quarter of the century, for early in the fifties we find English factors well established there. Nicholas (brother of Robert) Thorne and other Bristol merchants, according to Hakluyt, 'in the yeere of our Lord 1526 (and by all circumstances and probabilities long before). . . exercised usuall and ordinary trade of marchandise unto the Canarie Ilands', dispatching goods there from Seville to be exchanged for orchil (a local dye), sugar and kids' skins, which were shipped thence to England.[37]

---

[36] Hakluyt's sources clearly implied there had been no trade to Brazil since *c.* 1542. The Guinea trade begun in 1553 was a new trade to the Gold Coast, whereas Hawkins's earlier ventures were to the Grain Coast. Williamson suggested that the Guinea and Brazil trades might have stopped because the ships were diverted to Channel privateering in the French war, but Portuguese reactions to French interloping were probably more important – see Blake, *West Africa*, pp. 115ff.

[37] *PN*, VI, 124–5, 134; IX, 341.

The first evidence that Englishmen at Seville were taking part in Spain's New World trade occurs as early as 1509. In the 1520s Robert Thorne, his brother Nicholas and Roger Barlow were conducting business with Santo Domingo and other places in the Caribbean, employing as factors there not only Spaniards but the Englishman Thomas Tison. At least two other English traders resided in the Indies at this time, and others operated transatlantic business from Seville, but this seems to have been the height of the trade. Later in Henry VIII's reign the position of English merchants in Seville deteriorated owing to increasing political and religious tension between the two countries, though even then one or two Englishmen managed to have some trade with the Indies.[38]

The actions of the Inquisition against English merchants, beginning in the early thirties, caused increasing resentment in the latter part of that decade. No doubt the merchants' complaints were exaggerated, both by themselves and by Protestant propagandists then and later, but the fact remains that the Holy Office did imprison, maltreat and confiscate the goods of a number of Englishmen. Some were ruined, some withdrew from the trade, some accommodated themselves to the beliefs of their hosts and continued their business. All this embittered relations, not so much between the two states as between the two peoples. Anti-Spanish and anti-Catholic feeling developed particularly in the southwest ports, which had close ties with the Peninsula. Soon, moreover, maritime conflict between the two nations added fuel to these flames. In 1543 Henry VIII joined Charles of Spain in war upon France and licensed English ships to seize enemy vessels and goods at sea. Disputes then arose because English privateers attacked ships belonging to the emperor's subjects, Flemish as well as Spanish, alleging the presence of French goods aboard. This kind of trouble was common enough in time of war, especially when England and Spain were allied against France. But in 1544 Charles made peace with France, leaving Henry to continue the war alone. Hereupon the English privateers, hitherto held in check to some extent by the government, took to seizing and plundering Flemish and Spanish ships without restraint, the emperor retaliated by arresting English ships, property and persons in Spain and the Low Countries, and an unofficial campaign of maritime reprisals supervened.[39]

Prominent among these predators in the year 1545 were Thomas Wyndham, William Hawkins and Robert Reneger. Wyndham, already a leading naval commander, later became a moving spirit in the

[38] Connell-Smith, *Forerunners*, pp. 70–75, 97, 123; *PN*, x, 6–7.
[39] Connell-Smith, *Forerunners*, pp. 100–34.

opening of the Barbary and Guinea trades. As captain of the *Mawdelyn Russell*, a privateer owned by Lord Russell, he attacked Spanish shipping and in 1546 was in trouble over a quantity of pepper taken from a Portuguese ship. Both he and Hawkins had to restore some of their plunder and Hawkins spent a short spell in prison for illicitly selling Spanish goods taken by one of his privateers. Reneger was a Southampton man, much involved in the Spanish trade and one of the Brazilian venturers around 1540. As an important shipowner, he took up the maritime war with a will, obtaining letters of reprisal against the French in 1543. In 1545 he seized a cargo of treasure and other goods returning from the Spanish Indies, by far the richest prize of the war, and caused a major international incident. The immediate effect of such a sensational *coup* was to encourage others to join the fray in the hope of like success, so that the spoliation of Spanish shipping increased apace. But there also ensued a long diplomatic wrangle over the case, for although Reneger's action was patently illegal he had sufficient influence in high places (especially with the gold lodged in the Tower of London) to ensure the crown's backing. Henry VIII refused to restore the prize goods unless English property arrested in Spain were released, meanwhile keeping up the maritime pressure which Spain was unable to counter. Only after Henry's death was the matter settled by a compromise which strongly favoured Reneger and his supporters. The Spaniards interested had to be content with the restitution of less than a third of their goods, and this was made conditional upon the lifting of the Spanish embargo. The whole episode was a defeat for Spain and a significant triumph for the aggressive and predatory elements now entrenched in the English establishment, especially the naval establishment. Rightly has Reneger been called a forerunner of Drake.[40]

It is not difficult to discern in this fragmentary story some themes that were to ring loud and clear in the age of expansion ahead. Already the English declared an interest in the northeast shores of America. Already they began to poach upon parts of Africa and the New World claimed by the Iberian nations as their preserves. Already in the course of European conflicts they were preying upon Spanish and Portuguese shipping. To a great extent English oceanic enterprise derived its ideas and ambitions from Portugal and Spain, where most of its energetic exponents had business and connections. Out of these ties grew knowledge, emulation, rivalry, enmity – a cycle repeated in the

[40] Connell-Smith, *Forerunners*, pp. 127–203; Williamson, *Sir John Hawkins*, pp. 35–6; R. Tong, 'Captain Thomas Wyndham', *History Today*, 7 (1957), 221–8.

Elizabethan period and again in the Jacobean. But some major themes are as yet absent – the eastern drive for oriental trade for instance – and above all there is no coherent movement. Individuals or groups pursue their projects independently, without apparent contact, and there is no voice that speaks for them all, as Richard Eden is soon to do, and after him Richard Hakluyt. Ideas are raised and dropped again, initiatives are not followed through, there is a succession of false starts. All but a few committed persons are ignorant and indifferent.

At bottom the weakness of English oceanic enterprise at this stage lay in London. We have noticed throughout the pioneering rôle of Bristol men, Plymouth men, Southampton men, but London initiative and support were for the most part conspicuous by their absence. The crown, the court and government lent a helping hand often, and sometimes gave a lead, but the City hung back. At this time the community of London merchants was richer and more powerful than ever before, and its wealth and power were fast increasing, yet the range of London's overseas trade contracted during the reigns of the two Henries. For the basis of the nation's commerce was the production of woollen cloth for export, but although these exports doubled during the period they flowed increasingly into a single narrow channel: through London to Antwerp. Other branches of foreign trade – to the Mediterranean, northern Europe and the Iberian peninsula – fell away as the period progressed and the London–Antwerp sea link swallowed more and more, depriving the English outports of much of their business and making Antwerp the one great source for imports from far and wide, excepting only some special commodities – the wines of Gascony and the baysalt of Biscay notably. Antwerp was a most convenient centre for England's overseas trade, for it became the financial and commercial capital of Europe during these decades, and the great company of London cloth exporters, the Merchants Adventurers, had privileges there which multiplied the profitability of their privileges in England. Their interest lay in exploiting these advantages, not in looking for alternatives. Only when the Londoners began seriously to seek direct contact with ulterior or new markets, especially for access to highly profitable imports, would English oceanic expansion gain the momentum necessary for success. So far there was no consolidated success to record.

2

The Northeast

At Ratcliffe, a good mile down river from the Tower, on 10 May 1553 certain ships departed with the turning of the tide, bound northeast for Cathay by the north cape of Norway. The 'admiral' was the *Bona Esperanza* of 120 tons, commanded by Sir Hugh Willoughby, captain-general of the expedition, with 31 men. The *Edward Bonaventure* of 160 tons sailed under Richard Chancellor, pilot-major of the fleet, with 39 men, and the *Bona Confidentia* of 90 tons carried 25 men including the master. Each was 'new-built' – repaired with good timbers and planking, the keel sheeted with lead against worm. Each went fully armed, victualled for eighteen months and accompanied by a pinnace. Several merchants and a minister of religion made up the total complement of 116 men. The mariners in sky-blue uniform towed the ships down to Greenwich, and as they passed the palace a crowd of courtiers and common folk cheered from the river bank, the towers and windows, and the ships' guns thundered a salute to the dying king. Then the sailors changed into their slops and hoisted sail.[1]

In scale and importance this venture was quite different from all that had gone before. No less than two hundred subscribers put down the round sum of £6000 to launch it, and they included a whole galaxy of peers, privy councillors and other high officers of state, alongside a much larger number of wealthy City merchants. Sebastian Cabot, who returned to England in 1548, now emerged as 'governour of the mysterie and companie of the Marchants adventurers for the discoverie of Regions, Dominions, Islands and places unknowen'[2] – in effect a great corporation for the exploration and development of new trades by northern sea-routes, second only to the old Merchants Adventurers Company in commercial backing and political influence. The new company's charter, Cabot's instructions for the conduct of the

---

[1] *PN*, II, 212–14, 217, 244–5.
[2] *PN*, II, 195; T. S. Willan, *The Muscovy Merchants of 1555*.

voyage, and the royal letters missive carried by the commander all underline the decisively national and public character of this enterprise.[3] Its chief patron – John Dudley, duke of Northumberland, who had been Lord High Admiral at the end of Henry VIII's reign – was virtually ruler of England in 1553. It was his son-in-law, Henry Sidney, one of the leaders of English expansion under Elizabeth, who personally recommended Richard Chancellor to the assembled merchants and pledged the support of the nobility for the project.[4]

Thus Cabot and the City of London at last joined forces and the manner of their junction is instructive. Cabot, after all, was a northwest passage man, but this was a northeast passage expedition. His instructions for 'the intended voyage for Cathay' strangely omitted to specify the route, merely referring vaguely to the North Pole.[5] Since his return to England he seems to have been toying with various schemes: an Anglo-French venture to probe Peru by way of the Amazon, a Barbary voyage, a Thorne-style polar transit.[6] Flexible, eclectic, wily, the old man must have been the chief engineer of the 1553 enterprise, but Clement Adams, who engraved Cabot's northwest passage map in 1549, makes the Londoners responsible:

At what time our Marchants perceived the commodities and wares of England to bee in small request with the countreys and people about us, and neere unto us, and that those Marchandizes which strangers in the time and memorie of our auncesters did earnestly seeke and desire, were nowe neglected, and the price thereof abated, although by us carried to their owne portes, and all forreine Marchandises in great accompt, and their prises wonderfully raised: certaine grave Citizens of London, and men of great wisedome, and carefull for the good of their Countrey, began to thinke with themselves, howe this mischiefe might bee remedied. Neither was a remedie (as it then appeared) wanting to their desires, for the avoyding of so great an inconvenience: for seeing that the wealth of the Spaniards and Portingales, by the discoverie and search of newe trades and Countreys was marveilously increased, supposing the same to be a course and meane for them also to obteine the like, they thereupon resolved upon a newe and strange Navigation. And whereas at the same time one Sebastian Cabota, a man in those dayes very renowmed, happened to bee in London, they began first of all to deale and consult diligently with him, and after much speech and conference together, it was at

---

[3] The corporation dated from 1553, but letters patent were not formally issued until 1555 – *PN*, II, 201, 304–16. Cabot's instructions – *PN*, II, 195–205. Edward's letters missive were taken in Latin, Greek and other languages – *PN*, II, 206–11.

[4] *PN*, II, 242–3.

[5] *PN*, II, 204. The Spanish ambassador, writing after the departure of the ships, reported that some said they would follow a northwest route, while others thought they would go northeast – *Cal. SP Span.* (1553), p. 39.

[6] Taylor, *Brief Summe*, pp. liii–lvi.

last concluded that three shippes should bee prepared and furnished out, for the search and discoverie of the Northerne part of the world, to open a way and passage to our men for travaile to newe and unknowen kingdomes.[7]

Envy of the rich trades of the Iberian empires, the strongest and most abiding motive of English maritime enterprise, was thus at this juncture reinforced by a real and urgent economic need: to offset the disastrous fall in the country's cloth exports to the Continent since 1550. This was an immediate problem for the merchants, but a much graver one for the government, which was seriously concerned about the economic, social and political disturbance that the depression in the nation's main industry might cause. The subsequent history of relations between the government and the Merchants Adventurers Company shows that whereas the former desired to maintain the volume of exports, the latter was more interested in maintaining their price. It seems likely therefore that the initiative came from the government. Cabot himself suggested that not all the merchants were enthusiastic, referring to critics who had 'caused wavering minds, and doubtful heads, not onely to withdraw themselves from the adventure of this voyage, but also disswaded others'.[8] Whether the government brought pressure to bear upon the merchants we do not know, but it is reasonable to assume that one or the other or both brought pressure to bear on Cabot, obliging him to give priority to the search for cloth markets. Consequently his instructions said almost nothing about Cathay, emphasizing instead the need to investigate the trading potential of places on the way thither. This must have been the reason also for the adoption of the northeastern course.

The northern shores of America could not have looked promising for purposes of trade, but the northeast route offered contact with the vast regions known loosely as Scythia and Tartary, cold lands where English woollens might sell well. Indeed the promoters probably had more than an inkling of Russian prospects, for contact between Muscovy and the West had been growing for half a century, and in 1549 the detailed *Description of Moscow and Muscovy* by Sigmund von Herberstein was published in Latin at Vienna, with a second edition in 1551.[9] Adams relates that they sent for two 'Tartarians' from the king's stable to interrogate them 'touching their country and the manners of their nation'. Cathay remained the glittering prize, but 'every nation and region is to be considered advisedly. . . and not to tary long in one

---

[7] *PN*, II, 239–40. Adams's original Latin narrative, first published in 1554, survives only in the form of Hakluyt's transcript in *PN* (1589), pp. 270–9.
[8] *PN*, II, 204.
[9] Quinn, *Hakluyt Handbook*, pp. 254–6.

place, untill you shall have attained the most worthy place that may be found'. Cathay, it seemed, could only be approached by way of compromise in a spirit of opportunism. The commercial personnel were to compile reports on the trade and condition of all places visited.[10] But it would be wrong to conclude that Cathay was not an important objective. For the next thirty years the merchants, especially the leading members of the company, were to strive for that goal.

The leader of the expedition, Willoughby, was a soldier, chosen for his 'goodly personage' and authority as a fitting head for such a prestigious mission to far kingdoms. But it was Chancellor, according to Adams, 'in whom alone great hope for the performance of this businesse rested'. He was no ordinary seaman, but a navigator skilled in mathematics and astronomy, who evidently consulted John Dee and Thomas Digges, the mathematicians, in making the technical preparations for the voyage. He had served his apprenticeship to the sea in the voyage of the *Bark Aucher* to the Levant in 1550–51. Such a combination of theoretical mastery and practical experience was indeed rare in the England of Edward VI, and was to be severely tested.[11] Delayed by fickle winds and bad victualling, the ships did not reach Senja, in 69° on the Norwegian coast, until the end of July. Here they learned of a pilot to bring them to Wardhouse (Vardø) in Finnmark, but before they could take him aboard they were forced out to sea by violent flaws and lost sight of each other. Next day Willoughby, having lost both pinnace and ship's boat – a loss which already spelt disaster – met again with the *Confidence* and made sail for Vardø without the *Edward*. The surviving journal of the voyage shows that they missed it by many a league, running far north of the North Cape and eastwards into the Barents Sea until they sighted land in 72° – the forbidding shore of Novaya Zemlya. Unable to land for ice and shoals, they ran south along the coast and then west across the mouth of the White Sea to reach 'Arzina River' (Varzino) on the Lapland coast. Then for two days the ships made southeast towards the White Sea and safety, but turned back because they were unable to double the headland of Svyatoy Nos. So they came again to Arzina on 18 September, where, 'seeing the yeare farre spent, & also very evill wether, as frost, snow, and haile, as though it had beene the deepe of winter, we thought it best to winter there'.[12]

Southwest, southeast and west they sent out parties, but all soon returned 'without finding of people, or any similitude of habitation'.

[10] *PN*, II, 202–3.
[11] Taylor, *Tudor Geography*, pp. 90–91, 253–4.
[12] *PN*, II, 212–24.

The journal ends at this point. It was found next summer by Russian fishermen, among the frozen bodies of seventy men, who died, as was later realized, 'for want of experience to have made caves and stoves'.[13] A will found at the same time showed that most of them were still alive in January but, weak and wasted as they surely were already and ill-prepared for such an ordeal, they stood no chance of surviving a winter, including five weeks of continuous night, in that desolate place. So died the first pathetic victims of the search for northern passages. In 1555 the company's Moscow agent recovered the ships and manned them home the following year. Both went down with all hands off the coast of Norway.[14]

Chancellor meanwhile in the *Edward*, having waited seven days for his consorts at Vardø, sailed on to the White Sea and came ashore near one of the mouths of the River Dvina in the latter half of August. He made his way to Moscow by sled and presented the king's letters to the tsar, Ivan IV, who in due course replied welcoming English merchants to Muscovy. In 1554 Chancellor and his men returned to London with this encouraging news and vivid impressions of the country. In 1555 the body of merchants that came to be called the Muscovy Company was legally incorporated by royal charter and granted the monopoly of trade with Russia and all areas 'northwards, northeastwards or north-westwards' not known or frequented by Englishmen before 1553. Chancellor then voyaged once more to the White Sea, where the company's agents obtained full and formal privileges from the tsar. Chancellor was drowned in the wreck of the *Edward* on the Scottish coast on his way home the next year, 1556.[15]

His achievement was important, though not original. The route between the Atlantic and the White Sea was in fact known and used before, as Herberstein showed by his account of a journey from the Dvina to Denmark in 1496. The reverse trip was accomplished in 1501 and 1507.[16] Nor did he 'discover' Russia, in the sense of revealing a country unknown to western Europe. Italians, Germans and Flemings were in Moscow long before 1553. What Chancellor did was to make the northern sea-route a regular commercial highway, thereby increasing the volume of trade and communication between Muscovy and the West. In this he was assisted by Stephen and William Borough, who as master-pilots filled his place and consolidated his pioneering work.

[13] *PN*, III, 331.
[14] *PN*, III, 333–4.
[15] *PN*, II, 224–72, 291–316, 352.
[16] R. H. Major (ed.), *Notes upon Russia* (London, 1851), I, pp. 105–8. A. Ohberg, 'Russia and the world market in the seventeenth century', *Scandinavian Economic History Review*, 3 (1955), 123–62.

His voyage moreover had a great effect upon English overseas enterprise because it was the first breakthrough, starting a change that took
decades to unfold. The drama of the voyage, the charter, the royal
messages and embassies – these events made a cumulative impact
upon London. The City for the first time witnessed and took part in a
long-distance, heavily capitalized trade, run by a joint-stock company.
Formally endowed with the monopoly of the North, England's rightful
way to the Orient, the Muscovy Company naturally became the
leading sponsor and patron of geographical science and enterprise for
the next twenty or thirty years.

Not only did individual Muscovy men do much to promote other
oceanic initiatives – for example to Guinea, the Caribbean, Brazil,
Baffin Island – but the company itself notably advanced the intellectual
side of the movement. Most of the small band of men who in the fifties
began the dissemination of geographical knowledge and nautical
science were connected with the company. Dr Robert Recorde, the first
English authority to bring mathematics to the merchant and mariner,
wrote his *Castle of Knowledge*, a treatise on the sphere, expressly for the
company's navigators. Richard Eden, friend of Chancellor and Cabot,
dedicated his *Treatyse of the newe India* (1553) to the duke of Northumberland and commended his support for Willoughby and Chancellor.
His *Decades of the newe world or west India* (1555) gave special prominence
to Muscovy, and in 1561 the company paid him to translate Martín
Cortes's *Arte de Navegar* 'to have more store of skilful pilots'. It also
used the services of John Dee, Clement Adams and the elder Richard
Hakluyt. As for the younger Hakluyt, he was consulted too, and
acknowledged the importance of the company's contribution by
devoting more than a quarter of his *Principall Navigations* (1589) to
Russia. Meanwhile the company directly promoted not only commercial operations in Muscovy, but also persistent efforts to develop
eastern trade through Persia and by way of the northeast.

Among the company's protégés were the two young mariners who
sailed with Chancellor in 1553, Stephen and William Borough, sons of
the navigator John Aborough of Northam in Devon. Stephen went
master of the *Edward*, in which William, then aged sixteen, served as an
ordinary seaman. Both remained working sailors and based their
expertise as geographers and nautical consultants on continuing practical experience.[17] In 1556 the company entrusted Stephen with the
command of the pinnace *Searchthrift* for a voyage of exploration. The
task was to make a thorough survey of the route from Vardø eastwards

[17] *PN*, III, 209–12.

as far as the Ob and to reconnoitre the trend of the coast beyond. It was considered that the coast might incline east and south towards Cathay. Alternatively the Ob might give access to China overland. Sebastian Cabot, still governor of the company, no doubt did most to launch this new effort. Stephen's journal pictures him coming aboard to view the pinnace at Gravesend,

and then at the signe of the Christopher, hee and his friends banketted, and made me, and them that were in the company great cheere: and for very joy that he had to see the towardnes of our intended discovery, he entred into the dance himselfe, among the rest of the young and lusty company.[18]

At Vardø Stephen took command of the pinnace and eight men, including his brother, and soon fell in with several Russian fishing vessels, called 'lodias', bound for the River Pechora for walrus and salmon. These were large, shallow craft, supplementing sail with oar (one of them rowed with twenty oars and had 24 crew in all), better adapted for inshore work than the pinnace, and of course the Russians knew the coast. Luckily for the English, they were friendly, and one of their masters, a certain Gabriel, offered to act as guide. Without this help the Boroughs could not have achieved what they did: indeed the Russians at one point saved them from almost certain wreck. As far as the mouth of the White Sea Stephen's journal is a careful record, evidently checking and supplementing an existing chart. He notes the lie of the coast, landmarks, latitudes, tides, depths, shoals in anchorages, sand-bars, weather, compass variation, making virtually a rutter: 'In the bight of the Southeast shoare of the river Cola, there is a good roade in five fadome, or foure fadome and a halfe, at a lowe water: but you shall have no land Northnortheast of you then'.[19] Past the White Sea he used a blank chart, mapping this coast for the first time. The result was William's chart depicting the whole route from western Norway to Vaygach Island, though this probably incorporates some later as well as earlier information.[20]

Beyond Pechora the English made their own way as far as Novaya Zemlya. Here they met another group of fishermen, who gave them 'certain demonstrations of the way to the Ob' and accompanied them in that direction. This took them apparently along the Kara Strait

[18] *PN*, II, 322–44.
[19] *PN*, II, 327.
[20] William Borough's chart, a fine example of the explorer's art at this early stage, is reproduced in *PN*, III, opposite p. 224. In his 'Discours of the Variation of the Cumpas' Borough indicated that by 1581 charts of the northern route and the Baltic were in regular use by Muscovy Company seamen: Robert Norman, *The Newe Attractive* (1581), to which Borough's discourse was 'annexed'. Here he also mentioned that he gave Anthony Jenkinson the material on the northern coast for his map of Russia.

between Novaya Zemlya and Vaygach Island, at the northeastern corner of which one of the Russians took Stephen ashore to show him a great heap of idols belonging to the Samoyed people, much to the Englishman's disgust: 'the worst and the most unartificiall worke that ever I saw', all bloody from sacrifice. Although he did briefly meet one of these Arctic nomads, he derived his impression of them from the Russians, who assured him that these were not so 'hurtful' as the Ob Samoyeds, whom they believed to be cannibals.[21] From this place the Boroughs hoped to go on to the Ob, but turned back into the strait when they met 'a terrible heap of ice'. Shortly after this the Russians made off southwards through shoals the pinnace could not traverse. It was early August, and for the next fortnight the little group of explorers struggled desperately with fog and ice in increasingly stormy conditions. Finally they set course for the Dvina and spent the winter at Kholmogory, expecting to resume their efforts the next summer.

Instead they went on another mission and twenty-four years passed before the next attempt on the northeast passage. No doubt the failure of the *Searchthrift* to get past Vaygach Island was discouraging, and Cabot's death in 1557 perhaps deprived those interested of their chief support. For some years, moreover, the company pinned its hopes of eastern trade on Jenkinson's thrust southwards to the Caspian and beyond, but when Jenkinson returned from his second attempt in 1564 he resuscitated the northeastern project in a petition to the queen in 1565. Shortly afterwards Humphrey Gilbert put forward a contrary view and the two men argued their rival cases before Elizabeth herself. They then agreed to pool their efforts in a northwestern venture, but for reasons unknown failed to see it through.[22] Next, in 1568, William Borough drew up instructions for a voyage to the east from the White Sea, intended to complete the work interrupted in 1556. Though the voyage did not take place so far as we know, his notes indicate the methods and standards he expected. Latitudes were to be taken as often as possible, and the lie of the land 'set with your compasse . . . all alongst as you goe'. The pilots should 'draw the proportion and biting of the land, aswell the lying out of the points, and headlands' and show cliffs, etc. They should take soundings at least once every glass (half an hour) and should note the tides at each place, their direction, height and force, measured by the distance they would drive a ship in an hour 'as neere as you can judge it'. Borough himself taught them

---

[21] Richard Johnson, who accompanied the Boroughs in this expedition, wrote an account of the Samoyeds' 'devilish rites', based on personal observations after the voyage: *PN*, II, 345–9. In another account he alleged the Samoyeds to be cannibals: *PN*, II, 483–4.
[22] Quinn, *Gilbert*, pp. 6–10; Taylor, *Tudor Geography*, pp. 267–8.

how to use an instrument to find horizontal bearings and distances for purposes of mapping. And he charged them to keep their journal day by day, not forgetting or omitting to write it. He knew how hard that would be in the Kara Sea.[23]

Probably this plan was drawn up because the situation in Russia at the time was so threatening as to make a further Persian attempt seem unlikely. When these troubles were safely overcome and the Persian expedition went ahead, in 1569, the northeastern project was again shelved.[24] Then in the mid seventies the northwest monopolized attention, and only when the Lok-Frobisher bubble burst was Borough at last able to put his ideas into practice. In May 1580 the Muscovy Company commissioned Arthur Pet of Ratcliffe and Charles Jackman of Poplar to conduct a new search for a northeast passage. Borough supplied 'a plat of spiral lines' (a chart with true rhumbs) depicting a route in latitudes south of 70°.[25] The masters were to pass Vaygach and to follow the mainland coast 'whether it incline southerly or northerly' until they reached Cathay. If the land extended to 80° or more, barring a sea passage, they should winter in the Ob and explore that river at their discretion the next summer. Should this prove inconvenient, they should return through 'Borough's Strait' between Vaygach and Novaya Zemlya and follow the coast of the latter, which was assumed to run WNW, to see whether it led to 'Willougby's land', for it was supposed the land he had found in 72° lay west of Novaya Zemlya, a concept clearly expressed in Borough's earlier chart.

This commission represents the cautious and flexible approach of the practical explorer and was accompanied by his detailed instructions to the masters, similar to those of 1568. However, John Dee also supplied advice, together with his own chart. The whole course from Vaygach to the great promontory 'Tabin' lay in 70°, east of which the coast ran 'much southerly and eastwards' to the warm havens and cities of China, facts which he gathered from an old Arab cosmographer, Abulfeda Ismaël, as rendered down by Ramusio. He roundly rejected Mercator's world chart of 1569 in this respect. But Mercator, whom the younger Hakluyt asked for advice about the proposed itinerary, opined that Tabin (reaching on his map 76° – a good approximation to the actual Cape Chelyuskin) would be a great

[23] *PN*, III, 119–24. Borough attached a sketch map to his instructions: I am grateful to Sarah Tyacke of the Map Library in the British Library for this information.

[24] E. D. Morgan and C. H. Coote (eds.), *Early Voyages and Travels to Russia and Persia* (London, 1886), pp. 260–61; Willan, *Russia Company*, pp. 95–111, 145.

[25] This chart has not survived, but its depiction of the Asian coast may be deduced from the governors' hope that if it proved incorrect a passage might still be found between 70° and 80°: *PN*, III, 251–8.

obstacle, partly because it was too near the magnetic pole and partly because the Kara Sea was liable to be blocked by ice. He wisely counselled the English to seek a harbour west of Tabin and find their way by the great rivers towards the Grand Khan's empire.[26]

Long before these words of wisdom reached England, however, Pet and Jackman were on their way. Pet commanded the *George*, a bark of 40 tons, with nine men and a boy. He had been a mariner with Chancellor in 1553 and had sailed to Muscovy as a master at least once since. Jackman had been master's mate in the northwest passage voyage of 1577 and master and chief pilot 'for the discovery' in the following voyage. He now led five men and a boy in the *William*, of 20 tons. The commercial side of the operation was the responsibility of Richard Chancellor's son, Nicholas. Nor did he lack advice: the elder Hakluyt explained at some length the task of mercantile reconnaissance he cheerfully expected these two little barks to accomplish. They were to take all kinds of samples of English wares, from garters, girdles and gloves to 'glazen eyes to ride with against dust' (goggles, though English yet lacked the word), with comfits for the feasting of guests aboard – meaning Chinese, he hastened to add, not savages. But what he wanted was economic intelligence: of cloth markets, fisheries, dyeing processes and dumping grounds 'for the offals of our people', which might provide bases on the way for victualling and repairs. Maps and books ('the new herbal', for example) might impress the Grand Khan, and they should bring back a map of China and 'some old printed booke, to see whether they have had print there, before it was devised in Europe, as some write'.[27]

Great expectations and learned speculation thus wafted the mariners down the Thames. They reached and passed Vardø safely, but then Jackman, having trouble with the *William*'s steerage, put into Kegor while Pet went on in search of Willoughby's land, arranging to rendezvous at Vaygach. On the 10th he reached Novaya Zemlya and

[26] *PN*, III, 262–3, 275–82. Taylor, *Tudor Geography*, pp. 127–34. E. G. R. Taylor, 'John Dee and the map of North-East Asia', *Imago Mundi*, 12 (1955), 103–6. Mrs Tyacke of the BL Map Library advises me that the Philadelphia Library map is not by Dee, though Dee expressed a similar view in his map in the Marquess of Exeter's collection. Mercator's advice to Hakluyt sounds sensible, but he also wrote to Ortelius suggesting that the secret object of the Pet–Jackman expedition was to meet Francis Drake, who was expected to return from the Pacific by way of northern Asia, since that route would be half the length of the route round North America, which in any case according to Frobisher was obstructed by rocks. These remarks seem to contradict what he told Hakluyt and show that even the best of sixteenth-century cosmographers was inclined on occasion to wild surmise: Taylor, *Tudor Geography*, pp. 261–3; a facsimile and translation appear in H. P. Kraus, *Sir Francis Drake, a Pictorial Biography* (Amsterdam, 1970), pp. 86–8.

[27] *PN*, III, 264–75. Henry Lyte, *A niewe herball* (London, 1578).

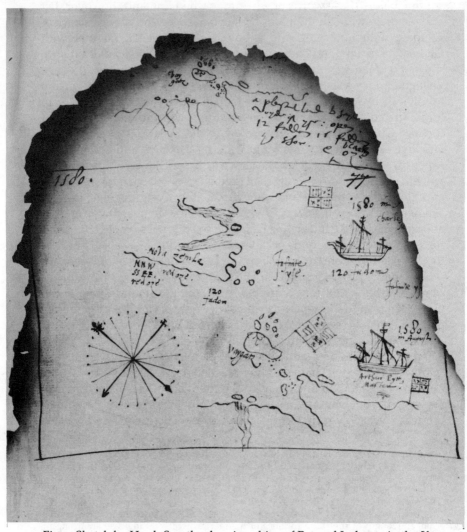

Fig. 2 Sketch by Hugh Smyth, showing ships of Pet and Jackman in the Kara Sea. (From BL, Cotton MSS, Otho E.VIII fo. 73.)

from then on the voyage became a continuous struggle with massing ice. Eventually he pushed through the more southerly strait into the Kara Sea, where on 25 July the *William* rejoined – in spite of a broken stern-post and useless rudder. Together the crews managed to repair her, but then, seeing no hope of advancing against the ice, returned. After many days of back-breaking labour and exhausted nights, when despair came very close, they found clear sea west of Vaygach and rejoiced 'as the bird which was escaped out of the cage, wherein she was kept long as prisoner'. On 22 August the barks lost contact for good. The *George* after a troublesome voyage entered the Thames on Christmas Day; the *William* was said (by Hakluyt eighteen years later) to have wintered in Norway and to have gone thence in February towards Iceland, accompanying a Danish ship, never to be heard of again.[28]

Pet and Jackman, like the Boroughs before them, were defeated by overwhelming physical difficulties, but their courage, endurance and seamanship were not entirely wasted. Others pursued their work, varying the approach. In the 1590s Willem Barentszoon, a great Dutch navigator, carried knowledge of Novaya Zemlya and the neighbouring seas an immense stride forward in three heroic voyages. Henry Hudson went northeast for the Muscovy Company in 1608 (the company's first attempt since 1580) and for the Dutch East India Company the next year, though he failed to reach the Kara Sea in either voyage. It was not until 1879 that the work begun by Willoughby and Chancellor was at last completed by Nordenskiöld's conquest of the northeast passage.[29]

[28] *PN*, III, 282–303: Hugh Smyth's journal of the *George*. Hakluyt here added the statement about the *William*'s fate to the version in his first edition, which also contains the journal by Nicholas Chancellor – *PN* (1589), pp. 476–82.

[29] In 1584 Anthony Marsh, a Muscovy Company factor interested in private trade overland to the Ob, received a letter from certain Russians informing him about the area, mentioning the feasibility of access by sea and stating: 'Heretofore your people have bin at the said River of Obs mouth with a Ship, and there was made shipwracke, and your people were slaine by the Samoeds, which thought that they came to rob and subdue them' – *Purchas*, XIV, 293. Nothing further is known of this episode.

From Muscovy to Persia

Both Elizabeth and Ivan welcomed the new link between their countries. The trade itself benefited Russia by widening the market for her hemp, cordage, flax, train-oil, furs, hides, tallow and wax, and by increasing her manufactured imports, especially of cloth. For England the new trade was valuable not so much in quantity as in quality. Russia did not become a major market for English goods, nor a major source of luxuries, but it made an important contribution to English sea power. In 1557 the company sent out ropemakers to organize the manufacture of cables, and soon the rope-walks of Kholmogory and Vologda were supplying the greater part of the crown's needs. In the year of the Spanish Armada Hawkins ordered 'great cables to be made this winter in Muscovia' to the value of £3000. Russian cordage was reputed the best and by the end of the century the navy was spending over £10,000 a year on it. After that the East India Company became an important customer. The nation's shipping also benefited because the trade employed merchantmen of the larger sort: six ships totalling 1050 tons in 1597, ten totalling 1360 tons in 1600, ten totalling 1580 tons in 1602, and these were typical years.[1]

The English, moreover, were privileged traders in Russia. They completely controlled the White Sea trade until the 1570s, when Dutch competitors began to appear, and they alone among foreigners had the right to trade in the interior of Russia without paying customs duties or tolls. With these and other advantages they rapidly deployed their commerce over a large area, concentrating on the north and Moscow. The company's investment of capital and personnel in Russia became a significant national asset, which Elizabeth and her ministers were concerned to protect, particularly in view of the trade's strategic value, the prospect of extending it eastwards, and the influence of the leading

---

[1] Willan, *Russia Company*, pp. 255–6 *et passim*.

shareholders, who included the queen's most powerful councillors.[2] Ivan, on the other hand, valued the English connection for political and military reasons. He wanted England as an ally against his Polish, Swedish and other enemies, including his own subjects, whom he came to fear and suspect increasingly from the 1560s as his own instability and unpredictable ferocity developed. Consequently he favoured the English merchants, but was inclined to use their privileges as a bargaining counter. Elizabeth had repeatedly to send special envoys to Moscow to defend the position of the company and its agents and at the same time to avoid any concessions that might embroil her in the Tsar's foreign or domestic difficulties.

The English in Russia, whether merchants, diplomats or others, were thus never secure and their position deteriorated and their trade declined after Ivan's death in 1584. Privileged though they were, they found life in Russia distinctly uncomfortable. Travel was extremely difficult, for the roads were few and bad, inns did not exist, and the housing and food were poor even by the abysmal standards of contemporary Europe. Foreigners were treated generally with mistrust and hostility. Resident merchants and craftsmen learned to cope with such problems, but the diplomat, who was peculiarly exposed to suspicion, surveillance, xenophobia, insolence and even violence, tended to suffer whenever the authorities chose to show their displeasure by letting him fend for himself. Frequently English ambassadors had to wait weeks or months before being permitted to see the Tsar, remaining meanwhile confined to house. Sir Jerome Bowes, who was in Moscow after the death of Ivan, was for over two months so closely confined that when any of his household looked out into the street they were 'beaten in with clots and such things as lay in the streets'. Though sick, he was not allowed a doctor, and he seriously expected his suite to be attacked on its way from Moscow to the White Sea.[3]

English reports of Russia in the later sixteenth century must be viewed in the light of these facts. The traders, who knew the language and the country more or less well, wrote chiefly about commercial transactions and conditions, usually leaving the rest unsaid. The significant exceptions were Richard Chancellor, Anthony Jenkinson

[2] Sir William Cecil and Sir Francis Walsingham. The best account of Anglo-Russian relations in Elizabethan times is K.-H. Ruffman, *Das Russlandbild im England Shakespeares* (Göttingen, 1952). See also Morgan and Coote, *Russia and Persia*; E. A. Bond (ed.), *Russia at the Close of the Sixteenth Century* (London, 1856); J. Hamel, *England and Russia* (London, 1854); Willan, *Russia Company*; M. S. Anderson, *Britain's Discovery of Russia, 1553–1815* (London, 1958).
[3] Anderson, *Britain's Discovery of Russia*, pp. 12–14.

and the interpreter Robert Best, who all recorded briefly their personal experience and observations in the early years of the trade, before the disastrous deterioration of conditions in the sixties, culminating in famine, plague, the Tsar's massacre of the citizens of Novgorod, the burning of Moscow by the Tartars, and so forth. These early reports are remarkable for their lack of prejudice, except in respect of religious matters. The Tsarist régime is seen as despotic, magnificent, powerful, benevolent. The poverty and drunkenness of the mass of the people appal them, though they have seen misery enough at home. Chancellor is struck by the physical endurance of the Russian soldier, Best cannot bear the brutality of Russian wedding customs and wifebeating. Of course there are misunderstandings and inaccuracies: it is hardly surprising that the English, who were rarely allowed to travel outside restricted areas, knew little of the geography of Siberia and other remote regions, repeated uncritically what the Russians told them about the Crim Tartars and the Samoyeds, or retailed fanciful legends about such places and peoples. It would be unjust to accuse these observers of narrow-minded ethnocentricity, or of fitting the facts to preconceived notions of Muscovy as a barbarous land, for in all essentials it was as they described it.[4]

They were not, however, responsible for the formation of English opinion about Russia. Much more influential in this respect were the well-publicized embassies which took place when that country was subject to extreme tyranny, oppression and disruption, and which were reported with considerable animus by aggrieved envoys who for the most part understood little of the language or the people. The most influential of these by far was Giles Fletcher, whose book *Of the Rus Commonwealth* came out in 1591, only to be rapidly suppressed at the instance of the Muscovy Company. Adversely critical of the régime, Fletcher blamed the government for the poverty, cruelty, drunkenness, ignorance, disorder and squalor in which the people lived. Fletcher wrote well and the scandal he created of course did much to make his book a success.[5] He depended heavily upon earlier writers such as Herberstein and on his contemporary Jerome Horsey, a servant of the company who knew Moscow well and served both Ivan and Elizabeth on special missions.[6] His own knowledge was limited and his book contained numerous errors of fact and interpretation. To what extent these vitiate the general picture of Russian society and

[4] *PN*, II, 224–38 (Chancellor); 418–25 (Jenkinson); 438–49 (Best).
[5] A. J. Schmidt (ed.), *Of the Rus Commonwealth by Giles Fletcher* (Ithaca, N.Y., 1966).
[6] Bond, *Russia*, pp. xliii–cxix. Horsey relied for patronage on Walsingham, who was a partner in some of his commercial dealings.

government he presents, however, it is hard to say. Russian liberals in the nineteenth century approved of Fletcher; Russian stalinists of the twentieth did not. Fletcher may have been often wrong, often misleading, but he did not decry or despise the Russian people. On the contrary he saw them as victims of ruthless robbery, culturally as well as physically deprived by 'the heavy yoke of this tyrannous government'.

Thus England's commercial penetration of Russia in the later sixteenth century did much to improve knowledge of that country in the West, and the English themselves, from being the most ignorant of the western nations in this respect, became by 1600 the best informed. The Muscovy enterprise was chiefly important as the first major step for England in extra-European trade, the first step towards the commercial empire of the future, but the Russia trade itself did not prosper after Elizabeth's reign. By the 1620s the Dutch had overtaken the English and reduced them to a minor rôle, and though the company compensated itself to some extent by promoting whaling and walrus-taking around Spitzbergen, it met fierce competition from the Dutch and others in this business also.[7]

In 1557 the leaders of the company in London – Andrew Judde, George Barne, Anthony Huse, William Garrard and William Chester – informed their agents in Russia that they were sending out 'one Anthonie Jenkinson Gentleman, a man well travelled, whom we mind to use in further travelling'.[8] Officially Jenkinson's status was that of a merchant at this time, for he did not obtain a grant of arms until 1568, but he was already a member of the aristocracy of trade by virtue of belonging to the Mercers' Company. Since 1546 he had journeyed in western Europe, in North Africa and in the countries of the Levant, and in 1553 he had witnessed the entry of Sultan Suleiman the Magnificent into Aleppo, receiving from him a safe-conduct permitting him to trade in Turkish ports. Jenkinson does not appear to have used this privilege, nor indeed did Englishmen conduct any considerable business in the Levant from that date for over twenty years, partly because they found the Mediterranean too dangerous. Whatever the reasons for the virtual cessation of the Levant trade, the Londoners now pinned their oriental ambitions upon the northern route by way of the White Sea, Moscow and the Caspian to central Asia, where they might conceivably tap the stream of east–west trade. Jenkinson's task was to reconnoitre the route and to discover whether it would be possible by a bold stroke of commercial strategy to outflank the

[7] *Purchas*, XIII, 11–26.   [8] *PN*, II, 390.

Venetian and the Turk, creating a direct link, company-controlled all
the way from London to Bukhara, Samarkand and beyond. It was a
difficult and dangerous mission, which only a man of Jenkinson's
capacity and character could have carried through successfully: a 'man
of business', in the contemporary phrase, a man who could deal with
Tsar, Shah or local khan, find his way half across Asia and back and still
show a profit, one of the greatest Elizabethan pioneers.[9]

Jenkinson left England in May 1557 in command of the Muscovy
Company's fleet for that year, which also carried the returning Russian
ambassador and his suite. He reached St Nicholas in July and Moscow
in December, where the Tsar received him in great state and gave him
permission to proceed southwards, with letters of recommendation to
'sundry kings and princes'.[10] In April he departed by water, joining
and passing down the Volga to Astrakhan through territory only
recently taken from the Tartars. This journey was safe, since Jenkinson
and his two English companions accompanied a substantial armed
force on its way to occupy Astrakhan, but he noted that not a single
trading centre on this waterway had survived the wars. Astrakhan
itself was a stricken place, ruined by famine and plague and overwhelmed by an influx of starving and dying Nogai Tartars from the
lands to the east. Its trade was 'small and beggerly', he said, 'not worth
the writing, neither is there any hope of trade in all those parts woorth
the following'.[11] And unfortunately this comment was to be repeated
like a monotonous refrain throughout his journey east and south from
Astrakhan to Bukhara. Beyond Astrakhan the travellers, no longer in
Russian territory nor protected by Russian soldiers, faced personal
danger and intractable problems of movement and communication.
With difficulty they negotiated the Volga delta and the waters of the
Caspian eastwards as far as the Mangishlak peninsula, where bad
weather forced them to land. Thence they rode in successive caravans
by stages to Bukhara, continually molested, held to ransom and
delayed by predatory princes, khans or bandit chiefs. Once at least
they had to fight for their lives and when they reached Bukhara,
exhausted after sixteen weeks of this overland ordeal and lacking
much of the merchandise they had started with, they found that
famous city a great disappointment:

There is yerely great resort of Marchants to this Citie of Boghar, which travaile
in great Caravans from the countries thereabout adjoining, as India, Persia,

[9] Morgan and Coote, *Russia and Persia*, pp. lxxxvi–cliv, 1–6 *et passim*.
[10] *PN*, II, 413–49 (Jenkinson's journey to Moscow and description of the country); 449–79
(Moscow to Bukhara).
[11] *PN*, II, 456.

Balgh, Russia, with divers others, and in times past from Cathay, when there was passage: but these Marchants are so beggerly and poore, and bring so little quantitie of wares, lying two or 3 yeeres to sell the same, that there is no hope of any good trade there to be had worthy the following.[12]

East of Bukhara all trade with China had been stopped by warfare, but even in times of peace the journey would take, as Jenkinson now learned, nine months. Since it had taken him eight months to reach Bukhara from Moscow, there was little to be said for this route at the best of times. He therefore decided to make southwards for Persia, but was again frustrated by news of warfare in that direction and so painfully retraced his steps to Moscow.

But Jenkinson was not easily defeated. As he told the company's chief agent in Russia, he had, in spite of a journey 'so miserable, dangerous, and chargeable with losses', brought back enough goods from the Caspian region to show a profit on the outlay. The rate of profit to be gained on kerseys and other wares would, he urged, justify the trade, if only they could sell them on a larger scale, provided, of course, they did not suffer the evil fortune that had plagued his Bukhara expedition.[13] The main problem of the Persia trade, as he had observed on his journey, was that it flowed westwards through Syria to the Levant ports. Considerable quantities of English goods, especially kerseys, came to Persia by way of Italy and the Levant, and it remained to be seen whether the company could compete with them in price. Only by underselling these other English exports could the company hope to purchase enough silk to make a profit 'worth the following'. On the other hand the company might be able to take advantage of the frequent and terrible wars between the Shah and the Grand Turk to divert Persia's western trade northwards, and in any case a foothold in Persia meant access to the oriental traffic of the Persian Gulf, inestimably profitable. Such were the considerations that inspired the company to send out Jenkinson once more in 1561. Taking with him letters to the Tsar and the Shah, he was instructed to obtain the necessary permission from both to establish trade through Russia into Persia. Failing this, he should either return to England or make some search for a passage east by way of Novaya Zemlya. In the last resort he was advised to carry his stock to Constantinople for sale.[14]

On arriving in Moscow in the summer of 1561, Jenkinson ran into difficulties. First he was denied access to the Tsar and then he was refused leave to travel south. Only after some six months' delay, when he was about to return to England, was he granted (thanks to the

[12] *PN*, II, 472.   [13] *PN*, II, 400.   [14] *PN*, III, 9–14.

intervention of the former Russian ambassador to England) permission to proceed. As a mark of favour Ivan, himself a great merchant, commissioned the Englishman to buy gems and silks for him in Persia. In May and June of 1562, therefore, Jenkinson voyaged once more down the Volga and, entering the Caspian, followed its western shore to land at Shabran, midway between Derbent and Baku. This area lay within the domains of the Shah, but effective local power rested with Abdullah Khan, ruler (Jenkinson called him king) of Shirvan. Centring upon the city of Shemakha, this province produced a wealth of raw silk. Abdullah welcomed Jenkinson in princely style and sent him on his way in safe company to the Shah's court at Kazvin, south of the Caspian. But here Jenkinson's luck ran out, for he arrived just in time to witness the conclusion of peace between Persia and Turkey, an occasion which was marked by much feasting and sealed by the murder of the Grand Turk's rebel son Bajazet, a refugee under the Shah's protection. The Turks of course opposed any attempt to turn Persia's trade away from the Levant and used their new influence with the Shah to rebuff the English initiative. In Jenkinson's own words:

For the Turkes Ambassadour being arrived and the peace concluded, the Turkish merchants there at that time present, declared to the same Ambassadour, that my coming thither (naming mee by the name of Franke) would in great part destroy their trade, and that it should bee good for him to perswade the Sophie not to favour me, as his highnesse ment to observe the league and friendship with the great Turke his master, which request of the Turkish merchants, the same Ambassadour earnestly preferred, and being afterwards dismissed with great honour hee departed out of the Realme with the Turkes sonnes head as aforesayd, and other presents.[15]

Consequently when Jenkinson eventually succeeded in delivering the queen's letters, the Shah abused and dismissed him: 'Oh thou unbeleever, said he, we have no neede to have friendship with the unbeleevers', which was true now that Persia was allied with Ottoman power. He even contemplated sending Jenkinson to the sultan as a present, from which course he refrained only at the instance of Abdullah Khan, who suggested it was inadvisable to treat strangers in that fashion. So Jenkinson was allowed to return north and came once more to Shirvan, where Abdullah Khan again received him generously. What was more, he assured the Englishman that the Shah approved of this cordiality. What subtleties of diplomacy or commercial interest lay behind that assurance we cannot know, but in this

---

[15] *PN*, III, 29. 'Frank' was a common term in Asia for Europeans. For Jenkinson's narrative see *PN*, III, 15–38.

single week at Abdullah's court Jenkinson obtained for the company safe-conduct for customs-free trade in the khan's domain. This was a major advance, for it gave the English not only access to the valuable silk of that region, but also a foothold from which they might open up the trade of Persia at large, which in turn could lead to a share in the spice trade. In Kazvin Jenkinson had already made contact with Indian merchants, who promised to bring spices there if the English could provide an assured market. Thus when he returned to Moscow in August 1563 the prospects for Persian trade looked favourable and he duly made arrangements for a fresh expedition into that country the following year, to be undertaken by two of the company's factors. Jenkinson himself capped his success by delivering to the Tsar a rich return of silk and jewels, and by obtaining for the company new and more ample privileges in Muscovy. He then sailed for England. In later years he led two further diplomatic missions to Moscow, but he left it to others to pursue the path he had pioneered into central Asia.[16]

The subsequent history of the Persia enterprise was one of hope continually raised and frustrated, of commercial success repeatedly offset by misfortune, and finally of failure. Five more expeditions followed Jenkinson's route into Persia in the next eighteen years down to 1581. The first three of these, in 1564, 1565 and 1568, were encouraging, even though one of the two merchants in the first was murdered and another died in the course of the second. Abdullah Khan also died in 1565, and this gravely prejudiced the English position in Shirvan, but Arthur Edwards, who soon assumed the leadership of English efforts in Persia and proved a worthy successor to Jenkinson, more than made up for this setback by securing full rights of trade from the Shah with exemption from customs duties. Now, moreover, the English expected to find plenty of silk in the province of Ghilan, to the south of the Caspian, and Edwards arrived at an understanding with certain Armenian merchants concerning future transactions in spices.[17]

Consequently the company equipped its next venture, in 1569, on a larger scale. Thomas Banister and Geoffrey Ducket, the leaders, embarked with a party of thirteen other Englishmen and some forty Russians in a 70-ton ship, the *Thomas Bonaventure*, in which they sailed down the Volga and across the Caspian to Shirvan. They spent three years and more in Persia, during which Banister and seven others died, but when Ducket and his remaining companions re-embarked for Astrakhan they carried a rich cargo of silks, spices and other goods.

[16] For the remainder of his career see Morgan and Coote, *Russia and Persia*, pp. xliv–cvii.
[17] *PN*, III, 40–72, 136–49.

On this voyage, in May 1573, they were attacked by Cossack pirates. Several of the Russian crew were killed and all the English wounded, the ship and goods being surrendered. The survivors struggled back to Astrakhan and even managed to recover some of their merchandise; indeed Ducket reported that the merchants, 'notwithstanding all misfortunes, lost nothing of their principall adventure, but onely the interest and gaine that might have risen by the use of their stocke in the meane time'.[18]

But it was undeniably an unfortunate voyage, and the company did not organize another until 1579. Again, however, the result was disappointing, and this time the reason was not simply 'misfortune' (though that was not lacking), but a forbidding change in the Caspian region: the conquest of Shirvan and neighbouring parts by the Turks, effectively obstructing the English route to Persia as well as devastating the entire area.[19] When the factors returned to Moscow in 1581 it must have been realized that this was likely to be the last attempt. The potential profit on silk and other goods bought in Persia was extremely high,[20] which explains the persistence of the company in the teeth of adversity, but now the hazards were becoming prohibitive. Persia had for some years past suffered internal disturbance and foreign war, and the northern route was unduly long, expensive and (as this last venture showed) dangerous. Above all, by 1581 a new English approach to eastern trade was afoot, reversing the commercial strategy of the Persian enterprise. That same year saw the incorporation of the Turkey Company and the formal establishment of English trade into the Levant by way of the Mediterranean. From that date the Muscovy route to Persia no longer mattered.

Jenkinson and the other English merchants who journeyed into central Asia made a minor contribution to European knowledge of the world. From the thirteenth to the early sixteenth centuries various Italians had frequented and described the region in maps as well as travel reports, which were supplemented by the Spaniard Clavijo's account of his journey to Tamerlane's Persia in 1403–1406. The English, coming to the area after an interval of half a century and approaching it from another direction, had a different tale to tell. They apparently knew little if anything of these earlier descriptions, which were in many respects superior to their own. Jenkinson's representation of the Caspian region, for example, in his famous map of Russia, certainly

---

[18] *PN*, III, 150–57.

[19] *PN*, III, 212–48. This account was written by Christopher, son of William Borough.

[20] See Ducket's remark above concerning the profits on his venture. Again the last expedition was said to have realized a profit of 6% in spite of the loss of two thirds of the goods acquired (*Cal. SP Span.* (1580–86), p. 367).

compares unfavourably with the Italian maps prepared a hundred years earlier. His map, first published in 1562, did not of course incorporate information gathered during his second expedition and, partly no doubt for this reason, followed the traditional error of giving the Caspian an approximately circular shape, showing Derbent, Shemakha and Baku to the south and omitting Kazvin altogether. He also gave a confused and misleading account of the regions to the east of the Caspian, particularly of their hydrography, basing his ideas, apparently, partly on Herberstein and partly on impressions gathered from Asian merchants in Bukhara. In fact Jenkinson's map was valuable on the central part of northern Russia, which the English knew fairly well, and on the northern coast, well charted as it was by the Borough brothers, but in other respects it was erroneous, not only in detail but in general, and included a surprising amount of legend and hearsay.[21]

As for the comments of the English on the politics, religion and customs of Persia and the neighbouring countries, they were brief and superficial. Jenkinson himself devoted very little space to such matters, his account being essentially a personal narrative. Edwards gave a great deal of commercial intelligence, no doubt accurate and useful, but little else. Only Ducket attempted a set description, dwelling upon some of the more obvious features of the country: the Shah's magnificence, the treatment of women, the abundance of oil. But this is not much more than a random collection of observations, marked by intolerant naïvety and woeful ignorance of Persian culture:

They have few bookes and lesse learning, and are for the most part very brutish in all kinds of good sciences, saving in some kind of silke works, and in such things as pertaine to the furniture of horses, in the which they are passing good. The lawes are as in their religion, wicked and detestable. And if any man offend the prince, he punisheth it extremely, not onely in the person that offendeth, but also in his children, and in as many as are of his kin. . . .What I heard of the maner of their marriages, for offending of honest consciences and chaste eares, I may not commit to writing . . . for there they use to put out their women to hire, as wee do here hackney horses. . . .The mutton there is good, and the sheepe great, having very great rumpes with much fat upon them. Rice and mutton is their chief victuall.[22]

Ducket and his fellow merchants had little time to achieve an understanding of Persian life. Their visits were fairly short and occupied with commercial dealings in an almost totally alien and often

---

[21] W. E. D. Allen, 'The Caspian', in Quinn, *Hakluyt Handbook*, pp. 168–75; Morgan and Coote, *Russia and Persia*, pp. cxiii–cxlviii.
[22] *PN*, III, 158–66.

hostile environment. In the face of adverse conditions which continually threatened their position they did remarkably well to maintain their trade for two decades and to renew direct European contact with a country so remote, producing in their pragmatic way at least a plain, unvarnished story of their experience. They were, after all, pioneers, and their reports have the virtues and limitations of most pioneering records.

4

The Levant

In the early Tudor period English merchantmen conducted a considerable trade with the Mediterranean, including its eastern part, where they resorted above all to Crete (which they called Candia or Candy) for its sweet wines and other luxuries, and to Chios off the Anatolian coast, still 'Genoa's right eye' though now in tribute to the Turk, for eastern spices and for the varied produce of the Near and Middle East, including that valuable bulk cargo, alum from the mines of Fokia, so needful to the cloth industry. Kerseys of various kinds were the main English export to the region. This trade into the Levant, according to Hakluyt,

> was very usuall and much frequented from the yeere of our Lord 1511, till the yeere 1534, and afterward also, though not so commonly, untill the yeere 1550, when as the barke Aucher under the conduct of M. Roger Bodenham made a prosperous voyage unto Sicilia, Candia, Sio, and other places within the Levant. Since which time the foresaid trade (notwithstanding the Grand Signiors ample privilege granted to M. Anthony Jenkenson 1553, and the strong and weighty reasons of Gaspar Campion for that purpose) was utterly discontinued, and in maner quite forgotten, as if it had never beene, for the space of 20 yeares and more.[1]

There is no good reason to doubt the essential truth of Hakluyt's statement: the silence of the most relevant series of records confirms his view, which was based directly on the knowledge of the merchants concerned, that English ships absented themselves from the Levant seas after 1550 until the early seventies.[2] Nor need we doubt the reason

---

[1] *PN*, v, 167–8. The trade was thriving before 1511, in the reign of Henry VII: P. Ramsey, 'Overseas trade in the reign of Henry VII: the evidence of the customs accounts', *EconHR*, 2nd series, 6 (1953), 173–82.

[2] Neither the London port books nor HCA examinations reveal traces of Levant voyages in the fifties and sixties: T. S. Willan, 'Some aspects of English trade with the Levant in the sixteenth century', *EHR*, 70 (1955), 400.

given by that same Gaspar Campion, a man of thirty years' experience
in the Chios trade, married and resident there for twenty-four of them:
'the Turke is growen mighty, whereby our ships doe not trade as they
were woont'.[3] Turkish maritime strength in the eastern Mediterranean
was at its height roughly from 1538 to 1571, when the English presence
dwindled and disappeared. The Venetians were able to maintain their
trade at this time with the permission and special favour of the Turk,
and English kerseys formed a most important component of their
cargoes for the Levant, kerseys carried overland from the Netherlands
across the Alps with other goods to the Italian cities, but above all to
Venice and Ancona for dispatch eastwards.[4] Once this great artery of
Continental trade was successfully in use merchants lost interest in the
sea-route.

In the early seventies, however, English shipping re-entered the
Mediterranean, frequenting first of all Leghorn in Tuscany and Civitavecchia in the Papal States. Venice and Antwerp, the poles of the
Continental axis, were now in serious trouble. The war of Cyprus
(1570–73) crippled Venetian trade for the time being, while the revolt of
the Netherlands from 1569 put Antwerp, already unsettled, in
jeopardy. From 1569 to 1572 a tidal wave of piratical depredation swept
Italian as well as Iberian shipping off the sea-route from the Straits of
Gibraltar to the North Sea. The Turks took over Chios in 1566: Civitavecchia now became the main source for alum and English ships went
there to fetch it, bringing to Italy herring from the North, tin and lead
for the wars, and of course their native cloths, especially kerseys.

There is some evidence that they were already pushing into the
eastern Mediterranean in the later 1570s. Thus in 1575 Acerbo
Velutelli, a merchant of Lucca, obtained, with the support of the earl of
Leicester and Sir Francis Walsingham, a monopoly over imports of
currants into England, and allegedly freighted English ships for the
voyage to Zante and Cephalonia, Venice's island colonies: two of John
Hawkins's ships in 1575 and two more of the same owner's in 1576.[5] In

---

[3] *PN*, v, 115–16.

[4] The Antwerp–Venice trade is documented in W. Brulez, 'L'exportation des Pays-Bas
vers l'Italie par voie de terre au milieu du XVIe siècle', *Annales ESC*, 14 (1959), 461–91;
W. Brulez, 'Les routes commerciales d'Angleterre en Italie au XVIe siècle', *Studi in
onore di Amintore Fanfani* (Milan, 1962), IV, pp. 121–84; P. Earle, 'The commercial
development of Ancona, 1479–1551', *EconHR*, 2nd series, 22 (1969), 28–44; F. Edler,
'Winchcomb kerseys in Antwerp (1538–44)', *EconHR*, 7 (1936), 57–62.

[5] BL, Cotton MSS, Vespasian F. IX, fos. 220–21. The paper outlines the dispute between
Velutelli and those challenging his monopoly, who alleged he had not used it to
import currants. Part of his defence was that 'Acerbo the first yeares of his lycence did
frayte twoo englishe shipps of Mr Jhon Hawkins for the voyadge of Zante and by that
voyadge loste 500^li and more. And the seconde yeare hee fraighted ij other shippes of
the said Mr Hawkins and Sir Frauncis Drake appoynted by him for that voyadge, but

1591 Oliver and Nicholas Stile and Simon Lawrence, then leading figures in the Mediterranean trade, claimed that they had been trading with the Levant since 1577.[6] Thomas Cordell, more prominent still in that business, evidently had a Turkish safe-conduct for Levant trade by 1577 and was probably using it for some years before 1580. Though later he was certainly a great shipowner, we do not know whether he sent English ships to Turkish ports at this stage.[7] Nevertheless in such ways the ground was being prepared for England's main break-through into the Turkey trade, for which Hakluyt is our key source:

Howbeit the discreete and worthy citizens Sir Edward Osborne and M. Richard Staper seriously considering what benefite might grow to the common wealth by renuing of the foresaid discontinued trade, to the inlarging of her Majesties customes, the furthering of navigation, the venting of diverse generall commodities of this Realme, and the inriching of the citie of London, determined to use some effectuall meanes for the reestablishing and augmenting thereof. Wherefore about the yeere 1575 the foresaid R.W. marchants at their charges and expenses sent John Wight and Joseph Clements by the way of Poland to Constantinople, where the said Joseph remained 18 monethes to procure a safe conduct from the grand Signior, for M. William Harborne, then factor for Sir Edward Osborne, to have free accesse into his Highnes dominions, and obtained the same. Which businesse after two yeres charge-able travell and suit being accomplished, the sayd M. Harborne the first of July 1578 departed from London by the sea to Hamburgh, and thence accompanied with Joseph Clements his guide and a servant, he travailed to Leopolis in Poland, and then apparelling himselfe, his guide, and his servant after the Turkish fashion (having first obteyned the king of Poland his safe conduct to passe at Camienijecz the frontier towne of his dominions next unto Turky) by good means he obtained favour of one Acmet Chaus the Turks ambassadour then in Poland, and readie to returne to Constantinople, to bee received into his companie and carovan. And so the fourth of September 1578 he departed with the said Acmet from Leopolis in Poland, and travelling through Moldavia, Valachia, Bulgaria, and Romania, gratifying the Voiavodes with certaine courtesies, he arrived at Constantinople the 28 of October next insuing. Where he behaved himselfe so wisely and discreetely, that within few monethes after he obtained not onely the great Turkes large and ample priviledge for himselfe, and the two worshipfull persons aforesaid, but also procured his honourable and friendly letters unto her Majestie in maner following.[8]

the greater of those shippes did make shipwracke aboute Dover wherby hee loste 700[li] and more. The thirde yeare whiche was 1577 hee did cawse Bonvisus to frayte the primerose for that voyadge to Zante and hee returned loden with currantes. . . .' In 1577 Alessandro Pallavicino chartered four ships of the Hawkins fleet to ship alum from Civitavecchia to England: L. Stone, *An Elizabethan: Sir Horatio Palavicino* (Oxford, 1956), pp. 49–52.
[6] *Cal. SPD* (1591–4), p. 58.   [7] Skilliter, *Harborne*, pp. 11–13.   [8] *PN*, v, 168–9.

Private initiative thus apparently began this course of events, but Harborne, setting out on his overland journey to Constantinople in 1578, was not merely the personal representative of Messrs. Osborne and Staper. His mission, though essentially commercial, was necessarily of interest to the state, nor was it by chance that it led directly to inter-state relations. 1578 was the probable date of a memorandum by Sir Francis Walsingham headed 'A consideracion of the trade into Turkey'.[9] Here he discusses the potential gains and the likely difficulties: the trade will 'sett a grett nomber of your grettest shippes a worke wherby your navie shalbe mainteyned'; the realm will sell its own commodities 'with most proffitte', whereas formerly they have fallen into strangers' hands, and direct access to the Levant markets will enable it to supply both itself and the hither part of Europe with Levant goods, much to its own enrichment. Thus Walsingham sees the English interest as essentially commercial – nowhere does he hint at any political advantage or Anglo-Ottoman entente. As for the difficulties, they will arise from attempts by Spain, France or Venice to 'impeach' us, by finesse, force or both. To meet such inconveniences a fleet of twenty ships will be needed for the voyage, adequately supplied for defence and trade. Furthermore,

the fyrst thinge that is to be done to withstande theyr fines is to make choice of some apte man to be sent with her Majestes letters unto the Turke to procure an ample safe conducte, who is allwaies to remaine there at the charge of the merchantes, as Agent to impeache the indirect practises of the said Ambassadours, whose repaire thither is to be handled with grett secrecie, and his voyage to be perfourmed rather by lande than by sea.

Harborne was that 'apte man'. A Yarmouth man of gentle birth, he had experience in trade, particularly as Osborne's factor in Spain, and was a founder member of the Spanish Company, formed in 1577. Secretary Thomas Wilson's letter to him in October 1579, addressing him as 'My good frend', congratulating him on his success and advising him how to proceed, leaves little doubt that he left England with the government's approval and support.[10] Although there is no evidence, we may reasonably assume, knowing the informality and indirectness of Elizabethan procedure in such matters, that he had unofficial instructions to open the way for English trade. In 1578 Turkey resumed war with Persia and was known to stand in desperate need of metals from the West: steel, lead and above all tin for the

---

[9] Skilliter, *Harborne*, pp. 28–30. The formerly attributed date of 1580 is no longer acceptable in the light of Skilliter's discussion.
[10] Skilliter, *Harborne*, pp. 75–6.

casting of bronze guns. The Papal ban on exports of munitions from Christendom to Turkey was generally observed in that age of Ottoman power, but the English, now drifting towards conflict with Spain, the Turk's main enemy, were prepared to break it. Walsingham's memorandum declares no such intention and speaks only of kerseys, but Harborne's message to the Porte may have conveyed much more, for the sultan's response was abnormally eager.

Contravening the Ottoman rule of never opening a correspondence (for Harborne evidently delivered no letters from the queen), he acknowledged the unofficial overtures and informed Elizabeth that he had granted a general safe-conduct to all English merchants to travel and trade in Ottoman territory. We now know that this was the sultan's message in his letter of March 1579, though the Latin translation actually received by the queen appeared to limit the privilege to Harborne and his two principals. Consequently she found it necessary in her reply, in October 1579, to request that the licence be extended to 'all our subjects in general', re-asserting in effect the national interest in this initiative, though also implying her sovereign right to limit the privilege herself. Still more revealing than this *contretemps* was another letter to Elizabeth, accompanying the sultan's, from Mustafa Beg, the interpreter who was responsible for dealing with Harborne and the English negotiation. For here Mustafa boldly proposed no less than 'a league and most holy alliance'. The most notable feature of the queen's reply to Mustafa is that it completely ignored this, pointedly devoting the main part of the letter to trade matters, adding only a plea for the release of English captives in the Turk's galleys. Her reply to the sultan took exactly the same line.[11] She obviously had nothing to gain, apart from the obloquy of Christendom, from any political commitment of the kind suggested. Nevertheless in 1580, possibly even before the end of 1579, cargoes including munitions of war were on their way from England to the Levant, and in May 1580 Sultan Murad III formally granted the English nation an elaborate charter of privileges, putting them on equal footing with the French. The grant was in the form of a unilateral treaty, conceded by the sultan at the request of the queen for friendship – a fictional request of course.[12]

The Elizabethan interest in the Levant was commercial. The state supported the merchants in their initiative because it regarded that trade as potentially valuable. From successful trade the realm would

---

[11] Skilliter, *Harborne*, pp. 49–75. My account of the royal correspondence is derived from Skilliter's expert critique of the Turkish materials, from which several significant revisions of older interpretations arise.

[12] Skilliter, *Harborne*, pp. 24–5, 86–103.

benefit in various ways, including the establishment of friendly inter-course with a foreign power, but the state did not attempt to substitute its own for its merchants' interests. Elizabeth's government usually adopted such a position in dealing with questions of foreign trade. Moreover it favoured the commercial élite, comprising chiefly the wealthier Londoners, by creating a series of chartered companies with monopoly rights over particular branches of foreign trade. In the case of the Turkey trade the crown granted a seven-year monopoly to Osborne and Staper in reward for their endeavours, joining with them two other named merchants and allowing them to adopt twelve other partners, operating together as a joint-stock company. Letters patent to this effect were issued in 1581 and the queen showed her special interest in the enterprise by reserving the right to appoint two stock-holding members herself.[13]

Meanwhile forces beyond her control were drawing her, willy nilly, into closer relations with the Porte. In April 1581 the English *Bark Roe*, returning from Chios where her crew had blithely hobnobbed with Harborne, piratically seized two merchantmen belonging to Greek subjects of the sultan. For this blatant crime Harborne was held responsible and arrested, the privileges being withdrawn. He obtained his release only through the good offices of the French ambassador, who now assumed the protection of English persons and property in Ottoman territory. In June 1581 Elizabeth was obliged to write a humble letter of apology and it became obvious that to obtain restora-tion of the privileges she would have to send a permanent ambassador to Constantinople. The Turks for their own reasons wanted the English trade to continue, as it did under French protection during 1582, and eventually Harborne, who returned to England after his release, went back as ambassador. He served there from 1583 to 1588, but at the merchants' expense, for the queen refused to finance him. As events showed, his presence contributed considerably to the pros-perity the trade enjoyed during those years. He appointed English consuls in Cairo, Alexandria, Aleppo, Damascus, Algiers, Tunis, Tripoli in Barbary and Tripoli in Syria, and he intervened repeatedly to secure justice for Englishmen against Turkish officials and the corsairs of Barbary. At the same time, as Anglo-Spanish relations deteriorated into open warfare, Harborne strove to embroil Turkey in renewed hostilities with Spain. He did not succeed in this, but his considerable influence was shown in 1587, when the Spanish envoy

[13] *PN*, v, 192–202. The queen lent 10,000 lb weight of silver to Osborne and some of his partners in October 1582: W. Murdin (ed.), *Collection of State Papers . . . in the Reign of Queen Elizabeth* (London, 1759), p. 781.

sent to negotiate an extension of the truce was sent away empty-handed.[14]

In Elizabethan commercial strategy the opening of the Turkey trade was the most important event between the forging of the sea link with Muscovy and the founding of the East India Company. English merchantmen could now fetch for the home market without inter-mediaries cotton wool and yarn, Turkish carpets and cloths, galls, Persian silk, and the sweet oils, sweet wines and currants of the islands; they could also reach much closer than formerly to the sources of pepper, cloves, nutmegs, cinnamon, ginger, aloes, indigo and other spices. In this respect the new trade fulfilled in considerable measure the hopes that the Muscovy Company had failed to realize. Perhaps indeed English merchants might go further, as some Venetians did, to the Persian Gulf and beyond, and set up a chain of trading posts stretching from Aleppo to India. Such was the nature of the scheme suggested to the new company in 1582 by the pioneering London merchant John Newbery.

Newbery had already travelled extensively in the Middle East. In 1579 he made a conventional trip to the Holy Land, but his second journey, begun in 1580, lasted two years and took him as far as Hormuz at the mouth of the Persian Gulf, whence he returned by way of Persia, Constantinople, Poland and the Baltic. On the voyage out to Tripoli in the *White Hinde* of London his companion was the merchant William Barret, who remained in Aleppo and later became consul there, and Newbery's account (evidently a rough but detailed journal later written up by Samuel Purchas) contains much valuable informa-tion about commodities, prices, customs duties, transport costs, caravan-routes and so forth. The outward journey, through Bagdad and Basra to Hormuz, was hardly pioneering, but the return route through southern Persia, Tabriz and Anatolia was less familiar to Europeans and most of it was quite unknown to Englishmen.[15]

In 1583 Newbery departed once more, this time with the backing of Osborne and Staper and bearing the queen's letters to 'Zelabdim Echebar, king of Cambaia' (Akbar the Great) and to 'the king of China'. With him in the *Tiger* sailed the merchants Ralph Fitch, John Eldred, William Shales, Ralph Allen and William Skinner, together with William Leeds, a jeweller, and James Story, a painter. At Aleppo they

---

[14] Skilliter, *Harborne*, pp. 159–200; *PN*, v, 189–91, 221–8, 243–319. S. A. Skilliter, 'The Hispano-Ottoman armistice of 1581', in C. E. Bosworth (ed.), *Iran and Islam* (Edinburgh, 1971), pp. 491–515.
[15] *Purchas*, VIII, 449–81.

spent £2000 on kerseys, cloths, tin and other goods, their plan being to leave Eldred and Shales with part of the stock to trade at Bagdad, Allen and Skinner likewise at Basra, while Newbery and Fitch would take the remainder and 'goe for the Indies'.[16] Jan Huyghen van Linschoten, however, who talked with Newbery in Goa, afterwards declared in his famous description of the East that 'although those wares amounted unto great summes of money, notwithstanding it was but onely a shadow or colour, thereby to give no occasion to be mistrusted, or seene into: for that their principall intent was to buy great quantities of precious stones, as Diamants, Pearles, Rubies, etc. to the which end they brought with them a great summe of money and gold, and that very secretly'. The inclusion of a jeweller in the party would appear to confirm this, and we may infer that Osborne, Staper and their factors were interested not so much in selling English goods as in acquiring the most profitable commodities, for which purpose they set up shop in Bagdad, Basra, Hormuz and, eventually, Goa. Immediate profit was not of course the main concern: as Linschoten observed, the company wished to see whether it could maintain factors in these places and so penetrate further into eastern trade.[17] It was in fact a planned commercial reconnaissance: Newbery and Eldred evidently reported their progress by letters to Harborne in Aleppo, while Newbery sent news at intervals to the merchant Leonard Poore in London, to whom Fitch also wrote; Newbery consulted John Dee and the younger Hakluyt before departing; Eldred and Fitch kept journals.

The expedition was not a success. All went well as far as Aleppo, whence Newbery wrote optimistically home. The trade at Bagdad and Basra impressed neither him nor Eldred, but they followed their prearranged scheme and about the middle of August 1583 Newbery, Fitch, Leeds and Story set sail from Basra for Hormuz. Arriving on 4 September, they set up shop and began business, but on the tenth they were all arrested. As Newbery reported from Goa,

There were two causes which moved the captaine of Ormus to imprison us, & afterwards to send us hither. The first was, because Michael Stropene had accused us of many matters, which were most false. And the second was for that M. Drake at his being at Maluco, caused two pieces of his ordinance to be shot at a gallion of the kings of Portugall, as they say.[18]

Drake did indeed fire upon a Portuguese galleon south of Mindanao on his way to the Moluccas in October 1579. More, he bought a large

---

[16] *Purchas*, ix, 496–7 (Eldred to G.S., 14 July 1583). For this expedition see also *PN*, v, 450–64 (letters of Newbery and Fitch), 465–505 (Fitch's report), 505–12 (Linschoten); vi, 1–9 (Eldred's report); *Purchas*, ix, 493–500 (letters of Newbery and Eldred).
[17] *PN*, v, 506.   [18] *PN*, v, 459.

quantity of cloves from the sultan of Ternate, who agreed with him informally to trade with the English in preference to the Portuguese in future. Worse still, Elizabeth had since 1580 countenanced the pretender to the Portuguese throne, the refugee Dom Antonio, against Philip of Spain, the established king, and Newbery was accused of carrying letters from Dom Antonio and of acting as his spy. Newbery of course repudiated any connection with Drake or Dom Antonio, but it is hardly surprising that the Portuguese authorities were less than pleased by the arrival of English merchants – heretics to boot – in their territory. What is surprising is that Newbery and co. had apparently not expected the Portuguese reaction and blamed the whole bad business on the Venetian merchant, Stropene. Linschoten, who heard Newbery's side of the matter only, did the same:

the Italians . . . fearing that those English men finding good vent for their commodities in that place, would be resident therein, and so dayly increase, which would be no small losse and hinderance unto them, did presently invent all the subtile meanes they could to hinder them: and to that end they went unto the Captaine of Ormus, as then called Don Gonsalo de Meneses, telling him that there were certaine English men come into Ormus, that were sent onely to spie the countrey; and sayd further, that they were heretikes.[19]

Stropene, acting upon advice from his brother in Aleppo, no doubt expressed the general hostility of the Venetians in the Near and Middle East to the advent of the English. Newbery and his companions must have seemed to them the advance guard of a force which would threaten their entire commercial network from Constantinople to Hormuz and beyond. Linschoten did not overstate their ill-will. Nor were the English hopes of penetrating the Portuguese empire in the East altogether illusory, for the attitude of the Portuguese to the Levant trade was not prohibitive but permissive: they were content to allow all kinds of merchants access to the Persian Gulf from east or west, provided they paid the dues imposed by the Estado da India.[20] The English case was of course difficult for the political and religious reasons mentioned, and this was probably why Meneses referred the whole issue to Goa, where the four English prisoners in due course arrived for interrogation. Fortunately they seem to have convinced the Dutch Jesuit who examined their faith that they were good Catholics, and they were even more fortunate in finding there a friend in Padre Thomas Stevens, an English Jesuit who had come out to Goa in a Portuguese ship in 1579. Indeed Newbery already had an introduction to Stevens from Richard Hakluyt, who had known him at Oxford.

[19] *PN*, v, 507.   [20] Steensgaard, *Asian Trade Revolution, passim.*

These two Jesuits and Jan Linschoten, servant to the archbishop of Goa, interceded for the English and secured their release after some three weeks in a Goan prison.[21]

In spite of these difficulties Newbery managed to carry on successful business: 'Many of our things I have solde very well, both here and at Ormus in prison', he wrote from Goa. 'Here is very great good to be done in divers of our commodities, and in like manner there is great profite to be made with commodities of this countrey, to be carried to Aleppo.'[22] Apparently at Hormuz he was let out of prison under guard each day and allowed to trade, though he paid the Portuguese commander and his officers heavily for the privilege, and lost some of his stock by pilfering. At Goa again pilfering and 'gifts' reduced the stock, and again they did good business after their release, but their position was still insecure. According to Linschoten the Jesuits, having got wind of the large sums of money the English possessed, tried to induce them to join their order by dwelling upon the dangers of their situation, and with Story, the painter, they succeeded, 'partly for feare, and partly for want of meanes to relieve himselfe'. He came out of prison before the rest, became a Jesuit and served the order as a painter. But the warnings of the Jesuits, to the effect that the viceroy intended to ship them all to Portugal, were not without foundation, for when they asked for the return of the money they had deposited as security, 'he made us a very sharpe answere, and sayd we should be better sifted before it were long, and that they had further matter against us'.[23]

Newbery, Fitch and Leeds therefore planned their escape and, leaving a considerable stock of goods behind, took their way through Bijapur to Agra and the court of Akbar, the Mogul emperor, which they reached in the summer of 1584. Towards the end of September, as Fitch relates, they separated:

and then Master John Newberie tooke his journey toward the Citie of Lahor, determining from thence to goe for Persia, and then for Aleppo or Constantinople, whether hee could get soonest passage unto; and directed me to goe to for Bengala and for Pegu, and did promise me, if it pleased God, to meet me in Bengala within two yeeres with a ship out of England. I left William Leades the Jeweller, in service with the King Zelabdim Echebar in Fatepore, who did entertayne him verie well, and give him an House and five Slaves, an Horse, and every day sixe S.S. in money.[24]

[21] *PN*, v, 452; vi, 377–85 (Stevens's letter to his father, which came into Hakluyt's hands and was lent by him to Newbery).
[22] *PN*, v, 461–2.
[23] *PN*, v, 471.
[24] *Purchas*, x, 174–5.

Leeds was luckier than Newbery, who disappeared after his departure from Fatepore and presumably died, as Purchas says, 'unknown how or where'. His mission was in fact a failure, but his initiative, energy and irrepressible optimism sustained a remarkable enterprise in the teeth of virtually insuperable difficulties. The geo-political circumstances were unfavourable at this time to such an approach on the part of the English to eastern trade, and Fitch's travels in the next few years only confirmed this negative conclusion. Fitch journeyed by river to the Ganges Delta and Hooghly, saw much of Bengal, visited Malacca and returned by way of Ceylon, Cochin, Goa, Chaul and Hormuz. In all these places he found the Portuguese, and though he found them friendly enough further east, Goa and Hormuz proved distinctly inhospitable places for an English merchant. Eventually, when he reached London via Persia and Aleppo in 1591, he was able to impart to those Londoners who were interested an impressive store of fresh information about the trade of the Indian Ocean, but what he had to say about the prospects of trading from the Levant to the Gulf and beyond must have been discouraging. From 1585 at least there could be no question of tolerating English traders in Hormuz or Goa, for the Portuguese acknowledged the rule of Philip of Spain, and he was at open war with Elizabeth.

From the 1580s until the 1620s and beyond English trade to the Levant prospered, overcoming a variety of political and commercial dangers. It was probably the most profitable branch of the country's overseas trade during this period, when 'Turkey merchants' became well known for their wealth and influence in the City. The war with Spain did not seriously interrupt this traffic: indeed it increased the value of the Turkish connection in English eyes and led to a marked strengthening of the English presence in the Mediterranean. The company's ships sailed in powerful convoys now and repulsed Spanish assaults with loss to the enemy; other English merchantmen entered the inland sea in increasing numbers and well armed, taking a growing share of the port-to-port trade; English privateers and pirates came also for plunder, attracted by the rich cargoes borne by shipping of many nations, and by the ready markets available in Barbary, where lawful prize was not subject to the taxes levied in England, nor illicit prize subject to arrest. These predators caused the Levant Company much embarrassment during the years around the turn of the century: the French, Venetian and other victims vehemently protested to the Ottoman authorities, pressing for redress at the company's expense, which (along with other worries at this time) led to some despairing talk of withdrawal from the trade, 'and that shortly if this corsair insolency be not in time depressed', as Henry Lello, then ambassador, remarked.[25] But the company survived this crisis and learned to live with the continual complaints and threats which arose from such depredations in the years and decades following.

It had meanwhile been greatly strengthened by re-organization in 1592. The original company's charter expired in 1588, about which time the joint-stock system of trading was evidently abandoned, and the government, in the person of Burghley, the Lord Treasurer, took this opportunity to consult the existing members and other interested groups about the opening of the trade to a larger body of merchants. In the event this was agreed and the number of members was substantially increased by the new charter of 1592, the most significant change being the admission of those merchants who had formerly constituted the Venice Company. This small group had gained in 1583 the sole right to import currants, wines and oil from the Venetian dominions, a most lucrative concession, which was exploited mainly by four merchants: Edward Holmeden, Paul Bayning, Thomas Cordell and William Garraway. The last three became important shipowners and promoters of privateering and oceanic enterprise, but their success, like Holmeden's, seems to have arisen from the currants of Zante, Cephalonia and the nearby parts of Greece. The merger of the Venice and Turkey companies strengthened the English Levant trade because the two monopolies had formerly competed with each other and because the currants trade supplied ships returning from further east with a marketable bulk cargo with which to fill their frequently half-empty holds.[26]

The most serious threat to the company's trade occurred when Dutch ships, quickly followed by English, established direct trade with the East Indies by way of the Cape of Good Hope, and the Dutch and English East India Companies came into existence in 1602 and 1600 respectively. At that time the Levant traders made much of their profit from goods originating east of Persia and many were inclined to view this development as a disaster, but in the event the trade continued to flourish. The westward traffic in spices, drugs and dyes did largely collapse, but by the 1620s the merchants were shipping large quantities of eastern goods from England to Turkey, as well as to Venice and other Mediterranean markets, a phenomenon which evoked the

[25] PRO, SP 97/4, fos. 209–10, cited in K. R. Andrews, 'Sir Robert Cecil and Mediterranean plunder', *EHR*, 87 (1972), 513–32.
[26] M. Epstein, *The Early History of the Levant Company* (London, 1908), pp. 20–39; Wood, *Levant Company*, pp. 15–20; E. P. Cheyney, *A History of England from the Defeat of the Armada to the Death of Elizabeth* (New York, 1914), I, pp. 375–406.

admiring comment of mercantilist writers.[27] Attempts to divert Persia's valuable raw silk from the Levant to the Gulf failed to make any impression at this stage, nor did the arrival of the Dutch as competitors in the Levant seriously disturb the prosperity of the English there, who at this time, in the first quarter of the seventeenth century, superseded both the Italians and the French as the dominant European 'nation' in the Turkish empire.

The advantages they successfully exploited were cloth on the one hand and shipping on the other. The kerseys which were the staple English export to Turkey in Elizabeth's reign enabled the English to rely to a great extent on their own commodities, supplemented by Spanish coin acquired in the Peninsula and Italy, but in the early seventeenth century, when kerseys gave way to dyed broadcloth from Suffolk and the West Country, these together with some re-exports normally sufficed to pay for the goods returned, whereas in Mun's words, 'a balance in money is paid by the other nations trading thither'.[28] As for ships, the English specialized at this stage in a type of merchantman most suited for this long and dangerous route: stout merchant galleons, well manned and strongly armed, 'defensible ships' as they were called. They were far less vulnerable than French or Venetian vessels and gave the English here what they had nowhere else – parity, in respect of shipping charges, with the Dutch. Not only the great ships employed by the company, of four or five hundred tons, but the middling merchantmen of 150–300 tons or so were now much in demand as carriers within the Mediterranean.[29] This was, in early seventeenth-century terms, sea power.

The Levant trade did not lead directly to empire in the conventional sense of territorial possessions overseas, nor even to the kind of domination that was later associated with imperial 'spheres of influence'. Nevertheless it made an important contribution to England's early expansion. The capital accumulated by the members of the company found its way into various forms of oceanic enterprise and above all into the East India Company.[30] The demands and opportunities of the Mediterranean were probably at least as important as any

---

[27] For example Lewes Roberts, *The Merchants Mappe of Commerce* (London, 1638), p. 193. Roberts was a 'husband' of the Levant Company.

[28] Thomas Mun, 'A discourse of trade from England unto the East Indies', in J. R. McCulloch (ed.), *Early English Tracts on Commerce* (London, 1856). Mun had been Thomas Cordell's factor at Leghorn and knew the Mediterranean field of commerce especially well. For details on the commodities exchanged see R. Davis, 'England and the Mediterranean, 1570–1670', in F. J. Fisher (ed.), *Essays in the Economic and Social History of Tudor and Stuart England* (Cambridge, 1961), pp. 117–37.

[29] Davis, 'England and the Mediterranean', pp. 126–30.

[30] Chaudhuri, *East India Company*, p. 11.

other factor in promoting the nation's resources of ships and skilled men fitted for the ocean trades. The ambassadors, consuls and factors in the Levant built up over the decades a valuable fund of commercial experience applicable in many respects to other parts of Asia. That they generally failed to bridge the cultural gap between Turkey and England or to develop meaningful contact with the Turkish people was not mainly their fault. As Giaours they had no right to expect friendly or respectful treatment and as merchants they were exposed to the extortionate and arbitrary demands (*avanias*) of Turkish officials. Contact with Turks led all too often to insult or injury, and contact with Turkish women was too dangerous to contemplate. Factors' acquaintance was for the most part limited to 'dragomen' (interpreters, often of Italian extraction), Jews, Armenians, Greeks and other Europeans. They led limited lives, which were apt to be brief, and stood little chance of surmounting the mutual repugnance and ignorance which governed relations between Turks and Franks.[31]

[31] Wood, *Levant Company*, pp. 205–49. On the treatment of the Levant in literature see S. C. Chew, *The Crescent and the Rose* (Oxford, 1937).

5

Western Africa

In the 1520s and 1530s the Portuguese dominated the Atlantic coast of Morocco from Agadir in the south to the Strait of Gibraltar, but in the 1540s a new dynasty – the Saadians – rose to power among the Moslems, forced the Portuguese out of Agadir, Safi and Azemmour and finally united the country under Muhammad al-Shaikh. By 1550 Muhammad effectively ruled Morocco: only Tangier, Ceuta and Mazagan remained in Portuguese hands. At this stage Portugal's claim to a monopoly of Moroccan trade became untenable not only in theory but in practice and the way lay open for English traders to enter the ocean ports of Barbary, an opportunity they were not slow to seize. Men already familiar with the trades of Lisbon, Seville and the Canaries found Morocco an easy and attractive extension of their business. English cloth sold well and the principal return, sugar, was in growing demand at home. Such was the substance of the Barbary trade as it actually developed after 1550, though the first promoters may have been at least as interested in gold.[1]

As Hakluyt tells us, the trade began in 1551 with the voyage of Captain Thomas Wyndham in the *Lion* of London. Wyndham had served Henry VIII and Edward VI as a commander at sea and had done his share of freebooting at Spanish and Portuguese expense: a hardbitten ruffian of gentry stock. Sir John Luttrell, his uncle, backed the venture, along with some others, though we cannot be sure who these were. One James Alday, a servant of Sebastian Cabot's, later claimed that he 'invented' the Barbary trade and was to have led the first expedition, but went down with the sweating sickness, 'whereon the chiefe of those with whom I joyned in that voyage died, that is to say, Sir John Lutterell, John Fletcher, Henry Ostrich and others'.[2] In the

---

[1] Ch.-A. Julien, *History of North Africa from the Arab Conquest to 1830* (London, 1970), pp. 213–25; T. S. Willan, *Studies in Elizabethan Foreign Trade* (Manchester, 1959), pp. 92–6.
[2] *PN*, VI, 136–7; Willan, *Studies*, pp. 96–102; Tong, 'Captain Wyndham'.

absence of supporting evidence Alday's claim cannot be accepted, for he was pleading his own cause, but there is no reason to doubt his identification of Luttrell, Ostrich and Fletcher as adventurers. Ostrich, kinsman of William Ostrich, governor of the Andalusia Company in 1538, was Cabot's son-in-law, which implies that Cabot was somehow concerned with the venture, while the other shareholders probably included William Chester, William Garrard and Thomas Lodge, prominent London merchants.

Of this first voyage we know only that the *Lion* (150 tons) and another vessel called at Agadir, but it was presumably successful because Wyndham set forth again in 1552 with the *Lion*, the *Buttolfe* (80 tons) and a caravel of 60 tons bought from certain Portuguese in Newport, Wales. His chief promoters this time were London magnates, including Garrard and Sir John Yorke. The ships first visited Safi and then Agadir, where they traded linen and woollen cloth, coral, amber, jet and other goods for sugar, dates, almonds and molasses. Returning homewards they put in at the Canaries for repairs and came into conflict with the Spaniards there. Lives were lost on both sides and although in the end the matter was settled by negotiation the whole incident was symptomatic of the suspicion and hostility which already poisoned Anglo-Spanish relations. As for the Portuguese, the narrator of this expedition, James Thomas, reported them

much offended with this our new trade into Barbarie, and both in our voiage the yeere before, as also in this they gave out in England by their marchants, that if they tooke us in those partes, they would use us as their mortall enemies, with great threates and menaces.[3]

But in spite of continued Portuguese protest this developed as a settled trade after 1552, financed mainly by the type of London merchant with an interest in rich grocery wares, in shipping or in both. Some conflict occasionally arose with the Iberians, but it was not until 1585 that the trade was incorporated and then for extraordinary reasons.[4] Even during the Spanish war, business continued much as usual, though many shipowners in the trade took out letters of reprisal and combined privateering with merchandizing to their best advantage.

The story of English trade to Guinea in the later sixteenth century

---

[3] *PN*, VI, 138–40.
[4] See Willan, *Studies*, pp. 163–87. The earl of Leicester was responsible for the formation of the company, which he foisted upon the merchants in order to secure control of the arms trade. He apparently induced the queen to grant a charter by assuring her that the company would maintain an ambassador in Morocco, who would serve the queen by working to embroil that country in warfare with Spain.

was altogether different. Guinea gold was the prize, one of the great prizes of oceanic empire. Portugal, though she grasped it but loosely, would resist any challenge here with fierce reprisal, as a threat to her vital interests. Conversely, English ambition to share those riches had strong thrust and a keen edge; powerful interests took up this enterprise and would not lightly give it up. The state itself became an interested party and the antagonism of the rival powers brought them close to war before they reached a tacit agreement.

Guinea in the middle of the century was a Portuguese sphere of influence only in the sense that the Portuguese controlled most of Europe's trade with the area and were the only Europeans established there. The king of Portugal was 'lord of Guinea' in name, but hardly in fact. Apart from the Cape Verde Islands and the islands in the Gulf of Guinea, which were effectively occupied and formed the strategic centres of an extremely dispersed commerce with the mainland, the sway of the Portuguese was confined to the immediate vicinity of a handful of coastal forts, of which the most important was São Jorge da Mina on the Gold Coast. In Upper Guinea considerable numbers of Portuguese and half-castes lived in scattered groups on the coasts and rivers of Senegambia and Sierra Leone, trading with the Africans, and here indeed Portuguese influence was more extensive and lasting than elsewhere, though far from sufficient to exclude other Europeans. Southward of Sierra Leone the Malagueta and Ivory Coasts, stretching almost to Cape Three Points, were little frequented, an area of intermittent contact and irregular trade, the haunt of French interlopers.

East and west of Cape Three Points lay the Mina coast, dominated by the castle of São Jorge. Under the walls of the castle the native town of Dondou was protected by the Portuguese, and these 'Mina Blacks' served well as allies, while additional fortified posts were maintained along the coast at Axim and (from around 1560) Samma and Accra, but these strong points by no means guaranteed the hold of the Portuguese over the Gold Coast as a whole. The numerous tribes, varying in power and all more or less independent, continually jostled with each other and often with the Portuguese, who could only maintain a modicum of security by mixing favours with brute force according to the shifting circumstances. Further east, Portuguese trade with the kingdom of Benin was by this time extinct. São Thomé and Principe looked mainly now to the Kongo and Angola, which do not concern us here.[5]

English efforts to penetrate the Guinea trade (leaving aside the earlier ventures of William Hawkins, already mentioned) began in

[5] Blake, *West Africa, passim*; Blake, *Europeans*, pp. 27–63.

1553 and lasted into the sixties. Two groups of men promoted them: leading London merchants on the one hand and important shipowning, naval men on the other. The first group included many Anglo-Iberian traders, particularly backers of the early Barbary trade such as William Garrard, William Chester, Thomas Lodge, Sir John Yorke, Francis Lambert and Edward Jackman, as well as the Canary Islands traders Anthony Hickman and Edward Castelin. These were all members of the Muscovy Company, as were many more of the Guinea promoters, like Sir George Barne and Thomas Lok. Indeed it has been shown that of thirty-four merchants interested in the 1558 Guinea voyage some twenty-two were named in the Muscovy charter of 1555.[6] Judging from this, the only voyage for which we have a full list of adventurers, the syndicates, which fluctuated in membership from one venture to the next, were large, presumably to distribute the heavy risk incurred in these expensive and dangerous expeditions, each voyage being separately financed as a terminable joint-stock.

We do not know precisely who owned the ships employed in the first Guinea venture, but in the three years following (1554–6) they were private merchantmen owned or hired by the London syndicates. In 1558, however, two royal ships sailed for Guinea in the company of two private vessels. This expedition, the last of Mary's reign, was evidently financed by some of the Londoners, who somehow secured the collaboration of the Lord High Admiral, Lord William Howard. The terms of the arrangement between the crown and the merchants are not known, but they probably resembled roughly those agreed for a later voyage in 1564. On this occasion a merchant syndicate chartered Elizabeth's *Minion*, a fairly old and light warship of 300 tons. The queen adventured the ship, fully equipped and armed, while the merchants were to provide trade goods worth at least £5000 together with the crew, their victuals and wages. Two persons appointed by the Privy Council were to act for the queen in checking the outward and return cargoes and the final reckoning, by which the queen should take one sixth of the 'cleare and holle gayne and proffit'.[7]

In this way the crown shared directly in the promotion of several expeditions to Guinea. On the other hand neither queen appears to have been involved personally, for the profits were paid, not into the privy purse, but into the hands of the treasurer of the navy, Benjamin Gonson. In effect, the adventuring of the royal ships in the Guinea trade was a business arrangement between the London merchants and the Navy Board. The interest of the latter was doubtless to keep its

[6] Willan, *Muscovy Merchants*, p. 27.
[7] BL, Lansdowne MSS, 113, fos. 9–17.

ships profitably employed, but it should be noted that Gonson had also a personal stake in Guinea venturing. In 1561 he was a member of the syndicate which chartered four of the queen's ships, and in 1564 he contributed his own ship the *Merlin* to the expedition led by the queen's *Minion*, for the provision of which he was officially responsible.[8] Another member of the Navy Board, William Winter, surveyor of the queen's ships and master of naval ordnance, set forth in 1565, in partnership with his brother George, their ship the *Mary Fortune*, which the Portuguese sank off the Guinea coast, taking the crew prisoner.[9] In fact the leading families in charge of the royal fleet – Gonsons, Winters and Hawkinses – were themselves shipowners and merchants, seafaring businessmen in the broadest sense, sometimes leading expeditions in person, regularly in contact with financial and mercantile circles of the City and particularly interested in types of maritime enterprise which called for shipping power – privateering and ventures into waters dominated by Spain or Portugal. They did not scruple to use their public offices to promote their private business – indeed they all accused each other of doing so – and inevitably their private concerns influenced not only their management of the royal ships and dockyards, but also their views on naval policy. All this was of course normal in the sixteenth century. Corruption was a necessary condition of public service, nor was it incompatible with devotion to duty.

As for the trade itself, it consisted essentially in the sale of miscellaneous items to miscellaneous Africans for gold and some minor returns. A list of 'the commodities and wares that are most desired in Guinie, betwixt Sierra Liona and the furthest place of the Mine', drawn up by William Towerson, the most experienced of the commanders, mentions first 'manils' (brass bracelets), tin basins and pots, wedges of iron, pearls and beads, blue coral, horse tails and 'linen cloth principally', as well as 'some red cloth of low price, and some kersie'. More basins follow, with other metal wares, coarse French coverings and 'packing sheets good store', and the last entry is a veritable rag-bag, from swords to leather bags and 'what other trifles you will'.[10] There is plenty of other evidence to show that West Africa beyond Morocco took no considerable amount of English cloth, nor indeed were the outgoing cargoes worth much, as the example of the *Minion*'s charter-party suggests. As it was pointed out in connection with the

[8] Williamson, *Sir John Hawkins*, pp. 48–57.
[9] Blake, *West Africa*, p. 169; R. G. Marsden (ed.), *Documents relating to the Law and Custom of the Sea* (London, 1915), I, pp. 184–9; *Cal. SPF* (1566–8), pp. 466–7.
[10] *PN*, VI, 252.

Winters' case for compensation for the loss the *Mary Fortune*, victuals, wages, fitting-out and armament were the chief charges incurred in a Guinea voyage, the merchandise being 'of the least value'.[11] The people who undertook this trade were interested in Guinea not as an export market but as a source of extremely profitable imports, gold above all, but also ivory and pepper.

Thomas Wyndham, who commanded the first Guinea voyage in 1553, left Portsmouth with two ships, the *Lion* and the *Primrose*, and a pinnace, the *Moon*, in August, backed by Sir George Barne, Sir John Yorke, William Garrard, Francis Lambert and other London merchants. King Edward VI had died a few weeks before, but this expedition was planned and prepared during his reign, with the knowledge and support of his government. Wyndham had the king's licence and it seems likely that the *Primrose* and the *Moon* were royal vessels. What made the project possible and perhaps inspired it was the defection of two Portuguese seamen expert in the navigation of West Africa: Antonio Anes Pinteado and Francisco Rodrigues. Pinteado, one of the foremost Portuguese commanders in Atlantic trade and naval operations, having lost favour at court, came to England in 1552 and agreed to sail with Wyndham as his 'petycapitaine' or second-in-command, Rodrigues accompanying him as pilot. Portuguese agents in England attempted to lure these renegades back to their country, but Wyndham, calling on the help of the Lord Admiral (then Lord Clinton), had the intruders thrown into prison. They were soon released, but the English went ahead with their preparations regardless of King John III's evident disapproval.[12]

Wyndham's voyage is remarkable in several respects, but most of all for his aggressive, predatory and brutal conduct of it. He made first for the Madeiras, where he plundered Portuguese shipping and raided the island of Deserta, being repulsed after some bloodshed. The River Sestos on the Malagueta Coast was their first Guinea landfall, but Wyndham was not content with grains for a return cargo and insisted on continuing to the Mina Coast, plundering his way thither. Carefully avoiding São Jorge, he trafficked east and west of it for 150 lb of gold. The season was now advanced and Pinteado advised completing their sales and returning, but Wyndham would have none of it, and 'fell into a sudden rage, reviling the sayd Pinteado, calling him Jew, with other

[11] BL, Cotton MSS, Nero B. I, fo. 149.
[12] Blake, *Europeans*, pp. 309–14; J. A. Williamson, *Maritime Enterprise, 1485–1558* (Oxford, 1913), p. 279. George Barne, one of the promoters, stated in court in 1555 that the *Primrose* was not hired, but belonged to the partners, but he may have been concealing the truth in view of the political circumstances at that time: the Lord Admiral referred to the venture in 1553 as 'certaine service of the kinges'.

opprobrious words' and ordering him to lead the ships to Benin. Here Pinteado, Rodrigues and some of the merchants who accompanied the expedition journeyed to the king's court and traded there for no less than 80 tons of pepper, but in the meantime Pinteado's worst fears were realized. Sickness invaded the fleet and the men died like flies, Wyndham among them. The Benin visit was cut short and course set in all haste for England. Pinteado, who was made the scapegoat for this misfortune, was one of the many who died during the return voyage. The *Lion* having been abandoned for lack of men to sail her, the two remaining vessels finally reached Plymouth in June 1554 with a complement of forty out of the original 140 crew. For the promoters it proved a highly profitable venture, but it was later alleged that they did not pay the surviving seamen for the entire period of their service, and the brother of one of the dead men had to take them to court to secure the wages bequeathed to him.[13]

A second expedition rapidly followed, financed by Barne and Yorke in conjunction with Thomas Lok, one of the sons of Sir William Lok, an outstanding figure in the City under Henry VIII, with Hickman and Castelin the Canaries traders, and doubtless with other investors. John Lok, brother of Thomas, took command of the three ships and two pinnaces and departed in October 1554. He called at the River Sestos to buy pepper and went on to the Gold Coast, where he traded successfully on either side of Mina, returning directly thence to England. It was a difficult homeward voyage owing to the strong Guinea current flowing east and contrary winds around Cape Verde, which made him work well out into the Atlantic, but in the end he came safely home with the loss of only twenty-four men in all and delivered a rich cargo of gold, ivory and pepper.[14]

Lok's prosperous venture had important repercussions. On the one hand it inspired many other English merchants to try their luck in the Guinea trade, so that a variety of projects were afoot in 1555. On the other hand the Portuguese reacted strongly. Lok's activities, added to those of French adventurers, who were now likewise pushing on from the Malagueta Coast to the Mina Coast, and to Wyndham's marauding violence, threatened grave damage to Portugal's gold trade. Extensive interloping would not only reduce the amount of gold available to the Portuguese, but would also strengthen the independence and bargaining power of the Africans. Resistance, both naval and diplomatic, became an urgent necessity, and in the summer of 1555 the envoy of King John III lodged a formal protest, demanding reparations for

[13] *PN*, VI, 145–52; Blake, *Europeans*, pp. 284–8, 309–26.
[14] *PN*, VI, 154–64; Blake, *Europeans*, pp. 289–91.

damage, restoration of merchandise, punishment of offenders and a veto on all further Guinea operations from England. This protest was not immediately successful. Privy Councillors sympathetic to the merchants' cause were probably responsible for delaying any reply and for summoning certain merchants to answer the Portuguese case, who denied that they had frequented places subject to the king of Portugal, indulged in forceful methods or traded otherwise than peaceably with people who welcomed them and assured them of their independence from Portugal. Indeed, 'the said inhabitauntes of that country offred us and our said factors ground to build uppon, if they wold make anie fortresses in their countrey, and further offred them assistaunce of certen slaves for those workes without anie charge'.[15]

But John III on this occasion had in his hand a card the English could not trump: King Philip of Spain, now husband to Queen Mary and joint ruler of England. By this time it was Spain's policy to support the Portuguese empire against intruders, for French oceanic aggression threatened the Iberian powers equally and English expansion was now beginning to take the same course. Towards the end of 1555 matters came to a head. Philip upheld the renewed Portuguese protest and Mary complied by officially prohibiting the Guinea trade. Even so, this check to English ambition was not fully effective. It stopped one particular project and perhaps deterred some who might otherwise have ventured, but at least one voyage – that of William Towerson – went ahead. His was a small expedition but gained a large profit with very few casualties, so that after his return in May 1556 merchants once again laid plans for Guinea trading and the government again took steps to frustrate them: prohibitions, sequestration orders, summonses to venturers to appear before the council, and so forth. Once more, however, the government, perhaps not wholehearted in implementing the ban, failed to prevent Towerson from sailing. This time Towerson found conditions on the Mina Coast less favourable. On the Grain Coast he fell in with a French fleet and joined forces with it in order to deal the better with Portuguese ships, which were reported to be patrolling the Mina Coast in strength. And so in truth they were, as the French and English soon discovered. They managed to trade at various places, and at one were invited by the chief to settle and build a fort, but they came into conflict more than once with strong Portuguese squadrons and eventually, finding themselves outnumbered, made for home. Though financially successful, this was a hard voyage, partly because the English, though allied with the French against the Portuguese, had to compete with the former for trade.[16]

Towerson's third voyage was even harder. It was a larger expedition of four vessels, including two royal ships, which got away in January 1558 in spite of Spanish opposition, but when it reached the Gold Coast all the dangers and difficulties of that trade converged: they came into conflict with both the Portuguese and the French; they found the Negroes sometimes unwilling to trade, sometimes even hostile, and finally attacked and burned one of their towns; and after a disastrous homeward voyage they reached port with only two ships and twelve men fit to work, most of their companions having died.[17] Towerson's failure this time seems to have arisen partly from the inability of the Africans to meet the increasing European demand for gold – 'over-trading' was the contemporary term – and partly from the growing naval strength of the Portuguese on the Mina Coast. The Guinea trade was rapidly developing into a kind of commercial war, and the accession of Elizabeth, shortly after Towerson's return, aggravated the conflict, for neither she nor her secretary, Sir William Cecil, was prepared to compromise in this matter. In the first two years of her reign Englishmen probably continued to frequent the Guinea region, for in April 1561 the Portuguese again protested. The queen's reply was that she saw no cause why her subjects might not trade to any country subject to Portugal, but that she would admonish them not to enter any ports in Ethiopia in which the king had dominion, obedience and tribute.[18]

What this implied she tartly spelled out when the Portuguese renewed their protest a year later: she thought the king was right in building forts only where need was, thereby saving charge; nor did it appertain to her to say where the king should build forts or whether he should levy tribute or not; nor did she question how much he possessed there, nor for how long, though she wished the king had the kingdoms of Guinea in like obedience that he had the kingdom of Portugal; if he was not satisfied with last year's proclamation, she suggested he should command the inhabitants of those countries not to trade with the English. In fact the crown was already fully committed to active participation in the Guinea trade, for in June 1561 it agreed terms with a London syndicate for the use of four royal ships in an expedition which set out under Captain John Lok in September with the principal object of selecting a site for a fort in the king of Habaan's

[16] *PN*, vi, 177–231; Williamson, *Maritime Enterprise*, pp. 288–302.
[17] *PN*, vi, 231–52; Blake, *Europeans*, pp. 292–4.
[18] *Cal. SPF* (1561–2), nos. 96, 97, 98, 128, 137, 138.

country on the Gold Coast. It was a carefully prepared operation, obviously based on a recent report, and it shows the readiness of the crown and merchants at this juncture to enter into open conflict with Iberian power for extra-European trade.[19]

This voyage, however, came to grief. Bad weather twice drove the unseaworthy *Minion* back to port. A pinnace was eventually arrested in the Canary Islands. Part of the fleet apparently reached Guinea and did some trade, but there was no more talk of a fort. In 1563 the syndicate set forth the queen's ships *Minion* and *Primrose*, but it was again an unfortunate voyage, marked by repeated fighting with Portuguese warships and galleys and by a negligible return of gold, Guinea grains and ivory being the chief goods acquired. All the same, these ventures evidently showed sufficient profit to justify the adventurers in launching another expedition in 1564, for which they again chartered the *Minion* (on the terms noted above), together with two private vessels, one of them Benjamin Gonson's. It was a disastrous voyage: Gonson's ship blew itself up – a common accident in those times; the other merchantman was taken by the Portuguese; as for the *Minion*, she lost her commander and twelve mariners, betrayed by Negroes to the Portuguese immediately they arrived on the Mina Coast, was beaten off the coast by galleys and reached the Azores with her victuals and her crew almost utterly consumed. Finally she came into the Thames, richly laden with gold, ivory and other wares, which meant that Garrard, Chester, Lodge, Hickman, Castelin, Gonson and the queen, along with lesser investors, probably secured a profit, since after all seamen's lives cost nothing.[20]

In the next few years plunder, reprisal and violence rose to overwhelm the English Guinea trade. In 1565 the Portuguese sank the Winter brothers' *Mary Fortune*, sending her surviving crew to join the other English prisoners in the castle at Mina. Already in 1564 Thomas Fenner, one of several shipowning, privateering members of that Sussex family, had gone for Guinea with three ships and returned with suspect Portuguese sugar and brazilwood. In 1567 George Fenner set forth in the *Castle of Comfort*, a powerful private warship, with two other vessels, which after some fighting and trading around Cape Verde made for the Azores, there to engage in a running battle, inconclusive, with a Portuguese armada. That year also saw the last of John Hawkins's descents upon Upper Guinea for slaves, which he acquired, as he put it, 'partly by the sword and partly by other means', including trade and plunder. Other intruders about this time included

[19] *Cal. SPF* (1562), no. 18; Williamson, *Sir John Hawkins*, p. 54; *PN*, VI, 253–4.
[20] Williamson, *Sir John Hawkins*, pp. 55–8; *PN*, VI, 255–65.

the Portuguese renegade Bartolomeu Bayão, who in 1565 in an English ship at the Ilhetas Islands near Cape Verde robbed a Portuguese caravel of 125 Negro slaves, presumably hoping to sell them in the Caribbean.[21]

Meanwhile the sovereigns continued to wrangle over the rights and wrongs of interloping and predation. Elizabeth still spurned the Portuguese demands that she should prohibit her subjects from venturing to Guinea, and she pressed for compensation for the Winters, just as the king of Portugal sought redress for the robberies committed by Hawkins and other Englishmen. During 1567 and 1568 these negotiations achieved no progress. The Winters obtained letters of reprisal in 1568 and began seizing Portuguese shipping and goods both at sea and in port. In reply English property in Portugal was sequestrated. At this time, moreover, Anglo-Spanish relations broke down and many English seamen took advantage of their government's blind eye to plunder Iberian shipping, joining the Dutch sea-beggars and the Huguenots of La Rochelle in an unofficial sea-war directed against all 'papists', which raged unabated throughout the four years from 1569 to 1572. Trade between Portugal and England ceased.[22]

Negotiations nevertheless continued and about the end of 1571 signs of a willingness to compromise were beginning to appear. In January 1572 draft articles of a treaty provided for mutual restitution of goods and for the queen to prohibit her subjects from passing to Ethiopia and India, excepting the Madeiras, the Azores and the African coast northwards of Cape Verde.[23] Although nothing came of this, other memoranda from 1572 indicate that the English were seriously con-templating sacrificing the Guinea trade in return for the withdrawal of Portuguese objections to their Barbary trade.[24] But no agreement was concluded, the diplomatic exchanges dragged on, and when at last a treaty was signed in 1576 it made no mention of the African dispute, merely referring matters of controversy over trade to certain commis-sioners yet to be appointed.[25] It is clear, however, that after 1571 the English effectively abandoned the Guinea trade. They did not resume the slave trade until after 1650, nor other forms of Guinea trade until the Anglo-Spanish war broke out in 1585. Portuguese naval measures

[21] K. R. Andrews, 'Thomas Fenner and the Guinea trade, 1564', *Mariner's Mirror*, 38 (1952), 312–14; *PN*, VI, 266–84; PRO, SP 70/95, fos. 260–61. Blake's account of Bayão's acquisition of these slaves (*West Africa*, p. 170) appears to be incorrect.

[22] Williamson, *Sir John Hawkins*, pp. 162–5; V. M. Shillington and A. B. W. Chapman, *The Commercial Relations of England and Portugal* (London, n.d.).

[23] *Cal. SPF* (1569–71), pp. 578–9; *Cal. SPF* (1572–4), p. 1.

[24] *Cal. SPF* (1572–4), p. 223; BL, Cotton MSS, Nero B. I, fos. 162–3.

[25] *Cal. SPF* (1575–7), p. 408; Shillington and Chapman, *England and Portugal*, p. 144.

on the Gold Coast certainly had a deterrent effect, for already in the later sixties the English limited their venturing to Upper Guinea.[26] Nor was it sensible to put at risk the immensely valuable Peninsula trade for the sake of an enterprise which, however promising in the fifties and early sixties, had yielded so little since and gave no hope of becoming a regular trade.

In fact it was this irregularity of the trade which lay at the heart of the English failure. Without a base on the coast they had to scramble from place to place hoping to pick up what trade might happen to be available at the moment. Such arrangements as they made with the Africans had to be provisional: the Negroes could not rely upon them to return and fulfil their promises, nor could they rely on the Negroes to resist Portuguese pressure or alternative offers from the French. The circumstances of the trade encouraged cheating, threats and acts of violence on both sides, whose mutual distrust was sometimes marked by the exchange of hostages. Unlike ordinary smuggling operations, however, it was of necessity exposed to easy detection and attack, for good harbours were few and ships usually had to lie well off shore, either waiting for the Africans to arrive in their canoes or else sending armed boats to conduct business ashore. By 1561 such difficulties had convinced the promoters of the need for a coastal base and they gave serious attention to preparing one, as did the French about the same time. Although it seems unlikely that the English could have held a position there for any considerable time, their failure to establish one made it practically impossible for them to retain the small share of the gold trade they had achieved in the fifties.

With the outbreak of war in 1585 the possibility of trade to Guinea returned, and in 1588 certain merchants of Exeter, Colyton, Barnstaple and London obtained a patent granting them a monopoly of English trade with the Senegambia region for ten years. The London merchant Anthony Dassell appears to have been the moving spirit of this enterprise and was setting forth ships to the area from 1587 until at least 1591. During these years his ships carried letters of reprisal, and the combination of privateering and African trade was probably highly profitable. His interest in the latter may well have continued after 1591, for three years later he was receiving information from Morocco (he was also a Barbary trader) about Timbuktu and Gao, then captured by Moroccan forces. The prospects of trade into Mali, whether from the north or from the west, were obviously affected by this dramatic development, probably for the worse. Dassell continued to set forth

[26] The *Mary Fortune* was taken near the River Sestos, George Fenner did not go beyond Cape Verde and Hawkins confined his attentions to Sierra Leone.

privateers until the end of the war, but nothing further is known of his Senegambia trade.[27] Meanwhile two London shipowning merchants, John Bird and John Newton, dispatched two successive expeditions to Benin for pepper and ivory in 1588 and 1590, but there is no evidence of any further Benin ventures.[28]

Although it is likely enough that some desultory trading to the coasts of West Africa occurred between 1591 and 1607, it is not until this latter year that a continuous history is available. From 1607 until 1618 the leading figure was the London merchant John Davies, who during that period conducted a profitable trade in redwood from Sierra Leone, and he it was who organized the formation of the Company of Adventurers of London trading to Gynney and Bynney in 1618, a chartered corporation headed by Lord Rich (second earl of Warwick from 1619), Sir Robert Mansell, treasurer of the Navy, and Sir Ferdinando Gorges. Of the thirty-six members of this company only about ten took an active part in the business, which was principally concerned with the promotion of three disastrous voyages to the Gambia (1618–21) in quest of gold mines that were supposed to be accessible by way of that river. Meanwhile Davies continued to ply the redwood trade, in which the London merchant Humphrey Slany developed a rival interest, though operating to the Sherbro River further south. Slany and his partners, William Cloberry and John Wood, joined the company in the 1620s, but conducted their trade privately without the company's licence, as did Nicholas Crispe, another London magnate, whose chief interest lay in the gold trade. Among other interested parties in the late 1620s was Sir Kenelm Digby, who – like Warwick, Davies, Crispe, Cloberry and the Slanys – played a prominent part in promoting privateering during the French and Spanish wars of 1625–30. The affairs of the company, however, went badly. Its history was largely one of unpaid debts and unsettled disputes until finally Nicholas Crispe, who acquired a controlling interest in 1627–8, re-organized it and obtained a new charter in 1631. In West Africa as in other spheres, the 1620s had been a time of much difficulty for English enterprise which, having begun to meet some success, found itself set back by adverse economic conditions, by inexperience of the trade and by its own weak organization and lack of capital, as well as facing Portuguese and Dutch competition.[29]

[27] *PN*, VI, 443–50; VII, 90–102. Andrews, *Elizabethan Privateering*, pp. 102–3. PRO, HCA, 13/31, 4 July 1595; 13/33, 21 June 1598, 14 February 1598/9; 13/36, 28 January 1602/3. PRO, HCA, 24/59, nos. 17–27 (1592), relate to infringements of privileges allegedly granted to Dassell and partners by Dom Antonio.

[28] *PN*, VI, 450–67.

[29] J. W. Blake, 'The farm of the Guinea trade', in H. A. Cronne, T. W. Moody and D. B.

The English visitors appear to have regarded the Africans of Guinea with a naïve mixture of suspicion and curiosity, tinged sometimes with respect, sometimes with condescension, sometimes with disgust. They came to these coasts not as masters but seeking barter, never sure of their welcome, dependent on the Negroes' goodwill. The physical force they could bring to bear on land would have been on many occasions insufficient to overawe the local people, and even the slave-trader Hawkins found that assaulting African towns and villages might cost English lives and prejudice any future business. Indeed his most successful slaving operation was his intervention in a major African war in 1568, when he acted merely as the useful ally of powerful African rulers, who paid him for his services in prisoners of war.[30] His reference to 'the Negro (in which nation is seldome or never found truth)'[31] would have been echoed by many an English Guinea trader, not because these English had preconceived ideas about black men, wide-eyed wonder being rather their typical state of mind, but because the particular conditions of their relationship with the Africans naturally bred mistrust. By 1565 the Africans on their side had plenty of reason to beware of the treacherous English.

As for the Negroes' appearance and ways of life, they are reported for the most part in neutral terms. Towerson's description of the 'king Abaan', his town 'as big in circuit as London', well stocked with 'the wheat of the Countrey', elaborately guarded, and of the making and drinking of palm-wine, is not unusual in its respectful tone:

All these ceremonies first done, the king took up a cup of gold, and they put him in wine, and hee dranke of it, and when he dranke, the people cried all with one voice, Abaan, Abaan, with certaine other words, like as they cry commonly in Flanders, upon the Twelfe night, The kinning drinks: and when he had drunke, then they gave drinke to every one, and that done, the king licensed them to depart, and every one that departeth from him boweth 3 times towards him, and waveth with both hands together, as they bow, and then do depart. The king hath commonly sitting by him 8 or 10 ancient men with gray beards.[32]

Their reports show that some of the English at least made distinc-

Quinn (eds.), *Essays in British and Irish History in Honour of James Eadie Todd* (London, 1949), pp. 86–106; R. Porter, 'The Crispe family and the Africa trade in the seventeenth century', *Journal of African History*, 9 (1968), 57–77; K. G. Davies, *The Royal African Company* (London, 1957), pp. 9, 39–40; J. C. Appleby, 'English privateering during the Spanish and French wars, 1625–1630' (unpublished Ph.D. thesis, University of Hull, 1984).
[30] P. E. H. Hair, 'Protestants as pirates, slavers and proto-missionaries: Sierra Leone 1568 and 1582', *Journal of Ecclesiastical History*, 21 (1970), 213–15.
[31] *PN*, x, 65.   [32] *PN*, vi, 228.

tions between African groups in terms of 'wildness' and 'civility'. Thus one reporter says of certain Cape Verde people: 'These men also are more civill then any other, because of their dayly trafficke with the Frenchmen, and are of nature very gentle and loving.'[33] Civility could, apparently, be acquired to some extent. The occasional reference to 'wild' Africans also implies that many were not, but the term seems to indicate simply people unfamiliar with European trade, these being already somewhat exceptional on the Guinea coasts by the later sixteenth century. Even so, there were Englishmen who reacted to blackness with horror and revulsion, as Robert Baker did in his atrocious verse accounts of two Guinea voyages in 1562 and 1563: 'And entring in, we see/ a number of blacke soules/ Whose likelinesse seem'd men to be,/but all as blacke as coles./Their Captaine comes to me/as naked as my naile,/Not having witte or honestie/ to cover once his taile./By which I doe here gesse/ and gather by the way,/ That he from man and manlinesse/ was voide and cleane astray.'[34] The almost hysterical tone of Baker's references to 'brutish black people' and so forth seems to be partly assumed for the sake of dramatic effect and partly the result of the bloody encounter which was his closest contact with black men.

Probably more typical a spokesman of English attitudes was Richard Jobson, whose book *The Golden Trade* (1623) was based on his experience of a voyage to the Gambia in 1620–21.[35] Jobson, when offered slaves for sale by the local ruler, replied: 'We were a people, who did not deale in any such commodities, neither did wee buy or sell one another, or any that had our owne shapes', but he also remarked on how surprising it was to see the Mandinga marriage ceremony performed with decorum, for the bride displayed 'modestie not to be looked for among such a kinde of blacke or barbarous people'. Such evidence of prejudice, however, is quite difficult to find in Jobson's book, which is generally a neutral and objective, though very lively and personal, account of the country and its people.

[33] *PN*, x, 15.
[34] *PN* (1589), p. 132.
[35] R. Jobson, *The Golden Trade* (London, 1623; reprint, 1968).

6

The Caribbean

William Hawkins of Plymouth, the merchant shipowner who had played so prominent a part in pioneering the Guinea and Brazil trades in Henry VIII's time, had two sons, William and John. When the old man died in 1554, William, aged about thirty-five, and his brother aged about twenty-two, took over the most important firm in Plymouth, with all the local influence which that implied. But they inherited much more than this. Their father had been a trusted servant of the crown, 'a man for his wisedome, valure, experience, and skill in sea causes much esteemed, and beloved of K. Henry',[1] active in the affairs of the West Country and in the French wars. In due course they too would assume such responsibilities. William was to devote his energies mainly to the family business and local affairs, while his brother launched himself upon a greater career in Atlantic commerce and naval warfare. Around 1560 their formal partnership was dissolved, but the brothers continued working together and assisting each other's enterprise until William's death in 1589.[2]

It was soon after Elizabeth's accession that John Hawkins began his climb to fame and power. In 1559 or thereabouts he married Katherine, daughter of Benjamin Gonson, treasurer of the queen's navy. Under the Lord High Admiral, Lord Clinton, Gonson was the senior member of the Navy Board, which managed the queen's ships. Thus Hawkins, though still young, became a man of some influence, a man to watch. Eventually he would succeed his father-in-law and run the royal navy. But first he had plans of his own to hatch. The Hawkinses as traders did business chiefly with the French and Iberian ports, like most of the West Country merchants who dealt overseas at all, and it was natural for them to extend their interests to the Canary Islands. Consequently, as Hakluyt tells us,

Master John Haukins having made divers voyages to the Iles of the Canaries,

[1] *PN*, xi, 23.   [2] Williamson, *Sir John Hawkins*.

and there by his good and upright dealing being growen in love and favour with the people, informed himselfe amongst them by diligent inquisition, of the state of the West India, whereof hee had received some knowledge by the instructions of his father, but increased the same by the advertisments and reports of that people. And being amongst other particulars assured, that Negros were very good marchandise in Hispaniola, and that store of Negros might easily bee had upon the coast of Guinea, resolved with himselfe to make triall thereof, and communicated that devise with his worshipfull friendes of London: namely with Sir Lionell Ducket, sir Thomas Lodge, M. Gunson his father in law, sir William Winter, M. Bromfield, and others. All which persons liked so well of his intention, that they became liberall contributers and adventurers in the action.[3]

In 1562, therefore, Hawkins embarked upon the first of a series of slave-trading expeditions, shipping Negroes from the western shores of Africa to the Caribbean, where he sold them to Spanish colonials. It was an ambitious project, involving a commercial offensive on two fronts challenging the exclusive policies of both Iberian powers, and Hawkins was the first of his countrymen to attempt it. On the other hand the enterprise can hardly be described as pioneering, for the transatlantic slave trade was a well-established business already. Nor was Hawkins the first interloper. Indeed he was one among many, as his Canarian friends well knew.

Spain's American colonies had been importing black slaves since the beginning of the century, Españóla being the chief market. Here the first three decades of Spanish occupation had gutted not only the island's accessible gold but the native population as well. The gentle Arawak people Columbus found there numbered at least a million; by 1520 they were almost extinct and from about that date the settlers looked to slave-grown sugar for their livelihood. For about fifty years the sugar plantations and the slave trade boomed and at the height of the boom, when Hawkins and his partners decided to enter the trade, Españóla had over thirty *ingenios* and about 20,000 Blacks, including the considerable number employed in the capital, Santo Domingo. By this time, moreover, African slaves were much in demand elsewhere in the Caribbean and beyond. The other islands of the Greater Antilles – Cuba, Jamaica and Puerto Rico – had few and could not yet afford many more, but the colonies along the Spanish Main, from Cumaná to Cartagena and Panama, cried out for slave labour, while the affluent citizens of Mexico and Peru provided a large and rapidly expanding market.[4]

[3] *PN*, x, 7.
[4] K. R. Andrews, *The Spanish Caribbean: Trade and Plunder, 1530–1630* (London, 1978), pp. 1–37.

Slaves for the Spanish Indies then came mainly from the region known loosely as Upper Guinea, stretching from the Senegal southwards to Sierra Leone, the kingdom of Kongo being the only other major source. Portuguese merchants of Santiago in the Cape Verde Islands and of São Thomé in the Bight of Biafra managed the trade under licences (*asientos*) from the Spanish crown permitting them to trade to America in accordance with the regulations laid down by the *Casa de la Contratación*, the official institution controlling all transatlantic commerce. These stipulated that slaves should be sent first to the Peninsula to be cleared from Seville, the monopoly entrepôt for American trade, but by the 1550s Portuguese dealers were in practice evading this rule, shipping cargoes not only from Lisbon but directly from Santiago and São Thomé, or indirectly via the Canary Islands. Merchants usually sent more slaves than their licences allowed, some dispatched ships without licence and many used the slave trade as a cover for exporting other merchandise.

In short, smuggling already flourished and it would flourish more than ever so long as prices, both of slave labour and of consumer goods, continued to rise in the Indies and Spain's rulers tried to restrict all American trade to Seville and to enforce a privileged monopoly, imposing heavy taxes on exports. Powerful the Spanish monarchy might be, but it lacked the means to keep intruders out of the Caribbean. It was not until the sixties that it attempted to provide some regular naval defence of that vast region and its scattered settlements, most of which were defenceless coastal villages. Even the authorities in Santo Domingo, Cartagena and Havana could do nothing to check alien activity in the rest of the Caribbean, nor indeed could they stop their own citizens dealing in smuggled goods. Most of this contraband, including slaves, reached the Caribbean in caravels from the Canary Islands, where Spaniards traded freely with Portuguese, Italian, Flemish, French and English merchants, sometimes doing transatlantic business on their behalf.

But the Caribbean already knew another kind of interloper: the corsair. From the late 1520s French privateers caused increasing havoc in those seas, plundering shipping and ports without mercy in wartime, allowing their victims no respite even in the brief intervals of official peace between France and Spain. The long campaign of pillage reached its climax in the 1550s in an offensive of unprecedented force and range, culminating in the sack of Havana by Jacques de Sores in 1555. This Franco-Spanish war came to an end in 1559 with the treaty of Cateau-Cambrésis, but by then the Caribbean had become, as it was to remain for centuries, a major focus of international rivalry, the scene of unending maritime conflict and predation. In part this was due to the peculiar commercial circumstances we have noticed, which attracted foreign ships – always regarded by Spain as pirates – to the region. Equally, however, it arose from the strategic importance of the Caribbean, through which the treasure of both Mexico and Peru passed on its way to Spain.

From the middle decades of the century this double stream of silver swelled to a flood, enriching the king of Spain and augmenting his offensive power, even though it impoverished his subjects and at length brought his country to ruin. The stream from Peru came through Panama and across the isthmus to Nombre de Dios, thence by sea to Cartagena and on to Havana. That from the mines of New Spain came by way of Vera Cruz on the Gulf of Mexico also to Havana, whence the combined bulk of bullion went north through the Florida Strait and east towards the Azores and the Guadalquivir. What a temptation that meant to the enemies of Spain the ensuing history of the West Indies would abundantly show. Hundreds of islands and thousands of miles of unoccupied shores afforded shelter and opportunities for trade and plunder on the way to the western Caribbean, which bore that greatest of all prey, the plate fleet.

But Spain and England were at peace in 1562 and there is no reason to suppose that Hawkins launched his venture with the intention of cruising the Caribbean as a pirate or in the spirit of reprisal. His three vessels, of 120, 100 and 40 tons burden, though doubtless well armed, were not very powerful, and his purposes appear to have been simply commercial, depending as they did upon collaboration with his friends in the Canaries and their contacts in Española. On the other hand this was avowedly a trial voyage, speculative not only in the financial sense. The English had no experience of the Caribbean and had to keep their options open, looking for suitable opportunities to make a gainful return and testing the Spaniards' response. Anglo-Spanish relations had been under some strain since the accession of the heretic Elizabeth. Neither Hawkins nor his partners were foolish enough to imagine that Philip II would permit them to infringe the Spanish monopoly of the western world. They knew perfectly well, if only from the recent history of the Guinea trade, that he stood shoulder to shoulder with the king of Portugal in adamant resistance to the penetration of their spheres of influence by foreign traders. Elizabeth of course scornfully repudiated Iberian claims over seas and lands not effectively in their possession and made no distinction between Spain and Portugal in this respect. It remained to be seen whether an Englishman could in fact conduct trade in the West Indies and whether

the king of Spain had sufficient real authority in the region to scotch the
attempt.

Consequently there was a dangerous ambiguity in Hawkins's slaving enterprise. The Spanish term for all such contraband trade was
rescates, which meant also barter or ransom, and the business of *rescates*
always involved deceit and distrust. Hawkins himself went about his
business in this first voyage 'trusting the Spaniards no further, then
that by his owne strength he was able still to master them'.[5] Spanish
colonial officials might countenance *rescates* or not as it suited them.
Even if they desired trade they might well be glad to do the foreigner an
injury, either to prove their loyalty or simply to express their abomin-
ation of the so-called *Luteranos*. On the other side the visitors might
well resent the devices used by their customers to achieve a hard
bargain and might be tempted, having armed force on their side, to
browbeat them with threats or demonstrations of strength, which
might turn into acts of aggression. The line between trade and plunder
was often difficult to trace. Corsairs themselves were accustomed to
trade with the colonists, not only by way of ransom but also by
bartering plunder for victuals. Traders for their part were inclined to
resort to force to get victuals or whatever else they strongly wanted.
Hawkins, who was nothing if not shrewd, could hardly have failed to
gather all this and much more about the conditions of Caribbean
venturing from his Canarian contacts, and in any case would have
learned it quickly enough from personal experience.

When, therefore, he declared to the governor of Burburata, in the
course of the second voyage, that 'for that there was a great amitie
betweene their princes, and the thing perteined to our Queenes
highnesse, he thought hee might doe their prince great service',[6]
Hawkins's tongue was undoubtedly in his cheek, and similar statements of his were equally disingenuous – at best vague and soothing
noises intended to reassure the colonists of his goodwill, so that they
might see their way to buying his slaves. There is no evidence that he
meant to serve the king of Spain in any other way than by doing
business with his subjects.[7] Neither he nor his London backers were
philanthropists – they wanted a share of the slave trade, which they

[5] *PN*, x, 8.

[6] *PN*, x, 33–4.

[7] It was Williamson's theory that Hawkins wanted to obtain licence to trade in the West
Indies from Philip II, as a reward for assisting him to eject the French from the region:
Sir John Hawkins, pp. 73, 77. In fact Hawkins never expressed any such intention, nor
any disapproval of the French presence, nor were these ideas attributed to him by
anyone until 1927. On the contrary, he helped the French in Florida and collaborated
with them in the Caribbean: Andrews, *Spanish Caribbean*, pp. 120–22.

believed would yield them a very high rate of profit.[8] Beyond that we do not know what hopes or dreams of American wealth crossed their minds, but we may be sure that they were conscious that their initiative could hardly help to repair that ragged cloak of 'amitie'. On the other hand it is worth noting that Gonson, Winter, Ducket and Lodge had all been active in the Guinea gold trade, which was now, for reasons we have observed, losing its attractiveness. Slaving would be less dangerous because the interlopers could limit their African operations to Upper Guinea and so avoid the miseries of the Mina Coast. Hawkins offered them a tempting alternative.

In his first voyage Hawkins called first at the Canaries, contacting there his business friend Pedro de Ponte, who supplied him with a pilot for the West Indies, having already prepared his own associates in Española for the English visit. Hawkins then passed to Sierra Leone, where he 'got into his possession, partly by the sworde, and partly by other meanes, to the number of 300. Negros at the least, besides other merchandises which that countrey yeeldeth'.[9] A few years later the Portuguese contractors of the slave trade in Sierra Leone brought a suit in Lisbon concerning the alleged piracies committed by Hawkins and his men in the years 1562–8.[10] Whether or not the charge of piracy was strictly justified is debatable,[11] and doubtless the damages were grossly exaggerated. It is unlikely that Hawkins carried away over 900 Negroes, for what we know of his transactions in the Indies suggests that Hakluyt's figure is nearer the mark. But Hakluyt himself goes on to speak of the human cargo as 'this praye', and there is no reason to suppose that Hawkins abstained from the use of force to acquire it.

On this voyage he sold his slaves on the northern coast of Española, aided and abetted by the very man whom the government of the island deputed ostensibly to stop him. The sales proceeded without a hitch and Hawkins laded his own ships and freighted two others with hides, ginger, sugar and some pearls. This seems to have been a straightforward smuggling operation, and his decision to consign the cargoes of the two freighted vessels to an English merchant in Seville, Hugh Tipton, was presumably another. Unfortunately these two consign-

---

[8] It is often suggested that Hawkins's enterprise was designed to help the home economy by opening up a new market for English cloth, but no contemporary statement to that effect has ever been brought to light. In fact textiles made up some 10% of the value of his sales in the Indies (slaves accounted for the rest) and most of those textiles were French linens. These *rouens* (Spanish, *ruanes*) sold well in those parts and became the staple of the illicit French trade thither: Andrews, *Spanish Caribbean*, pp. 109, 181–4.

[9] *PN*, x, 8.

[10] PRO, SP 70/99, fos. 1–49.

[11] Hair, 'Protestants and pirates'.

ments, though probably 'coloured' as Spanish property, were arrested on arrival because the authorities had received timely information of their true ownership from Española. Hawkins's appeal to the Spanish government for restitution of course received a dusty answer – what else could he reasonably have expected?[12] Even so, the course and outcome of the expedition as a whole must have been encouraging, for having returned in September 1563, Hawkins attracted much wider support for a second and larger slaving venture, which set out from Plymouth in October 1564.

In the meantime Anglo-Spanish relations had deteriorated. English acts of piracy against Spanish vessels from the Channel southwards led to the suspension of trade between England and the Netherlands and to arrests of English shipping in Spanish harbours. Commercial disputes were exacerbated by religious feeling and by charges of cruelties committed by the Spanish Inquisition upon English sailors. Hawkins's preparation of his second expedition thus took place against a background of developing antagonism between the two nations, and the Spanish ambassador officially protested at least twice to Queen Elizabeth asking her to prohibit the voyage. At the same time the Caribbean situation changed. In 1562 Captain Jean Ribault, with the backing of Gaspard de Coligny, admiral of France, had established a colony of Huguenot soldiers on the coast of Florida, directly threatening Spain's control of the Florida Strait and the security of her treasure fleets. But when Ribault returned to France that year to obtain supplies and reinforcements he found a civil war in progress and eventually, in 1563, he took refuge in England. Here a new plan for an Anglo-French expedition to Florida was hatched with the queen's support. This fell through, but English interest was now aroused and it was arranged that Hawkins should visit Florida in the course of his next voyage, by which time new forces under René de Laudonnière had revived the French colony.

The second slave-trade voyage had the support of the queen, the earls of Leicester and Pembroke and Lord Clinton, in addition to that of Gonson, Winter and the Londoners. It was a much more powerful expedition than the first. The queen contributed the mighty *Jesus of Lübeck* (700 tons) and with her sailed three smaller vessels totalling 220 tons. The queen and her associates were obviously interested in Florida, but their intentions with respect to it may well have been as obscure to themselves as they are to us. They knew next to nothing of

---

[12] Williamson argues that Hawkins sent these cargoes openly to Seville in order to test the willingness of the Spanish authorities to tolerate his activities: *Sir John Hawkins*, pp. 87–91. My view is explained further in *Spanish Caribbean*, pp. 114–15.

the country and the only special provision they made for this part of the voyage was to equip the expedition with a suitable pilot and a talented reporter, who included an account of Florida in his journal of the voyage. In this respect as in others the venture was essentially one of reconnaissance and the promoters no doubt trusted Hawkins to use his initiative and discretion to their best advantage, which they would certainly measure in terms of pocketable returns. As events showed, there could have been no serious question of replacing the French, for Hawkins was not equipped to establish a colony.

The first stages of the voyage repeated roughly the pattern of 1562: Hawkins contacted Pedro de Ponte, making certain arrangements with him, and went on to Sierra Leone, where he acquired about 400 Negroes by much the same methods as before. Across the Atlantic he touched at Dominica to water and thence sailed south to prospect the ports of the *Tierra Firme*, or Spanish Main. At La Margarita he obtained some victuals, but was refused a licence to trade; the governor evacuated the town and sent warning to Santo Domingo, thus treating Hawkins as a corsair. Justly or unjustly thus rebuffed, the English then moved along the coast to Burburata, where, in April 1565, they found the Spaniards in two minds: they wanted to buy slaves, but they insisted on making Hawkins wait while they got him an official licence from the governor at Coro. Meanwhile he grew impatient, suspecting that the delay was calculated to force down the price of his slaves. In a formal request for the licence he threatened, as the Spaniards reported: 'I protest that if from its refusal harm and damage follow, the fault and responsibility will be your honour's.'[13] Although this message may have been concocted later by the governor as an excuse for his having granted the licence, the threat of force, whether overt or concealed, was real enough, as the next stage in the negotiations proved. For on being required to pay, in addition to the normal duties, a levy of 30 ducats on every slave sold, the Englishman landed a hundred armed men and marched towards the town, and the fact this time comes from the English report.[14] Trade then proceeded satisfactorily.

Events followed a similar course at Río de la Hacha, Hawkins's next port of call. Here the colonists at first refused trade, but subsequently yielded to the threat of armed force, which Hawkins used again to secure favourable prices, though in this case some Spaniards alleged that only token resistance was offered. Even so, hostages were exchanged and the Spaniards kept their visitors nervous and ready for combat down to the day of their departure. Then Hawkins set course

[13] Wright, *Caribbean Voyages, 1527–1568*, p. 83.
[14] *PN*, x, 34.

for Española, where he probably intended to complete his return lading with hides and sugar. Lacking a pilot with sufficient knowledge of the Caribbean, however, he made the south coast of Cuba instead and finally groped his way into the Florida Channel and found the French colony at Fort Caroline. It was on the verge of breakdown. The Indians were hostile, the men mutinous and food supplies almost exhausted. The help expected from France had not arrived and Laudonnière had already made up his mind to evacuate.

Hawkins, upon learning this, offered to ship the French home, but Laudonnière, who 'stood in doubt least he would attempt somewhat in Florida in the name of his mistresse', refused, and instead accepted the gift of a 50-ton bark, victuals, shoes for his soldiers and other stores: 'as many courtesies', he wrote, 'as it was possible to receive of any man living . . . deserving to be esteemed as much of us all as if he had saved our lives'.[15] But most of those lives were destined to be short. In late August, a month after Hawkins's departure, Ribault arrived with reinforcements, but a few days later the entire French colony was overwhelmed by a powerful assault force dispatched from Spain for this purpose and led by the ferocious Pedro Menéndez de Avilés. Menéndez, having executed most of his prisoners, including Ribault, on the spot, went on to found a Spanish base at San Agustín and another at Santa Elena further north, effectively pre-empting Florida for Spain.

Nor was this an isolated success. Spain, in response to French offensive pressure, had already taken effective measures to improve the protection of her transatlantic trade by regularizing and strengthening her convoy system. Menéndez had played a leading part in this work and in 1567 obtained special responsibility, as captain-general of an *armada* of twelve galleons, for the naval defence of the Indies. In fact this never existed as a coherent force and such galleons as were available devoted their efforts chiefly to escorting the plate fleets, to the neglect of their Caribbean duties; nevertheless the Spanish state did in the later sixties substantially increase its efforts to suppress smuggling and marauding in the West Indies. In the circumstances it was virtually impossible to repel the tide of intruders, but these counter-measures aggravated the hostility already latent in the business of *rescates* and encouraged the use of armed force and reprisals, driving Hawkins and his ilk steadily towards the open adoption of their assigned rôle as corsairs. At the same time events in Europe were bringing England and Spain nearer to conflict. Civil unrest and religious dissent in the Netherlands gave rise to repression which culminated in 1567 in the

[15] *PN*, IX, 78, 80–81.

occupation of the country by Spanish forces under the duke of Alba. France, itself torn by intermittent warfare between Catholic and Huguenot, could do little to answer this menacing Spanish presence in northwest Europe. Elizabeth's room for manoeuvre was gradually contracting; she had now to rely increasingly on armed resistance and retaliation as diplomatic weapons. Neither she nor Philip wanted a hot war, but in the later sixties they drifted into a cold one.

The Spanish ambassador in England in October 1566, having realized belatedly that Hawkins was preparing a third expedition to the Indies, succeeded in persuading the government to forbid it. Nevertheless within ten days Captain John Lovell left Plymouth for Guinea and the Caribbean with three small ships provided by Hawkins. On the African coast he appears to have followed his master's example in assembling a cargo of slaves at Portuguese expense. He was next seen in company with the fleet of the French slave-trading corsair Jean Bontemps, at La Margarita, and followed the Frenchman into Burburata, where together they seized certain citizens, demanding licence to trade in exchange for their persons. But this ruse failed and only a few Negroes were disposed of, while at Río de la Hacha Lovell met with a blank refusal and had no choice but to put ashore 'ninety-two pieces of Blacks, all old, and very sick and thin' without payment.[16] Nothing more is known of Lovell's fortunes, but we may reasonably assume that his voyage was unsuccessful, probably because he lacked the armed strength to force trade as Hawkins had done two years before.

Hawkins's next slaving venture, the fourth and last of the series, became something of a *cause célèbre*, with the result that its historical significance has usually been overrated. It was, however, a substantially more powerful expedition than the rest. The *Jesus*, the *Minion*, the *William and John*, the *Swallow*, the *Judith* and the *Angel* made up some 1333 tons of shipping, the first two being warships of the queen's navy. The backing came from the same quarters as it had done in 1564, but this venture bore more emphatically the aspect of a national undertaking, combining private and public investment by way of a joint-stock. Although no object other than slaving is apparent, it may be that the queen wished to impress the king of Spain by a veiled threat, a demonstration of her own power and his vulnerability, in which case this should be reckoned the first of a series of such gestures. Of course this is mere speculation, but an ugly incident which occurred shortly before the departure of the expedition indicates the prevailing atmosphere. Towards the end of August 1567 a squadron of Spanish

[16] Wright, *Caribbean Voyages, 1527–1568*, pp. 95–112.

warships bound from Flanders for Spain put into Plymouth, where Hawkins rode with his fleet. When the Spaniards failed to salute, making as if to anchor side by side with him, Hawkins, perhaps sensing danger as well as insult, opened fire and forced the intruders out of the anchorage. He was well aware that the Spaniards suspected the intention of his fleet and consequently he suspected theirs. 'I know they hate me', he wrote to Cecil a few days before he sailed, and he evidently returned the sentiment.[17]

After the usual visit to the Canaries, the fleet moved on to the African coast in search of human cargo, spending nearly three months, chiefly between Cape Verde and Sierra Leone, in this work of plunder. In addition to robbing the Portuguese of a number of slaves, the English intervened in a tribal war, accepting prisoners-of-war as payment for services rendered. By the time he set out for the Caribbean, Hawkins had acquired nearly five hundred slaves and three more vessels for his fleet. Touching at La Margarita for victuals, he went on to Burburata, where he stayed more than a month, trading freely even though the governor refused him a licence. At Río de la Hacha, however, it was only by dint of burning part of the town and beginning to make off with some of the citizens and quantities of pillage that he finally brought the local government to heel. After that trade was brisk, and so it was at Santa Marta, the next port west, though here he took the town by agreement, having arranged with the governor to land 150 armed men and 'to shoote owte of the ships haulf a score of shott over the towne for a color'.[18] Finally the English, with some Negroes and other goods yet to sell, approached Cartagena, but there the Spaniards were far too strong to be coerced, and after some futile exchange of opinion and gunfire Hawkins left the harbour on 24 July. It was now time to head for home, the greater part of the cargo having been disposed of.

But what had been a prosperous voyage now turned into a series of disasters. In the Florida Channel the fleet encountered heavy storms. The *William and John* lost company and struggled home with severe loss, while the old and rickety *Jesus* was reduced to little better than a floating wreck. Hawkins decided to make for the nearest port to patch her up, and since the storm had driven him into the Gulf of Mexico his only recourse was to enter the roadstead of Vera Cruz, San Juan de Ulúa. When he arrived there the *flota* was hourly expected and the Spaniards, mistaking the English fleet for their own, allowed it to enter

[17] PRO, SP 12/44, no. 13. For a detailed account of the voyage see Williamson, *Sir John Hawkins*, and Wright, *Caribbean Voyages, 1527–1568*, pp. 115–62.

[18] BL, Cotton MSS, Otho E. VIII, fo. 36, printed in Williamson, *Sir John Hawkins*, p. 526.

unharmed. Luckily, too, the Spaniards panicked when they realized their mistake, abandoning to him the off-shore island that formed the harbour. The English could now proceed with their repairs and Hawkins hastened to reassure the authorities of his peaceful intentions.

Unfortunately the *flota* arrived the following day, under the command of the viceroy of New Spain, Don Martín Enríquez. Although Hawkins was in a position to deny him entry, he dared not commit so grave an affront to the king of Spain and instead allowed the Spaniards to enter unmolested. Both sides promised to keep the peace, hostages were exchanged and the English retained possession of the island for their security. But of course the viceroy had no intention of permitting a corsair to occupy a Spanish port in his presence. He made ready to attack. Hawkins, realizing something was afoot, sent his second-in-command to protest, but the viceroy arrested him and ordered the attack to begin. The island batteries were overrun, but Hawkins and his men rallied to drive the boarding parties from their ships, hauled clear and turned their guns on the Spanish fleet, sinking two and setting another alight. Now, however, the island guns concentrated a destructive fire on the English ships. The *Jesus* was immobilized and had to be abandoned. The other members of the fleet being also lost, there remained only the *Minion* and the *Judith*, which both withdrew out of range of Spanish fire. The next morning the *Judith* had disappeared. The plight of the *Minion*, with 200 aboard, was desperate. Hawkins had to land about half of them on the Mexican coast, where some died and others fell into Spanish hands. Many of those left in the *Minion* died in the passage home. Altogether Hawkins lost some 300 out of his original force of 400 men. Of the ships only the *Minion*, the *Judith* and the *William and John* reached England – 500 out of the 1333 tons of shipping that had set out from Plymouth. Financially the expedition was of course disastrous, even though Hawkins managed to bring home some gold, silver and pearls.

Yet the significance of the incident at San Juan de Ulúa for the English slave trade is often overstated. In fact the conditions and prospects of the slave trade remained much the same after 1568 as before. The efforts of Menéndez did not prove sufficient to cleanse the Caribbean of corsairs and smugglers; the demand for slaves continued to rise and Portuguese and French contrabandists continued to thrive in the seventies. Why then did not the English resume the trade? Part of the answer is to be found by an economic analysis of the Hawkins enterprise which suggests that the rate of profit on his ventures would have declined even if the mishap at San Juan de Ulúa had not occurred, because increasing resistance, both on the African coast and in the Caribbean, made him increase the scale of his armament.[19] Consequently the last venture was more like a naval expedition than a merchant voyage. Such power did, it is true, enable him to obtain slaves without having the local bases and regular trading arrangements enjoyed by the Portuguese, but it also reduced his margin of profit both there and in the Caribbean, where he had to compete with Portuguese slavers much less heavily armed and manned than his own vessels. As for the French, they had the advantage of controlling a specialized barter trade, exporting the Norman linens which commanded an excellent market in 'Pérou' (meaning the West Indies), in exchange for hides, which sold equally well in France.[20] In brief, the English did not resume the slave trade after San Juan de Ulúa because they could not compete with others who had obvious advantages.

Furthermore the political situation in Europe had already deteriorated, before the news of San Juan de Ulúa reached England, to such a point as to transform the existing prevalence of maritime disorder into a storm of violence, which in the years 1568–72 raged from the North Sea to the Canary Islands and beyond, finally leaping the Atlantic to invade the Caribbean. In this process San Juan de Ulúa played its part, not as a primary cause but as a secondary and aggravating factor. When Hawkins reached England in January 1569 western Europe had already entered a phase of acute political crisis. The flight of Mary Stuart into England in May 1568 created a growing threat of counter-revolution supported by French or Spanish intervention, while the summer and autumn of that year saw the duke of Alba triumphant over the rebel Netherlanders. The response of Cecil and his allies to these dangers was to develop offensive action to embarrass and contain both French and Spanish power. Hence on the outbreak of the third civil war in France in the autumn, La Rochelle, now the chief Huguenot privateering base, was supplied with arms and money, while English seamen were encouraged to obtain commissions from the Huguenot leaders and to join the assault on all Catholic shipping, whether French, Spanish, Flemish or Portuguese. William Hawkins was already deeply involved in this campaign when news of his brother's misfortune arrived. Finally in late November several vessels carrying a large consignment of treasure from Spain for the payment of Alba's troops were beset by English and French privateers in the Channel and driven into Southampton and other southern ports, where the money was taken ashore, ostensibly to ensure its safety, and

[19] For the economic analysis, see Andrews, *Spanish Caribbean*, pp. 127–33.
[20] Andrews, *Spanish Caribbean*, pp. 181–2.

a legal pretext was found for annexing it to the queen's use. The Spanish reply came at the end of the year, when Alba arrested all English property in the Netherlands. The English seizure of Spanish and Flemish ships and goods followed and an unofficial war of reprisal developed.

Now it was that the English openly adopted the course of plunder in the Caribbean, first joining and then outstripping the French. Anglo-Huguenot collaboration was nothing new – it had been a feature of Hawkins's voyages – but it became more important in the early seventies as both groups concentrated their attack upon the isthmus of Panama. Here the French were already active before 1570 and the Spaniards also suffered continually at the hands of two large communities of runaway Blacks, numbering together over three thousand and controlling much of the bush country north and east of Panama City. As the bishop of Panama reported in February 1570, 'This land is wearied of the *cimarrones* and the French; and certainly it is a great pity, for those who do business by sea and by river are readily despoiled, amid many affronts.' A year later he again lamented: 'human tongue cannot relate the ignominies which both the French and the *cimarrones* have this year inflicted here on all sorts of persons'.[21] But worse was to come, and in the course of 1571 Spanish complaints bracketed the English with the French.

In the years 1570–77 thirteen English expeditions to the Caribbean are known to have occurred, and probably there were others which went unreported, for these were all actions of piracy: undertaken, that is, without authority, licence or letters of reprisal in time of peace between the two countries and indefensible on legal grounds. Hawkins and his slave-trading associates were prominent among the promoters. They had sought redress for their losses in the High Court of Admiralty, but do not appear to have obtained letters of reprisal. Nevertheless in 1570 and 1571 the young Francis Drake made two voyages on their behalf to the isthmus coast. A kinsman of the Hawkinses, Drake had learned his craft as a boy in the Thames estuary. He first crossed the Atlantic as a seaman in Lovell's voyage and commanded the *Judith* in the last of the slaving ventures. A master mariner and a born leader of men, Drake was inspired by a passionate Protestant faith and a burning desire to revenge the wrongs done to him and his kind by the king of Spain. In these first two Panama raids he began a campaign of reprisal. In 1570 he sailed with two small ships, the *Dragon* and the *Swan*, and in 1571 with the *Swan* only, a bark of 40

---

[21] I. A. Wright (ed.), *Documents concerning English Voyages to the Spanish Main, 1569–1580* (London, 1932), p. xix.

tons. It was, according to the Spaniards, lucrative work: 'upon the coast of Nombre de Dios they did rob divers barks in the river of Chagre and in the same river did rob divers barks that were transporting of merchandise of forty thousand ducats and velvets and taffetas, besides other merchandise with gold and silver. . .'.[22]

This experience was valuable also in giving Drake familiarity with the whole coast from Acla to the mouth of the Chagre and up that river as far as Casa de Cruces, less than twenty miles from Panama. Here it was that the bulkier and less precious of the goods brought by mule from Panama would be shipped aboard small barks to be carried down-river and then eastwards to Nombre de Dios, while the rest, including most of the bullion, continued overland to that port. The commercial life of Nombre de Dios and the volume of isthmus traffic ebbed and flowed with the going and coming of the annual fleet, which normally arrived in January or February, when the Panama authorities would start to move their accumulated stocks of Peruvian silver northwards across that narrow neck of land at the centre of Spain's American empire. This portage, called the *trajín*, traversed by untold millions of treasure and rich merchandise, had taken a terrible toll of human life when the goods were carried by Indian slaves. Now black slaves manned trains of five or six hundred mules through the roughest of mountain country, across treacherous rivers and marshes in killing heat and humidity. By 1572, working with and learning from the French, Drake was ready to make a decisive change in the objects and methods of Panama raiding, realizing for the Spaniards their worst nightmare – an alliance of white piracy and black banditry.

The third expedition, again probably financed by Hawkins, the Winters and their friends, was carefully planned and well equipped: with arrows, firepikes and a variety of other weapons, with 'artificers' stuff and tools' and with pinnaces stowed aboard in pieces to be assembled when required. The seventy-three men and boys, all but one of them under thirty, were volunteers and they sailed from Plymouth late in May 1572 in the 70-ton *Pascha*, Hawkins's ship, and the 25-ton *Swan*. But the raid began badly. Drake's first action on arrival at the isthmus was to mount a night attack on Nombre de Dios, intending to gut the place of its treasure. Unfortunately the surprise was not complete, some of the Spaniards put up a fight and the English

[22] Bodleian Library, Ashmole MSS, 830. Knowledge of Drake's early West Indian operations (1570–73) is derived partly from the English narrative, *Sir Francis Drake Revived*, published in 1626 by his nephew, Sir Francis Drake, and partly from Spanish documents in the Archivo General de Indias, Seville, discovered and translated by Irene Wright: see Wright, *Documents, 1569–1580*, which contains most of the known material on the other English Caribbean ventures of that period.

withdrew in disarray, their leader himself wounded. The *flota* had in fact left some weeks before this, so that it is unlikely that Nombre de Dios would have yielded the raiders any considerable booty, though presumably none of them realized this, even after the event. For the next six months Drake operated up and down the Tierra Firme coast even as far as Curacão. His force was gradually dwindling and in January 1573 yellow fever reduced it to little more than thirty. But meanwhile he established contact with the *cimarrones* and so at last took the first step towards success.

In January these black bandits brought news of the arrival of the *flota* and Drake forthwith set out with thirty of them and seventeen Englishmen for Panama. The arduous march across the isthmus would have been impossible without the guidance of the *cimarrones*, and it was one of them who made his way into the city to discover that a mule-train was about to leave for Nombre de Dios. They ambushed it at Casa de Cruces, but again the surprise was not complete and the raiders lost the best of the prize. Returning to the north coast they resumed their routine operations and at length in March the tide of fortune turned with the arrival of a French privateer under Captain Guillaume le Testu of Havre. Le Testu was a protégé of Gaspard de Coligny, to whom he had dedicated his magnificent atlas, the 'Cosmographie Universelle', in 1556. A Huguenot, Le Testu had taken part in Villegaignon's colonial adventure at Río de Janeiro and must have been well acquainted with the strategic concept of *La France Antarctique*, a French South American empire challenging those of Spain and Portugal. What passed between him and Drake on this subject we do not know, but they agreed to pool their forces in another attempt on the treasure, and at last brought off the big *coup*. Twenty French, fifteen English and a party of *cimarrones* waylaid the mule-train outside Nombre de Dios. They drove off the guards, buried and hid a large quantity of silver near the road and made off with as much gold as they could carry. But Le Testu, wounded in the first assault, was unable to go far and the soldiers who soon arrived from the town killed and decapitated him. They also captured and executed another Frenchman and one or two of the Negroes and recovered most of the treasure left by the roadside, though the English managed to collect what remained of their hoard. The voyage was now made and after a perilous journey back to their ships the French and English divided their booty and departed. Drake and his crew reached Plymouth in August 1573 with a small fortune aboard.

Yet Drake's feat implied even more than it achieved: so at least it seemed to the Spaniards in Panama. It posed a new and altogether more serious threat to the security of the isthmus, that fragile waist of Spanish power in the New World, a threat of guerrilla warfare sustained from a base linked by sea to the ports of Protestant Europe. Worse, this combination of English and *cimarrones* might even conquer the isthmus:

We holde it certain [wrote the Municipal Council of Panama to the crown in February 1573, even before the final blow] that the principal design of these English is to explore and study this land, and what strength there is in it, in order to come from England with more people to plunder and occupy it. . . .This league between the English and the Negroes is very detrimental to this kingdom, because, being so thoroughly acquainted with the region and so expert in the bush, the Negroes will show them methods and means to accomplish any evil design they may wish to carry out.[23]

Drake certainly set great store by the Negro alliance, and the idea of using the *cimarrones* in further assaults on Spain's American empire became a characteristic feature of his strategic thinking, affecting his plans in 1577, in 1585 and even in the last and fatal expedition of 1595. For the Panama isthmus was less important for its own sake than as the key to what seemed then the greatest prize in the world, the kingdom of Peru. Peru, with its mountain of silver, Potosí, was in English eyes the source of Spanish power, and all the routes to Peru promised infinite wealth to the adventurer. The danger was clear to the Spaniards already in 1572, when the city of Panama warned the king: 'this realm is the key to the great province of Peru'. If Panama came into the power of the French or the English, 'this would mean the loss of Peru'.[24] As for Drake and his men, the strategic potential of the isthmus probably occurred to them about the same time, whether or not hindsight encouraged the author of *Sir Francis Drake Revived* to dramatize the point in that famous passage describing their first sight of the South Sea from a 'goodly and great high Tree':

After our Captaine had ascended to this Bower with the chiefe Symeron and (having as it pleased God at that time, by reason of the brize, a very faire day) had seene the sea of which he had heard such golden reports, hee besought Almightie God of his goodnesse to give him life and leave to sayle once in an English Ship in that sea. And then calling up all the rest of our men, acquainted *John Oxnam* especially with his petition and purpose, if it would please God to grant him that happinesse; who, understanding it, presently protested that unless our Captaine did beate him from his company he would follow him by Gods grace.[25]

[23] Wright, *Documents, 1569–1580*, pp. 49–50.
[24] Wright, *Documents, 1569–1580*, p. 34.
[25] Wright, *Documents, 1569–1580*, p. 300.

Both men were to achieve that ambition, and to sample the silver of Peru. But three years passed before Oxenham returned to the isthmus, three years in which the English and French continued their piratical raiding, but did little or nothing to renew the offensive on land in alliance with the Blacks. For these raiders were interested only in plunder, their forces being insufficient to undertake campaigns of the kind the Spaniards feared. Only with much more powerful backing could they have gone beyond the marauding, hit-and-run tactics of those years. Coligny might have provided that backing, but Coligny had been assassinated on the eve of St Bartholomew's day, 1572. In England the patrons of pirates had not the power to pursue a campaign across the Atlantic without the queen's approval, and that was now out of the question, for the year 1573 saw a *rapprochement* with Spain. In 1576, however, Oxenham returned, combined once more with the *cimarrones* and crossed the isthmus with their help, carrying a launch, in which he sailed to the Pearl Islands in the Gulf of Panama, whence he pillaged at will the treasure-bearing traffic of those waters. The Spanish colonial officials could foresee disaster:

They [the English] say that he is very happy to have opened a way from the Atlantic to the Pacific. He expects to be greatly rewarded by his queen for so doing and promises that next year he will enter there to settle with 2000 men and make himself master of all this realm, the strength of which is very little to resist such an onslaught as he announces.[26]

In reality Oxenham's threat was an empty one. With his own force of but fifty men and the help of some volunteer allies he could have achieved no more than nuisance raiding, profitable in itself, but strategically insignificant. Only the crown could have mounted an expedition strong enough to take Panama and even the crown would have found it practically impossible to hold. Queen Elizabeth was not likely to be inveigled into a war for the control of Panama at this or any other time – her attitude to the Panama expedition of 1595, when she was at open war with Spain, made that perfectly clear. In 1577 she was persuaded to send Drake to the Pacific on plunder bent, but that was a different matter from engaging the king of Spain on his own ground in a contest she could not hope to win. Elizabeth was a realist, not an imperialist. In any case Oxenham did not get the chance to beg her aid. The *audiencia* of Panama for once reacted quickly and forcefully to his initial success. One expedition searched the coast east from Nombre de Dios until it found the harbour where his vessels lay defenceless, capturing them and depriving him of his base. Another moved into the

[26] Wright, *Documents, 1569–1580*, p. 113.

bush from Panama and there located and defeated the English with their Negro allies on their way back across the isthmus with their booty. Perhaps also Oxenham was too casual and leisurely in his retreat and not sufficiently ruthless with the enemy: apparently the Negroes attributed their defeat to his refusal to kill his prisoners.[27]

The Spaniards achieved this considerable victory with local forces. But some of the English remained at large and the *cimarrones* were still a force to be reckoned with. The security of Panama required the rounding up of the enemy, the suppression of the Blacks and the establishment of effective naval control over the approaches to the isthmus, and it is a measure of the seriousness of the alarm created by Drake, Oxenham and lesser raiders that the Spaniards now dealt promptly and firmly with all these tasks. A strong body of volunteers from Panama invaded the heart of the Negro country, Vallano, and for six months scoured the bush, capturing most of the surviving English and many Negroes besides, burning their villages and crops and driving them to further places of refuge. In 1579 the Blacks submitted on terms and settled in a large *pueblo* on the Río Chepo, remaining free and handling their own affairs under Spanish rule, but returning to the Spaniards any fugitive slaves. A similar peace was concluded about the same time with the more westerly body of *cimarrones*. Both villages, after some initial mistrust and friction, settled down under Spanish tutelage, and the English hope of finding *cimarrón* allies thereafter was misplaced, as Drake learned to his cost when the Blacks of Santiago de Principe (near Nombre de Dios) opposed his troops in 1596.

Meanwhile in 1578 the Spanish crown authorized the dispatch of two galleys to Cartagena to protect the coast westwards from that base to Veragua. This proved to be a sound decision. As the Portuguese pilot Lopes Vas, who was in the Indies at the time and had a lively appreciation of the strategic problems of the area, noted: 'The first year that they were made they took six or seven French ships. So soon as this was known there used few English or French men of war to come on the coast, until this year 1586.'[28] Indeed by 1580 the threat to Panama was past and would not recur until for a brief space in 1586 Drake held Cartagena. In the years between, Drake and the Hawkinses turned their attention to the southern flank of Peru, seeking to approach their prize by way of Magellan's Strait and lands as yet unconquered by Spain or Portugal, 'beyond the equinoctial'.

[27] Wright, *Documents, 1569–1580*, p. 176.
[28] *PN*, XI, 234.

7

Beyond the equinoctial

Astounding though the explorations and conquests of the Iberian pioneers in South America were and are to this day, it is seldom realized how limited an area they were able effectively to occupy in the sixteenth century: certainly less than a hundredth part of that vast continent. In particular the territories now comprising southern Brazil, Uruguay, Argentina and southern Chile lay unconquered and largely unknown in the early seventies. After the conquest of Peru it had fallen to the *conquistador* Pedro de Valdivia to push southwards. In 1540 he moved into central Chile and began the long and bitter struggle with the Araucanian Indians in which he met his death in 1553. He succeeded in founding several Spanish towns: Santiago in 33°, with Valparaiso as its port, was established in 1541 and became the capital, but the smaller bases at Concepción in 36° (1550), Valdivia in 39° and Osorno in 41° were never safe from attack. Although in 1567 the Spaniards founded the city of Castro on the island of Chiloe as far south as 43½°, the boundary of their effective conquest lay around the fortieth parallel in the following decade, and the whole area from Concepción to Osorno remained a war zone for the rest of the century and long afterwards.[1]

Nor was the River Plate estuary occupied in the third quarter of the century. Pedro de Mendoza had created a settlement called Buenos Aires on the south bank in 1535, but by 1542 it had been abandoned. The main result of his expedition was the founding of Asunción, far to the north on the bank of the Paraguay in 25°, but Asunción was linked to Spain by way of Peru, as were the other scattered settlements of northern Argentina, the most southerly of which, Santa Fe, was not established until 1573 by Juan de Garay, who finally moved down river to refound Buenos Aires in 1580. As for the Portuguese, their southern-

---

[1] J. López de Velasco, *Geografía y Descripción Universal de las Indias*, ed. M. Jiménez de la Espada (Madrid, 1971), pp. 261–73. This work was completed in 1574.

most province in Brazil was São Vicente, which with its twin ports of
Santos and São Vicente in 24°, with São Paulo inland, grew and
prospered under the rule of Mem de Sá from 1558 to 1572.

Thus beyond the fringes of Iberian power in South America
stretched unsubdued a sub-continent the partial exploration of which
gave rise to continual rumours of gold and silver and reports of actual
routes to the fabled wealth of Peru. Given the obscure geography of the
region, it is not surprising that it inspired great expectations in certain
English breasts. They knew about Potosí already in the fifties, and
around 1570 they probably learned of Arauco, rich in gold, from
Zúñiga's epic poem about the Araucanian war, by which time they
must have been aware also of the existence of Valdivia's towns.[2] But
their location and the configuration of the Chile coast remained a
mystery. Juan Fernández Ladrillero's pioneering voyage in 1558 from
Concepción through the Straits into the Atlantic and back received
little public notice. The older maps left a blank between the Peru
conquests and the Strait, or linked the two with a purely speculative
line running southsoutheast. Valdivia's settlements first appear on a
map dated 1551, which has the old imaginary coast, but adds another,
running south and slightly west and then turning sharply east towards
the Strait, where a legend refers to Ladrillero, showing that the new
coast was added after 1558.[3] This more recent, but highly misleading,
outline became standard when Mercator adopted it in 1569. Drake and
his companions were shocked to find it so grossly in error and
suspected deliberate deceit.

The eastern side was of course better known. Even before 1526,
when Sebastian Cabot entered the estuary which later gained the
legendary title of Río de la Plata, the story of a 'white king' and of silver
mountains in the west had begun to lure Europeans towards the realm
of the Inca.[4] After Cabot's return maps showed to the west of the
Paraná a great *sierra* and his companion Roger Barlow reported:

On the west parte of this river within the lond toward the mountains 150 leges
of, is a serra or mount wheras thei saie is a king where is a grete aboundance of
gold and sylver. . . .This lond and the lond of pirro, which is in the southside
that the spaniards have dyscovered of late, is all one lond, wheras thei had so
grete riches of gold and sylver.[5]

[2] A. de Ercilla y Zúñiga, *La Araucana* (Madrid, 1569), the second part of which appeared
in 1578. Oxenham stated that Elizabeth 'had learned that beyond the Strait of Magellan
there were settlements made by Spaniards' (Z. Nuttall (ed.), *New Light on Drake*
(London, 1914), p. 9).
[3] H. R. Wagner, 'A map of Sancho Gutiérrez of 1551', *Imago Mundi*, 8 (1951), 47–9.
[4] C. E. Nowell, 'Aleixo Garcia and the White King', *HAHR*, 26 (1946), 450–66.
[5] Taylor, *Brief Summe*, pp. 162–3.

Cabot and Barlow seem to have passed on their special interest in the Plate region to other Englishmen. Richard Willes, for example, writing in 1577, mentioned Cabot's discovery of great and high mountains of silver, 'as he wryteth in his owne carde', meaning thereby Cabot's famous lost map.[6] This no doubt gave as badly distorted a view of the area as did the South American part of his 1544 world map, but would have been none the less stimulating to his Elizabethan successors. They would have seen other maps marking that interior 'Terra Argentea', would have read Hans Staden's account of his captivity, advertising incidentally São Vicente and the country south of it, and would have been aware, from Ulrich Schmidt's story, of the failure of the Iberians to occupy the lands east and south of Asunción.[7]

With Brazil English traders had established direct contact in the reign of Henry VIII, as we have seen, and in the early 1570s some mariners familiar with that coast were still in service.[8] Perhaps the most important link with that earlier generation was William Hawkins junior who, born in 1519, could well have played a part in his father's Brazil voyages. Well publicized, moreover, were the more intensive and persistent activities of the French, whose alliance with various Indian tribes, based on the barter trade, continually exposed the tenuous and fragmentary nature of Portuguese power in Brazil. In 1555 a French force under the chevalier de Villegaignon created a fortified base on an island off Río de Janeiro. The Portuguese finally destroyed it in 1560, but meanwhile the adventure caused a considerable stir in Europe, reported as it was most popularly by André Thevet. His book, *Les Singularitez de la France Antarctique*, came out in 1557 and appeared in English in 1568, soon becoming the chief printed source of information in England about Brazil.[9] Thevet pointed out that the Portuguese of 'Morpion' (São Vicente), though continually at war with the local Indians, had made great profit at first from sugar, but latterly 'have occupied them selves to a better worke, since that they have found out

[6] R. Willes, *The History of Travayle into the West and East Indies* (London, 1577), pp. 226–7. On Cabot's lost map see *PN*, VII, 145.
[7] A. Cortesão and A. C. Teixeira da Mota (eds.), *Portugaliae Monumenta Cartographica* (6 vols., Lisbon, 1960–63), I, plate 27; II, plate 108. M. Letts (ed.), *Hans Staden: the Story of his Captivity* (London, 1928, originally published at Marburg in 1557). L. L. Domínguez (ed.), *The Conquest of the River Plate (1535–1555)* (London, 1891), contains a translation of Schmidt's *Warhafftige und liebliche Beschreibung. . .* , originally published at Frankfurt am Main in 1567.
[8] BL, Lansdowne MSS, 100, fo. 142.
[9] André Thevet, *Les Singularitez de la France Antarctique* (Paris, 1557); translated by Thomas Hacket as *The new found worlde, or Antarctique* (London, 1568). The passages cited are from pp. 85 and 87.

Mynes of Silver'. He mentioned Spanish colonizing efforts in the River Plate and the interior, adding shrewdly:

Now to our purpose. This River of Platte with the countrey adiacent, is now very riche aswell in Silver as in stones. . . .The rest of the countrey hath not been frequented of christians, extending to the Caape Saint Dominik, or Caape Blanke, and from thence to the Promentary of the eleven thousand Virgins .52. degrees and a halfe beyond the Equinoctial, and thereby is the straight of Magellan.

Thevet's observations concerning the attractions of São Vicente and the parts beyond became accessible to the literate Englishman exactly when they were most likely to be noticed. The rift in the Anglo-Spanish alliance became an open one in 1568 and England entered into closer relations with France, especially Huguenot France. In the next few years Huguenot and English sailors and soldiers frequently fought side by side against the hated papist, whether French or Spanish. At this critical time, when Elizabeth and her Protestant régime were in grave danger, militant English patriots aligned themselves with Gaspard de Coligny, admiral of France, and associated with his Huguenot followers, from whom they gained insight into his grand strategy. In general he aimed to unite France by waging war on Spain, and to challenge Iberian power in the New World, not only striking at a major source of Spanish wealth, but winning for France a place in the sun. Coligny had been responsible for promoting Villegaignon's venture, which was intended as the first step towards a French empire in South America – La France Antarctique. When Coligny was assassinated in 1572 (the signal for the massacre of St Bartholomew's Eve) it was that same militant, expansionist element in England, personified by Richard Grenville, Humphrey Gilbert, Walter Ralegh, the Hawkinses and Drake, which fell heir to his Atlantic policy and American ambitions.

It appears to have been in the years around 1570 that notions of exploring and exploiting lands to the south of the Iberian dominions in America came to be discussed in England. It may be that they came from France, for as early as 1566 some such project had been proposed to the French crown by one Francesco d'Albagno, a citizen of Lucca, who himself derived the idea from a Portuguese cosmographer, Bartolomeu Velho.[10] In 1570, however, a Portuguese seaman,

[10] E.-T. Hamy, 'Francisque et André d'Albaigne, cosmographes lucquois au service de la France', *Bulletin de Géographie Historique et Descriptive* (1894), pp. 405–33; E.-T. Hamy, 'Nouveaux documents sur les frères d'Albaigne', *BGHD* (1899), pp. 101–10; E.-T. Hamy, 'Documents rélatifs à un projet d'expéditions lointaines', *BGHD* (1903), pp. 266–73; K. R. Andrews, 'On the way to Peru: Elizabethan ambitions in America south of Capricorn', *Terrae Incognitae*, 14 (1982), 61–75.

Bartolomeu Bayão, was talking in similar terms to councillors and merchants in London;[11] it is impossible, therefore, to award this concept a definite pedigree. Nor indeed can it be precisely defined, for all the references to it are couched in vague and mysterious language. D'Albagno was evidently anxious to convey the impression, by means of hints and cryptic talk of southern lands, that his purpose did not threaten Iberian interests, but was directed at 'ce dict reste non occupé par lesdicts Portugais ou Castillans'.[12] As for Bayão, the Spanish ambassador gathered that his object at first was 'to occupy one or two ports in the kingdom of Magallanes, in order to have in their hands the commerce of the southern sea, and that of Guinea and the coast of Africa, as well as getting as near as they wish to Peru'.[13] In fact, as events proved, Bayão had not the slightest intention of venturing anywhere near Magellan's Strait, but the ambassador was undoubtedly right in assuming that any such scheme must imply a threat to Peru and its seaborne treasure. The great southern continent of Terra Australis Incognita is not mentioned in the surviving documents relating to the d'Albagno project, but if it was implied as the objective (as some since have argued it was)[14] it may still have been merely a pretext for an enterprise involving direct infringement of Spain's New World monopoly, either by conquest of lands north of the Strait or by maritime plunder from some base in its neighbourhood. Such was the construction both the Spaniards and the Portuguese put upon the matter, and their worst suspicions were eventually to be confirmed by bitter experience when Drake translated these theories into action.

But the first stage in that translation was the work of Richard Grenville. In 1574 he and certain other gentlemen of the West Country, including William Hawkins of Plymouth, petitioned the queen to permit them to launch an expedition for 'The discoverie traffique and enioyenge' of lands south of the Equator not already possessed or subdued by any Christian prince.[15] Here and elsewhere in his submis-

---

[11] Andrews, 'On the way to Peru'.

[12] These words were used by his brother in his submission to Charles IX in 1571 – Hamy, 'Francisque et André d'Albaigne'.

[13] *Cal. SP Span.*, II, 243. The 'kingdom of Magallanes' may correspond to the 'Tierra de Magallanes Meridies' shown south of the Strait in Diego Gutiérrez's 1562 map of South America (BL, Maps, 183, no. 3, reproduced in J. H. Parry, *The Discovery of South America* (London, 1979), p. 275); but, as the use of the term 'meridies' suggests, that 'kingdom' was possibly envisaged as including the region to the north of the Strait.

[14] E.-T. Hamy construed the material in this way. For a different interpretation see Andrews, 'On the way to Peru'.

[15] The documents relating to Grenville's project are: a petition to the queen, dated 22 March 1573/4 (PRO, SP 12/95, no. 63); a letter of the petitioners to the Lord Admiral, evidently of the same date, together with articles explaining it (PRO, SP 12/95, nos. 64, 65; BL, Lansdowne MSS, 100, fos. 142–6, is a copy of the articles); a draft of letters

sion, Grenville took great pains to deny any intention to trespass upon Iberian-occupied territory, and it has been suggested that his real interest lay in Terra Australis Incognita, since the only southerly parts of America likely to have attracted him were already occupied by Portuguese and Spaniards.[16] This last assumption, however, is quite unwarranted, as we have seen, and furthermore the nature of Grenville's aims was made crystal clear a few years later by men who knew him and his plans intimately and could, after the event, speak frankly about them. These witnesses were John Oxenham and two of his companions, captured in Panama in 1577 and held by the Spanish Inquisition at Lima, where they answered questions about Grenville and Drake in 1579.[17] The first deposed that Grenville

had asked for a licence to settle on the River Plate towards the Strait of Magellan. For this purpose he had bought four vessels, and John Oxenham, who is here in this prison, had agreed to go with him. But as the queen did not give him the licence, they sold the ships. Questioned whether they had planned to found settlements on the coast of the North Sea [viz. the Atlantic], or to pass through the Strait of Magellan and populate the coast of the South Sea, he answered that he had heard it said that it was to be on the coast of the North Sea, towards the River Plate, in a country of which they had reports, from some Portuguese, that it was very rich. The queen had demanded that they were to give a security of thirty to forty thousand pounds that they would not touch lands belonging to King Philip, and on this account the expedition was frustrated.

John Oxenham admitted much more. The project was, he said, 'to come and found a settlement on the River Plate and then pass the Strait and establish settlements wherever a good country for such could be found'. The queen actually granted the licence, but then revoked it 'because she had learned that beyond the Strait of Magellan there were settlements made by Spaniards, who might do them harm'. The third witness declared that the intention was 'to come and pass through the Strait of Magellan and take possession of some land where King Philip had no settlements. The queen did not wish him to come for fear that he might do harm in the possessions of her brother King Philip.' These statements, though not exactly consistent with each other, leave little doubt about the real nature of Grenville's objectives. The River Plate

patent to Grenville and associates (PRO, SP 12/235, no. 1); a discourse of later date concerning the northwest passage (BL, Lansdowne MSS, 100, no. 4); depositions of English prisoners at Lima (Nuttall, *New Light on Drake*, pp. 5–12). All this material is reproduced in R. Pearse Chope, 'New light on Sir Richard Grenville', *Transactions of the Devonshire Association*, 49 (1917), 210–82.
[16] E. G. R. Taylor, 'More light on Drake', *Mariner's Mirror*, 16 (1930), 134–51.
[17] Nuttall, *New Light on Drake*, pp. 5–12.

was clearly his first target, and he intended then to proceed through the Strait to the Chile coast. That he had in mind the conquest of the southerly region of South America is equally clear from his own direct reference to that part of the New World as English by manifest destiny, arguing

The aptness and as hit were a fatall convenience that since the Portugall hathe atteined one parte of the newe founde worlde to the Este, the Spaniarde an other to the weste, the Frenche the thirde to the northe: nowe the fourthe to the southe is by gods providence lefte for Englande to whom the other in tymes paste have ben fyrste offred.[18]

Grenville himself was forbidden to pursue his plans. In 1574 the queen's relations with her brother Philip were tolerably amicable and it is clear that she did not then wish to upset him by countenancing or even covertly encouraging offensive ventures of this kind. But three years later, when those relations turned sour again, something very like the Grenville plan re-emerged and won her approval. This new project emanated from that group of naval men who had led the Panama Isthmus raiding campaign – Sir William and George Winter, John Hawkins and Francis Drake – and was closely linked to Grenville's, from which it clearly derived, in several ways. Oxenham was one link. As he told the Inquisition, before Grenville sold his ships 'he had spoken many times with witness, trying to persuade him to accompany him, but witness did not wish to do so. . . .The said Captain Francis [Drake] had often spoken to witness saying that if the queen would grant him the licence he would pass through the Strait of Magellan and found settlements over here in some good country.'[19] These discussions must have occurred after the return of Drake and Oxenham from the Panama Isthmus in 1573. What was the best approach to the Mar del Sur and Peru? It is not difficult to imagine Oxenham's arguments for the isthmus, nor those of Grenville and Drake for the roundabout route of Magellan's Strait.

Another link was William Hawkins – Grenville's partner in the 1574 project and no doubt associated with his brother John in the promotion of Drake's voyage. William and John were to show a persistent interest in South America and were probably the real engineers of the 1577 venture. They carried with them, moreover, one of the great men in

---

[18] In the light of this statement, the Lima depositions and the queen's refusal to permit the expedition, the contention that Grenville aimed to settle Terra Australis appears groundless. Indeed Grenville's discourse on the Pacific approach to the northwest passage, which refers to the 'waste ocean to the south' and completely ignores Terra Australis, conveys the impression that he did not believe in its existence.

[19] Nuttall, *New Light on Drake*, pp. 9–10.

the state: Clinton, earl of Lincoln, Lord High Admiral and a pillar of the Elizabethan régime, especially responsible in all naval matters. Clinton had been the chief sponsor of Grenville's project and probably did the same for Drake. As one of Oxenham's fellow-prisoners declared: 'he has heard it said that if the queen should die, Francis Drake would come [to Magellan's Strait], because the lord admiral has a great affection for him'.[20]

In the spring or early summer of 1577 a plan for a voyage through Magellan's Strait and home by the same route was drawn up. The document was later partly burned along with other manuscripts in the Cotton collection, but what remains is quite sufficient to indicate the nature and essential purpose of the expedition. The key passage, with interpolated letters and words in italics, runs as follows:

*shall enter the Strait of Magellan*as *lying in* 52 *degrees of* the powlle & *having passed therefrom into* the sowthe sea then *he is to sail so* far to the northwardes as *xxx degrees seeking* alonge the saied coaste af*orenamed like* as of the other to fynde owt pl*aces meet* to have trafick for the vent*ing of commodities* of thies her Maj*es*ties realmes, wh*ereas* at present they ar not under the obediens of *any* Christian prynce, so is ther great hoepe of *gold, silver*, spieces, druges, cochynillo, and *divers other* Speciall comodities, such as maye *enrich* her highnes domynyons, and also *put* shippinge awoork greatly and *having* gotten up as afore saied in to xxx de*grees in* the sowthe sea (yf hit shalbe thowght *meet* by the fore named fraunces Draek to proc*eed so* far) then he is to retorne the same way whome wardes, as he went owt. Which viage by godes favor is to be *performed* in xiij monthes all thoughe he shuld spend v. monthes in taryenge uppon the coaste to get knowledge of the prynces and cowmptres ther.[21]

The plan was, then, for a voyage of reconnaissance down the east

[20] Nuttall, *New Light on Drake*, p. 12.
[21] BL, Cotton MSS, Otho E. VIII, fo. 9. My reconstruction follows Taylor, 'More light on Drake', without her modernizations. A facsimile and a faithful transcript of the original are to be found in J. Hampden (ed.), *Francis Drake Privateer* (London, 1972), pp. 113, 176–7. The full argument for my interpretation is set forth in K. R. Andrews, 'The aims of Drake's expedition of 1577–1580', *American Historical Review*, 73 (1968), 724–41. The best analysis of the sources relating to this voyage is H. R. Wagner, *Sir Francis Drake's Voyage around the World* (San Francisco, 1926), pp. 238–302. Nuttall, *New Light on Drake*, gives the Spanish materials. W. S. W. Vaux (ed.), *The World Encompassed by Sir Francis Drake* (London, 1854), reprints *The World Encompassed* (London, 1628) and includes John Cooke's narrative, the 'anonymous narrative', the Doughty trial documents and the relevant extracts from *Principal Navigations*, viz. – *PN*, IX, 319–26 ('The course which Sir Francis Drake held from . . . Guatulco . . . to . . . California'); *PN*, XI, 101–33 ('The famous voyage of Sir Francis Drake'); *PN*, XI, 133–47 (Nuño da Silva's relation); *PN*, XI, 148–62 (Edward Cliffe's narrative); and *PN*, XI, 227–90 (the discourse of Lopes Vas). Francis Fletcher's narrative, inadequately rendered by Vaux, is printed in full in N. M. Penzer (ed.), *The World Encompassed and Analogous Contemporary Documents* (London, 1926). For Winter's declaration concerning the Portuguese prize see Nuttall, *New Light on Drake*, pp. 383–92, and for his report on his voyage, Taylor, 'More light on Drake'.

coast of South America to the Strait and northwards up the other coast as far as 30°s. or towards that latitude. The northward limit was left to Drake's discretion, presumably because it would depend on the local situation: the location of the frontier, the native reaction to his presence and so forth. These tasks and the investigation of the resources of the country would require a long voyage, which made the strait the obvious way home, or so it must have seemed to the planners. The scope of the expedition was thus expressly limited and the anti-Spanish implications left unstated, which reticence was no doubt thought necessary to obtain the queen's support. For as the document elsewhere reveals, the queen was to be asked to contribute her own ship, the *Swallow*, fully armed and equipped, as an investment in the venture. She could not be expected, in the light of Grenville's experience, to commit herself openly to any sort of South American project – that was presumably why the authors said she was to be 'made pryve to the trewthe of the viage, and yet the coollor to be geven owt for allixandria'.[22] But she might be induced covertly to subscribe if the voyage was presented as one of commercial reconnaissance without reference to colonization or Peruvian silver, and so might be drawn gently into more serious business.

Such evidently were the considerations in the minds of the projectors as they prepared to approach the queen. How she reacted in the event is not known, but it is clear that at some stage in the summer of 1577 she withdrew the ban she had imposed on Grenville and gave permission for Drake to sail. She did not allow the *Swallow* to be used, probably because she realized the aggressive implications of the voyage, but she may well have subscribed money privately, as Drake alleged. Drake's account of the queen's interest in the voyage, reported by John Cooke, was that, having first conferred with Walsingham about the queen's desire to be revenged on the king of Spain, and having refused to set his hand to anything, he was taken to Elizabeth, who told him:

[22] In June 1577 John Hawkins drew up an estimate for a voyage of the *Swallow* (300 tons) and the *Pelican* (120 tons) to Alexandria, Tripoli and Constantinople – PRO, SP 12/114, fos. 84–5, printed in Skilliter, *Harborne*, pp. 19–21. This is evidently the 'blind' called for in the plan, and it suggests that Hawkins was the author of the plan and that he wrote it in June or before. The care he took to camouflage 'the truth of the voyage' is shown in his attention to detail; he referred, for example, to a licence already obtained from Thomas Cordell: 'If it be found that the licence had from Mr Cordell be sure to traffique to Constantinople, then it were good to go thither.' The style of this document and its financial detail are typical of Hawkins's memoranda, as navy treasurer, addressed to Burghley, and it is reasonable to assume that it was intended for Burghley's eyes, though it would be quite wrong to assume that Burghley was deceived.

Drake, So it is that I would gladly be revenged on the Kynge of Spayne, for dyvers iniuries that I have receyved, and sayd fardar that he was thonely man that myght do this exployte, and withall craved his advice therein. Who told hir Maiestie of the smale good that was to be done in Spayne, but thonly waye was to anoy hym by his Indyes. Then with many more words he shewed forthe a byll of hir Maiesties adventure of a 1000 crownes whiche he sayde at sometyme before that hir Maiestie dyd gyve hym towards his chargs.[23]

In the light of the 1577 plan this story is difficult to accept in its entirety. For the plan clearly implies that the queen at that stage was not privy to the truth of the voyage and that the initiative came from the projectors, not from her. Indeed she was not in the habit of putting projects to other people: they came with their plans ready-made, seeking her yea or nay. By this time, moreover, the Winters, Hawkins and Drake had put up £750, £500, £500 and £1000 respectively and greater men had promised to subscribe: Lincoln, Leicester, Walsingham and Hatton.[24] Of these, Lincoln and Leicester had backed Hawkins in the slave trade, Leicester had promoted Andrew Barker's West Indies raid[25] and Walsingham was a militant enemy of Catholic Spain. It is reasonable to conclude from the draft plan, therefore, that the 1577 project emanated from Drake and his naval allies, who first gained the support of key men at court and then approached the queen. Either by luck or good judgement they did so at an opportune moment, for the situation in the Netherlands suddenly deteriorated in the summer of 1577, setting England and Spain at daggers drawn, with the queen in a hotly anti-Spanish mood.[26]

Thus Drake's famous voyage of 1577, which turned into a circumnavigation of the world, was a natural sequel to the Panama raids of reprisal and plunder. Consistently throughout the voyage Drake represented it as an act of revenge by way of predation. It was also, however, a colonial venture. Grenville had stressed colonization as his chief purpose, providing a variety of arguments – economic, social, military and political – to justify it. Conquest of the Plate basin and all the lands south of the viceroyalty of Peru, a strategic triangle commanding Magellan's Strait and forcefully abutting the rich Iberian dominions of Brazil and Peru – such was the hard core of the project Drake inherited from Grenville. As Oxenham told his inquisitors: 'with the aid of his relatives and companions [Drake] might be able to bring

[23] Vaux, *World Encompassed*, pp. 215–16.
[24] BL, Cotton MSS, Otho E. VIII, fo. 8. Hatton was knighted in December 1577.
[25] Andrews, *Spanish Caribbean*, p. 142.
[26] It is clear that she changed her mind, but not clear why. On the context see W. T. MacCaffrey, *Queen Elizabeth and the Making of Policy 1572–1588* (Princeton, 1981), pp. 332–3.

two or three vessels but that, after discovering a good country, they would be able to come with more ships'. The voyage of 1577 was to be the first step towards a South American empire, to be won by alliance with the people of Arauco and similar enemies of the Spaniard. As he told his prisoners in the Pacific, Drake came there 'for a greater purpose than that of seizing vessels'.[27] Those lands, adjacent to Potosí, the silver magnet of the western world, must surely contain rich mines of precious metal. After the voyage Drake's first thought would be to exploit them. Meanwhile it was not difficult to envisage circumstances in which the Spaniards of Peru would provide him with some of theirs. This is not to say that Drake and his backers were indifferent to the wider potential of the Mar del Sur. They, like Grenville, appreciated the importance of the link the Spaniards had in recent years created between Mexico and Manila, giving them access to the wealth of China and the Spice Islands, and they shared Grenville's interest in finding a western entry to the supposed sea-passage north of America into the Atlantic. In the long gestation of this project speculation about such prospects must have livened the discussions of the planners. Yet there is no indication that they chose to include any of these further ambitions among their immediate objects. What the plan of Drake's voyage implied was a practical, step-by-step approach to Pacific power.[28]

Drake's fleet consisted of his flagship the *Pelican*, of 150 tons burden, the *Elizabeth* of 80 tons under Captain John Winter, the *Marigold* of 30 tons under Captain John Thomas, the *Swan* of 50 tons under Captain John Chester, and the *Christopher*, or *Bark Benedict*, of 15 tons under Captain Thomas Moone. The *Pelican* was his own ship, built before February 1577, but perhaps not long before.[29] Though not a large vessel by contemporary standards, she was strong and very well equipped as a man-of-war, with eighteen cast pieces and a variety of other weapons – arquebuses, calivers, pistols, pikes, fire-bombs, fire-pikes, bows and

---

[27] Nuttall, *New Light on Drake*, pp. 10, 318.

[28] It is important to distinguish between the more speculative ideas and aspirations which drew the English into the Pacific at this stage, and the specific aims of the particular enterprise, which are clearly indicated in the plan of Drake's voyage and in Grenville's project. Grenville dwelt on the general attractions of the Pacific only in his second project, where they appear as arguments in favour of a western approach to the northwest passage and so are merely incidental to a proposal which was itself an afterthought: BL, Lansdowne MSS, 100, no. 4.

[29] P. Williams, 'The ownership of Drake's *Golden Hind*', *Mariner's Mirror*, 67 (1981), 185–6. This concerns a bounty paid to Drake for the ship in July 1577. But Nuño da Silva, who sailed in her, said she was 'not new', which suggests that Drake may have got the bounty for a re-building, not a new-building. Re-building was of course very common.

arrows. Some of the missiles were made aboard ship by the gunners and coal was taken for the smith's forge, as well as pickaxes, spades, shovels, mattocks, hatchets and crowbars. She carried four pinnaces in parts, to be assembled when required. Of the rest the *Swan* was a flyboat, used as a victualler. In the whole fleet Drake had about 160 men – roughly one man to two tons. This was heavy manning, but not excessive for such a lengthy and warlike expedition, where casualties from disease and enemy action were only to be expected. As it happened, Drake successfully avoided serious loss from these usual causes, and this alone, considering that the voyage lasted nearly three years, marks out the extraordinary quality of his leadership. Alto-gether about 100 men returned, most of the rest having been lost in the wreck of the *Marigold* and other mishaps. The original complement included a shoemaker, an apothecary, a tailor, a preacher (Francis Fletcher, who kept a detailed journal of the voyage), some trumpeters and viol-players, several boys, a number of soldiers and about ten gentlemen.

These last, according to Don Francisco de Zarate, one of Drake's prisoners, 'form a part of his council, which he calls together for even the most trivial matter, although he takes advice from no one. But he enjoys hearing what they say and afterwards issues his orders.' They also sat at his table, where he was served on silver dishes with gold borders and gilded garlands, displaying his coat of arms, but none of them would take a seat or cover his head in Drake's presence without his permission. He dined and supped to the music of viols. As for the crew, 'he treats them with affection and they treat him with respect . . . . He shows them great favour, but punishes the least fault.'[30] Drake had his own special style of command. Another Spanish witness describes him leading prayers and psalms. He had a table placed on deck at the poop, with a box and a kneeler at its head. He then sent for Foxe's *Book of Martyrs*, struck the table twice with the palm of his hand and was immediately joined by nine Englishmen, each carrying a book of psalms. 'Then the said Francis Drake crossed his hands and, kneeling on the cushion and the small box, lifted his eyes to heaven and remained in that attitude for about a quarter of an hour.' After that he read psalms for an hour and then sang to the accompaniment of four viols. A page-boy concluded the service with a dance 'in the English fashion', and afterwards Drake found occasion to lecture the witness angrily on the illustrations in Foxe and to justify his own conduct by referring to the damage suffered by Hawkins at San Juan de Ulúa.[31]

[30] Nuttall, *New Light on Drake*, p. 207.
[31] Nuttall, *New Light on Drake*, pp. 354–7.

The force of Drake's intense personality made an indelible mark on the minds of friend and foe, but to seamen like the Portuguese pilot Nuño da Silva, who assisted him in navigating from the Cape Verde Islands to the Pacific coast of Mexico, he was above all 'a great mariner'. Drake 'kept a book in which he entered his navigation and in which he kept delineated birds, trees and sea-lions. He is an adept in painting and has with him a boy, a relative of his [John Drake], who is a great painter'.[32] He certainly kept a journal, which he later presented to the queen, and this was probably illustrated with profiles of the coast, showing the lie of it and giving details of courses, shoals, tides and so forth: a journal-rutter such as Stephen Borough had compiled and William Borough's instructions had required.[33] He took da Silva's Brazil chart, had it translated and checked it closely as he worked his way down that coast. He wrote down all he could learn about the Portuguese sea-routes.[34] He carried with him three books on navigation – one in French and another in English, the third being described as 'Magellan's *Discovery*'.[35] As for maps, he took a Portuguese map of the world, which can have been of little use, and probably a copy of the 1570 Ortelius world map, which must have been worse than useless, particularly in respect of the Pacific coasts of South and North America.[36] The only cartographic aids likely to have been of any service were the charts he picked up in the course of the voyage from Iberian pilots. Drake's nautical achievement in what Hakluyt called his 'famous' voyage has been too often understated by writers who look upon him as a mere pirate. This was a voyage of exploration, conducted for the most part in seas utterly unknown to him and his companions, practically unaided as they were by the available maps and continually in danger of hostile action by Spaniards and Portuguese. No one in that age matched this feat of sustained seamanship.

The voyage began on 15 November 1577, but bad weather delayed the final departure, from Plymouth, until 13 December. On the way down the African coast they took several small Spanish and Portuguese vessels, appropriating whatever they wanted and then dismiss-

[32] Nuttall, *New Light on Drake*, p. 303.
[33] Nuttall, *New Light on Drake*, pp. 207–8, and see above, Ch. 2. Drake's paintings were probably coastal profiles like those made in his last voyage – see K. R. Andrews (ed.), *The Last Voyage of Drake and Hawkins* (Cambridge, 1972), pp. 258–9.
[34] Nuttall, *New Light on Drake*, pp. 308–9.
[35] Nuttall, *New Light on Drake*, p. 303. Nuño did not know in what language this was written. It may have been the English translation of Pigafetta by Richard Eden in Willes, *History of Travayle*. The French work was perhaps a translation of Pedro de Medina, *Arte de Navegar* (1545), and the English manual was possibly Eden's translation of Martín Cortés: *The Arte of Navigation* (London, 1561).
[36] Nuttall, *New Light on Drake*, p. 270.

ing them; one, however, was kept and another exchanged for the *Bark Benedict*. Finally a more valuable prize, Nuño da Silva's ship, was taken in the Cape Verde Islands. Her cargo of wines and other goods was much appreciated and her master's special knowledge of the Guinea and Brazil navigation proved even more welcome. Of course these were acts of piracy, but nobody in the fleet objected to these seizures, either then or later in the voyage. In fact trouble arose only over the division of the spoil, and this was certainly one root of the quarrel which led eventually to the execution of Thomas Doughty.[37] Doughty had served with Drake in Ireland under Walter Devereux, earl of Essex, in 1575. It is unlikely that he played a major part in the conception or the furtherance of Drake's project, but as Hatton's man and Drake's personal friend he seems to have been the most important of the gentlemen in the expedition. He was given charge of Nuño's ship but promptly fell out with Drake's brother Thomas over some matter of purloined valuables and was transferred to the command of the *Pelican*. Yet here again he quarrelled with Drake's men, being 'thought to be to peremptorye' and so was removed into the flyboat 'with utter disgrace'. A fatal pattern of conflict between gentlemen and sailors was now emerging. John Cooke remarks 'how hardly Mastar Thomas Dowghtye and some othar gentlemen were dealt withall in this theyr absens, by a sorte of badd and envyous people, as saylers and such lyke . . . for there the mastar put hym selfe from the mease of Master Dowghty and othar gentlemen, and dyd syt hymselfe amongst saylers'. Bitter words and blows followed, and Doughty appealed to the captain, another of the gentlemen: 'Mastar Chestar, let us not be thus used at thes knaves hands, lose nothinge of that aucthoritie that the Generall hath commytted unto yow, yf you wyll we wyll put the sworde agayne into yowr hands, and yow shall have the governement.'

Finally Drake placed Doughty and his brother John under arrest aboard the *Elizabeth*, accusing them of sedition and witchcraft and forbidding communication with them. Whether justifiably or not, he suspected Doughty of intrigue against himself, of trying to discredit him, of plotting 'the very ovarthrowe of the vyadge, as first by takynge away my good name and altogethar discreditinge me, and then my lyfe'. The danger of mutiny, so common in voyages of this sort, now became apparent and Drake characteristically met it head on, with ruthless, theatrical, almost demonic energy. After arriving at Port St

---

[37] John Cooke's narrative is the chief source for the Doughty affair, and all the quotations following are drawn from it. See also the trial documents in Vaux, *World Encompassed*, pp. 165–74.

Julian in 49° towards the Strait in June 1578, he impanelled a jury and tried Doughty on various trumped-up charges, leading inevitably to the capital charge of treachery:

Then it fell out upon fardar talke that Mastar Dowghty sayde that my lorde Tresorar had a plott of the voyadge. No, that he hathe not, q*u*od Mastar Drake. Thothar replyed that he had. How? q*u*od Mastar Drake. He had it from me, q*u*od Mastar Dowghty. Lo, my mastars, q*u*od he, what this fellowe hath done, God will have his trecheryes all knowne, for her Maiestie gave me speciall com*m*aundement that of all men my lord Tresorar shuld not knowe it, but to se he his owne mowthe hathe betwrayed hym. So this was a speciall article agaynst hym to cut his throte.

Doughty stood no chance – he had to die *pour encourager les autres*, and when this travesty of justice came to its bloody climax he gallantly performed his allotted rôle in the long-drawn-out ceremony which ended with his severed head raised and Drake's words: 'Lo, this is the end of traitors.' Before leaving Port St Julian on 17 August Drake took further steps to discipline the company. The stomaching between the gentlemen and the sailors must stop and the gentleman must haul and draw with the mariner, the mariner with the gentleman. He dismissed all the officers of the fleet and asserted his personal authority, derived as he avowed direct from the queen. Then, having humbled them, he forgave and reinstated them. The crisis was over.

By this time he had carried out a significant part of his task – the reconnaissance of the eastern shore of the continent. It was early in April that the fleet had sighted the coast of Brazil in about 31°, but almost immediately they found themselves in 'the most deadly fog', followed by a terrible storm as they clawed desperately off a lee shore, heavily shoaled. Alarmed by this experience, they cautiously coasted south, taking soundings, until they came to the north bank of the Plate estuary. They ran in seven or eight leagues and anchored under a cape, which Drake called Cape Joy, and then a further fifteen leagues, where they found a deep bay, probably the Bay of Montevideo. Here the fleet came together at anchor and the crews killed and ate seals. Then they ran another twenty leagues up the estuary until they were in only three fathoms of water, which was fresh: 'but wee staid not there, nor in any other place of the river, because that the winds being strong, the shoales many, and no safe harbour found, we could not without our great danger so have done'.[38] The point is further explained by Nuño da Silva:

The navigation from Spain to the Río de la Plata offers no difficulties if it is done

[38] Vaux, *World Encompassed*, pp. 41–2.

at the proper time, which is the month of August. Leaving Seville at that time, one can arrive . . . in the summer, which lasts there from September to February. At that season . . . there are no contrary winds, such as prevail in the other months when no vessels can remain in the river and no cables can withstand the strain. It therefore happened that, as the Englishman arrived there in April, he had only two days of good weather.[39]

Drake spent twelve days in the estuary, but 'could find here no harborowe as he expected' and so sailed out again, disappointed. The search for a harbour continued as they moved south, continually sounding, in very foul weather, the ships repeatedly losing each other, until they reached the harbour now known as Port Desire in 47°. Here they stayed for a fortnight, revictualling with seal and penguin meat, and made contact with the Patagonian people, who were friendly, but otherwise unimpressive. Then they pressed on south as far as 50°, but turned back with an adverse wind and came into Port St Julian on 20 June, having spent two and a half fruitless months reconnoitring those unpromising shores. As for Port St Julian, it was a forbidding place, the winter happened to be especially severe, and the Patagonians proved hostile. They killed two of Drake's men and some others died of sickness and exposure. The English must have been glad to see the last of it as they finally put to sea on 17 August, now reduced to three ships, the *Pelican*, the *Elizabeth* and the *Marigold*, making for the Strait.

Three days later they reached the mouth of the Strait and there, waiting for a wind, Drake ceremonially renamed his flagship the *Golden Hind*, in honour of Hatton. The passage of this dreaded entrance to the South Sea, so rarely traversed before, and never by an English ship, took only fourteen days. 'We found the sea to have no such current as some do imagine (following the course of the *primum mobile* from East to West) but to eb and flow as ordinarily as upon other coasts', wrote Edward Cliffe, and at the most southerly point of the Strait, 'where it bendeth like an elbow', they found three islands, which Drake named Elizabeth, St Bartholomew and St George, taking possession of the first for the queen of England. Here also his men barrelled an enormous store of penguin meat.[40] On 6 September they passed into the South Sea, the weather and Drake's superb seamanship having made that extremely difficult task seem easy. Then the three ships together held their course northwest – the supposed direction of the coast – for three days, covering a distance of some seventy leagues, making for the agreed rendezvous at 30°s. on the

[39] Nuttall, *New Light on Drake*, pp. 309–10.
[40] Vaux, *World Encompassed*, pp. 279–80.

coast of 'Peru'. Drake was certainly now following his instructions and carrying out the original plan to the best of his ability.[41]

But only the *Golden Hind* was to make that rendezvous. A heavy and continuous storm from the northwest now began to rage, driving the puny vessels helpless before the terrifying sea. Towards the end of September the *Marigold* disappeared and was never heard of again – whether she foundered then or came to grief later, after failing to rejoin, we do not know. On 7 October, the wind having dropped, the other two ships came near the entrance to the Strait, but were driven from their anchorage by a new storm and lost company. Winter, in the *Elizabeth*, took refuge in the Strait. For two days he anchored near the mouth, making fires at night in the hope that Drake would see them, and then he retired to a safer anchorage well within the Strait. Here he stayed three weeks and, as he explained later, 'looked still for Master Drake, and for a change of wind'. Finally, 'hopeless of my determined voyage, as also of the finding of Master Drake, and despairing utterly of the favourableness of the wind for to go to the Peru . . . the 11th of November I bare room with my country whilst I had the wherewithal'.

This much of Winter's story is straightforward enough, but he then added, 'I knew not where to revictual, except I had gone for the Moluccas'; indeed, 'Master Drake told me that he would go thither when I was last aboard of him.'[42] What can this mean? In the first place it is clear that Peru was the objective. The Moluccas are not represented as an objective, but as a place for revictualling. Secondly, this is the first mention of the Moluccas in all the material relevant to this voyage. There is no evidence whatever of any intention before this to return by way of the Moluccas and the inference is unmistakable: at anchorage after the first storm in the Pacific Drake's plans were changed. He would not return by way of Magellan's Strait because it was now obvious that to do so would be to court disaster. Seeking the mouth of the Strait in a storm driving towards a maze of jagged rocks was practically suicidal – no seaman would contemplate such a course unless he knew when he could expect favourable weather. Drake did not have that knowledge and so was compelled, as Hakluyt's 'Famous

---

[41] 'Our Generall having aforehand given order, that if any of our fleet did loose company, the place of resort to meet againe should be in 30 deg. or thereabouts, upon the coast of Peru' – Vaux, *World Encompassed*, p. 83. Nuño da Silva also states that this was the next objective 'according to previous agreement' – Nuttall, *New Light on Drake*, p. 298. This shows that Drake had no intention of seeking Terra Australis and that the objective of 30°s. mentioned in the plan of the voyage was a South American one.

[42] Taylor, 'More light on Drake', pp. 147–51.

Voyage' relates, to consider alternative routes home – after he had done whatever he had to do on the coast of Peru.[43]

So Winter returned, reaching England in June 1579. Meanwhile Drake was driven south again and found shelter in the lee of an island on the southern side of the archipelago south of the Strait: 'whereat wee arriveing', says Fletcher, 'made both the seas to be one & the self same sea & that there was no farther land beyond the heights of that Iland'.[44] This was probably Henderson Island in 55°s., and the discovery, pictured in Fletcher's sketch of the southern end of South America, that the oceans met there, was important in casting the first doubt upon the myth of Terra Australis and in anticipating the Dutch discovery of the Cape Horn route to the Pacific. It was not, however, widely publicized, nor generally accepted by cartographers in that century, and it is a curious fact that none of the Elizabethans who followed or tried to follow Drake into the Pacific attempted the passage of Cape Horn. In 1582, when Fenton thought the Spaniards might intercept him in the Strait, he apparently did not think of circumventing them, though he had with him a number of men who had been with Drake to the south of Tierra del Fuego, including the pilot Thomas Hood, who boasted of such special knowledge that the earl of Cumberland selected him as 'pilot for the Streights' in 1586.

Having spent a week or so among these islands, which he christened the Elizabethides, Drake set course once more for Peru, sailing northwest. After two or three days he realized that his maps were wrong in their account of the trend of that coast; he therefore turned northeast and on sighting land continued tacking northwards as far as the large island of Mocha in 38°. Mocha, reached on 25 November 1578, looked very promising. Fletcher enthused, 'this Iland is most Rich in Gold & silver and it aboundeth in many good things necessary for the maintainance of Gods good people flourishing with trees & fruit continually wanting nothing but a people feareing God to injoye it'. It stood in relation to the 'golden province' of Valdivia as the Isle of Wight to England, 'a doore barr to the Land . . . which being possessed by one Prince would make the one & the other invincible'.[45] The reference to

---

[43] *PN*, xi, 118. The winds ruled out a westerly course for the Moluccas; Winter's idea (though he may not seriously have contemplated it) was to go east by way of the Cape of Good Hope and Madagascar: Lansdowne MSS, 122, fos. 22–8.

[44] Penzer, *World Encompassed*, p. 134.

[45] Penzer, *World Encompassed*, p. 141. In a set of instructions for a voyage to North America in 1582 or 1583 it is said that two or three of Drake's men opined that the 'excellentest place that they sawe in all their Vyage . . . was about 45 Degrees of Latitude . . . an island in Marii de Sur called de Malco which lay in 46 degrees of Latitude' – Quinn, *New American World*, iii, p. 245. As Quinn suggests, this could have been Melchor Island in the Los Chonos archipelago. But other sources indicate that

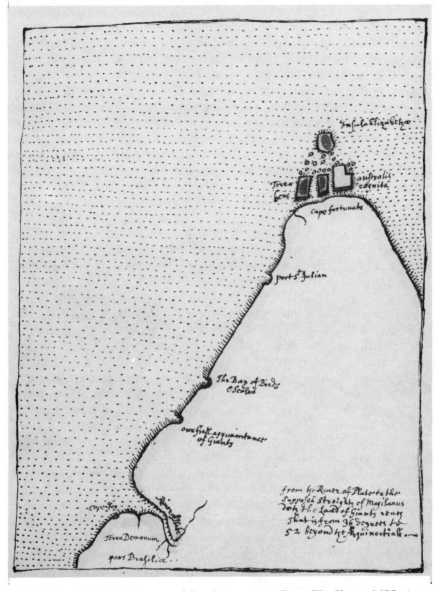

Fig. 3 Francis Fletcher's map of South America. (From BL, Sloane MSS, 61, fo. 35r.)

colonization is as significant as the strategic assessment. Here if anywhere, not far from Arauco itself, was a site suitable for exploitation, both as an anti-Spanish base and as a colony yielding precious metal. Moreover the Indians seemed eager to trade. But Drake was again unlucky. The natives, who appear to have been Araucanians, refugees from Spanish rule, mistook the English for Spaniards. Drake and a shore party of eleven, expecting no trouble, were received with a deadly hail of arrows. Two of his men were taken by the enemy and two more were wounded fatally, he himself being badly wounded in the face. Drake's reaction to this incident is again significant: he withdrew rather than attempt to recover the two prisoners, for he 'would rather have beene a patron to defend them [the Indians], then any way an instrument of the least wrong that should have beene done unto them'.[46]

After leaving Mocha, Drake followed the mainland north to about 32°, where he learned of the presence of a well-laden ship in the harbour of Valparaiso fifteen miles south. Two days later he took that prize and sacked the small settlement as well, after which, with the prize, her pilot and his chart in custody, he made leisurely way north some two hundred miles to latitude 30°s. and waited a week at this appointed rendezvous, clearly still hoping to see his lost companions. When a Spanish force attacked a watering party and killed one of the men, he moved further north again to about 28° and there spent a whole month careening and greasing the ship, assembling a pinnace and in general preparing for action. On 19 January 1579 he resumed the northward course and so, having devoted about ten months to his official task of reconnaissance, turned his attention fully and doubtless cheerfully to that unofficial business his promoters expected him to transact – the 'making' of the voyage.

On 5 February he reached Arica (19°s.), taking one valuable prize of silver and coin and burning another. Then, disposing of his prize-ships, he pressed on to Callao, the port of Lima. The dozen or so ships he found in the harbour here were empty, but Drake cut their cables, possibly in the hope that he could seize and exchange them for John Oxenham, whom he now knew to be held prisoner there. The ruse did not work and Drake was reduced to threatening condign revenge should the viceroy harm his friend. At Callao, however, he learned that the *Nuestra Señora de la Concepción*, nicknamed the *Cacafuego* (*Shitfire*), had recently left for Panama with a rich cargo of silver.

Drake did not put in to land in these latitudes – e.g. da Silva's log: Nuttall, *New Light on Drake*, pp. 286–7. Probably Drake's men meant Mocha, mistaking the latitude.
[46] Vaux, *World Encompassed*, p. 99.

Outstripping two ships sent from Callao in pursuit of him, Drake gave chase. Taking two or three lesser prizes on the way, he eventually caught up the *Cacafuego* near Cape San Francisco, just north of the equator. About nine o'clock at night on 1 March he came alongside and ordered her to surrender. The master, San Juan de Antón, replied: 'What old tub is that which orders me to strike sail? Come on board and strike sail yourself.'[47] Hereupon the English opened fire and at the same time boarded from a pinnace which had slipped round to her other side. There was no resistance, for the prize was defenceless. The cargo of silver bars, gold and coin had a value of over 400,000 *pesos* (say £140,000 in contemporary sterling), all of which went into the hold of the *Golden Hind*, while Drake entertained Antón and his crew, whom he released after a few days with handsome gifts.[48]

Drake's main concern now was to get home with the booty. Steering well clear of the Gulf of Panama, he reached the Nicaraguan coast about mid March and there had the good fortune to capture a bark carrying two pilots expert in the Philippines route and equipped with charts and sailing directions. He then moved north again, taking another minor prize, and on 13 April landed at the little Mexican port of Guatulco and sacked the place. He seems to have been anxious to secure plenty of water at this stage, and this was probably the main reason for the attack. He left the port with fifty days' water supply. All this gives the impression that he had now decided to make directly for the Moluccas. One of the Pacific pilots (whom he had meanwhile put ashore) was convinced the English intended to return 'straight to their country by the Molucca route'.[49] But Drake had also now released Nuño da Silva, who was equally convinced that they would look first for the northern strait to the Atlantic and then, if they failed to find it, make for the Philippines.[50] It seems reasonable to conclude from this contradictory evidence that Drake said different things to different people at different times, either because he was unsure which course to take or because he wished to confuse his enemies. In the event the Spanish authorities did nothing at all effective and the *Golden Hind* sailed away unmolested.

The sources do not give us a clear account of the course Drake now followed. Hakluyt's 'Famous Voyage' says that he went north to get a wind for the Moluccas, which hardly makes sense; the so-called 'Anonymous Narrative' describes Drake as 'sayling northwardes till he came to 48. g*rades* of the septentrionall latitud', which would certainly have been impossible in the time, given the prevailing winds; and only

[47] Wagner, *Drake's Voyage*, p. 361.   [48] Nuttall, *New Light on Drake*, pp. 155–79.
[49] Nuttall, *New Light on Drake*, p. 197.   [50] Nuttall, *New Light on Drake*, p. 317.

the *World Encompassed* offers a reasonable statement, namely that he covered 500 leagues in longitude (i.e. westwards) to get a wind and then went north as far as 48°, and it clearly implies that he was looking for signs of a northwest passage: 'though we searched the coast diligently, even unto the 48 deg., yet found we not the land to trend so much as one point in any place towards the East, but rather running on continually North-west as if it went directly to meet with Asia'. The 'Anonymous Narrative' confirms this: 'being afraid to spend long time in seeking for the straite he turned back againe'. Thus Drake probably did sail well into the Pacific and then northwards looking for the passage, which, had it existed in the form envisaged by the more optimistic cartographers of the day, would have provided the shortest and easiest way home. Whether he reached 48°N. is debatable: Hakluyt's 1589 text gives 42° and the maps showing the course of the voyage vary in this respect. Both Hakluyt and the *World Encompassed* say that although it was June the land was covered with snow and that the extreme cold caused him to turn south.[51]

There is no good reason to suppose, however, that Drake had instructions to seek the passage. As we know from the plan of the voyage, he was not expected to return that way, nor by way of the Moluccas. What he told Nuño and some Spanish prisoners about being 'bound to return by the Strait of Bacallaos, which he had come to discover, and that failing to find an exit he was bound to return by China' is not evidence about his mission, but about what he wanted the Spanish authorities to believe.[52] In 1577, it is true, the northwest passage was a matter of great interest in England because Frobisher claimed to have discovered the eastern end only the year before, and Grenville himself had, probably in 1576, advocated exploring the alternative approach, by way of Magellan's Strait and the Pacific.[53] But this indicates only that the idea was available to Drake and his promoters, not that they adopted it as part of their plan. The events of the voyage themselves sufficiently explain why Drake sought the passage: the instruction to return by way of Magellan's Strait had to be waived, not only for the nautical reasons we have observed, but also because by now the Spaniards were fully alerted and might well intercept him.

Having turned south, the *Golden Hind* coasted California until 'wee came within 38. degrees towards the line. In which height it pleased

[51] Vaux, *World Encompassed*, pp. 113–18; Wagner, *Drake's Voyage*, p. 277; *PN*, xi, 118–19; *PN* (1589), pp. 643–4.
[52] Nuttall, *New Light on Drake*, p. 317.
[53] BL, Lansdowne MSS, 100, no. 4.

God to send us into a faire and good Baye'.[54] The location of this bay has given rise to a great deal of controversy, but the question remains unsettled. The best arguments appear to favour Drake's Bay rather than Bolinas Lagoon or San Francisco Bay, the chief rival candidates.[55] In any case Drake chose well: he was safe there from 17 June to 23 July 1579 and well provided with the means to repair his ship, to refresh his men and to replenish his wood, water and victuals. The Indians there belonged to the Coast Miwok tribe and, far from resisting the English, seem to have regarded them with superstitious awe, lacerating themselves and offering what the English took to be sacrifices. Finally the chief and his people performed a ceremony which culminated in the setting of something like a crown on Drake's head, whereupon he, with characteristic opportunism, declared the whole country subject to the queen and named it Nova Albion. He certainly had no intention of creating a settlement then and there, and even a future colony must have seemed a very remote possibility, but a base on that coast would no doubt prove useful if the Strait of Anian, the supposed western exit of the northwest passage, were found to exist.

Leaving the California coast towards the end of July, the *Hind* sailed roughly southwest to catch the trade winds, and then pursued a course somewhat south of west, gradually nearing the line until, after sixty-eight days at sea, the islands of the Palau group, in 7° to 8°N., came into view. These belong to the Caroline Islands in Micronesia, but Drake's men accorded them the unflattering title of 'Islands of Thieves', for the natives, who came out to the ship in hundreds in their canoes, showed an acquisitiveness that soon led to trouble. Eventually the English fired on them, killing about twenty, and withdrew, their visit having lasted only three days.[56] Drake then sailed west as far as Mindanao and then south to the Moluccas, which he sighted on 3 November 1579. He was evidently making for Tidore, where the Portuguese were well established, when fortunately he was diverted to Ternate by a message from the sultan of that island offering trade.

The sultan controlled a number of other islands as well as Ternate and thus disposed of the greater part of the trade in cloves, but he was on bad terms with the Portuguese and seems to have welcomed the opportunity to establish trade with another European nation. Indeed, he offered 'to sequester the commodities and traffique of his whole Iland from others, especially from his enemies the Portugals (from

[54] *PN*, XI, 119.
[55] W. L. Hanna, *Lost Harbor: the Controversy over Drake's California Anchorage* (Berkeley, 1979).
[56] W. A. Lessa, *Drake's Island of Thieves* (Honolulu, 1975).

whom he had nothing but by the sword), and reserve it to the intercourse of our Nation'.[57] He followed this offer with a formal visit to the *Golden Hind*, but he did not actually go aboard, and Drake for his part refused an invitation to go ashore, sending a party of gentlemen in his stead. Relations with the sultan, in fact, were marked by mutual suspicion clothed in ceremonious courtesy. No formal agreement about future trade was reached, for Drake does not appear to have produced letters from the queen, presumably because he had none. Eastern trade was not, after all, an object of the expedition. At best an understanding was arrived at, and Drake, having taken aboard some 6 tons of cloves, departed rather hastily after only five days' stay, seeking a safer place to trim and water his ship.

Within a few days he found a small island near Celebes and having graved and furnished the ship, left there on 12 December, setting course for the Moluccas, which lay on his way homeward. Contrary winds, however, drove the ship off course along the eastern coast of Celebes, where the sea was a maze of islands and dangerous shoals. The ship was nearly through when on the night of 8–9 January 1580 she ran suddenly on a rock and stuck fast until four in the afternoon of the next day. Only by lightening her of 3 tons of cloves, two guns and some other stores were they able, with the aid of a good gale, to float her off. It was a narrow escape – so narrow that Fletcher, thinking they were lost, 'made them a sermon, and they receved the communion all together, and then every theefe reconciled him selfe to his fello theefe'.[58]

This was not the end of Drake's troubles. For the next month they endured bad weather in those strange and difficult seas of the East Indies. Eventually the weather improved and they made their way westwards, probably along the north side of Timor and then south of Java, where they came to anchor on 11 March and stayed a fortnight exchanging commodities and courtesies with the local rajahs. Thereafter the voyage was fairly uneventful. Passing by the Cape of Good Hope and touching Sierra Leone for water and provisions, the *Golden Hind* sailed into Plymouth on 26 September 1580.

Drake's triumphant return and the news of his success in circumnavigating the globe, plundering the Spaniards and making direct contact with the Spice Islands caused a considerable stir in England and elsewhere, but his reception was mixed and his achievement had confusing repercussions. Of course he became a popular hero, but he

[57] Vaux, *World Encompassed*, p. 138.
[58] Vaux, *World Encompassed*, p. 185.

had bitter critics, including not only some who had sailed with him but also the strong body of London merchants who now dominated Anglo-Iberian trade and had much to lose if King Philip chose to confiscate English property in retaliation for acts of piracy. In the event the queen, realizing that Philip was not prepared to make the matter a *casus belli*, stood by her captain and knighted him aboard the *Golden Hind* in April 1581, but at the same time she permitted negotiations for restitution of treasure claimed on behalf of Spanish merchants and some of the booty was in fact restored.[59] Indeed Drake's voyage did not have a decisive effect on international affairs. It occurred at a time when Anglo-Spanish relations were steadily deteriorating for reasons much more fundamental: the Netherlands revolt persisted, driving the two powers apart; the militant forces of the reformation and the counter-reformation tended to polarize the politics of Europe into two camps, led by Elizabeth and Philip respectively; and, more immediately, Spain's strength in Europe and the world at large was apparently magnified by Philip's accession to the throne of Portugal in 1580.

This last event came as no sudden shock: it had been expected since the death of King Sebastian of Portugal in 1578 and the succession of the aged Cardinal Henry. Philip II of Spain was the obvious heir to the throne, having a valid claim and the power to enforce it. His only serious challenger was Dom Antonio, prior of Crato, whose resistance Philip easily crushed in August 1580, after which Dom Antonio fled the country to seek support in France and England. Thus he became, for Catherine de Medici and Elizabeth, a useful pawn in the power game. He would one day be used to head an invasion of the Peninsula itself, but in the meantime they hoped he would focus Portuguese opposition to Spanish rule elsewhere, particularly in the East Indies, the Azores and Brazil. Each area offered inviting prospects, opportunities not only to damage or at least endanger Spain's interests, but also to promote the commerce and oceanic power of her rivals. These large issues of commercial, maritime and political strategy came onto the agenda of Elizabeth's government at approximately the time of Drake's return, which certainly stimulated English maritime ambition in general, but did nothing to give it the specific orientation it badly needed at this juncture. In the next three years English merchants, seamen and gentlemen were to consider a remarkable variety of ambitious enterprises, some of which took shape in action, but none of which succeeded. The occupation of Terceira in the Azores, trade with

---

[59] On the disposition of Drake's booty see Wagner, *Drake's Voyage*, pp. 196–205. As Wagner says, the total amount is not known and a good deal of exaggerated nonsense has been written about it.

Brazil, settlement in North America, completion of the commercial link with the Moluccas – all these ventures, hampered by unsureness of purpose, failed. In particular the South American enterprise projected by Grenville and launched by Drake petered out and was forgotten.

But the manner of this demise is worth considering. It was by no means immediate, nor was it a simple process. In the first place John Winter's return heightened interest in South America. He had spent four months on the east coast on his way back from the Strait and took special care to inspect São Vicente. Relations between ship and shore here were perhaps marred by mutual suspicion, but Winter made valuable contact with an Englishman, John Whithall, who had married the daughter of a rich Genoese sugar planter and had already, in June 1578, written to Richard Staper, Anglo-Iberian trader and promoter of the Turkey trade, proposing direct trade between London and São Vicente. In his letter to Staper, Whithall had called attention to the news 'that they have discovered certaine Mines of silver and gold, and looke every day for Masters to come and open the said Mines: which when they be opened will inrich this countrey very much'.[60] Winter talked with Whithall because, as he said, he wished to 'understande the state of the Countrey and the disposition of the people', and this was no idle curiosity.[61] When he reached England in June 1579 São Vicente took on a new importance in certain circles. The young Hakluyt interviewed Winter's men and thereupon entered the arena of grand strategy with a memorandum calling for the immediate seizure of Magellan's Strait.[62] He warned of the peril that would ensue to all princes of Europe if the king of Spain were suffered to enjoy Portugal with the East Indies and suggested that the Strait of Magellan be taken and fortified, that São Vicente be taken and kept as a supply base for the Strait, and that a further attempt be made to discover the northeast passage beyond the White Sea. Magellan's Strait, he argued,

is the gate of entry into the tresure of both the East and the West Indies. And whosoever is Lord of this Straight may account himselfe Lord also of the West Indies. . . . For the Symerones, a people detesting the prowde governance of the Spanyards, will easely be transported by Drake or others of our nation to the Straights, and there may be planted by hundreds or thowsands . . . for the defense of the Straights. And planting over them a few good English captens, and maintayning in the bayes of the Straights a good navie, there is no doubt but that we shal make subjecte to England all the golden mines of Peru and all

[60] *PN*, xi, 26–30.
[61] Nuttall, *New Light on Drake*, pp. 386–91.
[62] Taylor, *Writings of the Hakluyts*, pp. 139–46.

the coste and tract of that firme of America upon the Sea of Sur. And work the like effect on the hither side of that Firme.

He advised sending a force of pirates to seize and fortify the Strait in the first place, who could do it without 'the countenance of thenglish state', while 'To these Symerons we may add condemned Englise men and women in whom there may be founde hope of amendement'. Hakluyt was not an original thinker and it is likely that in this case his ideas corresponded to those of his informants, chief among whom was one Thomas Griggs, steward of the *Elizabeth* in Winter's voyage. Clearly the concept of an English South American empire was not the exclusive property of the Drake–Hawkins–Winter syndicate. Early in 1580, when the death of the cardinal-king brought matters to a head in Portugal, Hakluyt urged his project once again and offered to go and win Dom Antonio's approval for it.[63]

Meanwhile the Hawkins brothers were preparing to pursue their South American initiative. In January the Spanish ambassador reported that John Hawkins was fitting out three ships, 'the pretence being that they are taking merchandise to the coast of Brazil'. In fact, he added, they were lading trade goods. Next month he again referred to the venture, specifying São Vicente as the destination.[64] What the Hawkinses had in mind is revealed by a draft of letters patent, amended in Walsingham's hand, for 'W. Hawkins being sent to discover new trades'. This granted him rights and powers in connection with 'a voyage which he intendeth with the favour of almighty God to make into the coasts of Africa and America to the south and southwestwards for the better discovery of all trades of merchandises in the said coasts'. He was to have licence also to serve Dom Antonio 'against any his enemies' and to sell the proceeds of such actions in English ports. A clause forbidding any offence to princes in league and amity with her majesty did not disguise the fact that the expedition was designed to combine trade and plunder, and accordingly a reference to instructions to be drawn up by the queen or her council was deleted.[65]

What happened to this project we do not know. There is no further evidence of such an expedition in 1580 and Drake's return in September gave rise to new plans. His own first thought, apparently, was to follow up and exploit his discoveries in the southern hemisphere, for shortly after his return he submitted to the crown 'a project of a

[63] Taylor, *Writings of the Hakluyts*, pp. 163–4.
[64] *Cal. SP Span.* III, 3, 8.
[65] PRO, SP 12/142, fos. 149–52.

corporatyon of soche as shall venteur unto such domynions and contreys sytuate bayonde the equynoctyall line'.[66] The new company was to have monopoly rights in such dominions, in consideration of 'the late notable dyscoverye made by Francys Drake', who was to take 10% of the profits on all goods brought thence into the realm, while the queen was to have one fifth of the profits of gold and silver mines to be discovered there. The proposed corporation was not concerned with the Spice Islands, which in fact lay north of the equator and offered no prospects of precious metals, but evidently and logically with those lands Drake had set out to explore and had spent many months reconnoitring. These were the only lands 'beyond the equinoctial' he could reasonably claim to have 'discovered', and it may be inferred that he contemplated a fresh expedition, probably to the region of Arauco and Mocha.

Drake's intention, however, was obscured by the confusion of competing projects which ensued upon his return. His contact with the Spice Islands led to plans for an expedition to the Far East, which won strong support in the City and at Court. At the same time the earl of Leicester projected a scheme for the seizure of Terceira in the Azores by a powerful fleet under Drake's command in the summer of 1581. When the plans for this were changed in September to include a voyage to the East Indies via the Cape of Good Hope, Drake stood down, and after this neither he nor the Hawkins brothers took an active part in Leicester's project, which finally evolved into the ill-starred expedition led by Captain Edward Fenton in 1582, bound ostensibly for the Spice Islands by the southeastern route. The three Plymouth chiefs did send some of their men with Fenton, but meanwhile they preferred to pursue their own adopted course of trade and plunder beyond the equinoctial.

At the end of 1582 William Hawkins set out for Brazil. The promoters of the venture were William and John Hawkins and Drake, calling themselves collectively 'the company of discovery'. It was a strong expedition of four ships, well fitted for warlike action but also laden with merchandise. The programme indicated in the draft commission of 1580 was at last to be tackled and Drake's projected 'corporation' gave way to the purely private 'company of discovery'. In April 1583 Hawkins reached Santiago in the Cape Verde Islands and there decided not to proceed to Brazil, on the grounds that the year was too far spent, his cask (beer and wine) corrupted and his crew depleted, adding as his last and most telling excuse 'feare of 5. armados, set to

---

[66] Nuttall, *New Light on Drake*, p. 430. The document is in Walsingham's hand.

garde Brasile, as a prise advised'. Instead the fleet went to the Caribbean and returned towards the end of the year with a rich cargo acquired by smuggling, pearl-fishing and piracy.[67]

Those five Spanish warships, the news of which deterred Hawkins from his intended South American voyage, were part of a much larger fleet sent from Spain in December 1581 under the command of Diego Flores de Valdés. This was Spain's reaction to Drake's 'famous voyage', and it was immediately responsible for a decisive check to English ambitions and enterprise in South America beyond the equinoctial. Flores's instructions were to clear the coast of intruders as far as Magellan's Strait and there to establish a large force of soldiers and settlers under Pedro Sarmiento de Gamboa. Sarmiento, on the orders of the viceroy of Peru and in direct response to Drake's arrival in the Pacific, had already conducted a survey of the Strait (December 1579–February 1580), which he now planned to fortify. After setting Sarmiento and his people down, Flores was to proceed through the Strait to Chile and land there an army of 600 men under Alonso de Sotomayor, newly appointed governor of Chile, to pursue the Araucanian war. In addition to these defence measures, a body of eighty settlers sailed from Spain to the River Plate in May 1582 to reinforce Garay's colony, established there in 1580.[68]

Diego Flores arrived at Río de Janeiro in March 1582, wintered there, and set out for the Strait in November. A month later Edward Fenton, commanding two powerful warships – the *Galleon Leicester* and the *Edward Bonaventure* – together with two auxiliary vessels, reached the coast of Brazil. He had orders to make for the Moluccas by way of the Cape of Good Hope, 'not passing by the streight of Magellan, either going or returning, except upon great occasion incident',[69] but these orders he disregarded. On the flimsiest of excuses he changed course off Sierra Leone, making for the River Plate and Magellan's Strait. It is not unlikely that he and some of the promoters had intended this from the start. The decision certainly pleased the strong Hawkins–Drake faction in the fleet, led as it was by William Hawkins, son of that other William whose abiding interest in Brazil we have noted, and by John Drake, commanding his uncle's *Bark Francis*. It did not please the

---

[67] On the ships and investment see E. G. R. Taylor (ed.), *The Troublesome Voyage of Captain Edward Fenton, 1582–1583* (Cambridge, 1959), p. lv, these details being based on BL, Harleian MSS, 167, fos. 201–2; see also J. A. Williamson, *Hawkins of Plymouth* (London, 1949), pp. 219–24.

[68] On Flores and Sarmiento see C. R. Markham (ed.), *Narratives of the Voyages of Pedro Sarmiento de Gamboa* (London, 1895); *PN*, xi, 227–90 (Lopes Vas); and O. H. K. Spate, *The Spanish Lake* (London, 1979), pp. 268–78.

[69] *PN*, xi, 166–7.

factors of the Muscovy merchants who had invested in what they took
to be a trading voyage to the East Indies. But on the American coast in
28°s. the English learned that Flores was on his way to the Strait and
after much anxiety and debate they turned back for São Vicente. John
Drake hereupon slipped away, making for the South Sea and plunder,
but before long wrecked his bark in the Plate estuary and finally fell
into Spanish hands.

Ostensibly Fenton put into São Vicente in January 1583 for victuals
and trade, but the Portuguese refused trade because they feared the
wrath of their new king, Philip II, represented as he was in that vicinity
by a Spanish armada. They also felt threatened by the English galleons,
suspecting quite rightly that Fenton contemplated seizing the place.[70]
The *dénouement* came a few days after the English arrival, when three
Spanish men-of-war came into the harbour. They were a detachment
of Flores's fleet, sent northwards in search of the English when Flores
learned of their presence on the coast. Battle ensued and one of the
Spanish ships was sunk, but the other two withdrew to Santos. The
English could only depart, frustrated. They tried again for trade at
Espirito Santo further north, but were obliged, when news of the battle
reached there, to leave the Brazil coast for good.

These events virtually destroyed the prospect of English trade with
Brazil for many years. In November 1580, in response to John
Whithall's appeal, a group of Londoners had set forth the *Minion* for
São Vicente, emphasizing in their reply to Whithall 'that the just cause
of our comming is to trade as marchants peaceably, and not as Pirats to
commit any offence'.[71] There is no reason to doubt the sincerity of this
statement, but the report on the voyage by Thomas Griggs (Winter's
steward and Hakluyt's informant) shows that some of the English
busied themselves not only with trade but with intelligence, particularly concerning the 'Mines of treasure in these parts', the River Plate
estuary, the routes to Peru and the attitude of the Indians of the interior
to Spanish rule.[72] Griggs moreover concealed the fact that this was an
unhappy voyage. At Santos business was cut short by the intervention
of the religious authorities and subsequently at Bahia more trouble
over religion led to the arrest of some of the crew by the Portuguese.
They were released and the *Minion* made off in haste, but not before an
exchange of shots between ship and shore. Commercially the voyage
was probably a failure, for little trade was done. Two factors remained

[70] Taylor, *Troublesome Voyage*, p. 252; E. S. Donno (ed.), *An Elizabethan in 1582: the Diary of Richard Madox* (London, 1976), pp. 261–8.
[71] *PN*, XI, 32.
[72] *PN*, XI, 34–9.

behind in Bahia with a stock of wares for sale, but their London principals evidently arranged no further voyage to those parts.[73]

The next known Brazil venture was to Olinda in Pernambuco, set forth by a different group of Londoners in 1583. Again trading took place, but the enterprise ended badly after the departure of the ship, when Flores entered the port with his fleet, ordered the arrest of the two remaining English factors, confiscated their goods and sent them in irons to Seville.[74] In 1584–5 some further business was done at Olinda by the same group of merchants, but that was the bitter end of Anglo-Brazilian commerce for the Elizabethan period.[75] The king of Spain's authority had been secured and the Portuguese had learned to distrust the English and their ambiguous approach to Brazil. In 1585 war supervened and the English readily adopted the rôle of predators upon the sugar trade, in which Dutch and Hanseatic carriers filled the place the Londoners had hoped to fill.

The year 1583 marked the end of the English effort to explore and exploit the parts of America from the Tropic of Capricorn southwards. It was from the start an opportunistic enterprise, seeking plunder, trade or conquest as circumstances might permit, an approach which might and did prove advantageous in the first stage of pioneering. But in the second stage lack of direction and divided purposes ruined the continuation and consolidation of the work. Drake's experience of the southerly coasts was not very encouraging, and in respect of South America his voyage was rather an advertisement for the coast of Peru, whereas Winter's publicized the more accessible charms of southern Brazil. Moreover, the incoherence of the South American thrust was compounded by the general incoherence of purpose which overtook the oceanic movement around 1580. Varying geographical objectives and conflicting ambitions of trade and plunder dogged the Fenton venture from its confused gestation throughout its troublesome course until its miserable conclusion. On the other hand the Spanish reaction, though not formidable, played a significant part in scotching this initiative. It was perhaps a foregone conclusion that Iberian power, already well established in the South American continent and having so much at stake, would repel the tentative gropings of the English for a foothold. Flores did put Sotomayor and his men ashore in the River Plate, whence they made their way overland to Chile and continued the Araucanian war. And Sarmiento eventually, in 1584, began the

[73] Willan, *Studies*, pp. 5–10; Andrews, *Elizabethan Privateering*, pp. 201–2.
[74] Willan, *Studies*, pp. 9–10; Andrews, *Elizabethan Privateering*, pp. 205–6.
[75] Andrews, *Elizabethan Privateering*, p. 206; BL, Additional MSS, 14027, fos. 123–6; BL, Lansdowne MSS, 41, no. 44 (Southampton); PRO, E. 190/816/4 (Southampton searcher's book, outwards).

fortification and settlement of Magellan's Strait – yet another heroic episode in Spain's occupation of the New World, and one of the most tragic. Of the 350 people he took there some twenty remained alive when Cavendish passed through in 1587. Two years later Chidley's men found one only. In fact neither Sotomayor nor Sarmiento did much to strengthen Spain's real grip on South America, nor did the occupation of the Plate estuary bolt that door into the continent until much later. Nevertheless the events of 1582–3 were decisive: the English initiative was checked and turned aside by what amounted to a demonstration of force. After 1583 English ships on the southeastern shores of America were privateers, either bound for the South Sea and plunder, like Cumberland's men (1586), Cavendish (1586 and 1591), John Chidley (1589) and Richard Hawkins (1593), or bent on pillaging the trade of Brazil, like Abraham Cocke and James Lancaster (1595). If some of them harboured a residual interest in the area, it did not amount to any serious commercial or colonial intent.[76]

The English adventure beyond the equinoctial was thus a failure. But it had positive side effects: it brought the English into the Pacific, it led to their first contact with the East Indies and it provided the queen with a considerable war chest. Above all, Drake's circumnavigation of the globe greatly inflated English maritime prestige and ambition, which now took a decisive step towards oceanic power and overseas empire. In turn the Caribbean, the Panama Isthmus and the not-so-soft southern under-belly of Peru had been probed. There remained North America, the hopes and plans for which came to the fore as the South American prospects receded.

[76] In 1583 Edward Cotton, a Southampton merchant, promoted a voyage to the River Plate, São Vicente and São Sebastião Island, mainly for seal-hunting, but it came to grief on the coast of Guinea on the way out (*PN*, VI, 408–12); Cocke went to the River Plate with two ships in 1593 and was still on the Brazil coast in 1595; Cumberland's men in 1586 showed some interest in the River Plate; Chidley's venture was expressly intended for 'the famous province of Arauco on the coast of Chili' (*PN*, XI, 381–2). See K. R. Andrews, 'Beyond the Equinoctial: England and South America in the Sixteenth Century', *Journal of Imperial and Commonwealth History*, 10 (1981), 4–24, for further detail.

8

Northwest with Frobisher and Davis

By the reign of Edward VI English geographers were actively interested in the idea of the northwest passage. In the very year of Willoughby's departure Richard Eden expressed the opinion that if the northeast venture failed there remained the Strait of the Three Brothers, 'sufficiently known to such as have any skill in geography',[1] and it may be that an expedition did set forth to find the strait about that time.[2] Even so, it was difficult to get influential and moneyed persons to commit their purses, as Cabot had found in 1521 and again in 1553. After 1555, moreover, northwest projectors had to deal with the Muscovy Company, which obtained exclusive rights of northerly navigation to places not formerly known or frequented by Englishmen. Thus Humphrey Gilbert, the foremost advocate of the northwest passage in the sixties, soon ran into trouble with the vested interest of the company. His initial petition to the queen in 1565 asked for permission to undertake the discovery and for a monopoly of the passage, as did also his and Jenkinson's joint plan of 1566. We do not know why these proposals produced no result, but when at the end of 1566 Gilbert submitted another petition on his own behalf, he showed his willingness to make the discovery under the company's auspices,

---

[1] Sebastian Münster, *A treatyse of the newe India* (trans. Richard Eden, 1553), in E. Arber (ed.), *The First Three English Books on America* (Westminster, 1895), p. 9.

[2] A certain Philip Jones claimed in 1586 that he had sent out an expedition of two ships twenty-three years before, with the encouragement of Richard Chancellor, Robert Recorde and the pilot Pinteado. The fact that Pinteado died in the first Guinea voyage and Chancellor three years later suggests that Jones's expedition actually occurred around 1553 rather than 1563, and Jones's reference to Sebastian Cabot also supports the earlier dating. Jones says that his men 'shott themselves into the gulfe of terra labrathor, and ran farr into that lande, *which* in verie dede is in 60. degrees a lytle lesse towardes our pole Articke, and havinge the same lande on both sides, must nedes retourne the same waie they went in . . . for there is noe passage furder'. It is not surprising that the public never heard of this venture and its discouraging result. BL, Harleian MSS, 167, fos. 106–8.

abandoning his request for a monopoly. But the Muscovy men were still not satisfied. They made it clear that they intended 'to have the rule and orderinge of all discoveries' and would allow Gilbert no privileges that infringed their own. In effect, Gilbert was to carry out his enterprise as a servant of the company or else to give it up. At this point he evidently chose to give it up.[3]

The next to take an initiative in this matter was Martin Frobisher. Nephew of Sir John Yorke, a leading member of the Muscovy Company and a pioneer of the Guinea trade, Frobisher went to sea at fourteen in Wyndham's Guinea voyage and, unlike most of his shipmates, survived. He even went back the next year with Captain John Lok and returned only after having spent nine months a prisoner in Guinea. In 1559–62 he seems to have been involved in the plans for capturing or building a fort on the Gold Coast, and in the next ten years was arrested three or four times for piracy. By the early seventies he was known as a tough and able sea-captain and had made himself useful to the government.[4] Meanwhile, it seems, he had since around 1560 tried in vain to interest sundry merchants in a northwest project and finally found a sponsor in Ambrose Dudley, earl of Warwick. The Muscovy Company at first resisted the request of the Privy Council that it should license Frobisher's venture, but very soon, about the end of 1574, was forced to give way and granted a licence to Frobisher and Michael Lok, their own London agent, jointly. Lok, one of the sons of the London magnate Sir William Lok, had traded and travelled widely, was himself an amateur of cosmography and a northwest passage enthusiast. He now became Frobisher's partner and chief financial backer, whose audited account books and allied explanations reveal in unusual detail the economics of the whole enterprise from its auspicious beginning in 1576 to its inglorious collapse in 1579.[5]

In spite of the Privy Council's approval, subscribers were slow to come forward in 1575, and the promoters had to postpone the first venture until 1576 and to limit it to two small barks and a pinnace instead of the three ships originally envisaged. Lok later attributed this

---

[3] Quinn, *Gilbert*, pp. 6–11, 105–15.

[4] *PN*, VI, 160, 163, 253–7; Blake, *Europeans*, pp. 358–60; K. M. Eliot, 'The first voyages of Martin Frobisher', *EHR*, 32 (1917), 89–92; R. G. Marsden, 'The early career of Sir Martin Frobisher', *EHR*, 21 (1906), 538–44.

[5] PRO, E.164, nos. 35, 36; Huntington Library MSS, no. 715. Extracts are printed in Quinn, *New American World*, IV, pp. 193–200, and in Stefansson and McCaskill, *Three Voyages of Martin Frobisher*, II, pp. 215–23. This work reproduces the valuable documentation first printed in R. Collinson (ed.), *The Three Voyages of Martin Frobisher* (London, 1867), including Lok's writings about the enterprise. Many relevant state papers are published in W. N. Sainsbury (ed.), *Calendar of State Papers Colonial, East Indies, China and Japan, 1513–1616* (London, 1862).

shyness to Frobisher's reputation as a pirate, but by that time he was inclined to blame Frobisher for many adversities; more probably, deep-rooted doubts about the passage persisted. Lok found it necessary to stress alternative or additional prospects: the commodities North America might yield, the English goods it might consume, the fish and train-oil its waters held. He did not yet mention precious metals. The final list of stockholders for the first voyage numbered eighteen: eight eminent courtiers (Burghley, Walsingham, Leicester, Warwick, Sussex, Philip Sidney, Thomas Randolph and Edmund Hogan), six leading Muscovy men, and five others. But the total stock amounted to only £875, which fell far short of the gross outlay of £1613 19s. 3d. and Lok paid the difference out of his own pocket. He even paid Frobisher's debts 'to clere him out of England one the voyage'. These hard financial facts had an important bearing on the later development of the enterprise.

The geographical conception which had inspired Gilbert was expressed by Abraham Ortelius in his world map of 1564, showing America to have a north coast more or less in the latitudes of the British Isles, flanked by a wide northern sea, accessible from the Atlantic by several passages between Greenland, Labrador, Canada and the continent of America. This led towards the Strait of Anian between Asia and America, with Japan not far beyond. Gilbert expounded his views on the northwest passage in a discourse written in 1566, but this was not published until 1576.[6] Lok met him about Easter 1575 and welcomed his book as publicity, but repudiated any suggestion that his enterprise owed anything to Gilbert's ideas. In fact Gilbert's geography was already out of date, for Mercator's world map of 1569 radically revised the earlier picture of the North Atlantic and northeast America, showing the latter stretching continuously north to 74° and introducing major new features derived from the map published in 1558 by Nicolò Zeno. This map, illustrating the apocryphal voyages of Zeno's ancestors, showed various imaginary islands in the North Atlantic, the largest being 'Frisland', lying between 61° and 65°, and a large peninsula called 'Estotiland' jutting eastwards from the American mainland between 61° and 63°. The Mercator map, which Frobisher is known to have used, incorporated these errors and preserved alongside them Ortelius's erroneous placing of the southern end of Greenland in 66° – six degrees north of its true position. The result was a comedy of errors.[7]

[6] Quinn, *Gilbert*, pp. 4–11, 129–68.
[7] The relevant maps are reproduced in W. P. Cummings, R. A. Skelton and D. B. Quinn, *The Discovery of North America* (London, 1971).

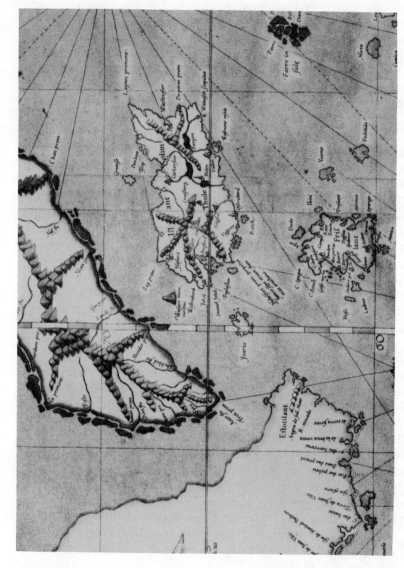

Fig. 4 Section of Mercator's world map of 1569, showing Frisland, Greenland, Estotiland and Iceland. (From Maritiem Museum Prins Hendrik, Rotterdam.)

In the geographical and technical planning of the expedition John Dee took an active part, at the invitation of Sir Lionel Ducket, one of the leading promoters. Dee not only went through the geographical evidence with Lok, Frobisher and others (including Stephen Borough), but undertook to instruct the masters and mariners in the rules of geometry and cosmography and in the use of the more impressive instruments of navigation they carried with them. These comprised some articles better suited to an astrologer's studio than to the cabin of a 30-ton bark in Baffin Bay: a great brass instrument called a 'horologium universale', an 'armilla ptolomei' and so forth. The expedition library bore the same academic stamp: André Thevet's *Cosmographie Universelle* (in French) and his *New found World or Antarctike* (in English), Pedro de Medina's *Regimiento de Navegación* (in Spanish), Mandeville's *Travels*, William Cuningham's *Cosmographical Glasse*, Robert Recorde's *Castle of Knowledge*, a 'Great Bible' and two unspecified French volumes. William Borough presented an astrolabe, gave advice about fitting-out and helped to find the crew, but, as Lok tells us, 'he was not so well perswaded of this enterprise, that he would venter his money therein'.[8]

On 7 June 1576 Frobisher left Ratcliffe in the *Gabriel*, 30 tons, with Christopher Hall master, Nicholas (son of Richard) Chancellor purser and seventeen crew; with him sailed the *Michael*, 30 tons, with a crew of at least twelve, and a 7-ton pinnace carrying three men. From Shetland in 60° they bore west and by north, expecting that course to take them clear north of America to the Strait of Anian. After a fortnight they came to the eastern side of the southern tip of Greenland, lying in 61°, but they of course assumed this to be Frisland, the south side of which according to their main charts lay precisely in that latitude, Greenland being shown far to the north. Longitude did not seriously enter into their calculations, for they were conscious of their own ignorance in that respect. As Hall relates in his journal, ice prevented their landing, but the 'discovery' proved important. In the next voyage it was confirmed that this was the Frisland of the Zeni brothers and afterwards Dee presented the queen with a treatise proving her title thereto. In the third voyage Frobisher went ashore and claimed it for Elizabeth.[9] These events consolidated the concept of

---

[8] Collinson, *Three Voyages of Frobisher*, p. 91. PRO, E.164/35, fos. 8–9. The instruments are listed in R. T. Gunther, 'The great astrolabe and other scientific instruments of Humphrey Cole', *Archaeologia*, 75 (1926), 315–16. Borough supplied an MS chart on which the results of the 1576 voyage were plotted: Waters, *Art of Navigation*, pp. 528–9 and plate 36.

[9] *PN*, VII, 288, 326. The references are to the narrative by George Beste, originally published as *A True Discourse. . .* (London, 1578).

Frisland and associated Frobisher strongly with its discovery. Such was the first act of the geographical comedy.

It was in the neighbourhood of Greenland, in the middle of July 1576, that Frobisher's companions in the *Michael*, 'mistrusting the matter, conveyed themselves privily away from him, and returned home, with great report that he was cast away'.[10] The little pinnace had already gone down in a storm and the *Gabriel* too might have been overwhelmed but for Frobisher's presence of mind and courageous example. And so towards the end of July the *Gabriel*'s men came to what seemed to them a 'land of ice' of 'marvelous great height', the southern end of Baffin Island, which was to be known as 'Meta Incognita'.[11] For some fourteen days they cast about amid towering icebergs and heavy fogs until in 63° they entered the inlet now known as Frobisher Bay and for eight days worked their way northwest. Then Frobisher, according to Lok, climbed a mountain:

and there he saw far the two hed lands at the furdest end of the straiets and no likelyhood of land to the northwards of them and the great open [sea] betwene them, which . . . they judged to be the West Sea, whereby to pas to Cathay and to the East India.[12]

Lok also suggested (and Beste likewise) that the land on the right of the so-called strait was Asia and that on the left America. These large and quite unwarranted claims rested chiefly upon wishful thinking and the knowledge that without something impressive to report there would be no second voyage. Perhaps Lok allowed himself to be deceived by Frobisher; perhaps Frobisher allowed Lok to varnish an otherwise plain tale; in any case an element of collusion is obvious, since neither was a fool.

Meanwhile the English made contact with the Eskimo. Inside the bay a number of kayaks approached the *Gabriel* and then retired ashore, whereupon Hall joined them and soon induced nineteen Eskimo to come aboard. But this promising beginning was ruined by a disastrous incident the next day, when five of Frobisher's men, escorting one of the Eskimo ashore, were apparently taken prisoner, together with their boat. Frobisher did his best to recover them by capturing one of the natives and trying to exchange hostages, but the ruse failed and he had no option but to head for home minus his boat and almost a third of his crew. On 27 August the *Gabriel* passed out of

---

[10] *PN*, VII, 279.

[11] *PN*, VII, 320: 'hir Maiestie named it very properly Meta Incognita, as a marke and bounds utterly hitherto unknown'.

[12] Collinson, *Three Voyages of Frobisher*, p. 83.

the bay and after surviving another terrible storm reached Harwich on 2 October with her men in a state of exhaustion.

Seven days later they entered London in triumph, displaying on their bowsprit a globe bought by Michael Lok for the occasion,[13] and 'bringing with them their strange man and his bote, which was such a wonder onto the whole city and to the rest of the realm that heard of yt, as seemed never to have happened the like great matter to any mans knowledge'.[14] The Eskimo made excellent publicity, especially because his Tartar-like features suggested the mysterious Orient, but he died shortly of a cold. Hereupon it was decided to embalm his body and send it back to his country, but for some reason this arrangement was abandoned in favour of burial in England. In the meantime Lok took great pains to have a likeness recorded. He hired a Dutch engraver to take a death mask and the Dutch painter Cornelis Ketel made 'a great picture of the whole body of the strange man in his garments' for the queen, and a similar one for the Muscovy Company, with another depicting him in English dress and yet another naked, in addition to two small pictures of his head.[15] An important object of the subsequent expeditions was to find out more about these strange people.

But the main object was something even more intriguing: gold. Frobisher brought back from the new land a piece of black stone, which Lok caused three different experts to assay. They declared it to be marcasite and to contain no metal, but in January 1577 Lok tried an Italian goldsmith, one Agnello, who claimed that the ore was rich in gold. Lok then revealed the secret to the queen by letter. Walsingham replied sceptically on the queen's behalf that he thought it 'but an alchemist matter' and he sent specimens of the stone to other experts, who all failed to find gold. There followed a protracted negotiation in which Lok sought to involve the crown while Walsingham continued to express doubts and Agnello offered to buy ore at £30 a ton, though the promise was not backed by sureties. These manoeuvres continued through January, February and March, during which time the news of a North American gold mine leaked out, with the predictable result that, in Beste's words:

the hope of more of the same golde ore to be found kindled a greater opinion in the hearts of many to advance the voyage againe. Whereupon preparation was made for a new voyage against the yere following, and the captaine more

---

[13] PRO, E.164/35, fo. 14.
[14] Collinson, *Three Voyages of Frobisher*, p. 87.
[15] E. G. R. Taylor, 'The voyages of Martin Frobisher', *Geographical Journal*, 91 (1938), 360–3. Ketel's paintings, some of which were shown to Eskimo in Meta Incognita, are lost. He also painted Lok, Frobisher, Hall and the *Bark Gabriel*.

specially directed by commission for the searching more of this golde ore than for the searching any further of the passage.[16]

Lok's own story suggests that the responsibility for this gold-rush was largely his. He it was who insisted on the validity of Agnello's findings, and it was his faith which seems to have moved the queen to invest in spite of Walsingham's doubts. Whether his faith was good or bad it is difficult to say. It was convenient for him thus to obtain a large capital stock sufficient to clear his charges on the first voyage and to provide for a second, and it is hard to believe that so capable and intelligent a businessman achieved this without careful contrivance. But Frobisher's charges – that he constructed false accounts, put no money of his own into the enterprise and was in short a bankrupt knave – were not justified. Lok's accounts were officially audited and in nearly all respects accepted. They show that he did invest large sums of his own and his family's and that he lost heavily. Perhaps he deceived himself as well as others.[17]

In March 1577 Lok launched a new company, called the Company of Kathai, to manage the whole business of discovery and exploitation. It was never endowed with the charter and extensive privileges he sought, but it served as a means of mobilizing capital.[18] New subscribers, chiefly from the Court and headed by the queen, raised the total investment to £5150, a sum which roughly met the deficit on the first voyage and the cost of the second. This was a much larger expedition: the queen's ship *Aid*, of 200 tons, together with the *Gabriel* and the *Michael*, carried 134 men, and the flagship's company included eleven gentlemen, twenty soldiers, three goldfiners, eight miners from the Forest of Dean and a party of convicts. Six of these last were to be landed to reconnoitre Frisland, Frobisher's orders being 'to do your best to speak with them in your return'. A bleak future was implied, but fortunately for them the convicts were discharged at Harwich when Frobisher realized he had too many people aboard.[19] Otherwise his instructions were to set the miners and others digging at a suitable site in Meta Incognita, leaving the *Aid* to receive the ore and using the two barks to explore westwards. Incidentally he should try to recover his five lost men and should bring back several Eskimo, including a few youngsters to be educated in England.[20] The enterprise now had not only a different purpose but a different complexion: one Edward

[16] *PN*, VII, 283.
[17] Collinson, *Three Voyages of Frobisher*, pp. 91–102, 359, 363. Stefansson and McCaskill, *Three Voyages*, II, pp. 119–51, 248–52.
[18] Collinson, *Three Voyages of Frobisher*, pp. 111–15.
[19] *PN*, VII, 284–6; PRO, E.164/35; Collinson, *Three Voyages of Frobisher*, pp. 103–10.
[20] Collinson, *Three Voyages of Frobisher*, pp. 117–20.

Fenton, the earl of Warwick's man, went captain of the *Gabriel*; one Gilbert Yorke, the Lord Admiral's man, commanded the *Michael*; George Beste, lieutenant to Frobisher, was Hatton's man; Dionyse Settle, who wrote a report on the voyage, was the earl of Cumberland's man. But the gentlemen were no drones: they pulled their weight at the capstan when necessary, and some of them used their intelligence and education to gain for Europe, from what would otherwise have been a futile exercise, a little knowledge, crude but new, of an alien culture.[21]

Leaving late in May and proceeding by way of the Orkneys and Greenland, where once again they were unable to get ashore, Frobisher and his men sighted Baffin Island on 16 July and after some delay, caused by ice, bore into the 'strait', landed and took formal possession of the country. Soon after this they settled down to the main task of mining and lading rock. Nothing was done to explore beyond the immediate neighbourhood of Frobisher Bay and after three weeks of hard labour the ships made for home, bearing nearly 200 tons of worthless rock.

Meanwhile Englishmen and Eskimo resumed their tentative and unhappy relationship. The first step was to lure the natives into contact by a form of silent trade. The English laid their goods on the ground and departed, after which the Eskimo approached, took what they wanted and left goods of their own in exchange. At length two of them put down their weapons and came to Frobisher and Hall, also unarmed. They exchanged presents. Then at an agreed signal the two seamen grabbed the others, but were unable to capture them. Joined by their fellows, the Eskimo chased them back to their boats and wounded Frobisher in the backside with an arrow. The English counter-attacked and captured one of them. Later a party of the English, believing they were on the track of their lost companions, attacked an Eskimo group, killed several and took prisoner a woman with her baby, incidentally wounding the baby. The visitors of course blamed the natives for such mishaps and hardened their hearts against those 'crafty villains'. They wanted to trade with them and to convert them to the true religion and they would brook no opposition. When the Eskimo resisted attempts to kidnap them, the intruders became hostile and contemptuous, determined to teach them a lesson. At the same time their curiosity, though tinged with disgust and a tendency to ridicule, remained intense. They showed their male prisoner pic-

[21] Settle's report was published in English (1577), French (Geneva, 1578), German (Nürnberg, 1580) and Latin (Nürnberg, 1580). See also Stefansson and McCaskill, *Three Voyages*, II, pp. 226–7.

tures of the Eskimo who had died in England and they watched the behaviour of the man and woman together. They described the Eskimo's clothing, weapons, boats and way of life as best they could. In all probability the artist John White, famous for his Roanoke pictures, sailed in this expedition. He made fine studies of the captive man and the woman with her child and he vividly recorded the skirmish mentioned above.[22]

Communication was of course a fundamental difficulty. Hall appended a number of Eskimo words, with their supposed English equivalents, to his journal of the first voyage, and Beste implies that the captives were taken 'for the use of language'. Unfortunately they did not survive to perform this function: within a month of their arrival in Bristol the man, woman and child were all dead. For the time being this was the end of any effective contact between the two peoples, for the third and last voyage achieved nothing in this respect. In the end the English came away with by no means wholly antipathetic feelings towards the country and its inhabitants. Beste, it is true, concluded by finding 'nothing that may be to delight in, either of pleasure or of account, only the show of a mine', and calling the Eskimo 'those base, cruel and man-eating people', but his detailed description of them showed considerable respect and he noted that the captives grew 'more civill, familiar, pleasant, and docible amongst us in a very short time'. Furthermore Meta Incognita, if thoroughly explored, would make England both rich and happy. It must have been a confusing experience for him and his companions.

After the return of the second expedition in September 1577 came the trial and processing of the ore. All through that winter Lok and his experts fed the government with promises, delaying the moment of truth. Independent assayers rejected their claims, but in March a new voyage was authorized. In May fifteen vessels left the Thames, with instructions to lade ore and to leave a colony of a hundred men to hold the country, to search inland and to explore the passage. Frobisher was permitted to use two barks to investigate the strait a further fifty or one hundred leagues, on condition that he rejoined the main fleet to bring it home. This was by far the hardest of the three voyages, an exhausting test of endurance and seamanship. They found the approaches to Meta Incognita choked with pack ice. Icebergs continually endangered the ships and soon after their arrival the 100-ton bark *Dennys* struck an iceberg and sank in sight of the entire fleet. Her men were saved, but part of the prefabricated house intended for the colony went down

[22] P. Hulton and D. B. Quinn, *The American Drawings of John White* (2 vols., London and Chapel Hill, 1964).

with her.[23] Throughout July and August the ships battled with storms and heavy ice.

Much of the time fog made matters worse, but it was also responsible for Frobisher's most remarkable discovery: that of the so-called Mistaken Straits, better known to later generations as Hudson Strait. This lay immediately to the south of Meta Incognita, and it is not surprising that, prevented by fog and snow from observing either latitude or landmarks, Frobisher found himself swept by a swift current into a Strait hitherto unnoticed. In fact it was far more impressive than the one he knew, as Beste reported:

And truely it was wonderfull to heare and see the rushing and noise that the tides do make in this place, with so violent a force that our ships lying a hull were turned sometimes round about even in a moment after the maner of a whirlepoole, and the noyse of the stream no lesse to be heard afarre off then the waterfall of London Bridge.[24]

The fleet entered the Mistaken Straits on 7 July. On the tenth four vessels, having lost sight of the rest, turned back, but Frobisher induced the main body to press on sixty leagues and more westwards. Had he not carried responsibility for the fleet as a whole, including the freighters and their intended precious cargoes, 'he both would and could', he avowed, 'have gone through to the South Sea'.[25] After nine days, however, he turned back and resumed the main business of the voyage – mining. He abandoned the idea of occupying the country, but used what materials were left to build a little house of lime and stone to test the effect of the weather in the coming winter. Inside it, 'the better to allure those brutish and uncivill people to courtesie', such tokens of English civilization as he could spare were left: bells, knives, pictures, looking-glasses and an oven with baked bread.[26]

The visitors then departed, nor did they ever learn what sense or use the Innuit made of the objects so laden with cultural significance, for they never saw Meta Incognita again. Frobisher's seamanship got the

---

[23] *PN*, VII, 329–31.   [24] *PN*, VII, 334.

[25] *PN*, VII, 336. Hall's log, however, suggests that Frobisher recognized his mistake only later, and that at the time he violently contested Hall's assertion that the strait was 'mistaken': *Cal. SP Colonial (1513–1616)*, pp. 38–40.

[26] Remnants of this structure and other traces of the Frobisher expeditions were found in 1861–2 by the American explorer Charles Francis Hall. The artefacts he collected then have since disappeared, but are described by him in Collinson, *Three Voyages of Frobisher*, pp. 367–74. Hall also reported that the local Innuit had inherited some traditional information about the Frobisher episode, including a story that the five captured Englishmen lived through the winter with the Eskimo and then built themselves a large boat, in which they sailed away. Another expedition visited the site in 1927, confirming Hall's findings: Stefansson and McCaskill, *Three Voyages*, II, pp. 240–7.

fleet home through stormy weather without heavy loss or mutiny, but in London he found the bubble collapsing. Lok had already been obliged in August to submit accounts of the three voyages for official audit, and Frobisher now insisted on a second audit. By the end of the year Lok's charges upon the adventurers had risen to £20,345, over two thirds of this being for outlays on the last voyage and the processing plant at Dartford. Many of the investors understandably resisted these demands, but they had by this time paid up £17,630 6s. 8d. and in January 1579 the wages of those who had served in the third voyage were for the most part settled. The outstanding debts of the company stood at £3658 14s. 3d. in October 1580.

Michael Lok complained bitterly that he was left to face his creditors alone and there is no doubt that he burned his fingers badly. Although born into the merchant aristocracy, he had never been a very wealthy man. He seriously overreached himself in this extraordinary adventure and evidently remained in some financial difficulty for a long time thereafter. But he was not ruined. When he told the auditors that he had turned all his goods into the stones at Dartford and left himself a house full of children 'which maye begge their bread yf the stones at Dartford be but stones', he was still in possession of substantial company funds on his own admission and he continued in business as a merchant for many years. More serious to him, perhaps, was the loss of reputation he suffered, for among the general public at least he became something of a scapegoat. Even so, he was not disgraced in official quarters, nor did he lose the respect of those who knew him well, notably John Dee and Richard Hakluyt the younger. Indeed Hakluyt, with his customary good sense and humanity, paid tribute to Lok in 1582 as 'a man for his knowledge in divers languages and especially in Cosmographie, able to doe his country good, and worthie in my judgement, for the manifold good partes in him, of good reputation and better fortune'.[27]

This remarkable testimonial occurs in Hakluyt's *Divers Voyages* (1582), where he published a map designed by Lok and dedicated to Philip Sidney, a map which is itself sufficient evidence of its author's geographical learning. It was in fact the best contemporary attempt to assess the geographical significance of Frobisher's explorations.[28]

[27] Hakluyt, *Divers Voyages*, p. 11; PRO, e.164/35, fos. 100–9, 138, 149; Collinson, *Three Voyages of Frobisher*, pp. 319–63.

[28] Lok's map is discussed in D. B. Quinn, *Richard Hakluyt, Editor* (Amsterdam, 1967), pp. 19–26. Beste, *A True Discourse*, included two crude maps, one of Frobisher's discoveries and the other a small world map. Dee drew a map of North America in 1580 (*PN*, viii, 486) and a simplified circumpolar chart in 1582 (Cumming, Skelton and Quinn, *North America*, p. 177).

Covering America and the Atlantic from the North Pole to 20°N., it showed, north of the heavily emphasized 'Mare de Verrazana', the western coast of America reaching northeast to Frobisher's strait in 61° to 63°. This lay north of 'R. Elizabeth' (Labrador) and south of the large island of 'Lok' (Meta Incognita), providing an easy passage between Atlantic and Pacific. The southern point of 'Frisland' is shown in 59°, but its northern coast is left undefined, while Greenland is rendered according to Mercator, with its southern cape on the Arctic Circle. Highly speculative even by contemporary standards, Lok's map gives an extraordinarily crude and inaccurate outline of the coast Frobisher discovered, and in this it no doubt reflects the latter's failure to produce (or at least to deliver) an adequate chart. Nevertheless Lok did locate the strait and its neighbourhood in the region of North America and so did better than the map-makers of succeeding generations. Their mistake arose from the second act of the geographical comedy, the northwest enterprise of John Davis.

John Davis, a sea-captain of Sandridge, near Dartmouth, was one of the finest navigators of his day and an expert explorer in the scientific tradition of Chancellor and the Borough brothers. His treatise on the northwest passage, entitled *The Worldes Hydrographical Discription* (1595) and including an account of his own voyages, indicates his deep interest in geography, while his handbook of navigation, *The Seamans Secrets* (1594), quickly became a standard work.[29] Such was his reputation as a mariner that in 1598 the Zeeland firm of Moucheron hired him as chief pilot for their East India voyage under Cornelis de Houtman and in 1600 the English East India Company appointed him pilot-major of their first expedition. Finally he sailed as pilot in Sir Edward Michelborne's East India venture of 1604–6, in the course of which he was killed by Japanese pirates.

Davis, born about 1550, was a neighbour and friend of the Gilberts, especially of Adrian, younger brother of Sir Humphrey, and he and Adrian were already in 1579 associated with John Dee, probably in occult experiments. In September 1580 Dee obtained rights of discovery northward of 50° from Sir Humphrey, whose patent of 1578 permitted him to make such assignments. Probably Dee, Davis and Adrian discussed plans for a northwest passage venture in the years 1580–82, but the first evidence of such planning dates from 1583, when the three of them discussed the project with leading Muscovy men.

[29] Both works were republished in A. H. Markham, *The Voyages and Works of John Davis the Navigator* (London, 1880), which volume provides most of the material for the following account.

The company, however, did not pursue the project and Dee removed himself abroad in September, leaving as principal promoter Adrian Gilbert, who in the next year obtained for himself and his associates a patent to seek a passage to China and the Moluccas by way of the northwest, the northeast or the north.[30] These associates, according to John Janes, author of accounts of two of the three voyages, consisted of 'Certaine Honourable personages and worthy Gentlemen of the Court and Countrey, with divers worshipfull Marchants of London and of the West Countrey', among whom William Sanderson, a London merchant, was 'the greatest adventurer with his purse'.[31] Ralegh was one of the gentlemen interested and we may guess the identity of others from the place-names Davis invented for his discoveries,[32] but the launching of the enterprise depended above all, as Davis gratefully acknowledged, upon 'the honourable care and some charge of Syr Francis Walsingham'.[33]

In June 1585 Davis set forth in the *Sunneshine* and *Moonshine*, barks of 50 and 35 tons respectively, taking what he describes as a 'northerly course' and so 'fell upon the shore which in ancient time was called Groenland'. Coasting southwards, he found the southern cape in 60° and named it Cape Desolation. He then pursued the western shore northwards to 64° 15' and brought his ships into one of the many inlets, calling it Gilbert's Sound.[34] Here he established friendly relations with the Eskimo – 'a very tractable people, voyde of craft or double dealing, and easie to be brought to any civilitie or good order: but wee judge them to bee Idolaters and to worship the Sunne'.[35] After a few days he set sail again northwest seeking the strait and made landfall at the point of Baffin Island on the Arctic Circle, which he named Cape Dyer. He then followed that coast south and entered Cumberland Sound for

[30] For detail on the genesis of Gilbert's project see Quinn, *Gilbert*, pp. 96–100, 483–9.
[31] Markham, *Voyages and Works of Davis*, p. 1.
[32] The persons Davis thus commemorated were, apart from those already mentioned, Sir Edward Dyer, the earl of Cumberland, John Chidley, Lord Lumley, the earl of Warwick, Edward Darcie, the earl of Bedford and the merchants of London, Exeter and Totnes.
[33] Markham, *Voyages and Works of Davis*, p. 205.
[34] Probably the site of the modern Godthåb.
[35] Markham, *Voyages and Works of Davis*, p. 8. In the second voyage, however, Anglo-Eskimo relations were less cordial. Davis at one point lost patience with the Greenlanders, whom he described as 'marvellous theevish' and fired on them, though evidently no harm resulted and friendship was restored. Later, however, the second bark of the expedition came to Gilbert's Sound and bloodshed occurred, though at first the reception was friendly enough, for the Eskimo 'did weave us on shore to play with them at the foot-ball, and some of our company went on shore to play with them, and our men did cast them downe as soone as they did come to strike the ball'. Markham, *Voyages and Works of Davis*, p. 36.

a distance of thirty or forty leagues.[36] This was encouraging, and after some further reconnoitring of the nearby coasts, Davis returned home. He had achieved a great deal more in one voyage than Frobisher had in three: he had clearly and correctly identified Greenland, demonstrating both its southerly extent and its relationship to northeastern America.

The second and third voyages, in 1586 and 1587, confirmed, extended and elaborated these discoveries.[37] Up the western coast of Greenland Davis forced his way as far as 72° in 1587, naming that place Hope Sanderson. Thence he made west for the American coast, but ran into pack ice and northerly winds and so came again to the Cumberland Peninsula, having observed to starboard 'a great sea, free, large, very salt and blew, and of unsearcheable depth' – a clear view of Baffin Bay. This time he reached the bottom of Cumberland Sound and then, further south, 'passed by a very greate gulfe, the water whirling and roring, as it were the meetings of tides'. This phenomenon, charted by Davis as 'A furious over fall',[38] marked the mouth of Hudson Strait, but he had no opportunity to explore the matter further and recorded it as an inlet or gulf. His hopes rested upon the far north, as he told Sanderson after his return: 'I have bene in 73 degrees, finding the Sea all open, and forty leagues betweene land and land. The passage is most probable, the execution easie, as at my comming you shall fully know.'[39]

Davis was an optimist. In the event this was the last of the northwest passage ventures until the next century, for 'by reason of the Spanish fleet, and unfortunate time of M. Secretarie's death, the voyage was omitted and never sithins attempted'.[40] Sufficient reasons, no doubt, but it is worth noting also that after the second venture most of the merchants had withdrawn their support, even though that second voyage had revealed excellent fishing grounds. Davis's performance could hardly have been bettered at that time, but it did not prevent men asking, as he himself put it: 'Why hath not Davis discovered this passage being thrise that wayes imploied?'[41]

Nevertheless Davis achieved an enormous step forward in

---

[36] His own statement. Janes says sixty leagues: Markham, *Voyages and Works of Davis*, pp. 11, 207.

[37] Markham, *Voyages and Works of Davis*, pp. 15–48, 207–10.

[38] See the reproduction of the globe in R. A. Skelton, *Explorers' Maps* (London, 1958), p. 122. Davis described this discovery in his log of the third voyage, from which it is clear that this was the mouth of Hudson Strait, though he thought it an inlet or gulf and mapped it as such: Markham, *Voyages and Works of Davis*, p. 56.

[39] Markham, *Voyages and Works of Davis*, p. 59.

[40] Markham, *Voyages and Works of Davis*, p. 210.

[41] Markham, *Voyages and Works of Davis*, p. 211.

European knowledge of the northwest and effectively started the continuous scientific exploration of that region. His charts have not survived, but their substance was incorporated in the terrestrial globe designed by Emery Molyneux and completed at Sanderson's expense in 1592. Davis and Molyneux had known each other long before the voyages and must have collaborated on the delineation of the northwest Atlantic. The globe shows 'Fretum Davis' between Greenland and North America, and gives each side of the strait its new nomenclature. The southern end of Greenland, however, is rendered as an island, separated from the main part of Greenland by 'Forbishers straytes', with Frobisher's discoveries adjacent. Frobisher's work was thus displaced, and the explanation of this curious error is to be found on the same globe, which displays to the east a prominent 'Frislant'. Davis and Molyneux accepted Frobisher's discovery of Frisland, not realizing that his Frisland was Greenland. Consequently they concluded that his next landfall to the west was Greenland, since they now knew that Greenland extended to the sixtieth parallel. Frobisher, they declared, had never reached America. We do not know what Frobisher made of that, though Davis and Molyneux might reasonably have expected an explosion, knowing his temper. Their verdict, moreover, was duly adopted in Edward Wright's world map published by Hakluyt in 1600, since this was based upon the globe, and this misconception of Frobisher's experience persisted until the nineteenth century, when Captain Hall discovered the actual remains of his presence on Baffin Island.[42]

[42] This geographical misunderstanding was first properly explained in M. Christy, *The Silver Map of the World* (London, 1900), pp. 26–36 and plate 10. On the Molyneux globe see H. Wallis, 'The first English globe: a recent discovery', *Geographical Journal*, 117 (1951), 277–90; and H. Wallis, 'Further light on the Molyneux globes', *Geographical Journal*, 121 (1955), 304–11.

9

Gilbert's ventures

Humphrey Gilbert, born probably in 1537, was the second son of Otho Gilbert of Greenway, near Dartmouth, and Katherine, daughter of Philip Champernowne. Katherine had five children by this marriage, including John, the eldest, and Adrian, and she afterwards married the Devonshire gentleman Walter Ralegh, by whom she had two sons, Carew and Walter. The Gilberts and Raleghs were related to many of the West Country landed families: the Champernownes, the Carews, the Drakes, the Grenvilles, the Chidleys and others. Katherine's brother, Sir Arthur Champernowne, became vice-admiral of Devon, a powerful figure among the Protestant, seafaring gentry throughout the third quarter of the century. Humphrey's step-father Walter Ralegh had first married the daughter of an Exmouth merchant. A shipowner, he traded to Bordeaux and Spain, and together with his sons by that marriage took to privateering and piracy in the wars of the forties and fifties, holding the deputy vice-admiralship of Devon in the later years of Queen Mary. Born into this milieu of aggressive maritime enterprise, Gilbert had the good fortune to be recommended to the princess Elizabeth by his aunt, Katherine Ashley, Elizabeth's governess, while still a young man of seventeen or eighteen and so entered her household a few years before she ascended the throne. His first important service came in 1562, when he led a company of foot in the English expedition to Havre, where he was wounded, returning to England upon the collapse of that enterprise in 1563.[1]

It must have been about this time that he became interested in the New World. The French attempt to colonize Florida began in 1562 and Jean Ribault arrived in England in 1563, publishing his account of the expedition in the same year.[2] Among those in London who now began

---

[1] Quinn, *Gilbert*, pp. 1–4; M. J. G. Stanford, 'The Raleghs take to the sea', *Mariner's Mirror*, 48 (1962), 18–35; W. G. Gosling, *The Life of Sir Humphrey Gilbert* (London, 1911), pp. 10–35.
[2] J. Ribault, *The whole and true discoverye of Terra Florida* (London, 1563).

to take notice of America and its prospects, Gilbert was certainly to the fore, but it was the northwest passage that occupied his attention chiefly at first, as we have seen, and when the Muscovy Company frustrated his efforts in that connection he turned to Ireland. Here Sir Henry Sidney, having become Lord Deputy in 1565, was engaged in suppressing the rebellion of Shane O Neill during the next two years, while at the same time he sought to persuade the government to adopt a forward policy for the more effective subjection of Ireland to English rule. His scheme included provision for the development of English colonies by private enterprise, notably in Ulster and Munster, and Gilbert, who in 1566 led a company of soldiers to Ulster to serve in the campaign against O Neill, quickly associated himself with the proposal of Sir Arthur Champernowne and some other gentlemen of Devon to plant a colony there, with the assistance of Bristol and London merchants hoping to exploit the fish and timber resources of the region. This idea came to nothing when it became clear that crown support was not forthcoming, but for Gilbert it was the beginning of a strong and enduring attachment to colonial enterprise in both Ireland and America.[3]

In 1569, probably in association with West Country men who had espoused the Ulster project, he joined forces with Sir Warham St Leger and Richard Grenville, who had recently begun to settle people in the neighbourhood of Cork Harbour. Their joint aim evidently was to develop the colonization of Munster on a large scale, to monopolize the fishing of the entire coast from the town of Ross to Blasket Sound, and to exploit the timber and other resources of the province as a corporation under the crown. It was an ambitious project, dependent upon the approval of the government, which was expected to assist the adventurers to conquer and confiscate the lands of the Gaelic Irish in return for rents and dues – to accrue later. The crown would also gain, they argued, the security of the region and of Ireland in general against rebels and foreign invaders, in particular the Spaniards, who would be driven out of the trade and fishing of the coast. During 1569, however, before terms could be settled with the government, the people of Munster gave their own answer to that argument by rising in rebellion, and the infant colony of Grenville and St Leger was destroyed.

Gilbert himself played a prominent part in the suppression of this rebellion. As colonel of the army in Munster he was in command of the operations, and conducted them with such ferocity and such contempt for the Irish as to shock even those accustomed to the brutality of warfare at that time. He deliberately killed women and children along

[3] Canny, *Elizabethan Conquest of Ireland*, pp. 66–76. Quinn, *Gilbert*, pp. 12–14.

with their men and laid waste the land in order to cause famine. He cut off the heads of his dead enemies and formed a lane of heads to the door of his tent, so that all his prisoners should pass through that lane, which, wrote Thomas Churchyard, brought 'great terror to the people when they saw the heads of their dead fathers, brothers, children, kinsfolk, and friends lie on the ground before their faces'.[4] The same writer relates that Gilbert 'thought his Dogges eares to good, to heare the speeche of the greateste noble manne emongest them', and Gilbert himself boasted to Sidney:

I slew all those from time to time that did belong to, feed, accompany, or maintain any outlaws or traitors; and after my first summoning of any castle or fort, if they would not presently yield it, I would not afterwards take it of their gift, but won it perforce, how many lives soever it cost, putting man, woman, and child of them to the sword.[5]

Gilbert continued to plan the formation of settlements in Munster until 1573, but without success. Such projects, like that of 1569, required large investment to cover the initial cost and could not obtain it without the wholehearted support of the crown. But the queen and her advisers had serious reservations, doubting the ability of the projectors to carry through their plans and fulfil their obligations, and fearing also the disturbance such a revolution in landownership would cause. Other schemes for English colonies in Ireland were afoot in the years down to 1576, and all of them failed. Sir Thomas Smith's grand concept of a colony in the Ards Peninsula envisaged something like an ancient Roman city in a barbarian land, the inhabitants of which would become a subject race like the Indians of Mexico, tilling the soil for English masters. Eventually in 1572 Smith had to launch his settlement on a much reduced scale and was able to maintain it little more than two years.[6] In 1573 Walter Devereux, earl of Essex, undertook to colonize Antrim. With the backing of the queen, who lent him £10,000 (taking as security the mortgages of most of his lands), he mobilized many of the former projectors, including Sir Arthur Champernowne, Sir Peter Carew and Sir Warham St Leger. But the impressive expedition he led to Antrim was soon wholly engaged in fruitless and bitter fighting. The colonizing venture thus turned into a hopeless war, for which the queen had to provide more funds, though with her usual

---

[4] Thomas Churchyard, *A generall rehearsall of warres, called Churchyardes choise* (London, 1579), cited in Quinn, *Elizabethans and the Irish*, p. 128, and Quinn, *Gilbert*, p. 17.

[5] Chope, 'New light on Grenville', p. 214.

[6] Canny, *Elizabethan Conquest of Ireland*, pp. 85–8; D. B. Quinn, 'Sir Thomas Smith (1513–1577) and the beginnings of English colonial theory', *Proceedings of the American Philosophical Society*, 89 (1945), 543–60.

reluctance, and in which Francis Drake and John Norris distinguished themselves by slaughtering the entire population of Rathlin Island in 1575. The death of Essex the following year brought a welcome end to this bloody and futile adventure and indeed to a whole phase of unsuccessful colonial experiment in Ireland.[7]

Gilbert meanwhile was occupied with other matters. In 1572 he commanded a force of English volunteers sent unofficially by the government to support the Dutch rebels. It was a mission of responsibility, requiring diplomatic tact and discretion as well as military skill, all of which qualities he conspicuously lacked. He presumably owed the appointment to the confidence he enjoyed at Court, confidence he seems to have retained despite his poor performance in this campaign and his growing reputation for unreasoning conduct and violent fits of rage. He does not appear to have been one of the 'gentlemen of the west parts' who subscribed to Grenville's South American project in 1574, though he could hardly have been unaware of their plans, especially since his uncle Champernowne was identified by Spanish intelligence as Grenville's chief partner.[8] Nor did he play any significant part in the Lok–Frobisher northwest enterprise of 1576–8, though he did discuss the project with Lok and did not stand in the way of the publication of his own *Discourse* on the passage in 1576. In 1577, however, appear the first indications that he contemplated striking at Spain in America.

In August of that year Henry Killigrew wrote from London to William Davison in Holland that Gilbert was in Devon, ready to sail and that some thought he would relieve 'one oxenden now in Perow that hath 150,000 li in gold but he hath no shipping nor meanes to bring yt thence'.[9] Although by then out of date, this was a true description of Oxenham's predicament in Panama, and it is also true that Gilbert was then in Devon, but if the latter did think of rescuing Oxenham and his loot he must have changed his mind, for in fact he sailed nowhere. In November of that year, however, shortly before Drake's departure for Magellan's Strait, when the queen's displeasure with her brother Philip was intense, he drew up for her eyes two papers suggesting how she might 'annoy' (viz. injure) the king of Spain.[10]

In both of these he laid great stress on the religious antagonism between Spain and England and the likelihood of war. To damage Spain's power he proposed, in the first place, that under colour of

[7] Canny, *Elizabethan Conquest of Ireland*, pp. 88–92.
[8] Chope, 'New light on Grenville', p. 227.
[9] Quinn, *Gilbert*, pp. 31–3, 169. Peru is evidently used here in the French sense, meaning the Caribbean.
[10] Quinn, *Gilbert*, pp. 33–5, 170–80.

letters patent 'to discover and inhabyte some strange place', he should himself set forth an armed fleet to capture all the shipping of France, Spain and Portugal at the Newfoundland Banks and take the best of the prizes (having burned the rest) either to Holland or to England, where they would appear in the guise of pirates under the protection of 'some certayne vice-admirall . . . who may afterwardes be committed to prison, as in displeasure for the same'. The return in fish would not only cover the cost of the expedition, but would finance another to the West Indies, also to be organized by Sir Humphrey (he had been knighted in 1570 for his services in Ireland) and his associates. The seizure of the West Indies would more than compensate for any loss of trade resulting from the first breach of the peace and would complete the destruction of Spain's sea power. By these means 'this Realme being an Iland shall be discharged of all forraine perills' and the queen would gain control of 'all the Northerne and Southerne viages of the world'. The second paper suggested one expedition for the capture of Cuba and Española and another to waylay the treasure fleet, using Bermuda as a base.

This rather wild and woolly project is interesting as a caricature of the strategic notions of the western militants, implying as it did that two or three piratical raids across the Atlantic, promoted privately but on the queen's behalf, could at once win the hero a fortune, cripple Spain and establish England's supremacy at sea, all at no cost to the crown. The ensuing war would presumably be conducted in the same fashion, as a privateering campaign, which was essentially how Ralegh, Hawkins and Drake conceived the conflict when it came, though their strategic views were more sophisticated and realistic than Gilbert's. But the curious feature of the 1577 memoranda is Gilbert's treatment of America, which he seems to have regarded at that juncture as no more than a theatre of warfare and piracy. Neither exploration nor colonization is considered, except as a cloak to hide a dagger. The occupation of some northerly place (probably Anticosti in the Gulf of St Lawrence was meant) is proposed only as a pretence. As for Cuba and Española, Gilbert described their resources merely to show that an occupying force could victual itself 'for the tyme of their continuance there if it shalbe found neadfull', clearly intending them to be held for the duration of hostilities only.

In the summer of the next year, 1578, Gilbert duly received letters patent for discovery and plantation overseas and set forth a substantial expedition, the objective of which remained secret. In the light of his recent recommendations it seems likely that he intended a raid of some sort, probably upon the Caribbean, especially since many of his men

were pirates, but there are also indications that he now had colonization seriously in mind.[11] The elder Richard Hakluyt's 'Notes framed by
a Gentleman heretofore to bee given to one that prepared for a
discoverie and went not', printed by the younger Hakluyt in 1582,[12]
may have been written for Gilbert and are concerned with the
establishment of a colony in Mediterranean latitudes. Anthony
Parkhurst of Bristol, who knew Newfoundland well, wrote two letters
at this time advocating its colonization, either or both of which may
well have been intended as advice for Gilbert. John Frampton dedicated to Gilbert in 1578 his translation of Martín Fernández de Enciso's
Suma de Geographia,[13] which was mainly about the West Indies, referring to Sir Humphrey's intention 'to take some noble voyage and
discovery in hand'. As for the patent, it mentioned 'this jorney for
discovery' and 'the seconde jorney for conquest hereafter'.

None of this is conclusive, for the relevance of the Hakluyt and
Parkhurst material is not certain and if the patent was intended to
deceive, those who drafted it would make sure that it did so, while
Frampton's dedication may mean anything or nothing. But the composition of Gilbert's expedition suggests that he intended something
more than piracy on the high seas, for he took over five hundred men
and victuals for a whole year. This was excessive for a voyage of
discovery, insufficient for the conquest of Cuba or Española, but
perhaps adequate for a raid of plunder through the Caribbean and the
establishment of a temporary base in that sea or somewhere within
striking distance of it to the north. The Spanish ambassador was
convinced by his spies that Gilbert intended to raid the West Indies,
and it is worth noting that Ralegh, who alone among the captains of
this expedition attempted to cross the ocean, 'tooke his course for the
west Indies'.[14] As to the whereabouts of the settlement, if such was
intended, Gilbert's ideas must have been extremely vague, for the
English knew little about the West Indies and practically nothing about
the east American coast. They would have to explore and make up
their minds on the way, keeping the Spaniards guessing meanwhile,
even to the extent of suggesting, as Gilbert did to the French ambassador, that he was bound for the far South, towards the Pole Antarctic.
The best-informed guess is that he looked chiefly to the region north of
Spanish Florida, known then by the mysterious name of Norumbega.[15]

---

[11] For analysis and documentation of Gilbert's 1578 enterprise see Quinn, *Gilbert*, pp. 35–
49, 169–238; Quinn, *New American World*, III, pp. 185–210.

[12] Hakluyt, *Divers Voyages*.

[13] John Frampton, *A briefe description of the portes, creekes, bayes, and havens, of the Weast
India* (London, 1578).

[14] Quinn, *Gilbert*, p. 237, citing Holinshed's chronicle.   [15] Quinn, *Gilbert*, pp. 35–45.

The queen appears to have committed herself to this venture only to the extent of granting the patent and permitting the voyage, and it was to Walsingham's patronage that Gilbert owed, as he acknowledged, this royal favour.[16] Otherwise the only great personage known to have helped him was the earl of Sussex. Of the forty-four named subscribers some were merchants, notably Thomas Smith, the Customer of London, one of the richest City magnates at that time, with a finger in many pies, especially public finance, and William Hawkins of Plymouth, but the majority were gentlemen, including of course Gilbert's brothers and half-brothers and nine or ten others who went on the voyage. Chief among these was Henry, son of Sir Francis Knollys, Elizabeth's vice-chamberlain and privy councillor, who commanded three of the ships as a fleet within the fleet. The remaining seven, under Gilbert's direct command, included the *Hope* of Greenway, Carew Ralegh captain and Jacob Whiddon master, and the *Falcon*, formerly the queen's ship,[17] captain Walter Ralegh and master Simão Fernandes. Whiddon was to reappear as one of Ralegh's captains and Fernandes had an important part to play in English Atlantic enterprise over the next decade. He was an expert pilot from the Azores, who had come to England around 1573 and had been involved in piracy along with John Callice and Ferdinando Fielding in the *Elephant*, a ship partly owned by Henry Knollys. Now in 1578 this was Knollys's flagship, in which Callice, one of the most notorious pirates of the day, sailed as pilot, with Ferdinando Fielding gent. an honorary member of the company. Walsingham had meanwhile taken the tough, unscrupulous, anti-Spanish and very useful Fernandes into his service and protection.[18]

It is not surprising that an expedition so constituted resulted in nothing but petty squabbles among the leaders and an outbreak of indiscriminate piracy. Gilbert had no real authority over Knollys, whose men were already resorting to piracy during the summer of 1578 and continued their depredations after leaving England for Ireland in November, making no attempt to sail for America. Gilbert with his ships left for Ireland a day later, but made no further progress: he apparently set out again for the west only to be forced back by bad weather. He denied all responsibility for Knollys's piracies, but one of his ships did take part in them and he was accused of complicity.

---

[16] Quinn, *Gilbert*, p. 199.

[17] The royal ship *Falcon* had been sold to one William Barnes in 1575: T. Glasgow, 'List of ships in the Royal Navy from 1539 to 1588', *Mariner's Mirror*, 56 (1970), 299–307.

[18] Quinn, *Gilbert*, pp. 209–13. Quinn, *England and the Discovery of America*, pp. 246–63 (on Fernandes). On Callice see C. H. L'Estrange Ewen, *The Golden Chalice: a Documented Narrative of an Elizabethan Pirate* (Paignton, 1939).

Whether he was really innocent in this respect is not clear, but in a general sense he was certainly to blame for the whole deplorable affair, including its criminal repercussions. In 1579 the government, perturbed at these disorders, instituted an inquiry, but the matter was not pursued and meanwhile Gilbert and his flagship were employed in official duties, chiefly concerned with the protection of Ireland against a threatened invasion.[19] He and his associates had certainly caused the government some embarrassment, but at no time was he in serious peril of disgrace – he was, after all, not only loyal and useful, but influential.

Nevertheless this misadventure of 1578 was a heavy setback, which deeply affected both the nature and the outcome of Gilbert's colonizing plans. As Edward Hayes, narrator of the last and fatal voyage, relates, 'by his former preparation he was enfeebled of abilitie and credit, to performe his designements', having 'buried onely in a preparation a great masse of substance, wherby his estate was impaired'.[20] Furthermore his patent, granted for six years, was due to expire in 1584 and he would lose all rights unless some settlement could be established by then. In order to raise money, therefore, he decided to grant 'certaine assignments out of his commission to sundry persons of meane ability, desiring the privilege of his grant, to plant & fortifie in the North parts of America about the river of Canada'. Thus in 1580 he disposed of his rights north of the fiftieth parallel to John Dee, who was to use this concession to promote Davis's northwest venture (though Dee personally soon retired from the project).[21] At this time he also licensed Edward Cotton, a Southampton merchant, to set forth a whaling and trading venture to the Gulf of St Lawrence – an unsuccessful voyage.[22] We do not know whether Gilbert made any other grants of land in the north, but in 1582–3 – again to raise money as well as to ensure the exploitation of his rights (since any settlement under the patent would give him rights of possession over lands two hundred leagues north and south of it) – he elaborated and partially put into effect a large scheme of assignments of land and commercial privileges to various individuals and groups.[23]

Thus by a series of agreements he granted 8,500,000 acres of the North American mainland and seven unspecified islands off the coast to groups of Roman Catholics led by Sir George Peckham and Sir Thomas Gerrard, with whom Philip Sidney associated himself. Until 1581 Elizabeth had treated the English Catholics mildly, but then the

---

[19] Quinn, *Gilbert*, pp. 40–9, 201–36.   [20] *PN*, VIII, 40, 77.
[21] Quinn, *Gilbert*, pp. 49–53; *PN*, VIII, 40–41.
[22] Quinn, *Gilbert*, pp. 426–7.   [23] Quinn, *Gilbert*, pp. 58–61.

government heavily increased recusancy fines and began to treat priests, especially Jesuits, as seditious. Peckham and Gerrard represented loyal Catholic gentlemen who hoped to escape their dilemma by founding estates in a New World where they would not be persecuted for their beliefs, a plan which met with the crown's approval, though not with the blessing of Mendoza and the pro-Spanish Catholic émigrés, who did all they could to discredit it.[24] Gilbert, as landlord and governor of the whole region, was to draw rent from the principals, who would also pay customs duties and contribute to the defence of the colony, enjoying jurisdiction, freedom of trade and membership of a colonial assembly, as well as lordship over their sub-tenants. The colony was thus to consist of a social hierarchy based on land tenure, dominated by landed gentlemen. The latter were expected to bring dependants who would take up farms of six-score acres in fee simple, paying fines of entry, yearly rents and heriot and relief upon death or alienation, with set shares in any mineral products. Poor persons sent over at the general charge of the realm or at their own proper charges would be the personal tenants of Gilbert or his heirs and would have 60-acre farms on similarly quasi-feudal terms. Gilbert himself would rule under the crown according to the laws of England, but the colony would be virtually independent, even providing its own defence.[25]

The principal purpose of Gilbert's new scheme, therefore, was to provide estates for gentlemen of landed families, especially for Roman Catholics and for that large class of relatively deprived gentry, the younger sons, with Sir Humphrey, in all his touchy pride and raging ambition, at their head. It was also assumed, however, that the colony would produce commodities for the home country, as if the natural *raison d'être* of any plantation must be supply. Thus land was not the only object. Hence the 'Merchant Adventurers with Sir Humphrey Gilbert', a corporation to be based at Southampton with an exclusive monopoly of trade with the colony. This was a joint-stock company, the shareholders being the subscribers to Gilbert's enterprise, including the adventurers of 1578, thirty-nine Southampton people, mainly merchants, Gilbert's relatives (his elder brother and Walter Ralegh had large shares) and a few others, notably Walsingham, who put in fifty pounds. Gilbert planned to get subscriptions from the towns of Totnes and Dartmouth and a number of courtiers and others, but their contributions are not recorded and probably many of them never

---

[24] Quinn, *England and the Discovery of America*, pp. 364–97, on 'The English Catholics in America, 1581–1633'.
[25] Quinn, *Gilbert*, pp. 266–78.

materialized. Those who did subscribe would have land in the colony as well as the right to trade thither.[26] The only interested parties for whom Gilbert made no provision at all were the aboriginal inhabitants of the lands he proposed to occupy. It is all too clear that he was not in the least concerned about their lot, for they had no evident place in his scheme of things.

Meanwhile Gilbert involved others in the active preparation of his second expedition. In 1580 his own 8-ton frigate, the *Squirrel*, sailed under Simão Fernandes to the New England coast, returning within three months, after which Fernandes paid a visit to Mortlake to discuss cartography with John Dee.[27] In 1582 Walsingham got together a committee, including Peckham and probably the younger Hakluyt as well as Gilbert, which examined David Ingram, one of the men put ashore by Hawkins in the Gulf of Mexico in 1568, concerning the journey he claimed to have made across North America. Ingram's story, which was published in 1583, was probably founded on fact, but so muddled and garnished with tit-bits from other travellers' tales as to mislead anyone credulous enough to take it seriously. Hakluyt printed it in his 1589 edition, but left it out of his revised version, having had second thoughts about it.[28] This committee obtained some slight information from two other Englishmen who had visited North America, and Hakluyt at this time compiled a list of North American products, which he published alongside his cousin's notes of 1578 and documents relating to the Cabots, Robert Thorne, Verrazzano, the Zeni brothers, Pet and Jackman, as *Divers Voyages touching the Discoverie of America* (1582), with a dedication to Philip Sidney. Hakluyt thus combined the functions of an adviser, providing relevant background reports, and a publicity agent, urging with manifest sincerity and enthusiasm the planting 'of our superfluous people into those temperate and fertile partes of America'. A year later, in June 1583, he even thought of taking ship for Norumbega himself.[29]

By this time, however, Gilbert's hopes and plans had gone somewhat awry. In the first place Peckham had to postpone the voyage he intended as many of his supporters withdrew, partly on account of Mendoza's counter-propaganda and partly because the government insisted that would-be émigrés must pay their swingeing fines in any case. Secondly, Gilbert himself had to delay his departure, frustrated by adverse winds, lack of funds and even by the queen, who

[26] Quinn, *Gilbert*, pp. 60–61, 81–2, 313–34.
[27] Quinn, *Gilbert*, pp. 51, 239–40, 282, 309.
[28] Quinn, *Gilbert*, pp. 64–6; Quinn, *England and the Discovery of America*, p. 217.
[29] *PN*, VIII, 81. Stephen Parmenius to Hakluyt, 6 August 1583.

at one point, with remarkable foresight, forbade him to take part in the voyage, 'as a man noted of not good happ by sea'.[30] She relented, but as Hayes explains, 'such were the difficulties and crosse accidents opposing these proceedings' that Gilbert, who had originally expected to sail in 1582, was not ready to leave until June 1583. In the meantime, however, Walsingham and his step-son, Christopher Carleill, with the assistance of the younger Hakluyt, succeeded in interesting the City of Bristol in Gilbert's plans, and in the spring of 1583 the Bristol men agreed to provide a thousand marks as well as a ship and a bark 'to bee left in the countrey under the direction and government of your sonne in law, M. Carlile'.[31] It was too late for this contingent to go with Gilbert's main expedition, but Carleill evidently hoped that it would form part of a second fleet for the supply and reinforcement of the colony, and that a number of London merchants could be induced to subscribe to this subsidiary venture.[32] In April, therefore, he drew up an elaborate and well-argued project appealing to the Muscovy merchants and others to support a North American colony, and in May a committee of the Muscovy Company agreed to recommend the scheme on certain conditions: Carleill must get a patent from the crown giving the adventurers an exclusive monopoly of trade and excluding all others from planting or trading within two hundred leagues of the first settlement. A new patent and a new corporation were perhaps necessary because the company could not claim privileges extending so far south as 40°N., the proposed latitude of the base, but these conditions do not appear compatible with Gilbert's patent, nor with his explicit exclusion of members of the Muscovy Company from his Southampton corporation. This was no doubt one of the reasons why Carleill's supporting expedition failed to materialize, though he did launch an abortive attempt to reach America in 1584.

The 'difficulties and crosse accidents' of the winter of 1582–3 tried Gilbert's patience hard and might well have broken the resolve of a less

---

[30] Quinn, *Gilbert*, p. 339.

[31] Quinn, *Gilbert*, p. 350.

[32] Thus Maurice Browne wrote to John Thynne about the end of April 1583: 'In A present supply divers of the cheife marchauntes of London, and the marchauntes of Bristowe dooe joyne in consort, and doth send fyve sayle more of good shipes with provision and men to Sir Humfrey' – D. B. Quinn and N. M. Cheshire (eds.), *The New Found Land of Stephen Parmenius* (Toronto, 1972), p. 204. Browne, a young gentleman servant to Walsingham, became involved in Gilbert's plans in 1582, was given command of the *Delight* in 1583 and went down with her, as did also the Hungarian poet, Parmenius. Browne's letters to Thynne provide much interesting detail on the preparation of the expedition. See also Quinn, *Gilbert*, pp. 76–81, 346–69, for an account of Carleill's project and an annotated text of his appeal, Hakluyt's text of which (*PN*, VIII, 134–7) was based on a printed pamphlet, described in D. B. Quinn (ed.), *The Roanoke Voyages, 1584–1590* (London, 1955), p. 3. See also Quinn, *New American World*, III, pp. 27–34.

determined man, but in the spring fortune and the queen smiled upon him once more. Walter Ralegh was now the rising star at court; his money helped, but still more valuable to Gilbert was the queen's favour, which wrought a marked change in men's attitudes to the enterprise. Nevertheless the delays had so consumed his provisions that he was obliged to choose a northerly course across the Atlantic to revictual at Newfoundland instead of the southerly route he would otherwise have followed.[33]

The classic account of Gilbert's last voyage, published by Hakluyt in 1589, came from the pen of Edward Hayes, a gentleman of Liverpool, who had subscribed to the 1578 expedition and in 1583 contributed the *Golden Hind* of 40 tons, in which he sailed as captain.[34] He was and remained an amateur of projects, but his interest in American discovery and settlement was deep and abiding, inspired by a sense of the duty of good Christians to bring light to the heathen. Colonial enterprise undertaken for worldly gain would never prosper, he preached, leaving the reader to fill in the culprit's name:

it behooveth every man of great calling, in whom is any instinct of inclination unto this attempt, to examine his owne motions: which if the same proceed of ambition or avarice, he may assure himselfe it commeth not of God, and therefore can not have confidence of Gods protection and assistance against the violence (els irresistable) both of sea, and infinite perils upon the land; whom God may yet use an instrument to further his cause and glory some way, but not to build upon so bad a foundation.

Hayes was careful to offset his censure of Gilbert's motives and conduct with a certain pious respect for the dead, but even when praising the lost hero he could hardly conceal his disapproval, exhorting his readers to 'judge charitably both of the cause (which was just in all pretence) and of the person, who was very zealous in prosecuting the same, deserving honourable remembrance for his good minde, and expense of life in so vertuous an enterprise'. Yet Hayes was not unjust. He stressed the difficulties under which Gilbert laboured, so 'incumbred with wants and woorse matched with many ill disposed people, that his rare judgement and regiment premeditated for those affaires, was subjected to tolerate abuses'.

Apart from the *Golden Hind*, Gilbert had his flagship, the *Delight* (120 tons), part-owned by Sir John Gilbert and by her captain, William Winter; Walter Ralegh's *Bark Ralegh* (200 tons); the *Swallow* (40 tons),

---

[33] See the above-cited letter of Browne for the change in Gilbert's fortune; and *PN*, VIII, 41–2, for Gilbert's decision concerning the route.

[34] *PN*, VIII, 34–77. The following quotations concerning the 1583 voyage are from this narrative.

which Gilbert had seized from the pirate Callice and treated as his own, though it rightfully belonged to its former owner, a Scottish merchant; and the *Squirrel*. Ralegh's bark put back to Plymouth after only two days at sea, either for want of victuals or because the crew were stricken by disease. The rest of the fleet took seven weeks to make Newfoundland, during which time the *Swallow*'s crew of pirates, having parted company, spoiled a fishing bark on her way home, 'whom they rifled of tackle, sailes, cables, victuals, & the men of their apparell: not sparing by torture (winding cords about their heads) to draw out else what they thought good'. In early August the ships forgathered at St John's harbour, where they found some thirty-six fishing vessels, Spanish, Portuguese, French and English, co-operating amicably under an English admiral, whose turn it happened to be to fill that position. They evidently suspected Gilbert's intentions at first, but received him generously when he showed the queen's commission, acceding to his demands for victuals. He then proceeded formally to take possession of St John's and of the coast for two hundred miles on either side in the queen's name, after which he obliged the fishermen to agree to rent from him their drying grounds. A colony now existed, at least in theory, and Gilbert could renew his patent.

The next fortnight was occupied with prospecting, and Hayes gave a favourable report of southern Newfoundland as a potential colony, playing down its coldness and somewhat overstating the richness of its natural resources. Gilbert, however,

was most curious in the search of mettals, commanding the minerall man and refiner, especially to be diligent. The same was a Saxon borne, honest and religious, named Daniel. Who after search brought some sort of Ore, seeming rather to be yron then other mettall. The next time he found Ore, which with no small shew of contentment he delivered unto the General, using protestation, that if silver were the thing which might satisfie the General & his followers, there it was, advising him to seeke no further. . . . My selfe at this instant liker to die then to live, by a mischance, could not follow this confident opinion of our refiner to my owne satisfaction: but afterward demanding our Generals opinion therein, and to have some part of the Ore, he replied: 'Content your selfe, I have seene ynough, and were it but to satisfie my private humor, I would proceede no further. The promise unto my friends, and necessitie to bring also the South countries within compasse of my Patent neere expired, as we have alreadie done these North parts, do only perswade me further.'

This false hope alone buoyed up the hapless leader in the weeks to come, as disaster followed disaster. During the two weeks at St John's sickness spread. Many died, others were too ill to work, others deserted, others again refused to continue the voyage. Gilbert therefore ordered the *Swallow* to return the sick to England and set out for the mainland with the remaining three ships. From Cape Race they were unsure of their course, there were arguments between Gilbert and the masters, and after eight days of dangerous navigation the *Delight* finally wrecked herself upon shoals, perhaps at Cape Breton Island, perhaps at Sable Island. Some managed to save themselves in a pinnace and of these a few eventually reached home by way of Newfoundland and France, but over eighty of her hundred men drowned then and there before the eyes of their shipmates in the *Hind* and the *Squirrel*.

Demoralized and in sore distress, the crew of the two surviving vessels would go no further and Gilbert, yielding to their pleas, set course for England. He had lost his notes and books in the wreck and – worse still to his mind – the precious ore and Daniel the Saxon along with it, but he refused to admit defeat, 'with demonstration of great fervencie of mind, being himselfe very confident, and settled in beliefe of inestimable good by this voyage, which [Hayes added a trifle wryly] the greater number of his followers nevertheles mistrusted altogether, not being made partakers of those secrets, which the Generall kept unto himselfe'. He had, he said, now become a northern man altogether, and reserved that part of North America for his own use, refusing to assign any more lands in those parts, especially at St John's, all of which convinced Hayes that Sir Humphrey had some evidence of a rich mine. In the spring he would set forth two fleets, one for the north and the other for the south, and when asked how he could pay for so great an expedition, he replied, 'I will aske a pennie of no man. I will bring good tidings unto her Majesty, who wil be so gracious, to lend me 10000 pounds.' He seemed to have forgotten Frobisher, or to have assumed that Elizabeth had forgotten, or – most likely – to have been whistling in the dark.[35]

It was in this pathetic mood of defiant bravado that Sir Humphrey Gilbert came to his death. In 'very foule weather, and terrible seas, breaking short and high, Pyramid wise', having refused to leave the tiny *Squirrel* for the safer *Hind*, on 9 September

the Generall sitting abaft with a booke in his hand, cried out unto us in the Hind (so oft as we did approch within hearing), We are as neere to heaven by sea as by land. Reiterating the same speech, well beseeming a souldier,

[35] On the other hand his optimism may have been based on the signs of goodwill which the queen showed him before his departure: Quinn and Cheshire, *Parmenius*, pp. 204–5.

resolute in Jesus Christ, as I can testifie he was. The same Monday night, about twelve of the clocke, or not long after, the Frigat being ahead of us in the Golden Hinde, suddenly her lights were out, whereof as it were in a moment, we lost sight, and withall our watch cryed, the Generall was cast away, which was too true.

Gilbert's own faults certainly helped to make his failure so calamitous, but the circumstances and conditions of the time greatly limited his chances of success. It was, as Camden observed, 'a difficulter thing to carry over Colonies into remote Countries upon private mens Purses, than he and others in an enormous Credulity had perswaded themselves, to their own Cost and Detriment'.[36] Even this is a harsh judgement, considering that Gilbert had little choice but to rely on his own and his friends' resources. Elizabeth, Walsingham and other responsible figures were happy to encourage his efforts but unwilling to provide the substantial backing needed by such an undertaking. Nor can they be blamed for regarding his efforts as a sideshow to the political struggle which occupied their attention or for failing to realize the scale of the task he set himself.

After the return of the remnant of Gilbert's expedition another colonial project appeared, written by Sir George Peckham and published about the end of 1583.[37] This makes an interesting comparison with Carleill's, since the two authors approached the matter differently and addressed their appeals to different sets of people. Carleill was closely associated with the Muscovy Company, being the son of a founder-member and a nephew of Sir George Barne and having commanded the queen's *Tiger* in 1582, when it escorted the company's fleet to the White Sea. His discourse displayed considerable knowledge of the Russia trade and a grasp of the problems of overseas trade in general, though he tended to exaggerate them for the sake of his main argument, which was that the difficulties and uncertainties of foreign trade made it highly desirable to develop colonial trade as an alternative. It would be steadier and safer, and in the long run – looking thirty years ahead – the commercial potential of North America was very great. His economic vision was thus far-sighted, if somewhat optimistic as to the pace of development, but his plan was quite realistic. He proposed to begin with a trading base in 40°, which could conveniently gather the commodities of the north, such as fish, tar, pitch, hemp, cordage, masts and furs, as well as those of the south – wine, oil, salt and so on. Many of the leading Muscovy men were in fact interested in southern as well as northern products already and

[36] W. Camden, *The History of . . . Princess Elizabeth* (London, 1688), p. 287.
[37] *PN*, VIII, 89–131. For bibliographical details see Quinn, *Roanoke Voyages*, pp. 3–4.

would find this prospect attractive. The first colony would be modest in scale and pioneering in its function: it would consist of a hundred men and would require an investment of £4000 (in £25 shares) to set up. Colonization would develop from this bridgehead as confidence in the venture built up at home and the natives learned civil ways. Carleill sensibly deprecated talk of mines, pointing rather to the likely growth of a large cloth market and the possible discovery of a new water-route to the East, and he dwelt upon the virtue of exporting the poor for their own good. But these were remote and hazy perspectives, the foreground being strictly commercial and practical.

Peckham directed his treatise principally at the 'noblemen and gentlemen, who doe chiefly seeke a temperate climate, wholesome ayre, fertile soile, and a strong place by nature whereupon they may fortifie, and there either plant themselves, or such other persons as they shall thinke good to send to bee lords of that place and countrey'. His intention was to attract subscribers to a scheme of landed settlement on the lines of those formerly agreed by his associates and Gilbert, though now his appeal was not confined to Roman Catholics. He was at pains to explain the case for plantation at some length, referring to the example of the Spaniards, whom he urged his countrymen to emulate, and showing how lawful and necessary it was for Christians to traffic with the savages and acquire land, settling colonies among them. If the natives resisted, the Christians would have the right 'to defend themselves, to pursue revenge with force' and so subdue them, taking possession of their towns and so forth, for which ample biblical precedent might be (and by Peckham tediously was) cited. After a feeble attempt to demonstrate the queen's title to North America, he proceeded to the conventional *pro bono publico* argument. The growth of fishing would strengthen shipping and so defence; the savages would 'take a marvelous delight' in coloured English cloths (though for export England in fact produced mainly undyed cloth); thus the cloth industry (of late run down, he wrongly believed, by the export of raw wool) would recover and the poor would be set on work. Readers who knew much about English industry would have found Peckham's vagaries in that respect less than convincing. He went on to indicate the benefits adventurers – merchants as well as gentlemen – would derive from planting, stressing the pleasantness of the climate, the richness of the animal life (for hunters) and the great variety of commodities. As for the savages, they would gain chiefly the blessing of Jesus Christ, but also the blessings of law and order and the mechanical arts. Colonization, moreover, was not difficult – and here he reverted to the inspiring deeds of the Spanish *conquistadores* and wound up for good measure with a short history of Portuguese expansion.

The differences between the early colonial projectors are at least as interesting as the common ground. They used the same platitudes about the benefit of the realm and the reduction of the savage people to Christianity and civility. But neither Carleill nor Peckham regarded colonization as a means to injure Spain or associated it with anti-Spanish policies, as Gilbert and Ralegh did. Peckham indeed seems to have admired the Spaniards and to have taken their experience of colonial expansion very much to heart. Whereas Gilbert ignored the American Indian and Hayes, at the other extreme, thought his conversion fundamental to colonial enterprise, Carleill hardly mentioned the gospel, concentrating entirely on the economic potential of the native as producer and consumer, while Peckham elaborated the process by which the recalcitrant heathen would be conquered and brought by force to worship the Christian god, with expropriation implied. In fact Anglo-Saxon attitudes to the natives of North America, whether more or less hopeful, more or less concerned, were as yet rather vague and formless, having little foundation in knowledge and practically none in direct experience. Experience would have a powerful effect upon such preconceived notions, which were by no means so clear, consistent and strong as to constitute a fixed idea.[38]

[38] The contrary thesis is expounded in Sheehan, *Savagism and Civility*.

10

Roanoke

When the remnants of Gilbert's expedition limped home in 1583 the future of North American enterprise must have seemed dark indeed. That disaster, unmitigated by any glimmer of hope, might well have deterred the boldest from similar attempts for years to come. Yet within a few months the venture was resumed with fresh energy and by the spring of 1585 had gained the support necessary to launch the first English transatlantic colony. It must be supposed that the surge of interest in oceanic enterprise was too strong to be set back even by so depressing a failure as Gilbert's. In fact several schemes arose in 1584 out of his: Sir John Gilbert had plans for Newfoundland, Carleill actually set out for America but was diverted to government service in Ireland, and Adrian Gilbert acquired a patent for the northwest quest.[1] But the main sequel was inspired by Gilbert's half-brother, Walter Ralegh, who in 1584 dispatched his first expedition to Virginia and so effectively began the plantation of North America by Englishmen.

Ralegh was now about 32 years of age. A younger son, he had early found his way from Devon to London and the Court. He had gained some experience as a volunteer in France in 1572 and took part, as we have seen, in Gilbert's 1578 adventure. After that he served as a captain of soldiers in Ireland under Lord Grey of Wilton against the force of Papal mercenaries which occupied Smerwick in 1580. What part precisely Ralegh took in the massacre of the Smerwick garrison after its surrender is not clear, but he emerged during his brief campaign as a vigorous exponent of harsh measures against rebels and enemies, and made himself known to ministers at home as an able and ambitious young man. The cleverness and arrogance he showed in criticizing Grey served him even better when he returned to Court in 1582. His handsome person, his elegance and wit adorned a strong, if dilettante intellect – he was, in short, just the sort of man to appeal to the queen

[1] Quinn, *Gilbert*, pp. 94–100.

and was already one of her favourite courtiers by the end of the year. In 1583 and 1584 she granted him lucrative privileges, including the sole right to issue licences for the sale of wine. More such revenues came to him later, making him unpopular as well as rich, but in 1584 his means were still insufficient for the launching of a major colonial experiment. These circumstances suggested a modest beginning, and in April 1584, having the previous month obtained a patent modelled on Gilbert's,[2] Ralegh set forth two barks to reconnoitre the coast north of Spain's Florida footholds.

In choosing for investigation the region that came to be called Virginia, Ralegh probably had in mind considerations both mercantile and strategic. On the one hand the latitudes of 35° to 40° seemed to indicate a Mediterranean climate and so to promise a rich output of southern commodities, such as oils, fruits, dyestuffs and sugar, profitable staples for a colony of supply and convenient substitutes for Iberian products. Such a climate would, it was thought, make settlement easier and more attractive. More important still at that historical juncture was the potential naval value of a foothold near enough to Spain's treasure route and the Caribbean colonies to serve as a base for privateering operations against them, yet far enough north to be relatively safe from attack from Florida. Such were the vague and hopeful notions, informed by hardly any geographical knowledge of that part of the North American coast, with which Ralegh's servants, Philip Amadas and Arthur Barlowe, left Plymouth in April 1584, taking with them as pilot the Portuguese, Simão Fernandes.[3]

Barlowe's record of the voyage, vigorously edited for publicity purposes after his return, provides nearly all we know about this expedition, and for that very reason deserves to be treated with some caution. The outward voyage was perhaps more difficult than appears, particularly in the negotiation of the passage from the Caribbean into the Florida Channel – a tricky piece of navigation for mariners not yet familiar with the currents there – and the coasting of the Carolina Banks can have been no easier. But eventually they found an inlet lying between the island that became known as Roanoke, to the north, and that called Hatarask to the south. They landed on the latter on 13 July

---

[2] Quinn, *Roanoke Voyages*, pp. 82–9. Ralegh's patent excluded Newfoundland from his authority, perhaps because Gilbert's other relatives reserved it, perhaps because it was thought best to leave the fishery alone.

[3] Quinn, *Roanoke Voyages*, pp. 78–117, for the Amadas-Barlowe voyage. Fernandes had been trained as a pilot in the Spanish transatlantic service and claimed some knowledge of the American coast north of Florida. It was probably the New England coast that he reconnoitred for Gilbert in 1580: Quinn, *England and the Discovery of America*, pp. 246–63.

and took possession of it for the queen. Two days later they made contact with the Carolina Algonquian Indians and soon established what seemed to be friendly relations with the Roanoke chief Wingina and his brother Granganimeo. There was a generous give-and-take of food and presents and a good deal of barter, chiefly of hatchets, axes and knives for deer-skins – a cordial kind of exchange accompanied by mutual curiosity.

The observant Barlowe described some of the commonest trees, roots, fruits and herbs, mentioning maize, 'their Countrey corne, which is very white, faire, and well tasted', and the obvious game animals. Apart from Roanoke and one or two other islands, the English visited only the nearby sounds and got vague impressions of the mainland from the Indians. Their interest centred upon the people themselves. Although in the course of the voyage there may have occurred another and less happy encounter with American Indians, on which occasion some of the English may have been killed and eaten, Barlowe omitted to mention this unfortunate episode, dwelling rather upon the friendlier sort of savages, whom he depicted as 'very handsome, and goodly people, and in their behaviour as mannerly, and civill, as any of Europe . . . most gentle, loving, and faithfull, void of all guile, and treason, and such as lived after the manner of the golden age'. Of course they were a warlike nation, but Barlowe succeeded in leaving the reader with the comforting sense that they were too engrossed in slaughtering each other to offer any real danger to outsiders. The discourse was obviously doctored after the event – it included information provided later by Manteo and Wanchese, the two Indians brought to England when the expedition returned in September – yet it retained the freshness and naïvety of a first impression because the English did not stay long enough to be disillusioned by the conflict and hardship that settlement would entail. In contemporary minds it helped to create the misleading picture of Virginia as a land of milk and honey, inhabited by innocent and amenable primitives.

Barlowe's discourse was designed to attract support among the public for the next stage of Ralegh's project, the founding of a colony. So too was the elder Hakluyt's treatise, 'Inducements to the liking of the voyage intended towards Virginia in 40. and 42. degrees of latitude', circulated in manuscript in 1585, though not published until 1602.[4] But more than private subscriptions Ralegh now needed official recognition and backing. In some measure he could count on both, for the queen favoured him and his project. She knighted him in January

4 Taylor, *Writings of the Hakluyts*, pp. 327–38.

1585 and authorized the name Virginia for the new land. She put one of her own ships, the *Tiger,* at his disposal and probably had it counted as her adventure. Her secretary, Walsingham, was a strong supporter and subscriber. All this was a sign of her personal regard for Ralegh, but she was also influenced by reasons of state. In 1584–5 the old amity between Spain and England was in tatters; the Spanish ambassador had been expelled in January 1584 and during the next fifteen months the international situation became ever more threatening. These circumstances no doubt helped Ralegh, for at such times Elizabeth inclined a more responsive ear to those who volunteered to 'annoy' the king of Spain. Ralegh, however, wanted more than that. Knowing well the fatal consequences of Gilbert's dependence on private funds, he sought to involve the crown in direct responsibility for the colonial enterprise. He was of course equally aware of the queen's reluctance to commit the state to any action that might precipitate outright war. His case would require persuasive argument, and it was for this purpose that he engaged the fluent pen of Richard Hakluyt the younger.

Hakluyt wrote his 'Particuler Discourse' (better known as the *Discourse of Western Planting,* a title it acquired later) in 1584, not for publication, but for the eyes of the queen and Walsingham.[5] In elaborating the case for colonization with specific reference to Virginia he therefore stressed reasons of state throughout, concluding with 'A brefe Collection of certaine reasons to induce her Majestie and the state to take in hande the westerne voyadge and the planting there'. His purpose was not to explain or justify Ralegh's initiative so much as to demonstrate that it was in the crown's interest to take this business in hand. What precisely that implied he did not say, but he evidently meant that the state should bear the main financial burden and underwrite the future of the plantation. As a champion of overseas expansion, he no doubt sincerely believed that the promoters' interests and those of the state coincided, but in seeking to establish this he wisely chose not to dwell upon the purposes of the former, preferring to imply that they were concerned only for the benefit of the realm. However it is not impugning their patriotism to suggest that they were looking for wealth and fame.[6] It is therefore mistaken to interpret the discourse simply as 'a record of the motives and intentions of the first colonizers'.[7]

Always the clergyman, Hakluyt put the cause of the gospel first. He

[5] Taylor, *Writings of the Hakluyts,* pp. 211–326. It was first published as *A Discourse on Western Planting,* ed. Charles Deane (Cambridge, Mass., 1877).
[6] Taylor, *Writings of the Hakluyts,* p. 37.
[7] G. B. Parks, *Richard Hakluyt and the English Voyages* (New York, 1928), p. 88.

deplored the backwardness of his countrymen in missionary work all the more because the boasted successes of the Iberians consisted in perverting rather than converting the infidel. The supporting argument – that setting some of the idle clergy 'on worke in reducinge the Savages to the chefe principles of our faithe' might incidentally reduce the amount of religious contention at home – was perhaps calculated to please the queen. Then came the economic case: 'all other englishe trades are grown beggerly or dangerous', whereas 'this westerne voyadge will yelde unto us all the commodities of Europe, Affrica and Asia, as farr as wee were wonte to travell, and supplye the wantes of all our decayed trades', as well as providing employment for innumerable people and a great market for English manufactures. These points were hardly original, but Hakluyt put them in his own way, which was both forceful and tendentious. He gave a rather distorted account of the country's overseas trade, exaggerating the difficulties without mentioning the commodities, proceeding then to an equally misleading picture of the North American prospects, listing all the commodities he could find mentioned in earlier descriptions and none of the difficulties. As for the unemployed, vagabonds and petty thieves, he offered an impressive catalogue of the tasks awaiting them across the Atlantic, from tilling the soil to drying, sorting and packing feathers. Sales of cloth there would soon equal and eventually exceed the maximum they had reached in the Netherlands, and the cloth would moreover be 'full wroughte by our naturall subjectes', unlike most of the exports to the Low Countries. The processing of imported raw materials from America would give employment to a multitude of the poor. Hakluyt drew a dark picture of the prevailing evils brought on by population pressure and his concern made this passage a moving one, but his argument that American trade would solve the problem would hardly have convinced an Elizabethan cloth exporter. As for the queen, she may have been more impressed by Hakluyt's promises of increased customs revenues.

Hakluyt gave roughly as much space again to strategic considerations. Bases on the east coast of North America would put Spain's treasure fleet and West Indian possessions at risk. The Indian enemies of Spain would prove powerful allies,[8] for Spain's hold upon her American dominions was weak, though her strength depended upon that treasure. By fortifying themselves near Newfoundland the English could easily dominate the fishery and seize Iberian shipping there if the need arose. But it was a Mediterranean type of colony that he envisaged, partly because that could supply the kinds of commodi-

[8] He specified the Chichimeca of Mexico and the Cimarrones of Panama.

ties hitherto obtained from southern Europe and especially from the Iberian peninsula, sources now threatened by the noise of war; and partly because a settlement around 36°N. would be well placed for purposes of defence and attack in time of war. The essential ideas were not new, but he bodied them forth (as he had done his economic arguments) with much plausible illustration, articulating in detail notions which by this time were familiar enough to Walsingham and Elizabeth, and backing them with a fierce denunciation, based on Las Casas, of the 'tyranies and devilishe doinges' of the Spaniards in the Indies.[9]

Although Hakluyt's memorandum had a distinctly academic flavour, referring frequently to literary sources and historical examples, there was commonsense in his advice that in order to forestall rivals the first reconnaissance should be quickly followed by the planting and fortification of the mouths of the main rivers, while naval forces should pre-empt the available harbours. Furthermore it was important in the first stage of settlement to find or produce goods to defray the initial cost of the enterprise: forest products offered the best prospects, he thought – timber, furniture, pitch, tar, soap-ashes, etc. He cited evidence to suggest that water-routes to the Pacific might well be found round or through North America, a reasonable enough supposition at the time, and he added lists of items that would be necessary for the voyage and for the colony: victuals, roots, seeds, breeding animals, artisans and other specialists, Bibles and so forth. In these and some other recommendations Hakluyt showed a certain interest in practical details, but of course he was not a practical man, nor had he or anyone else in England at that time any considerable knowledge either of the region in question or of how to found a colony. That indeed was the serious flaw in his case, as it was in Ralegh's actual project.

In spite of Hakluyt's thoughtful advocacy and Ralegh's eloquent lobbying, the queen's contribution to the launching of the Virginia enterprise did not come near taking it in hand. Her approval was of course indispensable and her favour gave Ralegh some useful advantages: authority to impound shipping, supplies and men in Devon, Cornwall and Bristol, for example. But the responsibility was left to him and he had to rely mainly on his own and his friends' resources to finance the expedition. Apart from Walsingham, Lord Charles Howard (Lord High Admiral from 1584), Sir Richard Grenville and

---

[9] Bartolomé de las Casas, *Brevísima Relación de la Destrucción de las Indias* (Seville, 1552), published in English in 1583 as *The Spanish Colonie*. Hakluyt also referred to Girolamo Benzoni, *La Historia del Nuovo Mondo* (Venice, 1572).

Thomas Cavendish were important subscribers, and without doubt
there were many others, enabling Ralegh to set forth a fleet and force of
men far stronger and better supplied than Gilbert's had been. As well
as the queen's *Tiger* (160 tons),[10] there were four ships and two
pinnaces, carrying about 600 men in all, under Grenville's command,
while Ralph Lane, an experienced soldier, was released from his post
in Ireland to lead the soldiers who were to form the main body of the
colony. These left Plymouth in April 1585 and a further squadron
under Bernard Drake and Amyas Preston was expected to follow them
in June.[11]

Making for the Caribbean, the *Tiger* was separated by storm from her
consorts, but safely reached Puerto Rico, where Grenville established a
fortified camp and was soon rejoined by the *Elizabeth* under
Cavendish. The advantages of the southerly route to Roanoke were
now demonstrated, for Grenville spent about a month here victualling,
watering, raiding and trading. He built a pinnace, took prize and sold it
back to the Spaniards, obtained livestock and plants for the colony and
trade-goods to sell in England. Finally the two ships and the pinnace
made their way through the Bahamas to reach the Carolina Banks
towards the end of June. But here a serious accident occurred: negotiating an inlet through the Banks, the *Tiger* went aground and was
damaged; much of the food provided for the colony was ruined by salt
water. Some blamed the flagship's master, Simão Fernandes, for this,
but in fact the whole Banks coast was dangerous for shipping. Indeed
this and the lack of any safe harbour made the chosen area quite
unsuitable as a site for a first continental foothold, especially a foothold
intended to serve as a naval base.

Experience was soon to convince the leaders of this, but meanwhile
they pressed ahead with their plans. During July the *Dorothy* and the
Roebuck rejoined, and by the end of the month the four ships and the
pinnace anchored in Port Ferdinando on Hatarask Island opposite
Roanoke. Manteo and Wanchese now did their job as intermediaries
and friendly relations were resumed with Wingina, Granganimeo and
the Roanoke tribe, who agreed to let the English build a fort and some
cottages at the north end of the island. Lane, it was decided, would
remain there with just over a hundred men – a much smaller colony
than was originally planned, since provisions were now so short that
they would have to live off the country: Drake and Preston had not

[10] T. Glasgow, 'H.M.S. Tiger', *North Carolina Historical Review*, 43 (1966), 115–21, shows
she was formerly the *Sea Dragon*, a private vessel owned by Sir William Winter.
[11] Quinn, *Roanoke Voyages*, pp. 158–9. My account of the first colony is based primarily on
pp. 159–313 of this work.

turned up, having been dispatched to Newfoundland instead to seize Spanish shipping there. Grenville therefore departed for home aboard the *Tiger* in late August, bearing Lane's preliminary and optimistic assessment of the prospects in letters addressed to Walsingham. On this return voyage Grenville captured a rich Spanish prize, which probably at least paid for the whole expedition. A maritime war of reprisals was now afoot – the result of the arrest of English ships and property in Spain in May – and privateering thus opportunely presented a most convenient and satisfying way of meeting the expenses of the colonial enterprise, an admirable solution, it seemed, to the problem Hakluyt had noted: how to realize some kind of return on investment in the early years of plantation. Was not the promotion of privateering, moreover, a major *raison d'être* of the colony? Commonsense, national loyalty and self-interest combined not merely to recommend but to demand the resort to plunder. Time alone would show that it might do the colony more harm than good.

Lane's main task, apart from that of keeping the colony alive, was to explore the region around Roanoke. Little was done southwards into Pamlico Sound, but a party was sent northwards to reconnoitre waters the Indians had indicated, where a satisfactory harbour might be found. They discovered Chesapeake Bay and spent part of the winter inland, making friendly contact with the Chesapeake tribe. Their report was most encouraging: 'But the Territorie and soyle of the Chesepians (being distant fifteene miles from the shoare) was for pleasantnes of seate, for temperature of Climate, for fertilitie of soyle, and for the commoditie of the Sea . . . not to be excelled by any other whatsoever.'[12] This was a valuable development, which had a strong influence upon Lane's plans for the future of the enterprise; but possibly for that very reason he left this part of his own report rather vague. The Spaniards already knew that the English had started a settlement north of Florida and in December 1585 they made an effort to find it, though without success. Lane was not aware of this, but when he wrote his report in the summer of 1586 discretion in respect of Chesapeake Bay was advisable.

Lane himself in the spring took another party westwards to the head of Albermarle Sound and then north up the Chowan River to Chawanoac, where the Chowan chief told him of metal, which sounded like copper or gold, further inland up the River Roanoke, and of a deep bay to the north where pearls were to be had. The latter was clearly a reference to Chesapeake Bay and although Lane appeared not

---

[12] *PN*, VIII, 321. Lane's report (*PN*, VIII, 320–48) and Hariot's (*PN*, VIII, 348–86) are the main sources for the following account of the first colony.

to recognize this in his report, he did attach great importance to the news and planned to march northwards from Chawanoac,

untill I had bene arrived at the Bay or Port hee spake of: which, finding to bee worth the possession, I would there have raised a maine fort, both for the defence of the harborough, and our shipping also, and would have reduced our whole habitation from Roanoak and from the harborough and port there (which by proofe is very naught) unto this other beforementioned.[13]

Removal to Chesapeake Bay was thus now Lane's firm intention, provided that the place offered the expected harbour and access for shipping, and he planned to resolve that question as soon as relief arrived from England, which would enable him to send a reconnaissance expedition by sea to find and investigate that bay. Meanwhile he decided to pursue the matter of the metal, which was reported to lie near a salt sea. The double lure – of gold and the Pacific – was very strong, for as Lane himself observed, 'the discovery of a good Mine, by the goodnesse of God, or a passage to the South-sea, or some way to it, and nothing els can bring this Countrey in request to be inhabited by our nation'.[14] He therefore set out in late March with a force of forty men to ascend the River Roanoke.

By this time, however, the Indians of the region were turning against the colonists. During the winter the latter relied increasingly upon the Roanoke Indians for food, as their own stores dwindled. They had arrived too late in the country to sow cereals themselves and consequently looked to the natives to supply maize, which they did happily in exchange for English goods so long as they had a surplus to dispose of. Lane's men, some of them gentlemen and the majority soldiers, no doubt obtained some fresh meat by hunting, but probably went short of protein, partly because they failed to master the native art of setting fish traps. They expected supplies to arrive from England before Easter and lacked any strong inclination to produce their own until the Indians, hard pressed themselves, refused to meet their demands. In March 1586 at Chawanoac Lane discovered that Wingina had already conspired with the Chowans and others to make war upon the intruders, planning at the same time to evacuate Roanoke, leaving the ground unsown and the colonists starving. Lane disrupted the proceedings at Chawanoac by seizing the Chowan chief and subsequently taking his son hostage, but the Indians remained hostile. As Lane's party made its way up the Roanoke River in search of metal, the natives, advised by Wingina, removed themselves and their corn. Desperately short of victuals, the English were attacked before reach-

[13] *PN*, VIII, 325.   [14] *PN*, VIII, 331.

ing the copper deposits, decided then to turn back, and had a very hard journey to Roanoke, arriving there to find the Indians in a dangerous mood. Lane's return in the face of such hardship seemed to change their attitude for a time, and in April they set up fish-weirs, sowed enough seed for a year's corn and allowed the colonists both land and seed for their own requirements. But the real cause of hostility remained: the harvest would not be ready before July and the promised relief from England was overdue. The threat of famine forced Lane to disperse his company to seek roots, oysters and shell-fish. In May he realized that Wingina was organizing a general assault to overwhelm the colony and he decided to forestall this by taking the offensive. On 1 June 1586 he took the Indians by surprise, slaughtered Wingina among others, and effectively crushed the opposition for the time being. A week later his men sighted a great fleet, reported as twenty-three sail, which to their relief turned out to be English, under the command of Sir Francis Drake.

Drake had left Plymouth for the West Indies on 14 September 1585, before the return of any ships from Roanoke, but he of course knew what Ralegh and Grenville intended and during his voyage bore in mind the welfare of the new-born colony.[15] His main object in this expedition was to inflict damage upon the Spanish Indies, specifically by sacking the chief accessible cities – Santo Domingo, Cartagena and above all Panama, the ultimate and supreme target. But some longer-term strategic gain was not ruled out. We have seen that Grenville set up a temporary base at Puerto Rico on his way out, after which, in August 1585, Ralph Lane wrote enthusiastically to Sir Philip Sidney exhorting him to undertake the occupation of that island and Española, 'an attempt most honorable and fesible, and proffytable, and only fytte for your selfe to be cheeffe commaunder in'.[16] In fact long before he received this letter Sir Philip had been expected to command the land force in Drake's expedition. He had since been replaced by Christopher Carleill, but the two men shared an active interest in Gilbert's colonial plans and probably in Ralegh's too.[17] Drake himself contemplated holding a base across the Atlantic – Panama was the main option, Havana another[18] – and the visit to Roanoke was

---

[15] On the West Indian events of this expedition see pp. 280–1 below. The chief sources are in Quinn, *Roanoke Voyages*; I. A. Wright (ed.), *Further English Voyages to Spanish America, 1583–1594* (London, 1951); M. F. Keeler (ed.), *Sir Francis Drake's West Indian Voyage, 1585–86* (London, 1981); and J. S. Corbett (ed.), *Papers relating to the Navy during the Spanish War, 1585–1587* (London, 1898).

[16] Quinn, *Roanoke Voyages*, p. 205.

[17] Sidney tried to join Drake's fleet at Plymouth in September 1585, but was recalled by the queen: Quinn, *Roanoke Voyages*, p. 250.

[18] Spanish evidence suggests that Drake's men expected to remain three years in Panama

undoubtedly on his agenda from the start. The events of the voyage increased its importance, for at Cartagena in February, March and April of 1586 he was forced to abandon the projected Panama raid and at that stage, having already recruited a number of Turks and Negroes at Santo Domingo for service in the isthmus, he took aboard further Turks and Moors from the galleys and runaway Negro slaves, some two hundred in all, in addition to three hundred Indians, mostly women.[19] On leaving Cartagena Drake may well have hoped to make Havana his next prize, but his passengers could hardly have been useful there: they must have been destined for Virginia, as reinforcements for the colony.

Drake did not attempt Havana, but made his way carefully up the eastern shore of Florida. He had learned that at Santa Elena (Port Royal Sound in 32°) there was a Spanish outpost, and he hoped, with the aid of a Portuguese pilot who knew the coast, to seek out and destroy this threat to the English colony before proceeding to Virginia. Before they reached that latitude, however, the pilot disclosed the location of the more important base at San Agustín. Here, therefore, Drake landed troops and devastated the fort and the town. The Spanish occupants managed to escape into the bush, but for the time being San Agustín as a base was crippled and Drake's men removed everything that might be useful at Roanoke.[20] The fleet then moved north again, but failed to find Santa Elena and reached Roanoke on 9 June.

Drake found the colonists in a poor state. Some of them were weak from lack of food or illness: these he offered to take home, leaving oarsmen, artificers and others of his own company in their stead. In addition he agreed to provide Lane with the 70-ton *Francis*, victualled for four months for a hundred men; a pinnace or two and boats, all with their crews, including two of his best masters, one of whom – Abraham Kendall – was an outstanding navigator; and fresh stores of clothing and weapons. Lane would thus be able to carry out the essential task that remained – 'to search the coast for some better

and that he intended to take pinnaces across the isthmus: Wright, *Further English Voyages*, pp. 55, 195. On Havana, *ibid.* p. 52 and Corbett, *Spanish War*, p. 73.

[19] Wright, *Further English Voyages*, p. 173.

[20] Wright, *Further English Voyages*, pp. 181–91. A foreign gentleman in London in August 1586 reported, presumably as hearsay from Drake's men, that at San Agustín Drake had learned that Pedro Menéndez Marqués, governor of Florida, had organized an expedition to destroy the English colony, and that Drake therefore went to Virginia with the object of 'rescuing Ralph Lane . . . and his people from death, and of bringing them all back home with him safely' – Quinn, *New American World*, III, p. 309. This statement cannot be accepted at face value, since Drake evidently did not intend to remove Lane. He presumably felt that he had weakened the immediate strike capability of the Spaniards enough to enable Roanoke, with such aid as he could supply, to survive for the time being.

harborow' – and then to return to England with the rest of his men. These plans were put in hand immediately, but before the arrangements were completed a great storm broke up the fleet, some smaller craft were lost and the *Francis*, with some of Lane's men aboard, disappeared. After the storm Drake offered another ship instead of the *Francis*, but it was a much larger vessel, suitable for bringing the colonists home but not for operating on and off that hazardous coast. Lane therefore decided – and with good reason – to take passage for England in Drake's ships, embarked all his men save three who were up-country and reached Portsmouth on 28 July.[21]

This was not quite the end of the first colonial adventure – an ironic last act was still to come. Ralegh had in fact organized the long-awaited relief, and his supply ship arrived before the end of June at Roanoke, only to find it abandoned. She returned with her stores to England and meanwhile Grenville set out with substantial reinforcements for the colony aboard a squadron of West Country privateersmen. These took a number of prizes on the way out and manned them home, which both delayed and depleted the expedition, so that when he reached Roanoke about the middle of July Grenville found the place 'desolate, yet unwilling to loose the possession of the Countrie. . . he landed 15. men in the Ile of Roanoke, furnished plentifully with all maner of provision for two yeeres, and so departed for England'.[22] This was an unfortunate decision. He would have done better to leave no men at all, since Roanoke was no longer thought worth holding, though he could not know this. On the other hand a strong force, such as he could have planted there, would have stood a fair chance of survival. Leaving a small holding party in those circumstances meant leaving them to the Indians. As it was learned later, they were attacked, driven off Roanoke and never seen again by English eyes. Grenville did not reach home until December, having spent the intervening time pursuing prize, which he did successfully enough to pay once again the expenses of the colonial venture, though this happy outcome hardly compensated for the harmful effect of his privateering activity upon western planting. It had prevented his arrival in time to reinforce Lane and it no doubt influenced his decision to leave only a handful of men on the island, since his company understandably preferred the prospects of a cruise to the rigours of Roanoke and he himself probably thought Roanoke of little use as a privateering base.[23]

The experience of the first Roanoke colony was not without value in

[21] Quinn, *Roanoke Voyages*, pp. 253–4, 288–312.
[22] Quinn, *Roanoke Voyages*, p. 480.
[23] Quinn, *Roanoke Voyages*, pp. 465–88.

spite of its disappointing end, value which was multiplied by the collaboration of two remarkable men – Thomas Hariot, a scientist, and John White, an artist. Hariot, a pioneer of astronomy, mathematics and navigation, joined Ralegh's household about 1580 to instruct him and his sea-captains in 'the mathematical sciences',[24] and in the event his original and questioning mind proved a whetstone to Ralegh's wit in other ways, for he was both philosopher and practitioner and his field of interest was unlimited.[25] Less is known about White, who first appears in 1577 as a painter of subjects connected with Frobisher's second northwest expedition. He probably took part in the Amadas-Barlowe voyage and in 1585–6 he and Hariot together produced a description of Virginia in words, pictures and maps, with particular emphasis on the life of the Algonquian Indians. Hariot learned the native language from Manteo and Wanchese well enough to investigate Indian society and religion in some depth. He and White moved around the mainland as well as Roanoke, recording their observations in detail – Hariot in written notes, White in accompanying drawings – studies of fish, birds, land animals, plants and above all of the people and their way of life. They also jointly surveyed and mapped the region.[26]

What survives of this work is incomplete, and what was published in De Bry's *America*, Part I, in 1590 did less than justice to the original work.[27] Even so, the result was to make that part of North America better reported than any other for a long time thereafter. The picture of Indian life was especially perceptive and valuable: 'a unique window – albeit a narrow one – through which we can look out on Indian life before the disruptions and dislocations caused directly and indirectly by the European invasions'.[28] White's original drawings show unusual fidelity in portraying the Indian people and Hariot's notes, though by no means flawless, generally attained a higher standard of objectivity than other contemporary descriptions of strange cultures. He had been, to use his own phrase, 'in dealing with the naturall inhabitantes specially imploied',[29] and the care and sympathy with which he undertook that most difficult task shine through his notes on Indian agriculture, warfare and religion. However, Hariot's ethnological

[24] Taylor, *Writings of the Hakluyts*, pp. 366–7.
[25] J. W. Shirley (ed.), *Thomas Harriot, Renaissance Scientist* (Oxford, 1974).
[26] Hulton and Quinn, *American Drawings of John White*; Quinn, *Roanoke Voyages*, pp. 390–464.
[27] Theodore de Bry, *America* (Parts I–XIII, Frankfurt, 1590–1634), I (1590).
[28] Hulton and Quinn, *American Drawings of John White*, p. 37.
[29] Quinn, *Roanoke Voyages*, p. 321. *Ibid*. pp. 317–87 for the collated and annotated editior of the report. Hariot here announced his intention to publish a chronicle of the colony but nothing more is known of this.

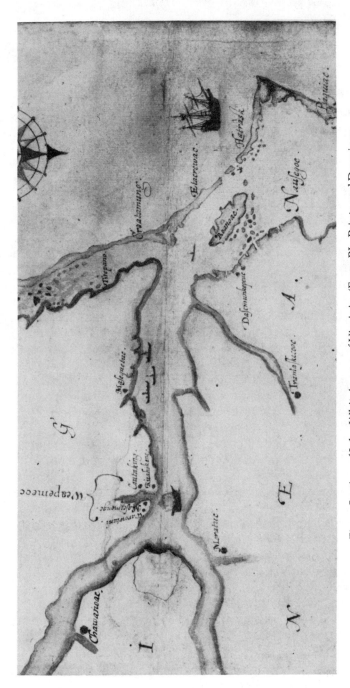

Fig. 5 Section of John White's map of Virginia. (From BL, Prints and Drawings, 1906-5-9-1(3).)

work came to be known more widely through the *Briefe and true report*, which was indeed brief, but not entirely true, since it was written quite expressly to counter the denigration of the country and its natives by the more disgruntled of Lane's men. Hariot's approach to the 'Indian question' in this context was hardly scientific:

These their opinions I have set downe the more at large, that it may appeare unto you that there is good hope they may be brought through discreet dealing and governement to the imbracing of the trueth, and consequently to honour, obey, feare and love us.[30]

Hariot had in fact done his best to achieve these ends himself. He took a Bible with him on his travels in order to propagate the faith and he displayed some of the wonders of European science to the Indians. They had the intelligence, he argued, to recognize the advantages of adopting a superior religion and culture, and to learn quickly. Friendship, education and good government would soon win them to civility and Christianity. He nevertheless respected the Indians, deplored as unnecessary the violence that had been used against them towards the end of the year of occupation and included excellent descriptions of their crops and cultivation, as well as rather optimistic accounts of the country's 'merchantable commodities'. This is the report of a committed observer, closely engaged with his subject – fascinated, for example, by the Indians' use of tobacco, which he did much to advertise in England. It is rightly regarded, despite its inevitable defects, as a major contribution to our knowledge of sixteenth-century North America.

The experience of the first colony was not wasted. Important lessons were evidently learned, for in 1587 Ralegh authorized White to make a new start along different lines.[31] For reasons by now obvious, the new settlement was to be planted not on Roanoke, but on Chesapeake Bay. Furthermore it was to consist of planters who would themselves have a stake in the country: 500 acres of land each, and more in proportion to their investment. These planters would bring their families, would work to make a living in the country and together would create 'the City of Ralegh in Virginia'. John White would be their governor, who would rule with twelve assistants under Ralegh's patent over a self-governing 'body politic and corporate' made up of the citizen-planters. Ralegh remained the overlord and supplied some of the capital, the rest being presumably subscribed by the planters themselves with

[30] Quinn, *Roanoke Voyages*, p. 381.
[31] On the 1587 colony see Quinn, *Roanoke Voyages*, pp. 497–552. The main documents are in *PN*, VIII, 386–403.

some merchant backing. Some of the planters were London tradesmen, some from farming stock, and there were probably some educated, middle-class people among the 110, including eighteen women, who eventually stayed in Virginia.[32] The constitution of the new colony represented not merely a change of tactics in response to the somewhat bitter experience of 1585–6, but a radical change in the character of the plantation envisaged. Whereas Lane's colony had been essentially a military establishment, White's was markedly civilian. The idea of a new 'inhabitation' (Hakluyt's term) for English commoners across the ocean now came to the fore. It had a certain kinship with Peckham's scheme, without its aristocratic emphasis, and so may be seen in retrospect to anticipate the popular and peaceful movement of the Brownist pioneers of the 1590s and the Pilgrim Fathers later, though we do not know whether any of White's planters were Separatists.[33] In various practical respects this kind of settlement stood a better chance of survival than Lane's and it had the great attraction of being cheaper to launch and maintain, but the price paid for this economy was that it could not be expected to contribute – at least for some considerable time – to the war effort. Thus it came at the wrong time politically, for in the years 1587 and 1588 the government was unlikely to attach much importance to a strategically worthless outpost. Lane's colony, had it lasted, might have appeared eligible for assistance even in 1588; White's could only be seen as a liability.

Nor did the events of 1587 improve its prospects. On 8 May the settlers left England in three vessels: the flagship *Lion*, of 120 tons, commanded by John White, with Simão Fernandes master; a flyboat, master Edward Spicer; and a pinnace under Edward Stafford, a gentleman who had served with Lane in the first colony.[34] White's journal of the voyage is a depressing tale of continual quarrels between himself and Fernandes, who were probably temperamentally incompatible and in any case disagreed about the conduct of the voyage. White was interested in the Caribbean as a potential source of

---

[32] William Sanderson and Customer Thomas Smith may have invested in the 1587 colony. Sanderson and Ralegh jointly borrowed money from Smith in that year and both of these merchants were among Ralegh's assignees in 1589: Quinn, *Roanoke Voyages*, pp. 539–43, 544, 557–8, 569–78.

[33] On the Brownist pioneers see Quinn, *England and the Discovery of America*, pp. 337–63.

[34] Sir George Carey, Captain of the Isle of Wight, sent out three ships early in 1587 for the West Indies under Captain William Irish, who visited Roanoke on his return voyage, presumably arriving and departing before White's arrival. Grenville also probably prepared ships for Virginia in 1587, but there is no evidence that they crossed the Atlantic. Quinn, *Roanoke Voyages*, pp. 499, 782. On Spicer see K. R. Andrews, 'The voyage of the *Jaquet* of Falmouth to the West Indies and Newfoundland, 1585–86', *Mariner's Mirror*, 59 (1973), 101–3.

supplies (animals, plants, water, etc.) for the colony, but Fernandes, perhaps because he would have preferred privateering, seemed (according to White) determined to thwart him. Bad feeling between the sailors and the emigrants – a recurrent feature of colonizing voyages – in this case as in others injured the enterprise, since the result of these petty wrangles was that the Caribbean yielded neither prizes nor provisions. And worse troubles were to grow out of this personal antagonism. On arriving at Hatarask on 22 July White went aboard the pinnace, accompanied by forty of his best men, intending to pass up to Roanoke in search of the fifteen men Grenville had left there the year before. Having consulted them about the state of the country, his intention was – as he stated in his journal – to go on to Chesapeake Bay and establish the colony there in accordance with Ralegh's instructions. However,

> assoone as we were put with our pinnesse from the shippe, a Gentleman by the meanes of Fernando, who was appointed to returne for England, called to the sailers in the pinnesse, charging them not to bring any of the planters backe againe, but leave them in the Island, except the Governour, and two or three such as he approved, saying that the Summer was farre spent, wherefore hee would land all the planters in no other place. Unto this were all the sailers, both in the pinnesse, and shippe, perswaded by the Master, wherefore it booted not the Governour to contend with them.[35]

White implies here that he had no real authority over the sailors, who, led by Fernandes, decided the course of the voyage to suit themselves. They wanted the rest of the summer for hunting prizes and were not prepared to waste that time looking for a new site in Chesapeake Bay. This is all credible in the light of what we know about the behaviour of Elizabethan crews, but doubts must arise about White's acquiescence. Was he really so spineless as to yield without so much as a protest to this blatant defiance of Ralegh's orders or was he content to let Fernandes have his way? It is conceivable that when confronted with this change of plan the governor was less unhappy with it than he afterwards claimed, since the Roanoke he knew may well have seemed at that time a more hospitable place than Chesapeake Bay, a region virtually unknown to him. If so, Fernandes became a convenient excuse.[36] Any attachment White may have felt to

---

[35] *PN*, viii, 391.

[36] It is equally possible that Fernandes knew more about Chesapeake Bay than White did, and consequently thought Roanoke the safer place. It would be wrong to take White's version of this episode for granted. The English obviously thought highly of Fernandes as a pilot, since they employed him over and over again, but as a foreigner he was eminently blameworthy. See Quinn, *England and the Discovery of America*, pp. 246–63, for an account of Fernandes.

Roanoke must have suffered some erosion in the next three weeks, however: Grenville's men were not to be found; it was learned from Manteo at Croatoan that they had been driven off Roanoke by hostile Indians; the Roanoke fort had been damaged and its earthworks razed; one of White's men was ambushed and killed; the estranged Indians eluded White's attempts to restore contact and (subsequently) to attack them. In the light of these developments it is not surprising that the colonists contemplated moving to the mainland forthwith.[37]

By 21 August the *Lion* and the flyboat were almost ready to depart for England and controversy arose between the governor and his assistants, none of whom was willing to return with the ships to organize the fresh supplies that were generally agreed to be urgently needed. Eventually, according to White, the entire company pleaded with him to make the voyage himself. He at first refused, arguing the discredit he – and consequently the enterprise itself – would suffer by an act which might be construed as desertion, but the colonists insisted he was the best man for that task and finally persuaded him, much against his will, to undertake it. White was certainly not a deserter, but his own account of these proceedings leaves the impression that his fellow-planters thought him better employed in organizing support at home than in leading them in the wilderness. And so on 27 August he boarded the flyboat, leaving behind his daughter Elenora, her husband Ananias Dare and their daughter, born in Virginia and called by that name, as well as the rest of the colonists and Manteo, now christened and made Lord of Roanoke, Ralegh's vassal. The voyage began with a disastrous accident at the capstan, in which most of the crew were injured, and it continued badly. Death and sickness so reduced the men that they could not sail the ship beyond Smerwick, where White took passage in another, arriving in England at last in early November, only to find that the *Lion* had come home in even worse case.

Having gone so far as to back White's project in 1587 in spite of its unwarlike, even vulnerable appearance, contrasting so sharply with the first design for Virginia, Ralegh could not forthwith abandon it without losing face and friends as well as self-respect. White's report can have offered no real hope that the colony would open the way to the creation of a naval base in the near future, but Ralegh's sense of personal responsibility was sufficient to produce an immediate

[37] In his 1587 journal White says 'they intended to remove 50 miles further up into the maine presently' (*PN*, VIII, 398) and in the 1590 journal he makes clear that this was no vague inclination, but a practical decision for immediate action: 'for at my coming away they were prepared to remove from Roanoak 50 miles into the maine' (*PN*, VIII, 417).

response. He ordered a pinnace to take out supplies as soon as possible, to be followed in the summer by a fleet under Grenville's command. In fact, however, the government had already ordered a general stay of shipping in English ports and Ralegh was unable, though he tried, to carry out his plans.[38] No relief pinnace was sent and Grenville's expedition, which he made ready for Virginia by the end of March, was then finally cancelled, the ships being sent to reinforce Drake's fleet at Plymouth. The only concession White, by dint of earnest pleading, was able to obtain was permission for two pinnaces – the *Brave* of 30 tons and the *Roe* of 25 tons – to sail with fifteen planters and provisions. These left Bideford, Grenville's home port, on 22 April, and at once began chasing every sail they sighted in hopes of plunder. On 3 May the two vessels parted company and shortly afterwards the *Brave*, in which White sailed, was badly mauled in a fight with a Rocheller. By the end of May she was back at Bideford, having abandoned the voyage, and there White learned that the *Roe* had done likewise. Nothing else was done in that year of the armada to relieve the colony, so far as is known, nor did the year 1589 see any fresh attempt.

In the winter of 1589–90 Hakluyt complained bitterly, in the preface to his *Principall Navigations* (1589), that the plantations were founded at the charges of sir Walter Raleigh, whose entrance upon those newe inhabitations had bene happie, if it had ben as seriously followed, as it was cheerefully undertaken'.[39] The evidence available to us suggests, however, that Ralegh did try to get Grenville to sea in 1588 and was overruled by the Privy Council. It was this government decision – one fully justified by the necessities of defence in that fateful year – which effectively sentenced the colony to death. Hakluyt, we may infer, held Ralegh personally responsible for the continued neglect of the settlers during 1589. In that year numerous English men-of-war cruised the Atlantic, some of them even the Caribbean. Ralegh himself had privateers at sea and his kinsman John Chidley led a major expedition to Magellan's Strait. Thus Hakluyt's charge is fair, though it may be said on Ralegh's behalf that the fatal die was already cast and the settlers already for all practical purposes forsaken in 1588, whereas in

[38] Ralegh wrote to Sir John Gilbert on 27 February 1587/88 ordering him to enforce the Privy Council's stay, but added the postscript: 'such as I have acquaynted yow withall to whom I have geven leve you may lett them steale away'. This, followed by the unequivocal orders to Grenville from the Privy Council, is sufficient evidence that Ralegh tried to have Grenville's ships dispatched but was overruled: Quinn, *Roanoke Voyages*, pp. 559–62. For White's account of the 1588 voyage see *ibid.* pp. 553–69.

[39] Sig. *4r. The preface was probably written towards the end of the new-style calendar year 1589 or (if Hakluyt chose to use the old style) between 1 January and 24 March 1590.

1589 there was more important work to be done against the enemy at sea. Moreover he did at least take steps to provide the framework for a broader and more regular organization of the colonial enterprise, associating himself and White's planters with a new group of nineteen partners, headed by the London merchants Thomas Smythe and William Sanderson and including Richard Hakluyt the younger.[40] These nineteen agreed to invest money, shipping, victuals and so forth in exchange for rights of trade. Whether the new organization was as strong in substance as in appearance is to be doubted, but it was on Ralegh's part a move intended to strengthen the foundations of the City of Ralegh, not to leave them to rot, and it was Sanderson who eventually, in 1590, managed to mount another effort to help the colony, or at least to discover whether it still existed.

Early in 1590 John Watts, the greatest privateering promoter among the London shipowners, was preparing a squadron of three ships for a West Indies cruise when the Privy Council ordered the stay of all shipping in expectation of a new armada. Sanderson hereupon arranged with Watts that, in exchange for a licence to sail (to be obtained by Ralegh from the queen), the privateers would take White to Roanoke together with some planters and stores, while Sanderson's own ship, the *Moonlight*, should accompany them.[41] In the event Watts allowed only White aboard, without stores or fellow-planters, and dispatched his ships before the *Moonlight* was ready, but finally the latter rejoined in the West Indies and after some highly successful prize-hunting there Watts's flagship the *Hopewell* proceeded in company with the *Moonlight* to the Carolina Banks. They anchored off Hatarask on 15 August 1590 and three days later found the Roanoke fort. It was deserted. Where the houses had been now stood a high palisade of trees, on one of which the single word 'CROATOAN' was carved in capital letters, while elsewhere another tree bore the letters 'CRO'. These signals indicated, according to a code arranged before White's departure, that the planters had gone to Croatoan Island. Had they been in distress the message should have been accompanied by a Maltese cross, but no such marking was evident, and White therefore 'greatly joyed that I had safely found a certaine token of their safe being at Croatoan, which is the place where Manteo was borne, and the Savages of the Iland our friends'.[42] The captain of the *Hopewell*, Abraham Cocke, then agreed to run south to Croatoan, but the

[40] Quinn, *Roanoke Voyages*, pp. 569–76.
[41] White's letter to Hakluyt in 1593 explained the arrangement: *PN*, VIII, 404–6; Quinn, *Roanoke Voyages*, 579–82.
[42] *PN*, VIII, 418.

weather grew so foul that they were unable to recover their water casks from ashore and lost two anchors getting clear of the banks. Reduced to a single cable and anchor, without a pinnace and short of victuals, Cocke and his men decided, with White's consent, to leave that coast and return after wintering in the West Indies. The *Moonlight*, however, refused to accompany them and made for home, and after two days' sailing for Trinidad the *Hopewell*, again beset by heavy storms, changed course for the Azores and thence for England, reaching Plymouth in October.

The story of the Roanoke colonists does not end in 1590, for the mystery which still shrouds their fate continued to exercise minds in both England and Spain. Their ghostly influence upon the course of events down to and beyond the refounding of Virginia in 1607 belongs, however, to the Jamestown story, and will be examined in that context. The Roanoke venture was finally abandoned when the *Hopewell* and the *Moonlight* left the banks. That voyage of 1590 itself vividly illustrated the attraction of privateering, and in the following year Ralegh joined forces with Watts and other Londoners to fit out another successful West Indian cruise. In 1592 he took the lead in organizing Atlantic privateering on a grand scale and for the remainder of the war he pursued the enemy by sea, seeking spoil and victory. He had an interest in numerous privateering ventures and in 1595 staked no small part of his fortune, as well as his reputation, on the quest for *El Dorado*, the golden man of Guiana. Ralegh can hardly be blamed for throwing his energies and resources into the war with Spain once Virginia was apparently a lost cause. That his contribution took the form of privateering and similar enterprise with personal as well as national gain in view was at that time perfectly normal and proper. Others did likewise and the sea-war occupied the shipping, capital and manpower which might otherwise have been partly invested in colonization.

The Roanoke enterprise was in fact undertaken with inadequate resources and insufficient knowledge at an unfortunate time, so that every mishap, adverse circumstance and human error told heavily against success. The first reconnaissance was too superficial to enable the planners to brief their pioneers usefully. In particular, though they may have known of the existence of Chesapeake Bay,[43] they had apparently no prior warning of the dangers of the coast to the south and of the absence of good harbours. By the time they learned these lessons by experience they were already paying the price of their

---

[43] A crossed-out note in one of Lane's letters to Walsingham stated: 'Thys Porte in ye Carte ys by ye Spanyardes called St Marryes baye', which was a Spanish name for Chesapeake Bay: Quinn, *Roanoke Voyages*, p. 201.

mistake and had committed themselves to an unsuitable site, from which they found it extremely difficult to remove. Nor did they have a realistic conception of the nature of the country. Accounts of the French colonies in Florida were to hand, but Ralegh's men could hardly draw relevant conclusions from Ribault and Laudonnière until they knew something of their own region and its problems – they, like the rest of us, could only learn from their own mistakes. Their notion that they could make a commercial success of that raw land by developing the cultivation of Mediterranean export crops was not unreasonable, but they failed to realize how long and hard the initial process of settlement would be and how much money would have to be ploughed into that process before Virginia could begin to yield dividends.

Hariot's remarks about Lane's men suggest that by no means all were possessed of the true pioneering spirit: 'many that after gold and silver was not so soone found, as it was by them looked for, had little or no care of any other thing but to pamper their bellies . . . Because there were not to bee found any English cities, nor such faire houses, nor at their owne wish any of their olde accustomed daintie food, nor any soft beds of downe or feathers, the countrey was to them miserable.'[44] The gentlemen of the party no doubt found the going rough and Lane's men in general seem to have taken living off the country to mean little more than living off the Indians. Well before the last days of the occupation the Anglo-Indian relationship had evolved into a state of intermittent warfare. Lane's determination to evacuate Roanoke, already set in principle before Drake's arrival, must have been influenced by these problems, which arose largely from the nature of the first colony, as well as by the need to find a better site.

His intention was frustrated by the weather, which was doubtless fortunate for him, since what he planned was virtually a step in the dark, fraught with untold dangers. Even so, at the moment of Drake's arrival in June 1586 the Virginia venture still held promise of survival and eventual success. Thereafter confidence in its future dwindled as misfortune followed misfortune. The return of Lane's colonists must have come as a shattering blow to the hopes of the promoters, and it was followed by public denigration of the enterprise so notorious that Hariot was obliged to take notice and write what amounted to an apologetic report. Meanwhile Ralegh's relief ship returned from its useless voyage and Grenville made the mistake of leaving a mere handful of men to hold the site Lane had condemned. Privateering was already proving far more attractive than colonizing and it was clearer than ever that the latter required state aid, but state aid was even less

[44] Quinn, *Roanoke Voyages*, p. 323.

available now that Elizabeth was committed to war in the Low Countries. The plantation movement was thus at a low ebb when White came forward with his scheme for a colony which would be largely self-financing and self-sufficient, avoiding thereby dependence on either Queen Elizabeth or the chiefs of the Chesapeake. It is not surprising that such a plan proved acceptable, but it had much less relevance to the Anglo-Spanish war than the first colony and consequently could not expect any official favours. When White came home in 1587, having failed to site the planters as instructed, he can hardly have inspired the queen's ministers with much confidence either in his own capacity as a leader or in the future of the plantation. Their decision not to let Grenville go was as much a logical conclusion to the history of the enterprise as it was an expression of the crown's concern for the safety of the Channel.

Anglo-Spanish hostility thus played a large part in this abortive colonial adventure from first to last. On their side the Spaniards, anxious as they were for their Florida footholds, which guarded the treasure route, were quickly alerted to and alarmed by the presence of the English to the north and planned to attack them from San Agustín. Drake's action scotched this danger for the time being only. Unaware of the subsequent English withdrawal, the Spaniards set themselves to restoring San Agustín and preparing a descent upon the English colony. In March 1588 orders were sent from Spain to the governor of Florida to prepare to lead an expedition in May, but neither the orders nor the reinforcements arrived. Instead the governor sent a small vessel north to reconnoitre the coast in the summer of 1588. This explored Chesapeake Bay and on the return voyage discovered by accident traces of the English at Hatarask, from which the governor concluded that the colony existed nearby. However, he could do nothing about it that year and early in 1589 he learned almost the full story of Roanoke from one Pedro Diaz, a Spanish pilot who had, since his capture by Grenville in 1585, taken part in the events until, as pilot of one of White's two pinnaces in 1588, he had managed to escape. His conclusion was that the English colony either no longer existed or was at the end of its tether. When this report reached Spain, however, it was decided to mount an expedition to ensure the final destruction of the enemy and to establish a fort to hold Chesapeake Bay and so forestall any further attempts by the English on the southeast coasts of North America. The exigencies of the war with England prevented the execution of this well-considered design, just as they had prevented Grenville from reviving the second colony.[45]

[45] Quinn, *England and the Discovery of America*, pp. 264–81.

11

The sea-war
1585–1603

In 1585 England and Spain came at last into open conflict. In August Elizabeth formally allied herself to the Dutch rebels and at the end of the year sent an army under the earl of Leicester to the Low Countries to engage the Spanish forces of occupation. Meanwhile at sea that summer English privateers began a campaign of reprisal against Spanish shipping in retaliation for the arrest of English ships, men and goods in Spanish harbours ordered by Philip II in May. In September Drake, with two of the queen's ships and twenty-three others, apart from pinnaces, set out from Plymouth to menace the coast of Spain and to ravage the West Indies. Thus began a war which was to last eighteen years, until the accession of James I in 1603 and the Treaty of London in 1604. Seemingly an inconclusive, even at times half-hearted, struggle, this war in fact marked a turning-point in the fortunes of both nations and above all in their oceanic fortunes. This is not to say that the war itself decided the course of empire overseas, much less that the protagonists recognized its imperial implications or attached more than marginal significance to its extra-European dimension. Indirectly and unintentionally, however, it had an important bearing upon the genesis of the British Empire.

The Tudor rulers before Elizabeth had maintained friendly relations with Spain most of the time. The two countries found a common enemy in France and, when Charles of Habsburg acquired the Spanish crown, a common interest in the Netherlands. France and Spain, the two great powers of Europe, were continually in conflict, a conflict only aggravated by the growing dominance of the Habsburgs in Italy, Germany and the Low Countries as well as the Peninsula. England meanwhile, having lost all her former conquests in France save Calais, clung stubbornly to that and hankered yet to recover some other footholds to counter the growing menace of French power across the Channel. The great trade of the English at Antwerp prospered until the mid-century, strengthening the old bond between England and Burgundy. And when Elizabeth came to the throne the threat from France seemed greater than ever. Calais had fallen to the enemy, Mary of Guise ruled Scotland and her daughter, Mary Stuart, in Catholic eyes the rightful queen of England, was married to the French dauphin. In 1559 the latter became king and the treaty of Cateau-Cambrésis ended the long wars between France and Spain. The prospect of a Franco-British empire dominated by the Guise family, likely enough in 1560, receded with the death of Francis II and the success of the Lords of the Congregation, but the Guise remained a power to be reckoned with and Elizabeth had cause to fear the French and look to Spain for support. As for Philip II, he had no wish to alienate England in the years that followed Cateau-Cambrésis, for he needed an ally to hold France in check while he struggled to contain a more dangerous enemy – the Grand Turk.

Such were the circumstances that held Philip and Elizabeth in diplomatic accord for nearly a decade after her accession. But already the ground was shifting beneath their feet. France, torn by faction and religious hatred, was sinking into impotence; the Low Countries, deeply disturbed by the economic crisis of the fifties and by the spread of Protestant ideas, seethed with discontent and resistance to Spanish policy; and Anglo-Spanish amity itself was wearing thin. The cause of the reformed religion held no strong appeal for Elizabeth, who resisted pressure to become the champion of the Protestants against the Catholics. Nevertheless she was irrevocably a heretic in the eyes of Philip of Spain and his advisers, some of whom thought her overthrow necessary to secure the Catholic faith and Spanish rule in the Netherlands. And they may well have been right, for among the queen's ministers there were those, notably Cecil, who encouraged dissent and resistance among Philip's subjects. Furthermore the persecutions of Mary's reign had already taught many Englishmen to identify Spain with the counter-reformation, while anti-Spanish and anti-Catholic feeling was particularly strong in the sea-ports, where the stories of seamen and merchants who had suffered at the hands of the Inquisition in Spain lost nothing in the telling. We have seen that even as early as the 1540s West Country sailors were beginning piratically to prey upon Spanish shipping; in the mid fifties the Killigrews of Falmouth and others were at it again;[1] from 1562 piracy in the Channel and thence southwards grew virtually unchecked. Trade between England and Flanders was consequently suspended in 1563–4, which made matters worse, and Hawkins meanwhile, backed by the queen's

[1] A. L. Rowse, *Tudor Cornwall: Portrait of a Society* (London, 1941), pp. 317–18.

officers and from 1564 directly by the queen, openly flouted King
Philip in the forbidden waters of the Caribbean.

Thus the tradition of friendship between England and Spain had
already been undermined when the duke of Alba marched his army
into the Netherlands in 1567 to stamp out disorder and compel
obedience. That was why the fate of the Low Countries became a bone
of contention between the two sovereigns. To Philip they were an
important dominion and must accept his rule in faith and law: England
was another, and altogether more remote problem. But Elizabeth
would not allow him to dispose of those provinces in his own way
because she feared that a Spanish conquest of them would lead on to
her own destruction. Henceforth the Netherlands were a wedge
driving England and Spain apart, ultimately into open conflict. Indeed
the two countries were already at daggers drawn from Alba's arrival
until 1572, years of acute international crisis which only subsided
because Philip remained preoccupied with the Mediterranean while
France and England moved into an uneasy alliance, keeping the Dutch
revolt alive. In the ensuing lull it even seemed possible that Spain's
rule in the Netherlands might be reconciled with a degree of autonomy, a solution Elizabeth favoured, since it would mean the withdrawal of Spanish troops without admitting the French, whose
presence in force was to be dreaded above all. But this prospect proved
illusory and from the late seventies the clouds of war gathered
ominously.

In 1578 Alessandro Farnese, Philip's nephew, took command of the
Spanish forces in the Netherlands and began the systematic conquest
of that country. At the same time the Turkish danger in the Mediterranean faded and Philip could at last deploy his power in western
Europe. First he made sure of Portugal, which he successfully
occupied in 1580, thereby substantially enhancing his resources and
especially his power at sea. Then from 1582 he turned the full force of
Spain, augmented now by an immense surge of American silver
production, upon the Dutch rebels. Elizabeth's response was to
encourage the duke of Alençon, younger brother of Henry III and heir
to the French throne, to intervene, but Alençon soon lost the rebels'
trust by attempting a coup d'état and fled the country in 1583. In the
next year events moved quickly towards a crisis. Farnese quickened his
relentless advance; in June the prince of Orange was murdered,
leaving the Dutch leaderless and desperate; in October the death of
Alençon made Henry of Navarre, a Huguenot, heir presumptive to the
throne. France, already weakened by continual conflict between the
Huguenot party on the one hand and the Catholic League, supported

by the Guise and the king of Spain, on the other, stood now on the brink of civil war, with a king too feeble to resist the pressure of the League. Increasingly England, too, had felt the menace of Spain's more aggressive policy since 1580; in January 1584 the Spanish ambassador, charged with complicity in a plot to overthrow the régime by uprising and invasion, was expelled, and anti-Spanish, anti-Catholic feeling came to the boil.

Hostility towards Spain had in fact been growing steadily in England since the sixties, and was especially associated with the commercial, colonial and frequently piratical ambitions and attempts the course of which we have already traced. These activities, sometimes inspired by a desire to injure Spain, certainly exacerbated the tension between the two countries, but they were not the main cause of the war. It was not the battle of San Juan de Ulúa which precipitated the breach between Philip and Elizabeth in 1568, but the latter's seizure of the duke of Alba's pay ships. When it suited the queen to repair that breach she took measures to suppress piracy and shelved Grenville's South American plans. Later, when she unleashed Drake, encouraged Dom Antonio and those who conspired with him to subvert or penetrate the Portuguese empire, and finally authorized the Virginia venture, it was the European situation which decided her policy. Throughout these pre-war years the Atlantic movement gathered momentum from the maritime ambitions of merchants and gentlemen, which did imply rivalry with the Iberian nations, but what, for example, made Drake a significant figure in the international scene was the political context of his 'famous voyage'. This exploit focused the increasingly militant and Protestant nationalism that was now developing in response to the evident danger from Spain and the counter-reformation, and it helped to identify those feelings with the cause of maritime expansion. Thus Drake became a national hero and overseas expansion became associated more decisively with anti-Spanish sentiments and policies. As we have seen, Drake's extraordinary achievement did not have much effect on the international situation: it dramatized that situation, and so had a powerful impact upon public opinion. In fact Drake's depredations were not a matter of insoluble dispute between the two sovereigns and in general such disputes were secondary to the main struggle for power in Europe.

But Elizabeth did not want war with Spain. All along it had been her policy to avoid the confrontation which ensued in 1585, to keep Philip at bay in the Low Countries and induce him by indirect pressure to accept a compromise there. She would lend the rebels money, allow English volunteers to fight alongside them, play the French against

Spain and use every means short of war to embarrass and contain Spanish power. Her attitude in fact was fundamentally defensive and her main object was limited: a Netherlands settlement favourable to England's security. That security would not, in her view, gain by a demolition of Spain's power, nor did she dream, as Ralegh did, of beating that great empire in pieces and making their kings kings of figs and oranges as in old times.[2] Apart from her well-justified fear that any great weakening of Spain would only strengthen France – potentially a more dangerous enemy, especially in possession of the Netherlands – she was far too realistic a statesman to imagine that such a total victory was possible. Unlike Ralegh and some others of her 'men of war', not to mention later pundits of the Dreadnought age, the queen fully appreciated the political, financial, organizational and logistic difficulties any ruler – and particularly any ruler of England – had to face in conducting warfare at that time.

Politically, at every juncture of this conflict both powers were entangled in a net of international relations which restricted their freedom to manoeuvre. Above all, neither could ignore the fate of France. Philip became increasingly committed to frustrating Henry of Navarre, who succeeded nominally to the throne in 1589, and to reducing France to a Spanish dependency, but the military resources this required had to be drawn mainly from the Netherlands, to the great relief of the insurgents and their English allies. Equally, however, Elizabeth was obliged continually to lend Henry money to keep an army in the field, to finance German and Swiss reinforcements for him and to send forces from England to his assistance, so that until he made a separate peace in 1598 France remained an important theatre of Elizabeth's war. Beating Spain and Spain's allies in France had to take precedence over beating Spain's empire in pieces. And the same considerations applied with even greater force in the Low Countries, where the maintenance of a strong Dutch bulwark against the tide of Spanish aggression was always a prime concern of Elizabeth's government.

Moreover the mounting of campaigns or expeditions of war was so costly that even Philip of Spain, with all the riches of the Indies at his disposal, faced repeated army mutinies over pay, was driven into bankruptcy three times and so taxed the people of Castile that he left them severely afflicted by inflation, famine and plague. Yet Elizabeth's financial resources were far inferior to his. Her three million subjects amounted to less than half the population of Spain, let alone that of Philip's other dominions, and were lightly taxed. The ordinary

[2] E. Edwards, *The Life of Sir Walter Raleigh and his Letters* (2 vols., London, 1868), I, p. 245.

revenue of the crown amounted, by dint of rigorous exploitation in this time of war, to some £300,000 a year, and the government managed to raise about two million by direct taxation over the war period, which together with other extraordinary revenue probably brought gross income to between £400,000 and half a million a year, out of which it had to pay the normal expenses of the Court and the administration. What remained was not enough to pay for a full-scale war: Elizabeth had to cut her coat according to her cloth and confined her military effort to supplying the French and the Dutch with auxiliary troops and raising small expeditionary forces for specific actions such as the assault on Cadiz in 1596. Even so, these modest efforts and the heavy burden of the Irish wars after 1595 increased military expenditure to such an extent that it represented a very large proportion of the total budget and could not have been raised without bankrupting the state: as it was, the crown's debts exceeded its assets in 1603.[3]

Campaigning was expensive partly because military administration was inefficient and corrupt and partly because great efforts were required to make relatively small gains in the field. England in the reign of Elizabeth lacked a regular army and depended on an antiquated system of recruitment which tended to produce troops of poor quality. Losses by desertion and disease were heavy, far exceeding losses in action; the survivors usually turned into hardened veterans and valued soldiers, but they were few; vast sums of money were embezzled by unscrupulous captains and victuallers. English forces on land might here and there make tactical gains, but they could never achieve a major victory and stood no chance of winning an important campaign. Indeed major victories and successful campaigns were rare in European warfare at this stage, chiefly because defence tended to prevail over attack. Open battles between armies seldom occurred; the fortification of towns and even villages became so effective that warfare consisted largely of sieges and associated skirmishes for control of tactical strongpoints, especially in densely populated areas like the Netherlands. Occupation of territory and sheer numbers of effectives were very important, strategy was reduced to a struggle of attrition, money was the arbiter more directly than it usually is in war.

These considerations perhaps sufficiently explain why Elizabeth 'never believed she could strike her enemy a fatal blow'.[4] Such a blow

---

[3] Figures concerning Elizabethan public finance should not be taken too literally. There was no budget, nor is there an adequate modern analysis. The leading authority describes the last years of the reign as 'the bankruptcy of the Tudor state', which must be an overstatement, though the particulars show a severe strain: F. C. Dietz, *English Public Finance 1558–1641* (New York, 1932), pp. 86–99.

[4] Corbett, *Successors of Drake*, p. 4.

was not only politically unnecessary, even undesirable; it was impossible to deliver. Consequently from the start she waged a limited war – limited in scale as in purpose. The intention in sending Leicester's army was to maintain Dutch resistance in order to bring Philip to terms; the essential mission of Drake in 1585 was to interrupt the flow of treasure to Philip's war machine, damaging thereby his immediate power and demonstrating to him the penalty he would pay if he refused to compromise. Unfortunately the effect of these measures was to convince Philip of the need to eliminate England from the struggle by a direct offensive. It was in 1586 that he approved plans for a grand expedition against England and set in motion the preparations for the Invincible Armada. Elizabeth continued to prevaricate, to negotiate, to limit the conflict; even though she found herself engaged in a *de facto* war, she could never regard this as more than a provisional state of affairs, necessitated by an emergency, which must pass when the European system resumed its normal shape. France in time would regain the strength to counter-balance Spain; the Dutch in time would become able to fend for themselves. Meanwhile she would do what she could to maintain their resistance to the domineering armies of Spain and to ward off Spain's offensive blows at England or Ireland.

At sea, therefore, the vital issue was control of the waters between the Strait of Gibraltar and the North Sea. That would enable Spain to send troops and supplies directly to Flanders instead of by the circuitous 'Spanish Road', which would mean immense logistic gains and all but certain victory, for it would solve her fundamental problem of finding the means to deploy her undoubtedly superior land forces effectively in northwest Europe, the only important theatre of operations. But in fact the English, in alliance with Dutch and Huguenot seamen, had dominated that north–south Atlantic route since the late sixties and could whenever they wished deny the Spaniards its use. So long as they retained this advantage, moreover, the islanders could continually reinforce their Dutch allies and hold the army of Flanders in perpetual check. Likewise they could maintain their French allies and frustrate Spanish attempts to seize or use bases on the French coast. They could also disrupt the mobilization of forces in the Peninsula ports by raiding down that coast. Command of the sea gave them, in effect, the power to negate Spain's main purposes and the logic of the situation demanded that if Philip could neither keep Elizabeth out of the war nor persuade her to withdraw, he must try to knock her out of it by a frontal assault.

In reality of course the issue was much less clear-cut and the king's intention to mount the Enterprise of England took many months to harden into an irrevocable decision. From the spring of 1586 the marquis of Santa Cruz was accumulating forces, but it was by no means certain that they would be used against England. Philip had good cause to hope that the threat alone might bring Elizabeth to reason, while on the other hand he had to take seriously the need to protect the treasure of the Indies against the enemy in the Atlantic. It was always possible that Santa Cruz would sail for the Azores instead of the Channel, and in the summer of 1587 he did so with a powerful detachment of the fleet and consequently delayed the launching of the attack upon England for a whole year. Both sides attached much importance to the American bullion because upon it depended Spain's entire credit structure and in particular her ability to transfer funds to the Netherlands, without which the army there would quickly grind to a halt. The contest in the Atlantic at large was thus relevant to the main issue and it remained so throughout the war. Conversely, as we shall see, the contest in Europe and European waters had implications for the oceanic fortunes of both parties. Spanish merchants, especially those with an interest in the Indies trade, supported the Armada and threw the ships and men of the Indies fleets into that battle because to them the defeat of England meant the safety and prosperity of the American trade. The Armada campaign was also a battle for the Atlantic.

It is unnecessary here to relate the story of the Armada of 1588, but the naval and maritime significance of the campaign deserves examination.[5] The mere launching of this expedition was a remarkable achievement for Spain, for until his acquisition of the Portuguese navy in 1580 Philip II had possessed no high-seas fleet (as distinct from galleys) of his own. Until then the crown had relied on requisitioning the ships of private owners, some of whom – naval entrepreneurs – built, manned and set forth ships for the crown at agreed rates for agreed periods of hire. When not required for royal service such ships were used for trade. By 1588 the crown had still done little to create a Spanish royal fleet, though it was then able to supplement the twelve Portuguese galleons with eight new galleons of the 'Indian Guard', built on private

---

[5] The best general account is G. Mattingly, *The Defeat of the Spanish Armada* (London, 1959). Spanish documents are to be found in C. Fernández Duro (ed.), *La Armada Invencible* (2 vols., Madrid, 1884–5); E. Herrera Oria (ed.), *La Armada Invencible* (Valladolid, 1929); and G. Maura Gamazo (ed.), *El Designio de Felipe II y el Episodio de la Armada Invencible* (Madrid, 1957). English materials are in J. K. Laughton (ed.), *State Papers relating to the Defeat of the Spanish Armada* (2 vols., London, 1895). G. P. B. Naish (ed.), 'Documents illustrating the history of the Spanish armada', in C. C. Lloyd (ed.), *Naval Miscellany*, vol. IV (London, 1952), contains Spanish and English documents.

contract for service with the plate fleets, while the four galleasses provided for the Armada were royal ships. The rest of the expedition, consisting of about forty so-called great-ships and various other craft, were requisitioned merchantmen. The 130 vessels listed at Lisbon before departure were officially rated at 57,868 tons, a monstrous force the like of which no one had ever seen in those waters, set forth at the even more monstrous cost of some ten million ducats (equivalent to the total income of the English crown for five or six years).[6] Yet the Armada was fatally deficient in several respects. The ships themselves were generally inferior to those of the English as sailers; the galleons, with their high freeboard and lofty castles, were less seaworthy and handy than the queen's ships, while the leading Spanish merchantmen, though large, did not share the strength and speed of their English counterparts. Many of the seamen had died of disease or deserted before the fleet sailed – the inevitable result of maintaining a state of mobilization for nearly two years on end – and had been replaced by unskilled men. Above all the Spanish fleet could not match the enemy in artillery, a fact which the king of Spain himself admitted in instructing his commander to come to close quarters and grapple with the English ships. Recent research has proved beyond doubt that 'the Spanish Armada was at such a disadvantage in fire-power, in both weight of shot and range, that it was probably incapable of winning the sea battle on whatever terms it was fought'.[7] There is also evidence that its powder and shot were deficient in quality and quantity. As the admiral himself, the duke of Medina Sidonia, pointed out, success in such an offensive required superiority, but in fact the Armada was inferior to the English fleet in everything that mattered.

In terms of tonnage the shipping the English had available at the time in the area of the fighting was probably smaller. About 140 vessels appear to have been present – ninety under the Lord Admiral, Charles Howard, in the west, and fifty under Lord Henry Seymour in the east – but many of these were barks and pinnaces.[8] The core of this force,

6 The fleet included an important contingent of foreign vessels, including Ragusan and Italian, commandeered by *embargo*. The official list is in Fernández Duro, *Armada Invencible*, II, pp. 60–82, and in Laughton, *Defeat*, II, pp. 376–81. Tonnage tends to be overstated and the Spanish *tonelada* was in any case equivalent to only about ⅔ of the English ton. On the cost of the Armada see I. A. A. Thompson, *War and Government in Habsburg Spain, 1560–1620* (London, 1976), p. 70. The ducat was worth 5s. 6d. sterling.
7 I. A. A. Thompson, 'Spanish Armada guns', *Mariner's Mirror*, 61 (1975), 355–71. For Philip II's instructions and Medina Sidonia's remarks about the inferiority of the Armada, see Fernández Duro, *Armada Invencible*, II, pp. 5–13, 134–7, 225–8.
8 The English tonnages of the official lists are unreliable, with a tendency to overstatement, but allowing for this and for the difference between the ton and the *tonelada*, the Armada appears to have had the greater tonnage.

however, was strong: the thirty-four queen's ships included eighteen powerful galleons of 300 to 1100 tons and seven lesser galleons of sufficient force to count in battle. The pride and confidence of the English commanders in these ships contrasts remarkably with the almost defeatist comments of Medina Sidonia on the quality of his. Since the late sixties and still more since 1580 the Navy Board had pursued a vigorous policy of building and rebuilding the queen's ships to produce by 1588 a fleet of remarkably efficient warships, not only more seaworthy, weatherly and faster than others, but better designed for fighting, longer in relation to beam and generally reduced in their top-hamper. These changes, though not radical, significantly improved the sailing qualities of the ships and made more room for battery guns at the expense of secondary armament, while the guns themselves and their mounting appear to have been improved.[9] Nor should we dismiss all the private ships as mere auxiliaries. There were half a dozen of 300 tons and over – the *Galleon Leicester*, the *Edward Bonaventure*, the *Merchant Royal*, the *Roebuck*, the *Hercules* and the *Sampson* – which were substantial galleons, and at least another twenty in the 200 to 300-ton class were very useful fighters, as John Watts's *Margaret and John*, among others, proved herself to be in more than one engagement. The effective fighting ships on the English side thus numbered at least sixty – just about as many as those in the Armada – and the private ships, like the queen's, were unquestionably superior to their Spanish equivalents, as we know from the formidable record of many of them as privateers.

Circumstances moreover ensured that the defenders, both ships and men, were in better shape than the enemy when the moment of action arrived. The Armada had been two years and more in the making and as from month to month departure was delayed the ships deteriorated, victuals went bad, men sickened, died, disappeared. As Medina Sidonia set sail from Lisbon he was aware of a serious shortage of water and victuals, largely owing to defective cask, which was also spreading sickness throughout the fleet, and after he had decided to put into Corunna for fresh supplies a terrible storm broke, ruthlessly exposing the deficiencies of the ships and multiplying the sick. The respite at Corunna, which lasted a month, saved the Armada, but it could not make it sound. For the most part these difficulties of the attacking force resulted from the fundamental weakness of Spanish naval organization: the absence of royal dockyards, of a naval administration, indeed virtually of a royal navy, meant that the enormous task of preparing

[9] D. W. Waters (ed.), *The Elizabethan Navy and the Armada of Spain* (London, 1974), pp. 4–13; T. Glasgow, 'List of ships', pp. 299–307.

the Armada was carried out *ad hoc* and inadequately in spite of the efforts of Medina Sidonia to bring order out of chaos when he took over in March 1588. His problems and those of Santa Cruz before him were also due in part to Drake's forestalling and disrupting operations in Cadiz Bay and off Cape St Vincent in the spring of 1587, but those operations, conducted with quite a small force (four queen's ships and thirteen others with five pinnaces) were only possible because the Spaniards could not get a fleet to sea to drive him off, though they had been mobilizing for twelve months already.[10]

English naval organization no doubt left much to be desired, but in comparison with Spanish administration the Navy Board was a model of efficiency. With royal dockyards at Deptford, Woolwich and Chatham, a victualling department and ordnance stores, apart from the resources of the outports and especially of Plymouth, now rapidly emerging as an important naval base, the means of mobilizing a fleet and maintaining it in readiness for service at short notice existed. This it was that enabled Elizabeth, having made no preparations for naval action throughout the autumn of 1587, to mobilize a major fleet within a fortnight in December and then, as the danger seemed to recede, to cut back the strength by half until the spring. Some naval historians have called this niggardly and deplored the risk, but in fact the queen saved men's lives thereby as well as the sinews of war, so that the fleet was fit in every sense when the enemy came to the Channel.

Medina Sidonia left Corunna on 12/22 July with 131 vessels manned by approximately 7000 seamen and 17,000 soldiers. His instructions were to proceed to the 'Cape of Margate' and to 'join hands' with Farnese (now duke of Parma) to ensure the safe crossing of his army from Dunkirk and Nieuport to England. Parma had an assault force of about 17,000 men, the cream of the army of Flanders, waiting to embark in barges and flyboats, and 6000 soldiers of the Armada were to reinforce him once he had established a bridgehead. How the two forces were to effect a junction was not explained. It would be difficult because Dutch flyboats commanded the banks and shoals of the Flanders coast and would sink Parma's army with the greatest of ease unless he or Medina Sidonia found the means to drive them off. Parma certainly lacked such means, nor could Medina Sidonia do much to help him without first destroying the English fleet. King Philip clearly expected the Armada to engage and defeat the English and thereby to

[10] I. A. A. Thompson, 'The Armada and administrative reform: the Spanish council of war in the reign of Philip II', *EHR*, 82 (1967), 698–725. The council of war was reformed in 1586 to meet the demands of the war with England, but not until 1594 did a *junta* specifically responsible for the Atlantic war come into being. See also Thompson, *War and Government*, pp. 185–205.

obtain total and unchallenged control of the crossing,[11] but in fact the Spaniards were unable to join battle in earnest until it was too late. Tactically Medina Sidonia lost the initiative very soon after entering the Channel, when Howard won the weather-gauge, for from that moment onwards the superior sailing qualities of the English ships and their superior artillery prevented the duke from precipitating the close general engagement in which his 17,000 soldiers with their arquebuses, muskets, pikes and swords might well have won the day. It was only after they had been driven from the Calais roadstead by fire-ships and when they were retreating in disarray that Medina Sidonia and his galleons turned at last to face the enemy at Gravelines and were there defeated by those same guns.

The failure of the Armada was by no means a matter of bad luck, bad leadership or lack of effort on the part of its officers and men: it was outsailed, outgunned and finally broken in battle. After that the Spaniards could not turn back. Already mauled by storm and enemy action, grievously short of victuals and water, they had no choice now but to brave the storms of the North Atlantic and the inhospitable shores of Ireland. So far they had lost only a few ships; now many more were wrecked – probably as many as twenty on the Irish coast alone – and thousands of men died by drowning, starved to death or were captured ashore and slaughtered. In all some fifty vessels of the original fleet failed to return, and many of those which made Spanish ports were beyond repair. The force which embodied the naval strength of Spain lay in ruins and Philip II's bid to win the war by a decisive victory had failed.

Yet this was rather the beginning than the end of the war and the beginning rather than the end of Spanish naval power. In fact the fighting capability of Spain at sea had suffered much less than her merchant marine. Only four galleons were lost, while no less than eighteen out of forty of the substantial merchantmen (Biscayners and Levanters especially) failed to return, in addition to a number of hulks and small craft. The nucleus of a state navy remained, but the maritime resources upon which the sea power of the country must in the long run depend were impoverished. Moreover the strategic situation

---

[11] See Fernández Duro, *Armada Invencible*, II, pp. 5–13, for the instructions. Philip clearly expected his main plan to be carried out, but admitted the possibility of failure. Should Parma be unable to cross, Medina Sidonia was to occupy the Isle of Wight and then do his best to co-ordinate measures with Parma. Should Parma get to England but fail to win a decisive victory, he had sealed orders to negotiate terms ensuring freedom of worship for English Catholics, evacuation of the cautionary towns held by the English in the Netherlands and compensation for past injuries done to Philip and his subjects – *ibid.*, II, pp. 13–18. It is quite wrong to suppose, as some writers do, that Philip and his advisers were blind to reality or else engaged in a gigantic bluff.

created by the defeat of the Armada meant that for the rest of the war Spain's merchant fleet came under increasing pressure and continued to decline, while the crown made great efforts – and with some success – to develop a powerful navy. For on the one hand the defeat of the Spanish offensive returned the initiative at sea to the English, who could now once again range the Atlantic in search of prey, hounding Iberian shipping at will and forcing Spain to invest heavily in the protection of its most precious and vital trade, the Seville-Atlantic system. On the other hand the strategic position in northwest Europe was not essentially changed by the events of 1588: Spanish power there, still formidable, was still held in check by England. The way to win the war was to neutralize England first, but to do so by diplomacy and compromise now seemed less possible and less acceptable than ever. Would it not be preferable to build up the naval strength to do it by force? Philip II had the incentive and the will to try again, nor did he lack the means to launch more armadas against England.

In the palmy days of the British Empire before 1914, when many saw sea power as the be-all and end-all of strategy, this country's leading naval historians, Corbett and Oppenheim, severely criticized Queen Elizabeth's conduct of the war with Spain: she neglected her navy, they said, and failed to use the immense potential of English sea power to win decisive victory over Spain. Parsimonious and pusillanimous, she reined in the bounding ambition of her men of war, thwarted their efforts by her continual irresolution and excessive caution, prejudiced the chances of promising expeditions by imposing ill-advised instructions. Obsessed with the defence of her realm against attack by sea, she never realized the offensive capability of her ships but all the same expected their offensive operations to yield a profit, valuing prize more than the destruction of the enemy and letting the sea-war degenerate into mere commerce-raiding.[12] Nor were these charges without foundation. The queen was not an ideal minister of war, but would not entrust the responsibility to anyone else. She was temperamentally given to indecision and ambiguity and had to bear in mind political problems which did not complicate the strategy and tactics of a Drake or an Essex. Undeniably, too, she was an inveterate 'Little Englander' – and proud of it – for reasons already noted. No government of this

---

[12] Oppenheim took an extreme 'blue-water' view in *The Naval Tracts of Sir William Monson* (London, 1902–14), I, pp. 1–92; Corbett also condemned Elizabeth's naval policy in *Drake and the Tudor Navy* (2 vols., London, 1898), II, pp. 360 *et seq.*, and in *Successors of Drake*, pp. 3–4, but his final verdict in the latter book (pp. 406–10) was realistic and fair. Elizabeth's defence is presented in R. B. Wernham's cogent essay, 'Elizabethan war aims and strategy'.

country could, in the 1590s, have pursued an imperial strategy of expansion overseas, given the acute economic distress and financial straits of that decade, without risking the solvency and even the safety of the state. She did not double the power of her navy because that would have reduced even further the meagre resources available for the vital Continental fronts, nor could she find the money to create an efficient army, an essential requirement of any effective counter-offensive. It is true also that she feared the power of Spain to launch another attack upon her realm and that this to some extent inhibited her employment of her own ships, though whether her caution was excessive one may reasonably doubt. As for commerce-raiding, it was cheaper and more rewarding than the counter-attacks she did mount, and in practice did the enemy more harm. Perhaps those counter-attacks would have been more successful had Elizabeth supported them more generously and given their commanders more freedom of action, but in the light of the incompetence, mismanagement and peculation which marred all the great expeditions of the war, it seems far more likely that the results would have been even more disastrous than they usually were. Elizabeth was certainly not a Chatham or a Churchill – and fortunately not.

There were others who hoped and argued for more aggressive policies at sea – Hawkins, Drake, Ralegh, Essex, for example – but none of these was in a position to see the war as a whole with the knowledge and understanding that Elizabeth possessed. The two Cecils, who had much the same comprehensive grasp as the queen, shared her outlook on strategy. The so-called men of war had enough influence to push various schemes for naval counter-offensives, but they did not make policy and so always had to accept conditions which restricted or contradicted their intentions. Whether they would have achieved greater success without such interference may well be doubted, for their projects were marked by jejune optimism and disregard for the usual difficulties of contemporary warfare, but it must be said that the queen never gave them full and fair opportunities to prove their ideas in practice.

Their best chance certainly came in 1589, with Spain unable to offer effective resistance at sea. Drake and Sir John Norris, the best of the army officers in the Netherlands, proposed an expedition to destroy enemy shipping at Lisbon and Seville and to seize Lisbon and the Azores, establishing Dom Antonio as king in Portugal. If successful, this double blow would not only take the war into the enemy's camp but give England a stranglehold on Spain's Atlantic trade. Incidentally, Dom Antonio was expected to grant his promoters large trading concessions in the Portuguese empire. In the opinion of Sir William Monson, success would have 'restored Dom Antonio to the crown of Portugal, dissevered it from Spain and united it in league with England, which would have answered the present charge, and have settled a continual trade for us to the East Indies and the rest of the dominions of Portugal; for so we might easily have conditioned'.[13] The Portugal expedition thus expressed the commercial ambitions of that important section of the City which took an interest in extra-European trade, and it drew heavily on the merchants for financial backing. For this was a joint-stock enterprise, a large proportion of the funds being supplied by private adventurers who expected a return for their money. After the expenses of 1588 Elizabeth could not afford to promote a large-scale offensive without such help and as an investor herself she also expected a dividend, or at least a victory free of charge. Like other naval expeditions of the Anglo-Spanish war, the Lisbon voyage combined the resources of the state with those of its subjects to serve the purposes of both, and in the event served neither.

For whereas Drake, Norris and their supporters, who included the enthusiastic young earl of Essex, looked principally to Lisbon to win the greatest prize and inflict the greatest damage, the queen was more concerned to destroy the remnants of the Armada, which lay defenceless at Santander and San Sebastián. These ships might in a matter of months be refitted to form the nucleus of a second armada or to protect the treasure fleets, and the queen's instructions to her commanders therefore rightly emphasized their destruction as the first and chief task of the expedition. After this they might proceed to Lisbon and Seville to destroy more enemy shipping, but were to attempt the seizure of the former only if Dom Antonio's support proved to be 'so great as he pretendeth'. Finally the force should make for the Azores and capture some of the islands, this last being evidently considered a less doubtful venture than an invasion of the Peninsula itself.

To assign three major objectives to the same expedition was of course an elementary error, but it was typical of Elizabethan naval strategy and reflected its divided purposes and the weakness of the chain of command. For if the queen is to be blamed, she should be blamed for not imposing her will upon those 'men of war' and insisting upon their obedience. In this case the composition of the force itself suggests that the commanders did not intend to obey. They took 150 vessels, including seven of the queen's, sixty Dutch transports and many ships of less than 200 tons, carrying over ten thousand soldiers:

---

[13] *Monson's Tracts*, I, p. 178. The best modern study is R. B. Wernham, 'Queen Elizabeth and the Portugal expedition of 1589', *EHR*, 66 (1951), 1–26 and 194–218.

not the kind of strike force required to destroy ships in harbour, but patently an invasion force, though Elizabeth herself, annoyed by the excess charges she was obliged to pay, gravely weakened it by breaking her promise to supply a siege-train. The voyage was a story of failure: they landed at Corunna, but failed to take it completely, and unforgivably made no attempt on the Biscay ports; heavily depleted by sickness and desertion, they failed to take Lisbon and straggled home without visiting the Azores, bringing in return for the loss of several thousand men a modest haul of prize-goods, most of the proceeds of which found their way into private pockets rather than the public purse. Indeed the whole enterprise had been organized and conducted with an eye to plunder, as critical observers noted at the time. Many of the volunteers, it was said, went only for spoil, and the queen's comment that 'they went to places more for profit than for service' was just.[14] A contemporary chronicler, however, got nearer to the heart of the matter:

the principal cause why so many faults and oversights were committed, or that nothing was performed or put in execution according as had been resolved in council, was because this army was levied by merchants; whereas in matters of this kind, princes only ought to have employed themselves.[15]

The Portugal expedition was not only ill-conceived as a piece of strategy, it carried in its own vicious nature the seeds of corruption and disaster. Neither the queen nor her commanders can be excused from blame, but the root cause of their failure on this occasion and by and large throughout the sea-war lay in the very character of English naval power at this time. The Elizabethan state simply lacked the resources to create a professional navy of sufficient strength to undertake an offensive of the kind envisaged; it had to rely on private adventurers for the capital, ships and supplies to launch it and could hardly avoid the deplorable effects of this participation on its aims, its constitution, its conduct and its results.

Another kind of maritime offensive was the scheme drafted by John Hawkins in 1587 for the operation of what has been since called a 'silver blockade'.[16] He proposed to maintain a continuous patrol of twelve queen's ships – six of them major galleons – between Spain and the Azores. Each fleet would keep the sea for four months, being replaced by another of the same scale. One advantage of the plan was its

[14] PRO, SP 12/254, no. 50.
[15] F. F. Fox (ed.), *Adams's Chronicle of Bristol* (Bristol, 1910), p. 137.
[16] PRO, SP 12/206, no. 61. The scheme was submitted to Walsingham early in 1588 (Laughton, *Defeat*, I, pp. 58–62) and to Burghley in July 1589 (PRO, SP 12/225, no. 14).

cheapness, for Hawkins even offered to find private adventurers to pay for wages and victuals. Such measures, he claimed, would not only bring assured dividends by way of prize, but could not fail to stop the flow of East and West Indian wealth to Spain, compelling her to sue for peace. There is no explicit statement here of ulterior commercial aims, but what we already know of Hawkins's career and connections makes it obvious that this was a plan not merely to defeat Spain, but to break her commercial and naval power and to open the oceans to English enterprise. But the seductive appeal of Hawkins's project lay in its promise to wage war at a fabulous rate of profit. The dream of capturing the treasure fleet, or at least one or two treasure ships, had a powerful influence upon the strategic thinking of Elizabethan statesmen and warriors.

Yet Hawkins's scheme was never put into effect. In 1588 of course it was out of the question. In 1589 the main effort went into the Portugal voyage and it was left to the earl of Cumberland to cruise that summer about the Azores with an assortment of privateers led by the queen's *Victory*. This and lesser privateering forces did well that year at their proper business, but as a blockading force they achieved practically nothing. They did not operate a systematic plan of interception and consequently failed to capture any significant quantity of silver, while the Portuguese carracks and several valuable West-Indiamen slipped through their slack clutches. In September, while Cumberland was still at sea, Frobisher was sent with a small squadron to patrol the approaches to Seville and Lisbon and did succeed in taking four ships of the West India fleet, but these were minor prizes and the main body of the treasure fleet came home safely.[17] These events indicated that there was little point in a partial blockade, but the next year's effort, though certainly more impressive, produced no better result. This time Elizabeth set no less than thirteen of her own ships to the task – a squadron under Frobisher to the Azores and another under Hawkins to the coast of Spain – but they operated only from July to early September and caught little of significance, for the *flota* remained in Havana that year rather than run the gauntlet, while two fast-sailing treasure-frigates and all the East India carracks save one eluded the blockade. 1590 was not a good year for Spain's merchants and bankers, but Philip's finances stood the strain and by this time he was already acquiring a naval force capable of challenging the English in the Atlantic.[18]

In the summer of 1591 Lord Thomas Howard stationed himself at the

[17] *Monson's Tracts*, I, pp. 226–39.
[18] *Monson's Tracts*, I, pp. 240–52.

Islands with a strong fleet comprising seven warships and two pinnaces of the queen's, while on the coast of Spain and across the Atlantic
in the Caribbean privateers were more numerous than ever. The
treasure fleet, greatly swollen by the delay, was probably in greater
danger that year than at any time during this war, but Spain could now
protect it: over fifty sail under Don Alonso de Bazán, including some
twenty warships, descended upon the Azores and Howard, warned in
the nick of time, wisely withdrew. Sir Richard Grenville, in the
Revenge, either could not or would not, as Ralegh in a famous broad-
side related:

The L. Tomas with the rest verie hardly recovered the winde, which Sir
Richard Grinvile not being able to do, was perswaded by the maister and
others to cut his maine saile, and cast about, and to trust to the sailing of the
shippe: for the squadron of Sivil were on his wether bow. But Sir Richard
utterly refused to turne from the enimie, alledging that he would rather chose
to dye, then to dishonour him selfe, his countrie, and her Maisties shippe,
perswading his companie that he would passe through the two Squadrons, in
despight of them: and enforce those of Sivill to give him way.[19]

So Grenville and his crew fought the Spanish fleet alone until at last
they were overwhelmed by superior force. Later the treasure fleet
arrived to join Bazán's escort. Many as it happened were lost in
subsequent storms and Howard's ships and the privateers took not a
few gratifying prizes, but nothing like a 'silver blockade' was achieved.
Nor could the English do significantly better thereafter, for although
they frequently resorted in strength to the Islands and the coast of
Spain and took or destroyed an occasional carrack or treasure-bearing
West-Indiaman, by far the greater part of the silver and the spices
reached the Iberian ports. This was due in part to the increasing
strength of the Spanish royal navy, which was deployed chiefly in
defence of the treasure, in part to the employment of fast and well-
armed frigates, sailing independently of the *flota*, to carry the silver,
and in part to Spain's renewal of the threat to invade England, focusing
attention once again upon European waters and so inhibiting the
Atlantic counter-offensive.

By 1595 Spain's naval revival was an obvious fact and Elizabeth was
strongly impressed by reports of a new armada in the making,
threatening Ireland or even England itself with invasion that year or
the next. Nevertheless she was persuaded to allow Drake and Hawkins to attempt an assault upon Panama, the original intention being to

---

[19] W. Ralegh, *A Report of the Truth of the Fight about the Iles of the Açores, this last Sommer*
(London, 1591). See also *Monson's Tracts*, I, pp. 253–77.

block the isthmus for some time in order to divert the bullion of Peru into her treasury. The queen's fear of the Spanish fleet, however, caused her to limit the expedition to a mere hit-and-run raid, the prospects of which were prejudiced by a last minute decision to attack San Juan de Puerto Rico first, where a great galleon of silver lay crippled. Bad leadership, bad luck and a Spanish response which was good in parts turned the last voyage of Drake and Hawkins into a disaster: both leaders, along with many men and some ships, were lost in what had been from the start a gamble for treasure, essentially a privateering venture in which the crown was the largest shareholder. It represents the nadir of Elizabethan strategy.[20]

As the remnants of this expedition put into various home ports, a far more powerful force prepared to leave Plymouth on a far more plausible mission: to strike at the Spanish coast, capturing and destroying both ships and ports. An assault from Spain or from the Spanish base at Blavet in Brittany now seemed imminent and it was the Lord Admiral who proposed to forestall this by a vigorous counter-attack, his scheme being taken up with enthusiasm by the earl of Essex. Financed jointly by the queen, Howard and Essex, the expedition comprised about 150 sail, including eighteen ships of the royal navy, eighteen Dutch men of war and twelve considerable Londoners, with an army approaching ten thousand in number. Though much delayed and at the last moment almost cancelled or altered from its purpose by Elizabeth, the force was well organized and achieved a complete surprise when it descended upon Cadiz. In the ensuing action two of the king's galleons were destroyed and two others captured, while the army took and sacked the town. It was a famous victory, achieved with only minor losses by land or sea, yet a curiously disappointing one, for reasons Essex himself listed in a paper written after the voyage.[21] The outgoing Indies fleet, comprising forty or fifty vessels with their cargo lying helpless in the bay, might easily have been seized, but was in fact allowed the time to destroy itself; after pillaging the town for a fortnight, the English set it on fire and departed, much to the disgust of Essex, who had from the first envisaged holding it indefinitely both as a base for offensive measures at sea and as a thorn in the king of Spain's foot; no attempt was made to intercept the incoming treasure fleet; no attempt was made on any other Iberian port and worst of all Lisbon,

---

[20] Andrews, *Drake's Last Voyage*.

[21] L. W. Henry, 'The earl of Essex as strategist and military organizer (1596–7)', *EHR*, 68 (1953), 363–93. For modern studies of the Cadiz expedition see Corbett, *Successors of Drake*, pp. 56–133; *Monson's Tracts*, I, pp. 344–95, and II, pp. 1–20; Cheyney, *A History of England*, II, pp. 37–91; C. G. Cruickshank, *Elizabeth's Army* (Oxford, 1966), pp. 251–79.

which harboured the main strength of Spain's armada, was ignored. He might have added that most of the loot of Cadiz was embezzled at the expense of the chief promoters of the venture, which left the queen unamused and some others discontented.

Essex, however, seems to have been provoked into something more than retrospective criticism, for he now drafted a plan for a more decisive attack on Spain, a plan distinguished by a commendable grasp of strategic principles.[22] Comparing the 'seats of war' the English might conceivably take as targets of attack by sea – the Islands, the Indies and the coast of Spain – he picked the last as the most promising because a base such as Cadiz would give the English command not only of the treasure link, but also of Spain's equally vital supply line from the north, the Eastland trade in corn, timber, hemp and other war materials borne by the great hulks of Hamburg, Lübeck and Danzig. No sort of blockade was possible without a base close by because ships and men could not, given the logistical conditions of the day, stand the strain of prolonged periods at sea. But furthermore Essex recognized that to hold such a base, and so to break Spain's war effort, England must produce an army fit for the task: much smaller than the unwieldy masses taken in 1589 and 1596, and consisting of well-trained, 'choice' men. The Low Countries would no doubt spare some English veterans, as usual, but something would have to be done about the quality of the rest.

In 1597 this plan materialized in the shape of another great expedition, for Spain's offensive power had yet to be crushed. The 'omissions' of the Cadiz voyage had left Philip II the means to assemble at Lisbon an armada as large as that of 1588 to revenge the humiliation of Cadiz. In fact this fleet was far weaker and worse provided than the 'Invincible' had been and succumbed with heavy loss to a storm off Finisterre in October 1596. But meanwhile the invasion scare in England was real enough and persisted in 1597 because there remained in Ferrol and Corunna the naval material for yet another offensive, which the king of Spain would undoubtedly attempt unless he were forestalled. Essex, now at the height of his prestige and influence, took sole command, and in his capacity as chief of the country's land forces introduced reforms in the recruiting system to secure an army fit for his purpose, which was to take and fortify a base on the enemy coast after disposing of the Spanish fleet at Ferrol. At last it seemed that the English might deliver a damaging blow, but it was not to be. The great expedition, comparable in scale to that of 1596, was driven back to Plymouth by heavy storms, the ships battered and the

[22] Henry, 'Essex as strategist'.

troops sick. Most of the army was then discharged and the fleet finally left in August with orders simply to destroy the ships at Ferrol and after that to hunt the *flota* in the East Atlantic. In the end events at sea led Essex to abandon the Ferrol raid and to sail for the Islands, where by poor judgement and slackness he narrowly missed the treasure. Straggling home, dispersed and defenceless, the English ships were lucky to escape a conflict with the Spanish armada which had in fact sailed from Ferrol, only to be defeated once again by bad weather.[23]

Thus the most promising of the counter-offensive projects of Elizabeth's men of war turned into a fiasco. Spain and England sought in vain to strike each other across the sea in the years of war that remained. Another armada threatened in 1599, but was diverted to the Azores, while England waited with bated breath. After that her men of war pursued carracks and treasure and blockading action by fits and starts with no more success than before. Some have blamed the civil power for this failure, some the commanders, and truly there is as much to blame as to admire in the conduct of either, but still more damaging was the conflict between them, which repeatedly reduced English strategy to compromises which achieved nothing of importance. Even so, the faults of over-cautious ministers and irresponsible men of war cannot alone explain why the English were unable to win the war by sea, for what they faced was objectively a very hard task. Time and again they were defeated by wind and weather, distance and disease, the intractable forces of nature and the inevitable limits of their own resources, technology and skills. The naval power at their disposal was small; the army available was scarcely adequate for the capture of a major sea-port, let alone its tenure as a base in the heart of enemy territory; expertise in the mounting and handling of large-scale amphibious operations took many decades to mature, as some disastrous expeditions of the next century were to show; men had still to work out the strategy and tactics of oceanic warfare and tended to underestimate the difficulties of a blockade, for example, or the seizure of an Atlantic island or a West Indian base.

And while the Atlantic thus posed new and typically modern problems, the naval means available to meet them were slow to change and the traditional conception, organization and methods of sea-warfare persisted. The queen's navy was still but a small part of the force the country could exert at sea, nor did it differ radically in character from the rest of that force. Privateering was the characteristic form of naval war and the royal navy itself tended to conform to the

---

[23] Corbett, *Successors of Drake*, pp. 134–227; *Monson's Tracts*, II, pp. 21–83; Cheyney, *History of England*, II, pp. 92–103, 421–43.

main pattern. The queen employed her ships in privateering, investing them in joint-stock expeditions for a corresponding share in the profits, even in voyages over which she exercised no control, such as the earl of Cumberland's ventures of 1589 and 1593. The chief of her navy was also the chief of the nation's privateering forces: a great shipowner and promoter of private ventures, he sometimes took a personal share in the fitting out of royal ships, sold at least one of his own to the queen and commissioned others for official expeditions.[24] He became deeply involved in the whole business of setting forth ships of reprisal, for which he issued licences, and in all matters of prize and spoil, over which his court, the High Court of Admiralty, exercised jurisdiction. Indeed, by virtue of the 10% due to him on all prize, which his officers did their best to levy, he had a vested interest in the privateering world. Furthermore most of the queen's leading naval men had a substantial stake in private shipping, from entrepreneurs like the Hawkinses down to the ordinary captain who served in a royal ship one year and took out his own the next.

Far from being a professional navy, distinct from the mass of private shipping, the royal navy was dominated by private interests deeply entrenched in every department of its organization and activity, from the building of the ships to the settling of accounts at the end of a cruise. Those interests were concerned above all with privateering, and the queen's policy encouraged the use of her ships in expeditions of plunder, for she expected them to pay their way when not employed in the defence of the realm or the necessary operations of the Continental and Irish wars. Other naval campaigns she would seldom finance without the assistance of noblemen, seamen and merchants willing to adventure ships, goods or money for profit. In some great naval enterprises of the war – the Islands voyages of 1592 and 1597, for example, in both of which Ralegh had a strong interest – public and private elements were so entangled as to become difficult to distinguish, and when all parties looked thus to their peculiar advantage it surprised no one that these semi-official expeditions, in which privateers outnumbered the queen's ships, filled every purse except the public one. Nor should it surprise us that forces thus constituted and directed failed to inflict decisive defeat upon a powerful enemy. Ralegh blamed the queen because he did not recognize the real weakness of the weapon she wielded, a weakness he, with his privateering interests and privateering approach to the war at sea, personified.

Thus the main naval war achieved nothing more positive than the

[24] Andrews, 'Cecil and plunder', p. 526; BL, Harleian MSS, 598, fo. 61.

frustration of Spain's enormous efforts by land and sea to dominate the northwest. This meant, however, that in the little war which accompanied it the English were free to exercise and develop their maritime capability by the sort of private enterprise that suited them best.

Privateering consisted in the officially licensed operations of privately-owned vessels against enemy shipping and goods in time of war. It was customary for the crown thus to allow its subjects to wage war, as it were, on their own account, and in this war it did so by issuing letters of reprisal in the High Court of Admiralty to those who claimed damages by the confiscations of 1585, though before long proof of loss became little more than a legal fiction and ventures of reprisal were promoted by men who had never dreamed of trading in Spain. Thus in the summer of 1585 the first of a host of voluntaries took to the sea, and soon the reports of Drake's triumphs in the West Indies 'inflamed the whole country with a desire to adventure unto the seas, in the hope of the like good success, [so] that a great number prepared ships, mariners and soldiers and travelled every place where any profit might be had'.[25] It was natural for the English, not themselves possessed of a rich and vulnerable merchant marine, to take advantage of their initiative in the Atlantic to conduct an unceasing campaign against Iberian shipping. In the next eighteen years hundreds of private ventures were organized for plunder. Ships of reprisal normally accompanied the official and semi-official expeditions and many more sailed independently. John Hagthorpe's statement that in the 'queen's time' there were 'never less than 200 sail of voluntaries and others' on Spanish coasts may have been an exaggeration, but the number may well have reached that level in some years of the war and seldom if ever fell below a hundred.[26]

Among these a growing minority stood out as private men-of-war, like the Lord Admiral's ships, the earl of Cumberland's, one or two of Ralegh's, Richard Hawkins's *Dainty* and Sir John Gilbert's *Refusal*, while in the nineties some merchant promoters of privateering built powerful galleons with an eye to war as well as trade – John Watts's *Alcedo* and Paul Bayning's *Golden Phoenix*, for example. But all these made trading voyages and most of the privateers were primarily merchantmen, sometimes pursuing prize in the course of trade, particularly when bound for or from Morocco or anywhere within the

[25] W. J. Harte (ed.), *Gleanings from the Common Place Book of John Hooker . . .* (Exeter, 1926), p. 39.
[26] Andrews, *Elizabethan Privateering*, pp. 32–4.

Straits, sometimes setting forth simply for plunder. They came chiefly from London and the ports from Southampton round to Bristol, with London increasingly prominent, accounting for more than half the tonnage by the end of the war. By this time also the trading reprisal-man of under a hundred tons, operating from places like Bristol, which did not specialize in 'warfare voyages' (in contrast to Southampton, Weymouth and Plymouth, which did), was less in evidence, as privateering became a more organized and professional business, dominated by big merchant shipowners, especially Londoners.

The middling and small privateers carried no great armament – one or two demi-culverins (4½-inch nine-pounders) and some lesser pieces would be more than adequate for a 100-ton ship – relying rather on close fighting with minor artillery and hand-guns to subdue their prizes, and above all upon boarding with sword, dagger and pike. For it was manpower that mattered in this business, and the readiness of owners to cram their ships with men was only exceeded by the eagerness of seamen to serve in such ventures. Manpower was cheap. Although in a trading voyage where prize was expected the crew would receive their usual wages in addition to a third of all prize, those in a simple privateering venture would sail for their thirds and so-called pillage only.[27] After the capital outlay on the ship herself, therefore, promoters found victualling the chief expense as a rule, and the cost of setting forth a privateer was low enough to make it an attractive business. It was attractive to some people, of course, as a gamble (some even named their ships appropriately: the *Hazard*, the *Wheel of Fortune*, the *Poor Man's Hope* and the *Why not I?*) and to some as a path to fame and glory, and there were a few gentlemen who lost their lives and fortunes in unduly expensive, over-ambitious and ill-led ventures.

But for the most part the promoters were merchants and seamen, people already in the shipping world, usually working in joint-stock syndicates. Owner-captains, whether professional seamen who had worked their way to the top or men of gentry, especially southwest gentry, stock, would promote their own voyages allowing shares (bills of adventure) for victuals or funds provided by merchants or fellow seamen. These were usually one-ship ventures, but some of the London merchants like Watts and Bayning would collaborate to set forth squadrons of three or four powerful ships with a pinnace or two, particularly for West Indian cruises. Such Londoners and a few big

---

[27] Pillage consisted in the recognized right of a privateer crew to share among themselves, according to customary rules, such goods and valuables in a prize as did not belong to the cargo proper.

merchants of the outports dominated privateering enterprise not only as shipowners but also by way of their investment in all sides of the sea-war. They adventured their ships, their stores, their funds, their expertise and of course their own brood of captains and masters in the great expeditions of Drake, Ralegh, Essex and Cumberland, they lent money to gentlemen promoters who were disposed to borrow, like Thomas Cavendish and John Chidley, they led the way in the combination of trade and plunder, they controlled a large sector of the business of prize disposal.

Privateering was something more than a form of business. It attracted – indeed consumed – a multitude of poor men, especially poor seamen, who were willing to risk their lives in those ill-conditioned and disease-ridden voluntary ships in the vague hope of booty. Monson declared that 'the numbers of sailors and seamen are increased treble by it [privateering], to what they are in the navigations of peaceable voyages',[28] a rhetorical flourish no doubt, but indicative of the mass movement which occurred. Privateering did not merely absorb the numerous pirates of the pre-war period, it drew upon the whole maritime population and inducted landsmen as well as seamen into a kind of predatory voyaging which verged upon and often deteriorated into piracy. It was not without cause that the English became known abroad now as a nation of pirates, for those equipped with letters of reprisal were inclined to seize neutral ships or goods and to proceed as rapidly and quietly as possible to sell the same, often in places beyond the reach of Admiralty officials, such as the ports of Barbary or Ireland, or else in the many places where Admiralty men were only too pleased to co-operate. Seldom were the unfortunate victims able to recover more than a modicum of their property. The tide of maritime violence which had been rising since the middle years of the century reached its height in the nineties, when the pressure of population, repeated harvest failure and trade depression combined to magnify poverty and unemployment to proportions England had not known for generations. Privateering probably derived much of its popularity and its disorderly, piratical tendency from this background. Mass poverty meant cheap manning and so promoted the growth of privateering, though it created problems for owners in other ways.

Material forces and motives do not, however, seem fully to explain this great wave of maritime aggression. Broadsides and pamphlets celebrating the victory over the Armada and many a blow struck by Drake, Cumberland and other venturers were of course propaganda, but they unmistakably reveal widespread anti-Spanish, Protestant and

[28] *Monson's Tracts*, IV, p. 21.

nationalistic sentiments. Writings like those of Henry Roberts, a privateering poet and pamphleteer, suggest that the crude patriotism of the common man found a special vehicle in this form of voluntary participation in the sea-war, which was in some measure a popular movement, drawing upon the support, practical or moral, of people of all classes. His poem *The Trumpet of Fame* thus greeted the departure of Hawkins and Drake on their last West Indian voyage:

> Tis Englands honor that you have in hand,
> Then thinke thereof, if you do love our land.
> The gaine is yours, if millions home you bring,
> Then courage take, to gaine so sweete a thing.
> The time calls on, which causeth me to end,
> Wherefore to God, I do you all commend,
> For whom all subiects that do love our Queene,
> Shall truly pray, to send you safe againe.
> And for my part, I wish you alwaies health,
> With quick returne, and so much store of wealth,
> That Phillips Regions may not be more stord,
> With Pearle, Iewels, and the purest gold.[29]

The naïve juxtaposition of motives and the blatant beating of the nationalist drum here are typical of the popular literature of the war, expressing a mood that had been developing for decades before 1585 and now became strident and bellicose. The sea-war in general and privateering in particular did much to associate English nationalism with militant maritime expansion. In attitudes at least the war marked a turning point, signalized by the publication of Hakluyt's *Principall Navigations* in the year after the Armada and of its extended edition in 1598–1600. Hakluyt's message of oceanic imperialism conquered the reading public with such triumphant ease because the public mind was now ready to accept it.

The material effect of privateering upon the balance of sea power between the nations was important for the future. Commerce-raiding, it is true, could not win the war. Nothing like an effective blockade was ever achieved, scarcely even attempted, and the amounts of treasure the English captured during the war were insignificant in comparison with those that reached Spain. It was only when they occasionally caused the postponement of the Havana sailings that the corsairs impeded the operation of the Spanish war machine. Yet the cumulative impact of continual shipping losses upon the Iberian marine was heavy. English sources suggest that the English captured well over a thousand

---

[29] Cited in L. B. Wright, *Middle Class Culture in Elizabethan England* (Chapel Hill, 1935), pp. 518–19.

Spanish and Portuguese prizes during the war, losses which must have contributed as much as any other factor to the catastrophic decline of Iberian shipping noted in 1608 by a Spanish shipbuilding expert.[30] The system of the transatlantic *flotas* was of course maintained, partly by increasing use of Hanseatic and Dutch vessels and partly by providing much stronger naval protection in the shape of escorting galleons and armadas operating independently in the Atlantic. But the rest of Iberian trade was perforce abandoned very largely to foreign shipping. Spanish trade with France and Flanders, for example, was practically stopped by the end of 1585. Financially, too, losses of goods and ships on this scale ruined many Iberian merchant houses, sapping thus the foundations of Iberian overseas commerce. Already at the beginning of 1588 English corsairs were reported to have caused damage to the value of six million ducats in the previous three years.[31]

The Spanish economy suffered even more from the indirect consequences of the naval war. The replacement of ships lost, whether in the disastrous invasion attempts or in the ceaseless little war of Atlantic depredation, was increasingly costly; and so was the building of warships for the defence of the Atlantic, which now became a major concern and a major outlay alongside the growing burden of the military effort in France and the Netherlands. Inflation sent up the prices of war materials, such as timber, and of labour much more steeply in Spain than in England, so that the strain of defence upon that country's resources was proportionately greater, indeed in the long run crippling. An increasing supply of American treasure for the time being kept Philip's war afloat, but in the process it aggravated the financial difficulties of the state and hastened the onset of famine and plague before the end of the century. The contribution of the corsairs to the decline of Spain was of course one factor among many, but in the decimation of Iberian Atlantic commerce they played a leading part. Spain, it is true, responded by developing her naval power, but this served only to erode the maritime base on which lasting naval power must rest. The stock of skilled seafaring men, already gravely depleted by 1585, was nearly exhausted in the early seventeenth century in consequence of losses at sea, pestilence, low wages and ill-advised attempts at conscription.[32]

What did the English, for their part, gain from privateering? The answer is not simple.[33] The reprisalmen certainly returned a large and

---

[30] Andrews, *Elizabethan Privateering*, pp. 224–5.
[31] Thompson, *War and Government*, pp. 29, 311.
[32] Thompson, *War and Government*, pp. 204–5.
[33] Andrews, *Elizabethan Privateering*, pp. 124–49 *et passim*.

valuable quantity of prize, amounting to at least £100,000 a year and in some years much more, but not all this by any means came into the promoters' hands. The queen and the Lord Admiral no doubt received much less than the 5 and 10% to which they were respectively entitled, but what they lost went mostly not to the promoters but to the sailors, who similarly 'embezzled' (to use the contemporary term) as much of the remainder as they could, over and above their rightful pillage and thirds. Nevertheless those who pursued privateering in business fashion generally made it pay. The professional owner-captains had special advantages which enabled many of them to prosper, like Robert White of Weymouth, William Parker of Plymouth, Christopher Newport of Limehouse and George Somers of Lyme. But the most successful promoters were the large merchant-shipowners, especially Londoners, who had an interest in the powerful type of merchantman most suitable for privateering and who normally dealt in the more lucrative types of prize-goods.

For although many of the cargoes consisted of corn, salt, iron, fish and similar lowly produce, the greater part of the booty in terms of value and profit came in the form of sugar, dyestuffs, spices, silk, gold, silver, gems and pearls. The commonest prize of all, for example, was the Brazilman, carrying sugar and brazilwood, often with some hides or cotton, usually valued at two or three thousand pounds: thirty-four of them were taken in the three years following the Armada alone. The sugar captured in those years, including that from Morocco, the Canaries, the Azores and São Thomé, must have fetched well over £100,000 in the market, and in 1593 the surveyor of the London customs expressed the opinion that 'although the Hollanders and Hamburgers have the only trade of other commodities that the Spanish trade can afford them, yet sugars they cannot have now in any quantity but from us, as the case standeth, by reason of the great quantities taken by reprisal from Spain and Portugal'.[34] Hence also, as another observer noted in 1598, 'the cheapness that all Spanish commodities do now bear in England, having no trade with Spain, that they be for the most part of less price in England than in Spain or the Indias'.[35]

The prize business attracted particularly merchants who had traded to Spain and Portugal before the war. These formed easily the weightiest group in the general mass of privateering promoters, not merely because they had suffered losses by the confiscations of 1585, but also because taking reprisals for those losses seemed to them, as men who knew the market for such commodities, a worth-while

[34] BL, Lansdowne MSS, 75, fo. 105.
[35] *Cal. Salis.* MSS, VIII, 212.

venture. Such considerations must have influenced the promoters of James Lancaster's successful raid on Pernambuco in 1595, for example, who comprised Watts, Bayning and several other former Iberian traders now prominent in the Barbary and Levant trades and in privateering.[36] The merchant-shipowners of the trades to Morocco and beyond were especially well placed to practise the most profitable form of privateering, directly combining trade and plunder in the same voyage and so achieving a super-profit, for they traded right across the main Spanish and Portuguese shipping lanes. The Mediterranean trades provided similar opportunities, and on these routes the English had strong ships, armed and manned sufficiently to assert themselves, but the great shipowners of the Levant Company, such as Thomas Cordell and William Garraway, preferred to keep their trading and privateering operations apart, for the company was sensitive to disturbance within the Straits and the freighters tended to grudge the risk involved and time wasted in pursuing prize. Nevertheless Cordell, Watts, Bayning and a few other shipping magnates of the Mediterranean trades were among the greatest of the promoters of Atlantic privateering.

The men of the southward trades thus combined an appetite for prize-goods with the means to satisfy it: the powerful ships commonly employed in those trades. Hence these Londoners, with a few of like substance in the outports, did not merely set forth their own vessels. They dominated the whole business of sea-plunder, collaborating with each other, financing amateur and professional venturers, buying up prize cargoes and obtaining a large measure of control over privateering from Plymouth, Weymouth and Southampton as well as the capital. In doing so they furthered their own fortunes, and there is no mistaking the wealth and eminence they achieved, but much more important than their personal success is the larger phenomenon which it exemplifies: the accumulation of capital by a loose association of shipowners, traders, seamen and gentlemen interested in privateering, in shipping and in the rich trades.

In pursuing their little war of reprisal the leading merchants of the privateering interest were continuing their commerce by other means and extending the drive for luxury imports which was, as we have seen, the main motor of the expansion. They were, moreover, developing means of extending it further in the near future, for the capital accumulated by Watts, Bayning, Thomas Myddelton and their fellows played no small part in the launching of England's East Indies trade before the end of the war and in the founding of England's first

[36] Andrews, *Elizabethan Privateering*, pp. 209–12.

American dominion soon after it. The first expedition of the East India Company was organized by a committee of seven headed by Paul Bayning and including Thomas Cordell, James Lancaster, Thomas Allabaster (a merchant closely connected with the earl of Cumberland), Roger Howe, Richard Weych and Richard Staper, all except the last leading figures (or directly associated with such) in the privateering world, and before long they called in John Watts himself, the prince of privateering promoters, to assist them. In 1601 he became governor of the company and was succeeded in that office by Sir John Hart, who had been Cumberland's chief financial backer in the Puerto Rico expedition of 1598. Three of the four major ships of the first company voyage were privateers: Cumberland's *Dragon*, Garraway's *Ascension* and Bayning's *Susan* (the last two having been employed also in trade), and the captains and masters in the early East India voyages were for the most part products of the privateering war: Lancaster, John Middleton, William Broadbent, Henry Napper and Roger Hankin in the first expedition, David Middleton, Nicholas Downton, Anthony Hippon, Christopher Newport, William Parker, Martin Pring and others later.[37] As for the Virginia Company, it too owed much to the capital of London and West Country merchants formerly prominent in privateering, to gentlemen promoters of the sea-war such as Sir John Gilbert, Sir Ferdinando Gorges and Sir George Somers, and to seamen who, like Christopher Newport, had won their mastery of the Atlantic in the privateering service.[38] English commercial initiatives in Guiana and the West Indies in the early years of the seventeenth century likewise derived to a large extent, in terms of capital, shipping and personnel, from war-time privateering.[39]

The success of privateering brought about a remarkable boom in shipbuilding – specifically in the production of the larger sort of private vessel, of 100 tons and over. The official survey of 1582 had shown about 250 of 80 tons and up, whereas in the sixteen years from 1581 to 1597 no less than 133 of 100 tons and over were built. Of these 106 were Londoners and 72 were rated at 200 tons and over – England had possessed fewer than twenty ships of that size in 1582. The boom was still accelerating in the mid nineties and appears to have continued until after the end of the war.[40] Some of these new ships were intended primarily for privateering, like the *Neptune* of London, built by Francis Glanville, a leading London goldsmith, his son-in-law Christopher

[37] See Ch. 12 below.
[38] See Ch. 14 below.
[39] See Ch. 13 below.
[40] Davis, *Rise of the English Shipping Industry*, pp. 7–8; Andrews, *Elizabethan Privateering*, pp. 230–31.

Newport, and his brother Richard Glanville, a warship Spaniards in the Caribbean came to know to their cost.[41] Others worked in the Levant, Barbary or Muscovy trades. Many brought home prizes. England at the end of the war possessed a more powerful merchant marine than at the beginning of it, and it was better adapted to the conduct of long-distance and oceanic commerce. With the ships, moreover, there had grown up a race of skippers who knew the ocean as their forefathers had known the Channel, men like Newport, Lancaster and hundreds more, trained in the school of reprisals not only to navigate and to fight, but to manage the whole course of an expedition from the fitting out to the safe delivery of the privateers and their prize. Elizabethan statesmen were right in seeing ships and seamen as the key to mercantile power and wealth. These two decades of maritime warfare brought no clear victory; uncertainty and depression prevailed in the nation's traditional trades abroad; hopes of eastern trade, western planting, a northwest passage, all running high in the years before the Armada, were deferred. But the English kept the initiative in the Atlantic and used their peculiar form of sea power, dilute and pervasive, to tilt the oceanic balance in their favour, developing at the same time the resources – not only in ships and men but in commercial capital and momentum – to produce the new wave of enterprise which broke with the new century upon the East and West Indies, North and South America. Spain would and could still resist the encroachment, especially in the Caribbean, her most sensitive region, but the war so weakened her maritime and imperial system and so strengthened the forces of expansion in England that projects which had stood little chance of succeeding in the eighties became actualities in the Jacobean era.

On 24 March 1603 Queen Elizabeth died and James Stuart assumed the throne. James immediately made known his desire for peace and proclaimed an end to the hostilities.[42] In June he ordered the restoration of all prizes taken by his subjects since 24 April/4 May, and meanwhile opened negotiations with Spain for a formal peace, which was finally concluded by the Treaty of London in August 1604. Public opinion in England was divided between those – probably a majority of

---

[41] K. R. Andrews, 'Christopher Newport of Limehouse, mariner', *William and Mary Quarterly*, 11 (1954), 28–41.

[42] On the peace treaty, see F. Davenport (ed.), *European Treaties bearing upon the History of the United States and its Dependencies* (4 vols., Washington, 1917–37), I, pp. 246–57; J. C. Salyer, 'Algunos aspectos del tratado de paz entre Inglaterra y España del año 1604', *Simancas*, 1 (1950), 371–82; R. D. Hussey, 'America in European diplomacy, 1597–1604', *Revista de Historia de América*, 41 (1956), 1–30; K. R. Andrews, 'Caribbean rivalry and the Anglo-Spanish peace of 1604', *History*, 59 (1974), 1–17.

the political nation – who welcomed the end of a burdensome war, looking forward to a resurgence of trade which very soon became a fact as the Iberian ports were opened to English ships, and those who, like Ralegh and Richard Hawkins, urged the continuation of the war, pointing to Spain's weakness and the opportunity it gave for gain at her expense, whereas peace would only expose the Dutch to defeat, with evil consequences for England and the Protestant religion. Cecil, who was chiefly responsible for handling the negotiations, had considerable sympathy for the anti-Spanish case, and Nottingham, the most powerful of the other English representatives, had more, but James's softer attitude of course prevailed.

Even so, the official policy did not differ in substance from that embodied in Elizabeth's instructions to Cecil for the abortive Boulogne peace conference in 1600. The English did not betray the Dutch, for the latter were well able by now to fend for themselves, and the former categorically refused to hand over to Spain the so-called cautionary towns they held in the Low Countries. In respect of trade, the English gained for their merchants exemption from the recent 30% tax imposed by Spain on foreign imports and exports, and an assurance that they would not be molested in Spain on account of their religion. They also pressed hard for Spanish recognition of their right to trade freely with the Indies, East and West, offering to prohibit their own people from frequenting places actually occupied by Spain, but the Spanish delegates refused to accept this and for their part demanded that the English should explicitly renounce any claim whatever to commercial rights in the Indies. Finally both sides agreed to the ambiguous formula that there should be free trade between all the dominions of the two kingdoms 'where commerce existed before the war, agreeably and according to the use and observance of the ancient alliances and treaties before the war'. Cecil argued that this represented a tacit concession of the English case: 'you shall rather find it a pregnant Affirmative for us then against us; For so, where it is written that we shall trade in all his dominions, that comprehends the Indies; if you will say, *secundum tractatus Antiquos*, never treaty excluded it'.[43] The Spaniards on the other hand maintained that the treaty effectively excluded the English from the Indies. They knew well, however, and admitted in private that the dispute was still there and could only be settled in practice. The interpretation of the treaty was a matter not of words, but of deeds, and in fact the English continued to trade to the East Indies and to pursue the reconnoitring of North America and

---

[43] Cecil to Thomas Parry, 5 September 1604: PRO, SP 94/10, fo. 105.

Guiana for purposes of plantation which were soon realized. Spain was unable to prevent these encroachments, though in the West Indies she had more success, at least for the time being. The islanders thus retained in the peace the advantages they had gained during the war.

The East India Company

The records of the East India Company begin with a list, dated 22 September 1599, of 101 London merchants who had promised subscriptions totalling £30,133 6s. 8d. 'to venter in the pretended voiage to the Easte Indias'. Two days later a general assembly was held, which appointed directors for the voyage, and these proceeded to petition the Privy Council for a grant of incorporation as a trading company with special privileges. The petition was well received, but almost immediately orders came from the Court suspending both the formation of the company and the preparations for the voyage in view of the negotiations then in hand for peace with Spain, their lordships 'thinckking it more beneficiall for the generall state of merchaundize to enterteyne a peace then that the same shuld be hindred by the standinge with the spanishe Comissioners for the mainteyninge of this trade'. Only after the peace talks had failed were the merchants allowed to proceed with their plans, as they did in September 1600. On the last day of that year the East India Company received its first charter and in February 1601 the company's first expedition left the Thames.[1]

It was over twenty years since Drake had returned from the Spice Islands and since then the various attempts of Englishmen to re-enter the Orient had led to nothing. Edward Fenton's voyage of 1582, designed as a trading venture to the Moluccas, turned, as we have seen, into an ineffectual plunder cruise and got no further than Brazil. Thomas Cavendish in 1586 set out to emulate Drake's Pacific exploits and in that respect succeeded, returning with a great haul of loot and a stimulating report on Manila and the China trade, but his second attempt of 1591, in which he hoped to combine further plunder with eastern trade, was disastrous. None of his ships reached the Pacific and he himself died at sea.[2] John Chidley's fleet of 1589, which likewise

[1] H. Stevens (ed.), *The Dawn of British Trade to the East Indies* (London, 1886), pp. 1–12; W. Foster, *England's Quest of Eastern Trade* (London, 1933), pp. 144–55.
[2] D. B. Quinn (ed.), *The Last Voyage of Thomas Cavendish, 1591–1592* (Chicago, 1975).

failed to pass Magellan's Strait, was probably intended for Arauco and privateering, with no serious interest in trade.[3] The same applies to the expedition of Richard Hawkins, who was defeated and captured by a Spanish force off Peru in 1594.[4] Indeed all these ventures since Fenton's were primarily 'warfare voyages' and even James Lancaster, whose voyage of 1591–4 was promoted by London merchants, looked for prize rather than trade. The Londoners who originally proposed this Cape-route expedition for the Indian Ocean and beyond in 1589 included Paul Bayning and Thomas Cordell, both successful privateering magnates and both prominent in the formation of the East India Company later. On this occasion, however, their enterprise failed badly: all three ships and the great majority of their men were lost along with the booty obtained from various Portuguese prizes, while neither trade nor commercial reconnaissance was attempted.[5] Finally in 1596 Benjamin Wood, an eminent mariner who had sailed with Amadas and Barlowe in 1584, with Chidley in 1589, in command of a West Indies cruise in 1592 and to the West Indies again under Sir Robert Dudley in 1594, headed a force of three vessels provided by the same Dudley, bound for China by way of Magellan's Strait. Wood's aims were similar to those of Cavendish in 1591, but in fact he followed Lancaster's route and pursued much the same course of predation in the Indian Ocean, only with still worse results, losing all his ships and men, himself included.[6]

This deplorable record indicates not only the inadequacies of English shipping and seamanship in the late sixteenth century, but a certain lack of interest in the establishment of a commercial sea-link with the East. Those interested in the spoil of Iberian shipping or ports could do far better in the Atlantic, where privateering was generally profitable. As for oriental produce, home demand was more or less satisfied by imports from Emden, Stade and Hamburg, supplemented by the returns of the prospering Turkey merchants. Portuguese eastern goods came directly to England in very small quantities during these decades, except when from time to time privateers captured a carrack or its contents, and the glut of the pepper market in London on these occasions showed that English demand for that commodity was both

[3] K. R. Andrews, 'New light on Hakluyt', Mariner's Mirror, 37 (1951), 303–8.

[4] Williamson, 'Observations' of Sir Richard Hawkins.

[5] W. Foster (ed.), The Voyages of Sir James Lancaster to Brazil and the East Indies, 1591–1603 (London, 1940), pp. 1–30; Andrews, English Voyages to the West Indies, pp. 284–97.

[6] Foster, England's Quest, pp. 138–41. On Wood see also Purchas, II, 288–97; G. F. Warner (ed.), The Voyage of Robert Dudley to the West Indies, 1594–1595 (London, 1899) and Andrews, English Voyages to the West Indies.

limited and inelastic.[7] Nor, so long as the war lasted and trading difficulties with the Continent persisted, was there much prospect of re-exporting such goods, however they might be obtained. Meanwhile the Red Sea and Persian Gulf routes of Euro-Asian trade flourished and English merchants were happy with their expanding share in the markets of the Levant, where their advantages over their chief competitors earned them high profits. They failed in the early eighties, as we have seen, to establish their own chain of commerce through Hormuz, and that failure, together with the subsequent report of Ralph Fitch on his travels in the East,[8] whence he returned in 1591, left English merchants in no doubt as to the determination and ability of the Portuguese to resist attempts to penetrate their sphere of influence.

In reality, however, the Portuguese commercial empire in the East was more vulnerable towards the end of the century than observers in England could have known until Linschoten's famous account, first published in 1595–6, appeared in English in 1598.[9] The monopoly of Euro-Asian spice trade at which the Portuguese had originally aimed remained as ever beyond their reach. Their pepper, acquired mainly in India and carried around the Cape of Good Hope, amounted probably to over half the total sent to Europe from Asia between 1500 and 1550, but thereafter declined. This decline was offset by some increase in the volume of other and more valuable spices, the most important of which were cinnamon, cloves, mace, nutmegs and ginger, but even so it is clear that the Levantine routes bore a substantial share of the trade throughout the period.[10] In the Indian Ocean, it is true, the Portuguese were more than mere merchants: the *Estado da India*, having created the ring of powerful bases comprising Mozambique, Hormuz, Goa and Malacca, used these and minor strongpoints to deploy their superior naval power in order to control the major channels of maritime trade in

---

[7] The chief hauls of eastern goods during the war came in 1587 (the *San Felipe*, taken by Drake), 1592 (the *Madre de Deus*, taken by a combined fleet of privateers) and 1595 (taken at Pernambuco by Lancaster).

[8] *PN*, v, 465–505.

[9] A. C. Burnell and P. A. Tiele (eds.), *The Voyage of John Huyghen van Linschoten to the East Indies* (2 vols., London, 1885).

[10] This leaves out of account Persian silk, which went through the Levant. The size of the Portuguese share of the spice trade (including pepper) is a vexed question. The modern view until recently was that it comprised the greater part down to about 1550, but declined thereafter. Steensgaard, *Asian Trade Revolution*, pp. 154–69, reduced the significance of the Cape route even further, but C. H. H. Wake, 'The changing pattern of Europe's pepper and spice imports, ca. 1400–1700', *Journal of European Economic History*, 8 (1979), 361–403, argues that for most of the century it was responsible for over 75% of European imports – restoring credibility to a notion long since dismissed by modern historians.

the region, requiring Asian vessels to carry Portuguese passes and pay Portuguese customs dues. Their political skill in exploiting differences among the Asian powers and their ruthless determination in taking and holding their bases helped them to achieve this maritime dominance in the Indian Ocean, but it was never complete, nor did it gain them a monopoly of trade. In particular they failed to block the Red Sea route and in the later sixteenth century were content merely to tax the shipping which used it.[11]

East of Malacca, moreover, the Portuguese exercised no such dominance. Competing with Javanese, Chinese and many other traders in the huge complex of commerce ranging from Sumatra to Japan, they managed to secure a special position in the Moluccas by virtue of their alliance with the sultan of Ternate down to 1575 and in the rich trade between Macao and Nagasaki thanks to a fortuitous conjunction of circumstances. Thus they obtained regular supplies of cloves on the one hand (in addition to other spices from nearby) and of silver on the other, which commodities were important components in their system of inter-Asian exchange. Silver was the *sine qua non* of Euro-Asian trade, being Lisbon's main export to the East in the form of Spanish coin, and any supplement acquired in Asia was particularly welcome. The Indonesian spices were in effect bought largely with textiles shipped by the Portuguese from Gujarat and Coromandel in India.[12] The far-flung trade beyond Malacca was therefore integral to the entire structure of Portuguese oriental commerce and contributed valuably to the cargoes of the returning carracks, but the Far East lay wide open to any other European power that could find the means to conduct business there, as the Spaniards proved in the last third of the century by the development of their entrepôt at Manila. The real strength of the Portuguese eastern empire lay in its hold upon the western coast of India, whence it dominated Ceylon, the source of cinnamon, and stretched westwards to the Persian Gulf and the supporting East African stations. Its maritime power in the Indian Ocean was not seriously threatened in the sixteenth century. Yet even this was vulnerable, for the maintenance of these fleets and bases, in addition to the demands of western Africa and Brazil, imposed an intolerable strain upon Portugal's resources of manpower and shipping. The result was a deterioration in the quality of both, causing in the last two decades of the century an alarming rise in the shipping

---

[11] Steensgaard, *Asian Trade Revolution*, pp. 81–113.
[12] M. A. P. Meilink-Roelofsz, *Asian Trade and European Influence in the Indonesian Archipelago between 1500 and about 1630* (The Hague, 1962); C. R. Boxer, *The Portuguese Seaborne Empire* (London, 1969), pp. 39–63.

losses of the *carreira da India*.[13] Above all the *Estado da India*, despite its entrenched power and wide influence, was ill-fitted to deal with the kind of competition that finally appeared. For the Portuguese establishment in the East was not only corrupt, inefficient and hamstrung by aristocratic privilege; it was by nature parasitic, depending as much on tribute as on trading in commodities and generally preferring its own welfare to the realization of net gains. Neither the English nor the Dutch East India company was a model of business efficiency, but in this respect they far surpassed the *Estado da India*.[14]

The Dutch launched the first effective challenge. The maritime provinces of Holland and Zeeland had throughout the century played a major rôle in the trade and shipping of western Europe, especially in the Baltic and Iberian trades and the North Sea fishery. They had maintained that rôle in spite of difficulties caused by the revolt of the Netherlands – indeed the decline and fall of Antwerp directly assisted the rise of Amsterdam, which was soon to become the leading commercial centre in northern Europe. The 1590s saw a spectacular expansion of Dutch maritime enterprise and overseas trade, backed by a rapid increase in shipping and investment provided not only by the wealthy merchants of the regent class but by large numbers of lesser folk. It was to be expected, therefore, that they would try to break into the richest trade of all, especially because since 1580 Spanish embargoes of shipping in Iberian ports had repeatedly interrupted or threatened their trade with Lisbon, where merchants from the Netherlands had a considerable interest in the extra-European trades and in the marketing of spices, dyes, sugar and so forth north of the Pyrenees. The first Dutch venture, well prepared and financed, sailed in 1595 for Indonesia. Poorly led, it was a troublesome voyage, from which most of the men failed to return, but it established contact with Bantam in Java and brought home enough spices to inspire the formation of several new companies and the dispatch of 22 ships for the Indies in 1598. The most successful of these, led by Jacob van Neck, returned from Bantam richly laden in July 1599 and stimulated a still greater wave of competing companies and ventures, which were finally, on the initiative of the States-General, induced to merge in the United East India Company (known by its initials as the VOC) in 1602.[15]

[13] Boxer, *Portuguese Seaborne Empire*, pp. 215–19; C. R. Boxer (ed.), *The Tragic History of the Sea, 1589–1622* (Cambridge, 1959), pp. 24–5.
[14] Steensgaard, *Asian Trade Revolution*. Meilink-Roelofsz, *Asian Trade and European Influence*, pp. 116–35, gives a judicious account of the weaknesses of the Portuguese system.
[15] C. R. Boxer, *The Dutch Seaborne Empire, 1600–1800* (London, 1965), pp. 5–7, 18–24. For a more recent bibliography and a good general analysis of Dutch expansion see G. V.

It was van Neck's success which aroused the London merchants to their belated action in 1599, as the report of their assembly on 25 September 1599 implies in referring to 'the successe of the viage performed by the Duche nation', adding that the Londoners were 'stirred up with noe lesse affection to advaunce the trade of ther native Cuntrey then the duche merchauntes'.[16] It may be doubted whether they would have bestirred themselves had not the Dutch taken the initiative, for national rivalry clearly played a large part in the formation of both companies: the VOC in turn was created in response to the threat posed by the English company. In particular the Dutch triumph caused great alarm and despondency among the English merchants trading to the Levant. One merchant wrote from Chios that 'This tradinge to that Endyes have clean overthroughen our deallings to Allepo, as by experience ere longe we shall see', and expressed the fear that unless the Levant Company could find some other way of meeting its expenses it would have to give up its patent.[17] In the event the Levant Company survived this crisis and flourished more than ever, but at the turn of the century its position seemed so precarious that the Turkey merchants of London gave their attention seriously to the only practical alternative: to compete with the Dutch and the Portuguese on the Cape route to the Indies. Consequently the Levant traders played a leading part in the formation of the East India Company. They made up at least a third of those present at the first meeting and a majority of the fifteen directors then elected, and they dominated the committee that organized the first voyage. Alderman Paul Bayning, who headed that committee, was prominent in the Turkey trade and Thomas Smythe, the first governor of the new company, was at the time of his election governor of the Levant Company.[18] The two companies remained closely connected for some years even though their interests diverged.

By the charter of 1600 the crown granted the company a monopoly of English trade to countries beyond the Cape of Good Hope and Magellan's Strait for fifteen years, excluding places possessed by any Christian prince. Monopolies of this kind were characteristic of such charters and the company gained the usual rights associated with them, in addition to the special privilege of exporting silver to the value of £30,000 a year. The Privy Council welcomed the enterprise and

Scammell, *The World Encompassed: The First European Maritime Empires, c. 800–1650* (London, 1981), pp. 373–435.

[16] Stevens, *Dawn*, p. 8.

[17] W. Foster (ed.), *The Travels of John Sanderson in the Levant, 1584–1602* (London, 1931), p. 190.

[18] Stevens, *Dawn*, pp. 4–6, 12, 62, 281, etc.; Foster, *Travels of Sanderson*, p. 207.

threw its weight behind the company when some subscribers tried to withdraw. This was, it threateningly declared, 'a publike action and not to be dallied withall', and before the departure of the first expedition it took measures to discipline those who refused to supplement their initial subscriptions at the company's request.[19] On the other hand the company was jealous of its independence and determined to manage its own affairs. When Lord Treasurer Buckhurst proposed Sir Edward Michelbourne, one of Essex's soldiers, for the command of the first venture, it rejected him on the grounds that 'they purpose not to imploy anie gent in any place of charge',[20] undoubtedly because the subscribers would not permit another 'warfare voyage'. Since England was still at war with Spain and Portugal they were willing to authorize their commander to take prizes, but only on condition that this did not prejudice the main purpose, which was trade. Their business, as they clearly perceived it, was commerce, not fighting the country's enemies. If force proved necessary for that business, they were prepared to use it, but from the outset they made no attempt to capture Portuguese forts or otherwise to acquire bases or colonies in Asia, in which respect their policy differed radically from that of the Dutch.[21]

This restraint on the part of the Londoners was not a matter of principle but of expediency: they lacked the resources of their rivals. Although the capital available for investment had increased substantially in the later sixteenth century, merchants were reluctant to lock it up in the kind of long-term overhead expenditure that a more ambitious strategy would have required. Indeed the company found it hard to finance even the strictly commercial policy it chose to pursue: the sum raised for the first voyage alone amounted to about £70,000. Instead of establishing a permanent joint-stock, therefore, the company had to resort to the creation of separate and terminable stocks for each voyage, members having the option of subscribing or not as they pleased to any of the voyages. This arrangement of course hampered the development of the trade, but it was not until 1613 that a longer-term form of financing was introduced in the shape of the first joint-stock, which was paid up over four years and finally wound up in 1621, by which time a second and still longer-term joint-stock had been instituted.[22] Merchandising policy also posed for the founders problems which were to become familiar over the years. They knew very well that eastern trade required large amounts of specie, but neither

[19] Stevens, *Dawn*, pp. 61, 112–13, 164–5.
[20] Stevens, *Dawn*, p. 28.
[21] D. K. Bassett, 'Early English trade and settlement in Asia, 1602–1690', in J. S. Bromley and E. H. Kossmann (eds.), *Britain and the Netherlands* (London, 1968), pp. 83–109.
[22] Chaudhuri, *East India Company*, pp. 207–23.

the government nor other merchants nor the general public liked to see bullion or coin exported on the scale required. It was for this reason that the company initially and for some time sought to sell English broadcloths and kerseys in eastern markets, though with little success. They were not interested in cloth for the sake of industry or the public good, but as a convenient form of purchasing power with which to obtain pepper, spices and other oriental goods, the actual source of their profits, particularly because they could obtain English cloth more cheaply than their rivals could.[23]

The ships bought for and employed in the first voyage were the *Red Dragon* (600 tons), formerly the earl of Cumberland's *Malice Scourge*; the *Susan* (240 tons), formerly Paul Bayning's; the *Ascension* (260 tons), built for William Garraway in 1597; the *Hector* (300 tons); and the *Gift* (120 tons). The *Red Dragon* was a first-rate man-of-war, the other three major vessels were powerful Levant Company men and the *Gift* was used as victualler.[24] For the general command the directors chose James Lancaster, who had long experience not only as a captain and general of privateering forces but as a merchant and factor in Portugal.[25] With him in the *Red Dragon* as pilot-major of the fleet sailed John Davis, recently returned from a Dutch East India expedition in which he had served as chief pilot. John Middleton, John Havard and William Brund went as principal factors in the *Hector*, the *Susan* and the *Ascension* respectively: although effectively in command, they were not officially called captains, for they were appointed as merchants, each being assisted by three other factors. Brund, for example, was chosen as 'a grave and discreet merchaunt and one which hath the arabyan Spanishe and Portugall Languages'.[26] It was emphatically a 'merchant voyage' and for that very reason the masters carried large responsibilities as managers of the ships and crews. The whole company of the fleet amounted to about 500 men for 1520 tons of shipping – heavy manning for a merchant voyage, but in the circumstances justifiable. They included one Philip Grove, a Dutchman, as second pilot, and one Peter Frauncis of Bridgwater, a Portuguese sailor, who was appointed to advise Davis.[27]

On 29 January 1601 Richard Hakluyt appeared before the directors, 'and having read unto them out of his notes and bookes divers instruccions for provisions of Jewelles, was required to sett downe in wryting a note of the principall places in the East Indies wher Trade is

[23] Chaudhuri, *East India Company*, pp. 13, 111–17.
[24] Stevens, *Dawn*, pp. 34, 147–8.
[25] Foster, *Voyages of Lancaster*, pp. xiii–xiv.
[26] Stevens, *Dawn*, p. 93.
[27] Stevens, *Dawn*, pp. 38–9, 47; Foster, *Voyages of Lancaster*, p. 76.

to be had to thend the same may be used for the better instruccion of our factors in the said voyage'. In about a fortnight Hakluyt delivered detailed notes on the commodities of Portuguese eastern trade and was duly paid for this information and former advice as well as for three maps.[28] He did this job as well as could be expected, but his knowledge was academic and the directors' respect for it suggests how much they had yet to learn. Even so, their strategy was clear. The expedition would by-pass India and make directly for the Indonesian region, where the Dutch had already traded successfully. Factors would be left in suitable places to conduct trade pending the arrival of a second fleet. Private trade was strictly forbidden.[29]

It took Lancaster about fifteen months in all to reach Achin (Sumatra), a major source of pepper and hostile to Portugal. Though disappointed with the trade here, he captured a valuable Portuguese prize in the Straits of Malacca and pressed on to Bantam, where he traded freely, making good use of the calicoes he had acquired from the Portuguese, and left several factors, thus founding the first of the English company's factories in the East. Thence he set sail for home with a cargo consisting chiefly of pepper and after a difficult voyage of seven months reached the Downs in September 1603.[30] It was, however, a depressing situation to which he returned. The company had been unable, in spite of pressure from the government, to raise anything like the funds required for a second expedition, partly because in 1602 it devoted a considerable sum to financing George Waymouth's north-west passage venture, which in the event was a waste of money. Nor did Lancaster's cargo solve the problem. The plague of 1603 constricted the home market, such as it was, while Dutch competition ruined the market abroad. The first commercial achievement of the East India Company, it seemed to many, was to drain the country of silver by exporting almost £22,000 in specie, and its second was to create a pepper glut of unprecedented proportions.[31] Thus the first four years of the seventeenth century, which saw the dawn of English trade to the East Indies, also witnessed a dawning awareness, on the part of the company, its supporters and its critics, of the financial difficulties the company would face throughout its early years, when the pressure of shareholders for immediate dividends combined with a chronic shortage of capital to restrict operations in the East. Not until 1611 did the company open its second factory there, nor was it able in the

[28] Stevens, *Dawn*, pp. 124, 143; Quinn, *Hakluyt Handbook*, pp. 313–16; Taylor, *Writings of the Hakluyts*, pp. 476–82.
[29] Stevens, *Dawn*, pp. 129–37.
[30] Foster, *Voyages of Lancaster*, pp. 75–166.
[31] Chaudhuri, *East India Company*, pp. 115–17, 153–4.

following years to withstand the aggressive policy of the Dutch in Indonesia. Its relative failure in this region hindered in turn the creation of the integrated trading system necessary to success. Confronted with these interconnected problems, the company could not rely upon the crown for steady support and consequently had to endure a hard infancy.

The original aim of the company was, as we have seen, to obtain a share of the Indonesian trade in pepper and spices. Consequently the second voyage, dispatched in 1604, was designed to renew trade at Bantam and to extend operations to the Spice Islands, this second objective being all the more important now that the directors appreciated the need to balance pepper with cloves, nutmegs and other valuable spices.[32] They employed the same four ships and chose as their general Henry Middleton, brother of John, who had been one of the principal factors in the first voyage, and of Robert, a leading member of the company and cousin to the London magnates Thomas and Hugh Myddelton. Henry was accompanied by his brother David, who was later to command the company's fifth voyage. Christopher Colthurst, captain of the *Hector*, had long experience in privateering and represented a London family of shipowning merchants prominent in the Levant trade. Roger Stile, captain of the *Ascension*, belonged to a similar London family closely allied with the Colthursts. The captain of the *Susan*, William Keeling, gave the company long and valuable service, becoming eventually its 'factor-general' in the East.

Middleton, his crews much reduced and enfeebled by scurvy, reached Bantam in December 1604 only to find in the road a fleet of twelve Dutch vessels and ashore an English factory demoralized by sickness and other troubles. He nevertheless managed to lade two of his ships with pepper and dispatched them home, proceeding eastwards himself with the other two for Amboina. Here the Portuguese, dominating the island from their fort, effectively denied trade to the English by grossly overpricing the cloves and Middleton, who had orders not to quarrel with the king of Spain's subjects, could do nothing about it. Shortly after this the Dutch arrived and, being at war with Spain and determined to secure control of the Spice Islands, promptly captured the fort and refused the English permission to trade so that, as the anonymous journal of the voyage put it, 'all hope of trade in this place was gone'.[33] With this bitter foretaste of things to

[32] W. Foster (ed.), *The Voyage of Sir Henry Middleton to the Moluccas, 1604–1606* (London, 1943).
[33] Foster, *Voyage of Middleton*, p. 24.

come, Middleton sent the *Ascension* to the Banda Islands for nutmegs and himself made for the Moluccas in the *Dragon*. Though well received by the Portuguese at Tidore and by their enemy the sultan of Ternate, the English, having laded a fair quantity of cloves, were obliged to stand by once more as the Dutch took over Tidore and decisively shut them out of both islands. The *Ascension* had meanwhile traded successfully at the Bandas and rejoined the *Dragon* at Bantam to make for London. On the way home, nearing Table Bay, Middleton found the *Hector* 'driving up and downe the sea . . . with tenne men in her', having lost 53 men dead since she came out of Bantam nine months before, and having lost touch with the *Susan*. The *Hector* he managed to rescue, but the *Susan* was never heard of again.[34]

Middleton's voyage can hardly be described as an unqualified success, but it was so profitable that the company aimed to make annual voyages henceforth. Bantam and the Spice Islands were still the main targets, for as yet Dutch competition there did not seem overwhelming, but the directors planned now to help their Indonesian trade by opening up commercial relations with Aden and Gujarat, either or both of which should provide Indian goods, especially calicoes, for sale in southeast Asia. This was all the more necessary since English textiles were clearly failing to find any considerable market and exports of treasure were mounting. Keeling, in command of the third voyage, set out in 1607 with the *Dragon* and the *Hector*, making for Aden first on the plausible assumption that a factory there would stand a better chance than one at Surat, so near the heart of Portuguese eastern power.[35] In the event, however, the two ships, having taken over a year to reach Socotra Island, were unable to make Aden itself. Keeling therefore sailed for Bantam in the *Dragon* while the *Hector* took William Hawkins, his lieutenant, to Surat and then proceeded also for Bantam. Thus began the course of events which led to the formation of the English factory at Surat and to rivalry with Portugal for the trade of that region. This sequence, though related to the developments in southeast Asia, will be examined later.

The third voyage included a third ship, the *Consent*, which sailed directly under David Middleton to Bantam and then to the Moluccas, where he found that the Spaniards and Portuguese had repulsed the Dutch. The Iberians refused the English permission to trade because Middleton would not support them, but he managed to secure a cargo in spite of these difficulties and returned to England safely. Keeling arrived at Bantam later, sent the *Dragon* home and himself conducted

---

[34] Foster, *Voyage of Middleton*, p. 69.
[35] *Purchas*, II, 502–49; Foster, *England's Quest*, pp. 184–7, 198–202.

the *Hector* to the Bandas. Soon after he reached there, in 1609, a powerful Dutch force arrived and began conquering the islands, a process he could do nothing to stop, though he successfully completed his lading and returned via Bantam to England. The next year David Middleton in the *Expedition*, the sole ship of the company's fifth voyage,[36] came likewise to the Bandas and acquired a cargo in spite of the Hollanders, who had not yet completed their conquest, but when he reached London at the end of 1610 it was obvious to all concerned that the Dutch, having concluded a twelve-year truce with Spain, were determined to use their superior power to exclude their rivals from the Spice Islands by imposing commercial treaties and contracts upon the local rulers.

In 1611 the company addressed a petition to Lord Treasurer Salisbury (formerly Sir Robert Cecil) detailing their grievances against the VOC and begging him to mediate on their behalf with the States-General.[37] They rehearsed the 'uncyvell and inhumaine wronges' done to them and their servants, Henry and David Middleton and Keeling, and they argued that the Hollanders had no right to exclude them from the East Indies, particularly because Drake, Cavendish and Lancaster had traded there before the Dutch entered the region. James I and his ministers certainly had no desire to allow this quarrel to aggravate their already rather strained relations with the Hague, nor did the States wish to endanger Anglo-Dutch amity in Europe on this account. Talks therefore began and conferences were held in 1613 and 1615 in the hope of reaching a settlement. The Dutch company's case was that it had waged war at great expense on the Portuguese and Spaniards in the Indies and that the English could not reasonably expect to reap the benefit unless they were prepared to contribute to the past and continuing cost of Dutch naval and military operations. The English merchants for their part referred pointedly to the Netherlanders' own doctrine of freedom of the seas, claiming this as a right no friendly nation should deny them. As for contributing to hostilities with the Iberian powers, it was out of the question in view of the existing state of peace and King James's concern to remain on good terms with Spain. The suggestion that the two companies should merge or trade jointly, a solution favoured by both governments, proved unwelcome to the

---

[36] *Purchas*, III, 51–60; Foster, *England's Quest*, pp. 202–5. The company's fourth voyage (1608) was disastrous. Of the two ships one, the *Union*, lost nearly all her men on the return voyage and had to be abandoned on the coast of Brittany; the other, the *Ascension*, was wrecked near Diu: *Purchas*, III, 61–82.

[37] G. Birdwood and W. Foster (eds.), *The Register of Letters etc. of the Governor and Company of Merchants of London Trading into the East Indies, 1600–1619* (London, 1893), pp. 429–32.

merchants on both sides and so for the time being the negotiations made no progress.[38]

Meanwhile relations between the companies' men in the field went from bad to worse. In the Spice Islands generally, and especially at Amboina and the Banda Islands, the English persisted in their efforts to trade and to encourage local resistance to Dutch domination. Ladings were thus acquired, but during the years from 1611 to 1617 the VOC steadily tightened its grip on the area as a whole and on its lucrative trade. These years saw the rise to power of Jan Pieterszoon Coen, the most vigorous exponent of an aggressive and exclusive policy, and his appointment as Governor-General of the Dutch Indies in 1618 signalled the endorsement of his strategy by the seventeen directors of the VOC. It was precisely at this juncture that the English company decided to mount at last an open and strong challenge to Dutch supremacy in Indonesia. A fleet under Sir Thomas Dale and another under Martin Pring converged upon Bantam, headquarters of the English factories in the Far East, and from there John Jourdain, the champion of the forward policy, launched the attack late in 1618. An unofficial war ensued, in the course of which the Dutch brought their superior force to bear. Jourdain was killed in July 1619, and repeated defeat had severely weakened the English when in March 1620 they were saved by the news that the governments in Europe had at last reached an agreement.[39]

At home the United Provinces were now under threat. War had broken out on the Continent in 1618 and it seemed impossible for the Netherlands to avoid becoming embroiled when the Dutch-Spanish truce expired in 1621. King James, on the other hand, was anxious to dispose of a dispute in which he was not vitally interested at a time when his cherished foreign policy was beset with acute difficulties. The two powers therefore resolved their difference in the East by the so-called 'Treaty of Defence' of July 1619. The English were to have one third of the Spice Islands trade, while the pepper trade of Java was to be shared equally. In return for this concession the English company was to contribute to the cost of defending the trade of the whole area, including the Coromandel coast, against Iberian attacks.

This was of course a paper solution and it failed to work. The Dutch in the East disliked it because they felt they had been cheated of victory and obliged to make large concessions to a weaker power which had invested far less in the contest for commercial supremacy. As for the

[38] Foster, *England's Quest*, pp. 205–7; G. N. Clark, *The Colonial Conferences between England and the Netherlands in 1613 and 1615* (2 vols., Leyden, 1952).
[39] *Purchas*, IV, 508–35; V, 1–241. Foster, *England's Quest*, pp. 253–75.

English merchants, they resented the sacrifice of their independence and found it impossible to meet the cost of so large a share of the trade and of the preparations of the Dutch for renewed war with Spain and Portugal. The strength of English shipping and factories in southeast Asia had already been seriously injured by the hostilities of 1618–19 and a further contraction of trade in that region followed. The Bantam headquarters had been closed in 1620 and moved to Batavia (Jakarta), whence the President and Council wrote despairing reports in the next two years concerning their lack of capital and inability to sustain a profitable trade. It was decided to withdraw the English agents from the Spice Islands as an economy measure, to leave Batavia for some more suitable centre and to recall the company's factors from Patani (Malaya), Ayuthia (Siam) and Hirado (Japan), since trade in these places was unprofitable.[40] Thus the company was already losing ground in the Far East and retiring from the unequal struggle with the Dutch when, in February 1623, ten English merchants at Amboina were executed by the Dutch authorities after being tried for conspiring to seize the fortress. This so-called 'massacre of Amboina' roused a storm of protest and resentment in England which raged for many years and helped to cause the first Anglo-Dutch war, but it had less influence upon the struggle for commercial power in Indonesia than some used historians think. In fact it was the culmination of years of jealous and frequently violent hostility between the two nations in that region and its effect was merely to put an end to their unwilling collaboration and to confirm the English decision to vacate the Spice Islands.[41]

Indeed the company continued to drive a considerable trade after 1623 in the westerly parts. At Macassar in Celebes, where the Dutch had no foothold, they developed a factory deservedly described by the Bantam Council in 1627 as 'one of the especialest flowers in our garden',[42] receiving smuggled cloves from the Dutch islands. Macassar remained a thriving international emporium until the Dutch captured it in 1667. In Java also the English persisted, re-establishing their presence at Bantam in 1628, while Jambi in Sumatra became a major and regular source of pepper for the home market. To these stations the factory at Masulipatam in the kingdom of Golconda on the Coromandel coast formed a valuable complement from its foundation

[40] For a general account of the factory established at Hirado and dissolved in 1623 see Foster, *England's Quest*, pp. 217–25. The story of William Adams is related in *Purchas*, II, 326–46; *ibid.* III, 516–70, concerns the Japan factory.
[41] Bassett, 'Early English trade and settlement', pp. 90–91; Foster, *England's Quest*, pp. 276–7; Chaudhuri, *East India Company*, pp. 60–62.
[42] Cited in Chaudhuri, *East India Company*, p. 168.

in 1611, supplying the cotton piece-goods indispensable to the south-eastern trade. Before the middle of the century the company extended its operations thence southwards to Madras, which in 1652 replaced Bantam as the seat of its eastern presidency, and northwards to Bengal.[43] The 1620s, it is true, saw the failure of the high hopes which had inspired the company in its early years – hopes centred upon Indonesian pepper and spices – and the difficulties in southeast Asia were chiefly responsible for the general crisis of confidence which in 1627–8 brought the company in London seriously to contemplate suspending all business.[44] This crisis, however, passed and the company held on, encouraged by its much better prospects in India and Persia.

When the directors decided in 1607 to make contact with the Gujarati port of Surat in western India, their main purpose was to use it as a supply point to assist the development of their Indonesian trade. For this reason and because it took some years for the English to establish themselves securely at Surat and at Agra, where the Mogul emperor kept his Court, this centre at first occupied a secondary place in the company's eastern system. Indeed it was not until 1615 that the factors dispatched a ship directly from Surat to England.[45] Soon, however, its great potential value emerged more clearly. Already in 1613 Thomas Aldworth, the head of the factory there, described it as 'the fountain-head from whence we may draw all the trade of our East Indies; for we find here merchandise which we can take and sell in nearly all parts of these Indies and also in England', and four years later Sir Thomas Roe echoed his words: Surat was 'the fountain and life of all the East India trade'.[46] Gujarat itself was a highly productive region. Apart from the calicoes so much in demand elsewhere in Asia, it yielded indigo, which in 1623 was thought to be 'the best commodity the company had from the parts of Surat',[47] as well as sugar and saltpetre. Surat gave access to Agra, a rich market for luxury wares, and to all the westerly parts of the Mogul empire. It was a major shipbuilding centre and its trade stretched not only all along the western coasts of India, but much further afield to the Persian Gulf, the Red Sea and the East Indies.[48]

From the arrival of William Hawkins at Surat in 1608 it took the company about ten years to establish a firm commercial foothold in that part of India. A mixture of force and diplomacy was required to

[43] Foster, *England's Quest*, pp. 208–15, 244–52, 321–2.
[44] Chaudhuri, *East India Company*, pp. 68–70.
[45] Chaudhuri, *East India Company*, p. 17.
[46] Both cited in B. G. Gokhale, *Surat in the Seventeenth Century* (London, 1979), p. 93.
[47] Chaudhuri, *East India Company*, p. 176.
[48] Gokhale, *Surat*, pp. 10, 90–94.

overcome the resistance both of the Portuguese and of those local merchants and officials who found their interests threatened by the newcomers. Hawkins himself made a remarkable impression upon the impressionable emperor, Jahangir (son of Akbar the Great, who had conquered Gujarat), but having the support of no one but the single English factor at Surat, he found himself continually frustrated by Portuguese influence and had made no real progress towards establishing an English presence when he finally left the country, discomfited and discredited, at the beginning of 1612 aboard one of Sir Henry Middleton's ships.[49] Middleton, commanding the company's sixth voyage, had arrived in September 1611 with the intention of settling a factory at Surat, but was rudely rebuffed, in reprisal for which treatment he sailed for Aden and the Red Sea and proceeded to seize numerous Indian ships, forcing them to trade on his terms and exacting ransoms from those that belonged to Gujarati ports.[50] These violent measures, which might have been expected to ruin English prospects at Surat, in fact improved them, since they exposed the defencelessness of that port's most valuable traffic. Consequently when Captain Thomas Best arrived some months later with the *Dragon* and the *Hosiander* (213 tons),[51] the English merchants, led by Thomas Aldworth, succeeded at last in founding a factory, which thenceforth flourished until the Gujarat famine of 1630–31.

Aldworth did more than anyone to develop English trade at Surat, but this commercial progress owed much also to the gun-power of the East-Indiamen and the ineptitude of the Portuguese. When a force of four Portuguese galleons came from Goa in November 1612 to attack Best's ships, he routed them so conclusively that Portuguese prestige suffered a damaging blow. This was not sufficient, however, to secure the English position, for their opponents remained influential at Agra while Best removed the commanding presence of his ships early in the new year, and it was not until October 1614 that the next company fleet arrived, under the command of Nicholas Downton.[52] Fortunately for the English, the Portuguese in the interval overplayed their hand. In September 1613 they deeply offended the emperor by seizing a rich Surat merchantman belonging to his mother and aggravated the ensuing rupture by preparing an armada at Goa to attack Surat. Downton was consequently greeted as a protector who would save the

[49] *Purchas*, III, 1–51; Foster, *England's Quest*, pp. 184–97, 234–43, 280–87, covers the Surat story from 1608 to 1619.

[50] *Purchas*, III, 170–93, 250–91.

[51] W. Foster (ed.), *The Voyage of Thomas Best to the East Indies, 1612–1614* (London, 1934).

[52] W. Foster (ed.), *The Voyage of Nicholas Downton to the East Indies, 1614–1615* (London, 1939).

city from fire and slaughter. Even now the viceroy could easily have reached agreement with the Gujaratis at the expense of the English, but he determined instead to crush both at once. At the beginning of 1615 he attacked and was repulsed with heavy loss. This victory was not final, for Surat's commerce with Goa remained important and Portuguese influence at Agra soon recovered, but the emperor could no longer be expected to heed demands for the expulsion of the English, for that would not only leave Surat at the mercy of Goa, but would also expose the shipping of Gujarat to English vengeance.

Nevertheless Aldworth and his fellow factors at Surat found their position far from satisfactory. The imperial officials of Gujarat, led by the powerful Mukarrab Khan, looked upon the English as intruders who had little to offer in exchange for the wealth of that country and who deserved, as mere merchants, nothing but contempt and arbitrary exactions. Nor had the English endeared themselves to the people of Surat. The local merchants valued the Portuguese trade far more than the English and still resented Middleton's piratical conduct. Meanwhile the company's successive agents at Court lacked the diplomatic skill and presence to impress the emperor. The only hope of improvement lay, as Aldworth had already reported in 1613, in 'a suffitient man . . . that may bee Resident in Agra withe the kinge, and sutch a one whose person may breade regarde, for they here looke mutch after greate men'.[53] After considerable argument in London this was accepted and the company decided to send a full ambassador accredited by King James, for which service they chose Sir Thomas Roe. Roe was a gentleman of merchant stock, favoured at Court by Elizabeth and later by Prince Henry. Knighted already in 1605, the young courtier won distinction by his Guiana expedition of 1610–11, but Henry's death in the following year left him without a patron. He served in 1614 as a member of Parliament, but for financial reasons was glad to accept the diplomatic post offered him that same year, since it brought him a salary of £600 a year and a handsome expense allowance—all paid by the company.

It was no easy task that Roe faced on his arrival at Surat in September 1615 but, having resisted with dignity the attempts of the local governor to humiliate him, he journeyed on to Agra and soon won the personal esteem of the Mogul himself. Unfortunately this did not lead to the concession Roe was expected by the company to win: a formal treaty embodying capitulations which would guarantee the safety and free development of the company's trade in the emperor's dominions.

[53] W. Foster (ed.), *The Embassy of Sir Thomas Roe to the Court of the Great Mogul, 1615–1619* (2 vols., London, 1899), I, p. iii.

Though he remained there over three years Roe was unable to achieve this objective. As he wrote resignedly to the company in 1618, 'You can never expect to trade here upon Capitulations that shalbe permanent. Wee must serve the tyme. Some now I have gotten, but by way of *firmaens* and Promise from the Kynge. . . .You shalbe sure of as much priviledge as any stranger, and right when the subject dares not plead his.'[54] Thus the English factors acquired a measure of protection against abuses and were permitted to trade freely and govern themselves according to their own religion and laws. Roe's patient diplomacy substantially improved their position and finally defeated Portuguese efforts to secure their expulsion. Their trading base secured, the English merchants rapidly developed a number of other factories in Gujarat and some further afield, including one at Agra and one as far north as Lahore.[55] On the other side of India, as we have seen, the company was already established at Masulipatam in 1611 and thereafter steadily extended its operations from that base. Thus by 1630 English commercial penetration of the Indian sub-continent was well under way.

Sir Thomas Roe was also personally responsible for the opening of company trade between Surat and the Red Sea port of Mokha (the modern Al Mukna in the Yemen). This was a trade of great potential value to the company since, as Roe pointed out, the Egyptian merchants who frequented this and other Red Sea ports paid for Indian and East Indian products largely in specie. The factors in Gujarat at this time depended heavily on silver sent from England, for the early hopes of selling English goods there had not been realized. If the company could dispose of English and Indian exports in the Red Sea it would not only gain a highly profitable extension of its commercial network but also remedy to some extent a deplorable loss of treasure to the commonwealth. Furthermore, Roe argued,

seing those of Surat cannot trade saufely thether without the Company of the English into the Red Sea, wher it is said that Trade is for two Millions yearely, they wilbe glad of the companie of the English. . . .[56]

so glad, he thought, that they would be prepared to pay for the privilege. Better still, the company of the English would also be conferred upon the pilgrims coming back from Mecca: 'which shippe of theirs retourning is of very great valewe, having 1000 of their people in her, wilbe as a pawne and assurance for the good usage of our

---

[54] Foster, *Embassy of Sir Thomas Roe*, p. 469.
[55] Foster, *England's Quest*, pp. 314–15.
[56] Foster, *Embassy of Sir Thomas Roe*, p. 524.

people at Surat'. The merchants of Surat had of course traded for generations to the Red Sea without the benefit of such 'protection' and would not take kindly to it. As Thomas Kerridge, now chief of the Surat factory, put it to Roe, the English had already ruined the local merchants' trade to southeast Asia, so that 'since our coming, this porte is undone, which in their greefs they spare not somtymes to tell us'.[57] The Red Sea traffic was the only important commerce left to them and if the English tried to usurp that too their Gujarat factories would suffer for it. And suffer they did. After the company's initial, single-ship venture to Mokha in 1618, obstruction by the Surat merchants developed into a general boycott, intended to compel the company to abandon that trade, and when the factors appealed to the emperor's viceroy in Gujarat they received a dusty answer.[58] This dispute was aggravated by another, concerning the company's importation of large amounts of coral, to which the Gujarati merchants objected, and by the English habit of seizing Indian vessels or goods at sea in reprisal for losses ashore. The opposition was sufficient to prevent a company voyage to the Red Sea in 1620, but the trade was resumed the following year and continued with varying fortune thereafter. The local merchants were in fact unable to hold their own against so powerful a corporation which, once established in the country, could easily outdo them in bribery, in physical force and in commercial efficiency.[59]

More important, however, than the Red Sea enterprise was the successful establishment, between 1614 and 1622, of company trade with Persia.[60] Persian raw silk, one of the most valuable commodities of international trade, flowed to Europe through the dominions of the Grand Turk, but Shah Abbas, the sultan's great enemy, was keenly interested in having it exported by way of the Persian Gulf. Since it was well known that English cloth commanded a substantial market in Persia, it is not surprising that the East India Company took advantage of this excellent opportunity. That it did not respond sooner was probably the fault of the first champions of such a scheme—the Sherley brothers.[61] Sir Anthony went out to Persia in 1599 with his younger brother Robert, intent upon a grandiose scheme to ally Persia with the European powers against the Turks, to promote English trade there

---

[57] Foster, *Embassy of Sir Thomas Roe*, p. 166.
[58] W. Foster (ed.), *The English Factories in India, 1618–1621* (Oxford, 1926), pp. xiv–xx.
[59] Gokhale, *Surat*, pp. 147–71, on the relations between European and Gujarati merchants.
[60] For a general account see Foster, *England's Quest*, pp. 295–313. Steensgaard, *Asian Trade Revolution*, pp. 209–414, is largely concerned with Hormuz and the struggle for the Persia trade.
[61] On the Sherleys see Chew, *Crescent and Rose*, pp. 239–98, and E. D. Ross, *Sir Anthony Sherley and his Persian Adventure* (London, 1933).

and (last but not least) to win fame and fortune for himself. The Shah sent him back to the West with his blessing, but Sir Anthony, an adventurer with little money and less sense, failed to convince those who mattered in Europe and died in obscure poverty in Madrid some time after 1635. In 1608 Robert, who had remained in Persia meanwhile, followed his brother on the same errand, hoping particularly to win support in Madrid for a combined Ibero-Persian strategy in the Indian Ocean, which would include the channelling of the silk trade through Hormuz, accompanying this with pointed references to the Shah's ambition to take that base from the Portuguese. He failed, however, to move the government of Philip III and so resorted to London. Here, as in Madrid, he inspired only mistrust, while neither the Levant Company nor the East India Company welcomed the idea of diverting the silk trade, the former for obvious reasons and the latter for lack of the large amounts of cash demanded for the launching of the operation. Consequently Robert returned to Persia disappointed in 1614.

That same year, however, the idea of opening up the Persia trade by way of the Gulf was taken up as a practical proposition by the English factors at Surat, at the instance of an English merchant, Richard Steel, who had journeyed through Persia to India. Encumbered as they were with surplus English cloth, they welcomed the chance and sent Steel back to Persia in 1615, where he luckily met Sherley and obtained through him licences to trade in certain ports. In spite of Roe's doubts about their handling of the matter, the Surat factors pressed on with their initiative and in 1617 their agent in Persia, Edward Connock, effectively opened the trade at the port of Jask, on the Gulf of Oman, under extensive privileges granted by the Shah. But then difficulties slowed down the progress of the enterprise. On the one hand the company in London adopted a cautious approach, stipulating the conditions it would require in any contract with the Shah for the silk trade. On the other hand the Shah himself would not sign any such contract, having now been driven by the Turks to make peace with them. Before 1622 the company had achieved no more than a modest trade through a somewhat remote port.

Once again, however, the Portuguese reaction resolved the company's problem. In 1619 an envoy from Goa to the Shah's Court demanded the exclusion of the English, a monopoly of the Gulf trade and restitution of certain territory on the mainland which they claimed belonged to Hormuz. Thereafter relations between Portugal and Persia deteriorated and reached the point of open war in 1621. Meanwhile the viceroy dispatched from Goa a squadron of warships to destroy or drive off English shipping frequenting Jask. This force was roundly defeated by a fleet of East Indiamen at the end of 1620 and a year later another company fleet joined forces with the Persian army, reduced the Portuguese fort on Kishm Island and went on in 1622 to capture the stronghold of Hormuz. Hormuz thus passed into the Shah's hands, but the Portuguese were not effectively excluded from the Gulf, since they soon developed alternative bases at Masqat and Basra, nor did the English reap much reward for their naval prowess. They gained valuable concessions in respect of customs duties at Hormuz and Gombroon (Bandar Abbas), moved their factory to the latter, which was an improvement on Jask, and developed their trade from there; but they failed to secure the silk contract with the Shah and for lack of capital found themselves at a disadvantage in competition with the VOC.[62]

These events at Hormuz demonstrated the formidable naval power exerted by the company in the Indian Ocean. The English had quickly achieved superiority over the Portuguese in this respect and frequently exploited their advantage to take Portuguese prizes even though the two countries were officially at peace. Although the East-Indiamen of this period did not compare in size with the carracks of the *carreira da India*, they were strong fighting ships, heavily gunned and fairly heavily manned. The company's policy was to build its own ships and it created dockyards at Deptford and Blackwall to do so. Of the 76 ships acquired between 1600 and 1640, 49 were of 300 tons and over, ranging to over 1000 tons, and the great majority of these were built by the company before 1626. In 1615 the directors declared that 'ships of 300 tons at least and so fourth to 600 or 700 tons were fittest for them', being the most economical as carriers, but because they were so heavily armed such vessels were well capable of dealing with any opposition they were likely to meet apart from the fleets of the VOC. As the Surat factors advised in 1613, 'your Worships are to provide 5 or 6 good ships which will be very sufficiently able to withstand all the force the Portingales can make here'.[63] East of Malacca the company's ships for the most part acquitted themselves well in conflict with the Dutch and lost the struggle there mainly because they were outnumbered. Many of the company's captains and masters, like Nicholas Downton, David Middleton, Anthony Hippon, Martin Pring and Christopher Newport,

---

[62] On the English company's commercial problem at this time see Steensgaard, *Asian Trade Revolution*, pp. 346, 368–75. The influence of the English Levant traders may well have played a part in the company's failure to secure the silk trade.

[63] Chaudhuri, *East India Company*, pp. 89–105.

had learned their trade in privateersmen and put that experience to good use in a service where sea power was essential.

Shipping therefore occupied much of the time and trouble of the directors and their servants at home and constituted, along with the dockyards, the greater part of the company's fixed capital. The company preferred ships to bases chiefly because it had not sufficient capital to maintain the latter, and in the 1620s its problem of capital supply became critical. The expanding scope of operations in the East increased the factories' demands for ships, goods and money, while at home a severe economic depression was followed in the later twenties by wars with France and Spain. These financial difficulties were the fundamental cause of the relative failure of the company in Indonesia and other parts of the Far East and of its inability to take full advantage of the fall of Hormuz. Necessity apart, however, a reasonable case could be made for pursuing a well-armed trade without bases. Sir Thomas Roe, who at first favoured the idea of an English fort at Surat, came to the conclusion that

the Chardge is greater than the trade can beare; for to maintayne a garison will eate the Profitt. . . .A warr and trafique are incompatible. By my consent, you shall no way engage your selves but at sea, wher you are like to gayne as often as to loose. It is the beggering of the Portugall, notwithstanding his many rich residences and territoryes, that hee keepes souldiers that spendes it; yet his garisons are meane. He never Profited by the Indyes, since hee defended them. Observe this well. It hath beene also the error of the Dutch, who seeke Plantation heere by the Swoord. They turne a woonderfull stocke, they proule in all Places, they Posses some of the best; yet ther dead Payes consume all the gayne. Let this bee received as a rule that if you will Profitt, seeke it at Sea, and in quiett trade.[64]

This was of course the policy followed consistently by the company throughout this period. It had not the resources to challenge either the Dutch or the Portuguese, nor did it seek a conflict with either. Both in Indonesia and in India, as we have seen, it was driven by the aggressive measures of its rivals to defend itself by force, unsuccessfully in the first case though successfully in the second. In spite of difficulties and setbacks this concentration on commercial methods and objectives backed by naval strength enabled the directors and their agents in the East slowly to build up by trial and error a complex system of trade. By way of experience which was sometimes bitter they learned the business of eastern trade in these early decades: how to diversify their spice trade so as to depend less on pepper, how to market an increasing proportion of their oriental produce by re-exports

[64] Foster, *Embassy of Sir Thomas Roe*, p. 344.

to the Continent, how to provide the precious metals so necessary in the East, how to integrate the Indian with the southeast Asian trades and Surat with the Persian Gulf and Red Sea trades. This process of growth was heavily checked by defeat in the Spice Islands and the subsequent contraction of trade in Indonesia and elsewhere in the Far East, but at the same time the more westerly development continued. It was unfortunate that the company had to go through a most difficult phase of re-deployment in the 1620s, a time of great financial stringency and commercial depression affecting the whole range of England's overseas trade.

Nor could the merchants depend upon the crown for aid and comfort at this juncture. James I and Charles I of course recognized the need to uphold English trading interests abroad and relied even more than Elizabeth upon the City for loans, but their relations with the East India Company were marked by mutual mistrust. James I had aroused much resentment among the leaders of the company by granting Sir Edward Michelbourne licence to fit out an expedition for discovery and trade in the Far East in 1604—a flagrant violation of the company's charter—and Michelbourne's piratical proceedings in eastern waters caused the company such trouble and anxiety that in 1607 they began a suit in the Admiralty Court against the courtier, though they soon dropped it, fearing no doubt the king's influence in that court.[65] In 1617 James again jeopardized the company's monopoly by granting a patent to a group of courtiers calling themselves the Scottish East India Company. In conjunction with the Muscovy Company, which was also threatened by the new patent, the English East India Company was obliged to buy out the courtiers and to subscribe to a royal loan for good measure.[66] After the fall of Hormuz the company again came into conflict with James because his favourite, the duke of Buckingham, claimed as Lord High Admiral a tenth share of the prizes taken in that campaign, offering them the alternative of being charged with piracy and having all their gains confiscated. The upshot was that Buckingham received a sum of £10,000, upon which James protested to the directors, 'Did I deliver you from the complaint of the Spaniard and do you return me nothing?', and so obtained the same amount.[67]

The so-called 'Treaty of Defence' concluded between James and the States-General in 1619 was, as we have seen, a compromise which proved of little benefit to the company. It may be that the crown could

[65] Foster, *England's Quest*, pp. 170–71.
[66] W. R. Scott, *The Constitution and Finance of English, Scottish and Irish Joint-Stock Companies to 1720* (3 vols., Cambridge, 1912), II, pp. 55, 104; Chaudhuri, *East India Company*, p. 31.
[67] Chaudhuri, *East India Company*, p. 64.

not have done much more than than it did to protect the interests of the company against the VOC, but it was certainly more concerned with the European implications of an Anglo-Dutch accord. Right and proper as was this royal stance, it did not entirely please the company, which was bitterly aggrieved when, after the Amboina incident, the royal navy, having received orders to arrest VOC ships in the Channel, allowed the returning Dutch fleet to sail past them unmolested. The result was a majority vote in the company's general court (comprising all the shareholders) threatening to 'give over the trade for the Indies' unless the crown took measures to obtain compensation from the Dutch'.[68]

Relations between the company and the crown were therefore less than happy at the accession of Charles I and were rendered less happy still in the following few years by the factious behaviour of a group of courtiers within the company. These, under the leadership of Thomas Smethwike and with the king's support, carried on a persistent campaign in the company's general court against the directors, criticizing their handling of the trade and demanding greater powers for the shareholders. Both sides were well aware that the real intention was to gain greater strength for the royal party and in particular to obtain the admission of the king as a member of the company holding one fifth of the stock, which the company was expected to concede in return for nothing except the royal protection. This proposal was rejected in 1628 with some asperity, and in this and subsequent arguments the merchants' attitude towards the courtier element in their midst was clarified. In effect, they were welcome as subscribers and would be kept informed about the business, but their interference with the conduct of trade was not to be tolerated. In 1628 the reaction of the merchants to Smethwike's agitation probably influenced their refusal of the king's request for a loan to help finance the La Rochelle expedition, and the continuance of discontent on both sides eventually led to the king's grant of a charter to a rival East India Company headed by Sir William Courteen.[69] The political relations of the company with the state were not settled satisfactorily until it was virtually refounded by Cromwell in 1657.

In other respects too its difficulties persisted until the Restoration, when its days of prosperity and grandeur may be said to begin. In the meantime it was only the perseverance of its servants in the East – factors and sailors alike, both much-abused groups of working men – which saw the company through the hard times from the twenties to the fifties.

[68] Chaudhuri, *East India Company*, pp. 65–6.
[69] Chaudhuri, *East India Company*, pp. 58–60, 73; R. Ashton, *The Crown and the Money Market, 1603–1640* (Oxford, 1960), p. 171.

❧ 13 ❧

The West Indies
1585–1630

The history of the British West Indies begins with the founding of English settlements on the islands of St Kitts, Nevis and Barbados in the 1620s. These important events and the immediate circumstances which gave rise to them were well reported and have often been described, but they cannot be explained satisfactorily without some further exploration of their historical background, which has long remained obscure. What connection, if any, can be seen between these tiny, precarious, tobacco plantations and the invasions of the Caribbean and Guiana in former times by Drake and Ralegh? What happened in that region, including Guiana as well as the islands and mainland shores of the Caribbean, to turn the invaders from raiding by sea to planting by land, from plunder to colonization? The answer is not simple. A variety of developments combined to change both the aims of the interlopers and the opportunities open to them – developments which involved Spanish, Dutch and French at least as much as English interests.[1]

When Drake departed for the Caribbean in September 1585 he was not primarily concerned with English prospects in that area. Walsingham thought that upon this voyage depended 'the life and death of the cause',[2] and the queen, though less worried about the 'cause' than about Philip II's reaction, was at one with her secretary in treating the operation as a move in the game of European politics. The purpose of the expedition was to injure Spain's financial security and prestige by capturing the plate fleet or sacking cities on the treasure route. There was, it is true, some talk of holding Panama or Havana in order to strangle the king into submission, but nothing like a permanent

---

[1] A. P. Newton, *The European Nations in the West Indies, 1493–1688* (London, 1933), provides a general overview. For more detail on the transition in question see Andrews, *Spanish Caribbean*.

[2] J. Bruce (ed.), *The Correspondence of Robert Dudley, earl of Leicester* (London, 1844), p. 341.

colony was envisaged. As in Drake's last expedition and Cumberland's Puerto Rico exploit of 1598, the most that was contemplated was a base that would confer on the holders a temporary strategic advantage, perhaps diverting Spanish forces from Europe, perhaps shortening the war. Even so, none of these notions came to fruition. Practical difficulties invariably frustrated them and responsible leaders must have recognized that the maintenance of any such base would pose insuperable political, financial and logistic problems, since they could hardly count upon the queen for the generous and persevering support it would certainly need. Drake and his English contemporaries saw the Caribbean simply as a theatre of war and plunder.

Yet within a few years of Drake's death and before the end of the war with Spain this attitude began to change and indirectly Drake's own raid of 1585–6 helped to bring that change about. He attacked first Santo Domingo, the old capital of the Indies, which fell almost without resistance, and went on to win an astonishingly easy victory at Cartagena, a very much stronger place.[3] In fact the promoters of the enterprise were disappointed with the booty, which evidently failed to meet the expense, while the actual damage done at those two centres and at San Agustín in Florida was soon repaired. But the shock effect was much more serious. Not only was Philip II's prestige and credit in Europe shaken, but the strategic implications of the assault caused panic in the Caribbean colonies and real concern in Madrid. The primary bases of the treasure route, the *flotas* and the bullion supply itself, so vital to Spain's war machine, were under threat. The Spanish government reacted with unaccustomed dispatch: it immediately ordered new galleons for the guard of the transatlantic fleets and in 1588 inaugurated the use of fast, well-armed war frigates for the delivery of the silver to Seville. It sent two galleys each to Santo Domingo, Cartagena and Havana for the defence of those cities and the adjacent coasts. At the same time, in 1586, the Italian engineer Juan Bautista Antoneli and an experienced soldier, Juan de Tejeda, undertook the task of planning adequate fortification for the main stations of the treasure route – Cartagena, Porto Belo, San Juan de Ulúa, Havana, Puerto Rico – and for Santo Domingo. In effect, the crown now belatedly launched, in direct response to Drake's raid, a major defence programme.

But this was not a programme for the defence of the Caribbean. Nothing was done, for example, to create a locally based fleet to defend the region against corsairs: although the concept of an *armada del*

[3] *PN*, x, 97–134: Walter Bigges's account of the expedition. See also Wright, *Further English Voyages*, and Keeler, *Drake's West Indian Voyage*.

barlovento was familiar enough, it was not accepted in principle until 1601 and not implemented in practice until over thirty years later still.[4] In Philip II's time at least the crown could hardly have chosen its priorities otherwise. The treasure, the *flotas* and the bases that served them had to be secured. The outer parts of the Caribbean, east of Cartagena and Havana, were relatively unimportant strategically, unattractive commercially and indefensible physically. The sugar plantations of Española were now in decline and the pearl beds of eastern Venezuela were failing. Eastern Cuba, Jamaica, Española, Puerto Rico and Venezuela were poor relations of the rich mainland empires of Mexico and Peru, remote and difficult to reach from the western centres of trade and power. Their scattered, often decayed or struggling settlements left huge areas and long stretches of coast unoccupied. Neglected by the Council of the Indies and the *Casa de la Contratación*, such places seemed often to get more serious attention from foreign smugglers and pirates, but their complaints on this score fell upon deaf ears. By and large they were expected to fend for themselves. As for the outermost arc of islands, the Lesser Antilles, they were left to the fierce and formidable Caribs.

The necessities of maritime defence in the war against England thus widened the gap between the favoured and the under-privileged colonies and exposed the latter to continual harassment by the Elizabethan privateers, who preferred to seek their prizes in these less dangerous backwaters. For in fact such powerful fleets as Drake's, menacing the major ports and silver convoys, were exceptional. He and Hawkins led a similar force to the Caribbean in 1595, which suffered heavy loss and gained nothing to speak of in return (a defeat due rather more to English faults than to Spanish strength), and the only other large-scale invasion of that area by English ships during the war was that led by the earl of Cumberland, who in 1598 captured San Juan de Puerto Rico. The great majority of the English intruders in that period sailed in much smaller ventures, consisting often of one or two and rarely of more than four vessels (leaving aside very small pinnaces, boats or shallops). Although such petty expeditions would sometimes collaborate to form considerable squadrons, particularly on the Havana coast, and were sometimes capable of assaulting minor ports like La Yaguana in Española and Caballos in Honduras, they never reached sufficient strength to attempt the capture of a treasure fleet or a main base such as Cartagena.

Cumulatively, however, the operations of these lesser predators did far more than the great invasions to weaken Spain's grip on the West

[4] J. H. Parry, *The Spanish Seaborne Empire* (London, 1966), p. 262.

Indies. They swarmed thither in large numbers: apart from Drake's two fleets, 74 ventures comprising 183 ships are known to have sailed those waters between 1585 and 1603, and there were certainly many others, as yet unidentified. Nor did this raiding diminish in the later years of the war (as used to be alleged before such detailed facts and figures were available): we know of 77 voyages in the seven years from 1589 to 1595, and 82 in the seven years from 1596 to 1602 (omitting Drake's 1595 fleet).[5] Haunting the islands and the Tierra Firme coast, they patrolled the sea lanes frequented by the shipping upon which those colonies depended for their livelihood: the frigates, caravels and round ships bearing sugar, hides, tobacco, ginger, sarsaparilla, pearls and so forth bound eventually for Spain, and manufactures of all kinds and foodstuffs bound for the settlements. They bottled up Santo Domingo, the very hub of the westerly Caribbean, for months on end and they infested the approaches to Havana and Cartagena as well. When the galleys put out from those centres they occasionally caught a privateer, but most of the time the galleys remained in port, unable to move for lack of money or supplies or crewmen.

These petty depredations, which might in other circumstances have amounted to little more than a temporary nuisance, had a serious effect because they aggravated the existing commercial difficulties of the outer colonies, increasing their isolation and eroding their security. Along the Tierra Firme coast La Margarita, Cumaná, La Guaira, Burburata, Coro and Río de la Hacha, and in the Antilles San Germán in Puerto Rico, Puerto de Plata, Bayahá, Guanahibes and La Yaguana in Española, as well as other ports in eastern Cuba and Honduras, had long experience of the business known as *rescates* – illicit trade with foreign smugglers, mainly Portuguese and French. The town clerk of La Yaguana, Jerónimo de Torres, an authority on these matters, wrote a lengthy description and analysis of them in 1577:

These French and Portuguese bring many slaves and many fine cloths of all kinds, many linens; and they have brought soap, wax, quicksilver and every type of merchandise one can imagine; they exchange a slave for fifty or sixty hides, and a *vara* of fine cloth for two or three hides, four or five *varas* of *ruan* [Rouen linen] for a hide, five or six *varas* of coarse linen for a hide, a pipe of wine for twenty or twenty-five hides. These are the normal prices and by comparison all the goods cost more in Seville and Medina.[6]

[5] Andrews, *Spanish Caribbean*, pp. 156–7. Detailed accounts of privateering in the West Indies at this time are given in Andrews, *English Voyages to the West Indies*, and Wright, *Further English Voyages*.

[6] 'Relación sobre cosas de la isla Española', in E. Rodríguez Demorizi (ed.), *Relaciones Históricas de Santo Domingo* (Ciudad Trujillo, Dominican Republic, 1945), pp. 128–43.

Of the French some were corsairs and some combined trade and plunder at will, but from the mid seventies they came mainly to barter the linens of Normandy (Fr. *rouens*, Sp. *ruanes*) for the hides of north and west Española, the so-called *banda del norte*.[7] The men from Dieppe, Le Havre, Cherbourg, St Malo and La Rochelle, who described their destination as 'Pérou', grew bolder and more numerous in the nineties as the Atlantic war brought increasing pressure to bear on Spain's American trade. French merchants interested in the Seville-Atlantic trade now laboured – as did others, Spanish or foreign – under a double handicap: the tax (*avería*) on all merchandise for the cost of convoys and oceanic defence rose steeply, pushing up the prices of the goods exported, while the risk of capture by English privateers nevertheless worsened. The privateers would not interfere with the Norman smugglers, who were their friends in the Caribbean, but any ships or goods found on the routes between Spain and America were claimed and normally condemned as lawful prize. These incentives to interloping also began to produce a Dutch response in the same decade. Dutch overseas enterprise at this time advanced with enormous strides particularly because their interests in the Iberian Peninsula were threatened by the arbitrary embargoes imposed by Philip II on their shipping. One effect of these interruptions of Dutch-Iberian trade was to stop the supply of salt to the Netherlands from Setúbal in Portugal. Salt was of course essential for the herring trade, one of the pillars of the Dutch economy, and the immediate Dutch reaction was to resort elsewhere – first to the Cape Verde Islands and then, after the embargo of 1598, to Venezuela.

Here, at the great natural salt pan at the western end of the Araya Peninsula lying between La Margarita and Cumaná, thirteen or fourteen hulks – bulk-cargo ships of 200, 300 or 400 tons – arrived in the summer of 1599 and in full view of the impotent Spanish authorities filled their capacious holds with free salt. Eight more came in the autumn and then in May 1600 they began to swarm: fifty came that month and from then until 1605 they numbered over 100 a year.[8] Even before this massive invasion of the Caribbean Dutch ships had begun to visit the region as smugglers, but the presence of the hulks brought a change in the scale of *rescates*. The salt-laders themselves brought various merchandise and used their watering places as *rendezvous* with

---

[7] On the French trade to 'Pérou' see C. and P. Bréard, *Documents rélatifs à la Marine Normande* (Rouen, 1889), pp. 148–78; J. Hayem (ed.), *Mémoires et Documents pour Servir à l'Histoire du Commerce et l'Industrie en France* (Paris, 1911, etc.), v, pp. 47–209: Ph. Barrey, 'Le Havre transatlantique de 1571 à 1610'.

[8] E. Sluiter, 'Dutch-Spanish rivalry in the Caribbean area, 1594–1609', *HAHR*, 28 (1948), 165–96.

people from Cumaná and La Margarita who would give pearls for cloth and hardware. On their way homeward, too, some of the hulks would tarry in the outports of Cuba, Española or Puerto Rico to buy sugar and hides. Along with the hulks, moreover, there came pinnaces which would range down the Tierra Firme to Cumanagoto and La Guaira, port of Caracas, chiefly for tobacco. But apart from the hulks and their pinnaces came smugglers, laden with the linens and fine cloths, metal wares and other European manufactures that the Venezuelan settlements could no longer obtain from Spain in any quantity at reasonable prices. At the same time the Dutch expanded their share of the islands trade, vying with the French in the *banda del norte* and the south Cuban ports while conversely the French used the umbrella of the salt-hulks to exploit the Venezuelan market.

It was this boom in contraband, led by the French and Dutch, which prompted English merchants to re-enter West Indian trade in 1602 after more than thirty years of abstinence. In May of that year the 400-ton *Prosperous* of London, probably owned by Thomas Allabaster, a prominent figure in the East India Company, arrived with a cargo reputedly worth 30,000 ducats at Guanahibes, where she stayed at least two years trading for hides and other goods, which were brought home by several other ships. In the same year Thomas Myddelton and several other London magnates combined with Richard Hawkins to promote a similar venture by the *Vineyard*, while John Eldred (the Turkey Company pioneer and East India Company leader) in partnership with Richard Hall set forth the *Mayflower* (300 tons) and three other London vessels for the same purpose.[9] Circumstantial evidence suggests that Sir Robert Cecil and the earl of Nottingham, who together now dominated the government of the kingdom, may have sponsored or at least encouraged this initiative in order to strengthen English commercial claims in the peace negotiations which they foresaw must soon ensue.[10] But the Spaniards for their part were desperately worried now about the security of the Caribbean. Western Española and eastern Cuba in 1603–4 appeared to be given over to *rescates* and dominated by alien shipping. The contrabandists worked hand in glove with corsairs who used the area as a base for large-scale assaults on other places. Thus in 1603 Christopher Newport led a powerful Anglo-French force from Guanahibes to Puerto de Caballos and there captured two Spanish war galleons and held the town for

[9] K. R. Andrews, 'English voyages to the Caribbean, 1596–1604: an annotated list', *William and Mary Quarterly*, 31 (1974), 243–54. Other English traders in the Caribbean, 1602–5, included the *Peter*, the *Diana*, the *Dorothy*, the *Golden Phoenix*, the *Aid*, the *Mary*, the *Arthur* and the *Lark*.
[10] Andrews, 'Caribbean rivalry'.

eighteen days. Eastern Venezuela likewise seemed in danger of slipping out of Spanish control.

Spain therefore responded with concerted measures to turn back the tide of invaders. Already in 1602 new governors had been dispatched to Havana and Santo Domingo with instructions to put down *rescates* by prosecuting the offending colonists without fear or favour. In Cuba the outcome was a mild mixture of fines and pardons, but in Española the government eventually, in 1605, mounted a campaign to remove the population from the north and west of the island. Many were resettled in the south, some took refuge in Cuba, some joined the enemy ships. Meanwhile the local commanders did what they could to arrest the foreign smugglers and executed those they caught with deliberate brutality, *pour encourager les autres.*[11] In 1605 the Spanish admiral Luis de Fajardo led a powerful expedition from Spain against the Dutch hulks at Araya, capturing twelve of them along with one French and three English ships. His prisoners he treated with scant mercy. Early in 1606 a detachment of this force engaged and pursued a large group of alien ships, mainly Dutch, off southern Cuba, but with little success. In Venezuela the new governor of Caracas in 1606 seized and hanged twelve Dutchmen who came ashore to trade at La Guaira, while a royal decree banned the planting of tobacco throughout the province and ordered the depopulation of Cumanagoto, the chief centre of that trade. The prohibition of tobacco production seems to have had little effect, but here as in the islands the local measures to repel intruders and suppress *rescates*, measures scarcely sufficient by themselves to meet the case, were powerfully reinforced by the ending of the Anglo-Spanish war. On his accession James I almost immediately declared an end to privateering and soon made it clear that Englishmen trading to parts of the Indies effectively occupied by Spain must do so at their own risk. In December 1604, after the Treaty of London had been concluded, his attitude emerged still more clearly: a Spanish envoy then reported that James had promised to execute any who 'set forth to disturb your majesty's seas'.[12] Subsequently protests about the treatment of English West Indian venturers were in fact relayed to Madrid, but James, holding to his pro-Spanish policy, was not inclined to press them. The main effect of the peace upon the Caribbean, therefore, was to diminish the alien presence. The privateers for the most part withdrew and as the Seville trade recovered, the incentive to direct trade faded. In 1607 negotiations for

[11] See for example Andrews, *Spanish Caribbean*, pp. 206–7.
[12] Archivo General de Simancas, E. 841, no. 201: Juan de Tassis to the crown, 9 December 1604.

peace between Spain and Holland brought the salt-hulks back to Setúbal.

This deliberate co-ordination of civil discipline, physical violence and international diplomacy did largely achieve the desired object of halting the penetration of the Caribbean by foreign shipping. The crisis of 1598–1605 passed and for some years the settlements, though still troubled from time to time by pirates, were left in peace. But for the most part it was a peace of exhaustion. The Antillean sugar boom was long past, the hides trade dwindled and the pearl fisheries of the eastern and western Main, plagued with many problems, produced little. In the west Cartagena and Havana looked towards the continental empires and flourished, but eastwards of those transatlantic terminals Caribbean commerce stagnated. Of course the illicit tobacco trade, having once taken hold during the contraband boom, grew mightily, but it flourished only on and beyond the southeast border of the Caribbean until new circumstances in the 1620s brought back the northerners to trade, to plunder and to settle.

In his famous account of his first voyage to Guiana—*The Discoverie of the Large, Rich, and Bewtiful Empyre of Guiana* (1596)—Ralegh declared that he had learned about 'that great and Golden Citie, which the Spanyards call El Dorado' many years since, 'by relation'.[13] He was presumably referring to the information he had obtained from Pedro Sarmiento de Gamboa, when that pioneer of Magellan's Strait had fallen prisoner to Ralegh's privateers in 1586. Sarmiento was an authority on the Incas and impressed the Englishman with the legend, then generally believed in South America, that a second Inca civilization existed deep in the interior, ruled by El Dorado, the gilded one, from his capital Manoa on the shore of a great lake, in which he performed the ritual of bathing after having covered his body with gold-dust.

Since 1530 Spaniards had mounted many expeditions into the heart of the continent in search of this golden empire, but no one had devoted more effort to the quest than Antonio de Berrío. A veteran of the wars, Berrío was over sixty when he took up the enterprise in 1584, journeying east from New Granada and down the Orinoco to the Atlantic. In two further expeditions, in 1585–8 and 1590–91, he strenuously advanced Spanish knowledge of Guiana, of which he was officially appointed governor, and focused attention on that province as the supposed location of El Dorado. On returning from his third

[13] V. T. Harlow (ed.), *The Discoverie of the large and bewtiful Empire of Guiana, by Sir Walter Ralegh* (London, 1928), p. 4.

expedition he found his efforts to pursue and consolidate his explorations thwarted by rivals who aspired to capture the great prize themselves, but he managed to dispatch his partner, Domingo de Vera Ybarguen, on a further expedition in 1592–3, who returned to confirm Berrío's reports and to place Manoa more precisely in the highlands to the south of the Río Caroni, a tributary of the Orinoco. Berrío meanwhile had established his headquarters in Trinidad, which had been left unoccupied by Spain until 1592, when its value as a base for the conquest of Guiana became apparent. Here at San Josef he was impatiently awaiting authority and reinforcements from Spain to embark on the final push to Manoa when Ralegh descended upon him.

Sudden and unexpected though this assault was, Ralegh had been preparing it for some years. Whether or not he promoted the mysterious venture of 1587, when two English boys were left among the Indians on Trinidad and two more in the mouth of the Orinoco,[14] in the early nineties he must have heard reports of that island from the privateering captains who were resorting there to barter with the Indians for victuals and tobacco. In the years after the Armada he was one of the chief promoters of the privateering war and in 1592 he planned to lead a great expedition to the West Indies. In the event this plan fell through, but a combined fleet in which he had a large interest took prize the great carrack *Madre de Deus* that summer.[15] Ralegh, however, reaped no reward. Disgraced and imprisoned for his secret marriage to the queen's maid of honour, Elizabeth Throckmorton, he was lucky to be allowed a share at all in the proceeds and to be released from the Tower. It was at this juncture, 'left of all, but of malice and revenge', as he put it, and 'in the darkest shadow of adversitie',[16] that he looked to Guiana as a means of recovering the queen's favour and his own fortune.

In 1593 he joined with a syndicate of London merchants to fit out his own *Roebuck* and three other ships led by Sir John Burgh, who attempted to take the island of La Margarita with a force of 400 men, being repulsed with some loss.[17] Although there is no evidence to support Sir William Monson's statements that Burgh visited Trinidad and Guiana, it seems likely that he had some instructions to reconnoitre the region or perhaps to prepare the way for Ralegh by destroy-

[14] J. Lorimer, 'Ralegh's first reconnaissance of Guiana? An English survey of the Orinoco in 1587', *Terrae Incognitae*, 9 (1977), pp. 7–21. Dr Lorimer argues that Ralegh was probably responsible for this initiative.
[15] *Monson's Tracts*, I, pp. 278–96.
[16] Harlow, *Discoverie*, p. 3.
[17] Andrews, *English Voyages to the West Indies*, pp. 225–35. Burgh had commanded Ralegh's squadron in the Azores in 1592.

ing the Spanish settlements on La Margarita. In the following year Ralegh's faithful lieutenant, Jacob Whiddon, went out to Trinidad, making useful contact with the Indians there and gathering what little he could from them about Guiana, though he lost eight men in an ambush set by Berrío. Ralegh also obtained geographical information about the West Indies (including a Spanish rutter) from Captain William Parker and was advised about the difficult navigation of the Gulf of Paria, between Trinidad and the mainland, by English sailors who knew those waters. When he sailed for Trinidad himself in 1595 he was equipped with no less than four Indian interpreters.[18] Thus carefully prepared, he cannot have been pleased when he heard that Robert Dudley, Leicester's illegitimate son, had anticipated him, though in fact that young man achieved nothing of significance during his visit to Trinidad and the Orinoco Delta in February and March of 1595.[19]

Ralegh's own account of his enterprise represents it in terms of high strategy. He invited the reader to consider the king of Spain's enormous offensive power, a capacity for aggression continually renewed in spite of repeated and terrible losses:

these abilities rise not from the trades of sackes, and Civil Orenges. . . . It is his Indian Golde that indaungereth and disturbeth all the nations of Europe, it purchaseth intelligence, creepeth into Councels, and setteth bound loyalty at libertie, in the greatest Monarchies of Europe. If the Spanish king can keepe us from forraine enterprizes, and from the impeachment of his trades, eyther by offer of invasion, or by besieging us in Britayne, Ireland, or else where, he hath then brought the worke of our perill in great forwardnes.

It was therefore essential to take the war to the enemy and 'to advance al those attempts, that might eyther promise return of profit to our selves, or at last be a lett and impeachment to the quiet course, and plentiful trades of the Spanish nation'. The empire of Guiana would afford the queen and the kingdom 'no lesse quantities of treasure, then the king of Spayne hath in all the Indies, east or west'. Petty assaults on the outports of the Indies would neither harm Spain nor enrich England, whereas Guiana would be 'a better Indies for her majestie then the king of Spain hath any' and would bring her victory.[20] Private ambition he disavowed: had he not refrained from plundering the chiefs of Guiana in order to win them as allies for the queen? And had

---

[18] Harlow, *Discoverie*, p. 117 (Pedro de Salazar's account of the events at Trinidad).

[19] G. F. Warner (ed.), *The Voyage of Robert Dudley to the West Indies, 1594–1595* (London, 1899), pp. xx–xxi. It is not clear whether Dudley intended to steal Ralegh's thunder or to co-operate with him, but this was certainly an impromptu venture – his original purpose was a South Sea voyage, which the queen forbade.

[20] Harlow, *Discoverie*, pp. 4–10.

he not preferred the great task of empire-building to mere privateering, which he now affected to despise? – 'It became not the former fortune in which I once lived, to goe journeys of picorie . . . to run from Cape to Cape, and from place to place, for the pillage of ordinarie prizes.'[21]

Ralegh no doubt believed his own rhetoric and saw himself as a statesman, champion of the royal and national interest. Behind that arrogant manner, however, lay a deep anxiety. He knew then, after his return from Guiana, that his project could not succeed without the queen's backing. His *Discoverie* was nothing if not an appeal to the crown to take this matter in hand and therefore cannot be taken at face value as a statement of motive or purpose. In fact many had declined to subscribe to his venture. He was still something of an outsider, disliked by some and distrusted by others—not least those who remembered Virginia. The talk of gold aroused scepticism, as it had done ever since shiploads of rock from Baffin Island had been used to mend the highways. Nor did the privateering interest respond, preoccupied as they were with journeys of pickery and ordinary prizes. His most important supporters were Sir Robert Cecil, now the queen's secretary, and Lord Charles Howard, the Lord Admiral. The latter contributed his ship the *Lion's Whelp*, but Ralegh owed even more to Cecil who, having adopted him as a political ally against Essex, used his own influence to help the enterprise in various ways. For example when Whiddon was arrested at the suit of certain Dutch merchants he wrote to the judge of the Admiralty Court requesting his prompt release: 'I pray Sir take some paines in the matter, and let it be so carried as Whydden may be forthwith at lybertie, for I assure yow, it concernes Sir Walter very nere, and yow shall therby doe such a curtesie to me and him as wee shall both thincke our selves beholdinge unto yow.'[22] Neither Cecil nor Howard minced their words in dealing with Sir Julius Caesar. Cecil himself invested in the voyage and no doubt encouraged Thomas Myddelton and Sir John Hawkins, both clients of his, to do so.[23] But Ralegh had to turn to his relatives and personal friends for most of his backing, particularly to William Sanderson, the London merchant who had married his niece. Shortly before he sailed Ralegh quarrelled bitterly with Sanderson, refusing to acknowledge a debt of £1600 or £1700 to him. Financially he was skating on rather thin ice at this time.[24]

[21] Harlow, *Discoverie*, p. 4.
[22] BL, Lansdowne MSS, 158, fo. 395.
[23] PRO, PCC, 26 Drake: will of Sir John Hawkins, 3 March 1595. National Library of Wales, Journal of Sir Thomas Myddelton's accounts.
[24] R. McIntyre, 'William Sanderson: Elizabethan financier of discovery', *William and*

On 6 February 1595 Ralegh set out with some 300 men in four ships: the *Lion's Whelp* under George Gifford, a small Spanish prize described as a 'gallego' under Lawrence Keymis, a small bark contributed and commanded by Captain Robert Crosse, and his own flagship under Jacob Whiddon. Meanwhile Amyas Preston and George Somers, West Country privateering gentlemen like most of Ralegh's seafaring partners and lieutenants, prepared two ships and a pinnace for a supporting venture, in which they were joined by Captain William Prowse and a certain Captain Jones commanding two Southampton ships. This second force was delayed and probably for that reason did not attempt to join Ralegh at Trinidad, but after touching at La Margarita and Cumaná went on to take and burn Caracas and Coro, since it was part of Ralegh's strategy to isolate Guiana by destroying Spain's bases along the Tierra Firme coast.[25] Ralegh himself reached Trinidad late in March and quickly won the friendship and co-operation of the Indians. He fully recognized that alliance with the natives here and on the mainland would be vital not only for the discovery and exploitation of Manoa, but also for the defeat of Spanish forces in that region and possibly elsewhere. Consequently he took great pains to cultivate the people of Trinidad and Guiana, to inflame their hostility to Spaniards and to induce them voluntarily to accept the queen's protection.

Before embarking for the mainland Ralegh secured his base on the island by destroying the Spanish settlement at San Josef and capturing Berrío. Some of Berrío's companions managed to escape but, partly in revenge for Whiddon's men and partly to impress the Indians, Ralegh put to death all the Spaniards he caught, sparing only the old man and his second-in-command for the intelligence they might provide.[26] He professed in his book to admire Berrío as 'very valiant and liberall, and a Gent. of great assuredness, and of a great heart: I used him according to his estate and worth in all things I could', but the governor of La Margarita heard that at one stage he threatened to have both prisoners executed by the Indians unless they showed him the way to Guiana.[27] From Ralegh's own account the Spaniard emerges as a wily opponent, ready enough to tell the story of his enterprise, but keeping geographi-

Mary Quarterly, 13 (1956), 184–201. Sanderson had assisted Ralegh's Virginia ventures and had largely financed Davis's northwest voyages as well as Molyneux's globes. It is not clear how far his generous contributions to pioneering enterprise helped to bring him to the debtors prisons where he spent seven years or more between 1613 and 1622.

[25] On the Preston-Somers expedition see Andrews, *English Voyages to the West Indies*, pp. 377–98.

[26] Harlow, *Discoverie*, p. 118 (Pedro de Salazar's account of events at Trinidad) – see also pp. 121, 125, 127.

[27] Harlow, *Discoverie*, pp. 15, 119.

cal details to himself and exaggerating the dangers awaiting the English in the hope of discouraging them.[28] Time moreover was on his side, for the longer the English delayed and the longer they spent finding their way, the more likely it was that de Vera's force from Spain or another from New Granada would trap them in the Orinoco.

But Ralegh was not to be deterred. About 17 May 1595 he set off up the delta with about a hundred men distributed in the gallego, cut down to make a small galley, two wherries, a barge and a ship's boat. It took fifteen days to get through the delta, struggling against the current in extreme heat, short of victuals and drink and at times on the verge of exhaustion and despair. Once in the main river, however, progress was faster and Ralegh's policy, imposed upon his men by steady discipline, won the help and apparent friendship of the local *caciques*. After five days he approached the confluence of the Orinoco and the Caroni and made contact with Topiawari, an old chief and overlord of that area, at a place called Morequito. Here he was able to collate what he had learned from Berrío and his own experience with the knowledge and ideas of Topiawari to build the concept of Guiana which he expressed both in the *Discoverie* and in Thomas Hariot's map.[29] Southwards from the Orinoco lay the nations of the ancient people of Guiana stretching to the valley of Amariocapana, but beyond the mountains on the other side of that valley the land had been conquered, said Topiawari, in his father's time

by a nation from so far off as the *Sun* slept (for such were his own words,) with so great a multitude as they could not be numbered nor resisted, and that they wore large coats, and hats of crimson colour . . . and that they were called Oreiones, and Epuremei, those that had slaine and rooted out so many of the ancient people as there were leaves in the wood upon all the trees, and had now made themselves Lords of all. . . . those Epuremei had built a great town called Macureguarai, at the said mountaine foote, at the beginning of the great plaines of Guiana, which have no end: and that their houses have many roomes, one over the other, and that therein the great king of the Oreiones and Epuremei kept three thousand men to defend the borders.[30]

This must be the lost Inca empire of El Dorado, Ralegh concluded, and forthwith, dividing his men into three parties, he set out to find a way thither. It soon became clear, however, that towering falls made a passage up-river impossible and that it would be unwise to spend

---

[28] Harlow, *Discoverie*, pp. 29, 34.
[29] The map, drawn by Hariot on the basis of Ralegh's notes and writings, corresponds closely to the account in the *Discoverie*. The original in the British Library (BL, Additional MSS, 17940A) is reproduced in Harlow, *Discoverie*.
[30] Harlow, *Discoverie*, pp. 51–2.

further time marching south while summer rains swelled the Orinoco itself into a raging torrent. He therefore turned back and in further talks with Topiawari agreed to return the following year to lead a general assault of the 'Guianians' upon the empire of 'Inga'. To have gone for the gold immediately would have meant risking defeat, but in any case, Ralegh argued,

it woulde have been in my opinion an utter overthrowe to the enterprize, if the same should be hereafter by her Majestie attempted: for then (whereas now they have heard we were enemies to the Spaniards and were sent by her Majestie to relieve them) they would as good cheape have joyned with the Spanyards at our returne, as to have yeelded unto us, when they had proved that we came both for one errant, and that both sought but to sacke and spoyle them, but as yet our desier of gold, or our purpose of invasion is not known unto those of the empire: and it is likely that if her majestie undertake the enterprize, they will rather submit themselves to her obedience then to the Spanyards, of whose cruelty both themselves and the borderers have alreadie tasted.[31]

Here political shrewdness is more in evidence than any moral or humane consideration for the Indians. Ralegh's real aim was to present the queen with gold. His own fame and fortune would follow. The welfare of the people of Guiana was merely a tactical factor. It was probably Thomas Hariot who later worked out the more thoughtful, systematic and statesmanlike argument embodied in the treatise 'Of the voyage for Guiana', where first place is given to saving the Indians' souls from idolatry, ignorance and incivility and their bodies from 'the intollerable tirrany of the Spaniards'.[32] Here, referring to Spanish controversy about the status of the Indian and the justice of 'invasive warrs uppon infidells', the author condemned the *conquistadores*, called for peaceful conversion of the natives and concluded that 'it is more safe and commendable for us rather to seeke to bring Guiana to become tributory, then to conquer it'. This could be done by uniting all those nations, 'borderers' and 'Epuremei' alike, against the Spaniards and in allegiance to the queen. Here too the strategic implications of English possession of Guiana are taken a step further by a proposal to arm the people of Guiana and to instruct them in the use and manufacture of modern weaponry to wage war on the Spaniards and win back Peru. Ralegh may have concurred in and approved of all this, but the attitudes expressed differ markedly in emphasis from those to be discerned in the *Discoverie*.

---

[31] Harlow, *Discoverie*, p. 62.
[32] Harlow, *Discoverie*, pp. 138–49.

Meanwhile Ralegh departed from Morequito, leaving behind with Topiawari as hostages one Francis Sparrey and a boy, Hugh Goodwin, with instructions to learn the language, gather information about gold, and so forth. The remainder of the English returned to Trinidad after some four weeks' absence and embarked with the whole force to attack the Tierra Firme ports on the way home. At Cumaná, however, they suffered a bruising defeat, for which the subsequent spoil of Río de la Hacha and Santa Marta was small consolation. Reaching England in September, Ralegh was disappointed by his reception. Although in fact everything he had discovered was already known to Berrío, his expedition had been remarkably well conducted and in its own terms successful. The way to the beautiful empire of Guiana, to gold and to eventual victory over Spain seemed clear. Unfortunately few were impressed. His specimens of allegedly gold-bearing rock and precious stones convinced no one and some said he had not even crossed the Atlantic. Unpopular, distrusted and frustrated, he failed to win either the queen or the general public with his *Discoverie* and had to be satisfied with sending out Lawrence Keymis with two ships in 1596. Keymis returned with the discouraging news that Berrío, whom Ralegh had released at Cumaná, had established a fort before the entry to the Caroni River, blocking the way to Manoa, but he also reported the existence of a better route to El Dorado by way of the Essequibo, which was said to lead to a great lake, presumably the fabled lake of Manoa. Ralegh's hopes were thus sustained and in 1597 he dispatched a pinnace under Leonard Berry which reconnoitred the Wiapoco, the Marawyne and the Corentine rivers and further encouraged the promoter's belief in Manoa and its accessibility by one or more of the Atlantic rivers.[33] In these years 1596 and 1597 Ralegh had much else on his mind – the Cadiz expedition and the Islands voyage – and thereafter he was busily engaged in public affairs until his trial and imprisonment for treason in 1603. It was after this that his old dream of an empire in Guiana returned and finally lured him to his last adventure and extraordinary death.

The large region which came to be called the Wild Coast, stretching from Trinidad and the Orinoco Delta to the Amazon, attracted English attention in the early seventeenth century for two main reasons. On the one hand, hopes of finding gold there persisted and in Ralegh's case at least were associated with anti-Spanish manoeuvres. On the other hand, attempts to develop tobacco production proved even more

---

[33] *PN*, x, 441–501; XI, 1–15. The rivers are now known as the Oiapoque, the Maroni and the Corantijn.

persistent, associated as they were with the rapid growth of the home market for tobacco. Curiously interwoven, the themes of treasure hunting and tobacco planting shape the main plot of this story, but nothing substantial emerged from either. The Wild Coast sent home vastly more tobacco than gold, but the enterprises were generally unsuccessful and the settlements shortlived. A brief account may suffice to explain both the persistence and the failure of these efforts and to show how they nevertheless led on to the more permanent West Indian colonies.

Demand for tobacco began to expand fast towards the end of the sixteenth century in England. By 1604, when King James published his pamphlet, *A Counter-Blaste to Tobacco*, denouncing it, the smoking habit was widespread and tobacco a regular import listed in the Book of Rates for customs duties. Imports in 1610 were estimated to be worth over £60,000 and the quantity increased at such a rate that the price collapsed in the 1620s and 1630s from over twenty shillings to a few pence a pound.[34] Profits were so high in the first two decades of the century that they over-stimulated production, particularly because tobacco was fairly easy and cheap to grow, prepare and transport, requiring neither the range of skills nor the intensive labour that sugar demanded. For nascent or young colonies with little capital, labour, technical equipment or business organization it was an ideal crop, which in consequence was a major incentive to Dutch, French and English trade and settlement in the accessible parts of America from Chesapeake Bay to the Amazon at this time.

During the first phase of expansion in the 1590s and early 1600s the northerners' main suppliers were the Spanish colonies of Cumaná and Caracas, though they also frequented Trinidad to barter with the Indians there. In these years Cumanagoto appears to have been the main centre of tobacco smuggling. About 1607, however, the measures against *rescates* caused the centre to shift eastwards to Trinidad and the Orinoco River. These places evidently received tobacco from the more westerly areas of production, which were now effectively closed to foreign shipping, but by this time they were themselves producing for export. Here Fernando de Berrío had succeeded to the government on the death of his father in 1597, inheriting a country ruined by the disastrous expedition which Domingo de Vera had brought from Spain the year before. Disease, starvation, Indian attacks and desertions all but annihilated an army of 1500 men and women within a year. In 1598 the stockade of Santo Thomé de Guayana (founded to guard the gate to

---

[34] C. A. Harris (ed.), *A Relation of a Voyage to Guiana, by Robert Harcourt* (London, 1928), p. 105; Davis, *English Overseas Trade*, p. 35.

Manoa in 1596) held but 160 people and the men of San Josef in Trinidad numbered only 40.[35] Fernando and his followers resorted to tobacco planting to recoup some of their losses and in 1607, when the ban was imposed on the other provinces and the foreigners resorted to Trinidad and the Orinoco instead, a phenomenal boom started. This lasted until 1612, when official measures to suppress it finally came into effect and the London merchants, who had conducted a large part of the trade, retired, unwilling to face the displeasure of their sovereign lord, who not unreasonably thought the tobacco trade less important than Anglo-Spanish amity.[36]

Until this date, therefore, eastern Venezuela provided English importers with good tobacco in plenty and English venturers upon the Wild Coast to the south were not particularly interested in trying to compete. Charles Leigh, the first of the Jacobean colonists, had been associated (as we shall see later) with certain Separatist Protestants in an attempt to settle the Magdalen Islands in the Gulf of St Lawrence in 1597 and since then, in 1601, had commanded a privateering voyage to the Mediterranean promoted by Sir Robert Cecil, the earl of Nottingham and others, including his own brother, Alderman Oliph Leigh.[37] In 1602 he had undertaken a voyage of discovery to Guiana and had determined to found a colony in the Wiapoco. Two years later he set forth in the *Olive Plant* (50 tons) with 46 men and boys to carry out that intention, financed chiefly by his brother and sponsored politically by Cecil and Nottingham, who apparently secured the approval of King James and the Privy Council. This was before the Treaty of London, when Cecil and Nottingham were particularly concerned to repudiate Spanish claims over places not in Spain's effective possession, but it is also worth stressing that they were carrying out thereby a policy inherited from Queen Elizabeth and fully accepted by James, who did his best to adhere to it throughout his reign. It is not clear, however, what specific purpose Leigh had in mind. There is no evidence that any of his companions were Separatists: in a letter to his brother some weeks after arriving in the river, he showed a strong interest in converting the Indians, and concluded by reminding Sir Oliph to send out preachers, but he specified that they should be 'sober and discreete men, and such as are well perswaded of

[35] P. Ojer, *La Formación del Oriente Venezolano* (Caracas, 1966), pp. 567–71. J. Lorimer, 'The English contraband tobacco trade in Trinidad and Guiana, 1590–1617', in Andrews, Canny and Hair, *Westward Enterprise*, pp. 124–50.

[36] Lorimer, 'English contraband tobacco trade'.

[37] Quinn, *England and the Discovery of America*, pp. 328–36; Andrews, 'Cecil and plunder'. Leigh's Wiapoco colony is authoritatively analysed in J. A. Williamson, *English Colonies in Guiana and on the Amazon, 1604–1668* (Oxford, 1923), pp. 29–41.

the Church government in England'.[38] In this letter he also discussed the commodities the country might produce, pointing to flax, cotton and sugar as the best prospects. Although he looked for gold and had a refiner with him, the expedition was by no means a treasure hunt. As for tobacco, the settlers obtained some from the natives and planted some themselves, but there is nothing to suggest that they considered it important.[39]

After two years Leigh's colony collapsed, broken by sickness and by the failure of reinforcements and supplies, dispatched by Sir Oliph in 1605, to reach the river: the ship's company, hostile as seamen often were to such passengers, abandoned them on the island of Santa Lucia where most of them died at the hands of the Caribs. Robert Harcourt, a gentleman favoured by Prince Henry, made another attempt to colonize the Wiapoco in 1609. Disappointed in his initial hope of gold, he too looked to sugar, cotton and flax to make the colony pay, leaving tobacco to the last, but predicting a brilliant future for it. The sort of colonization he envisaged, however, is indicated in his *Relation of a Voyage to Guiana* (1613), where he mentions 'the things which the Indians desire from us by way of trade in exchange for the above named commodities'.[40] The Indians were to produce the goods, presumably under the direction of groups of Englishmen stationed in factories at suitable places. Harcourt's men appear to have managed to operate along such lines for about three years, but with limited success, since at the end of that time Harcourt proposed a quite different project, offering land to planters in a joint-stock company framework. Nothing came of this, perhaps because potential investors doubted the chances of such a land-based colony in that region, where Dutch experience already suggested the superiority of factory methods.[41]

Meanwhile Sir Thomas Roe, another protégé of Prince Henry, had renewed the search for gold with the backing of Ralegh, the earl of Southampton and others. Departing in 1610, he spent over a year on the voyage, penetrated 200 miles up the Amazon and far up the Wiapoco, exploring other rivers also and finally reaching Trinidad, where he found, as he informed Cecil, '15 sayle of ships freighting smoke'.[42] In this letter from Trinidad he made no secret of his anti-Spanish sentiments nor of his attempts to gather intelligence from

[38] *Purchas*, XVI, 323.
[39] *Purchas*, XVI, 320–22, 344, 349.
[40] Harris, *Harcourt's Relation*, p. 105; *Purchas*, XVI, 386.
[41] G. Edmundson, 'The Dutch on the Amazon and the Negro in the seventeenth century: part 1', *EHR*, 18 (1903), 642–63.
[42] Williamson, *English Colonies in Guiana*, p. 55.

disaffected Spaniards about the Orinoco, which in his opinion was 'infinite ritch and weake, and may easely be taken away, and as easely held'. Roe sent two further expeditions of discovery to Guiana and for a few years kept some twenty men in the Amazon, who turned with apparent success to tobacco planting, as did other Wild Coast venturers in this decade, including groups of English, Irish, French and Dutch pioneers, sometimes working together, among whom Dutch traders formed the dominant element. This was a period of prosperity for the northern tobacco planters in Guiana, before the competition of Virginia undermined their profits and before Spain, aroused by Ralegh's aggression, mobilized physical force and diplomatic pressure against the intruders.

Ralegh's biographers have told the story of his last exploit often enough to cloud the issues with sentiment, but the main facts are not in doubt.[43] Ralegh was released from prison, though not pardoned, in 1616 in order to prepare a voyage to Guiana. He proceeded to mount a powerful fleet of fourteen ships with almost a thousand men for Trinidad and the Orinoco, knowing full well that the Spaniards occupied both the island and the river. Keymis had persuaded him that gold was accessible by way of the Orinoco and the ostensible object of the expedition was to mine a considerable quantity thereof and ship it back to England. Ralegh explained all this to King James and James duly informed the Spanish ambassador, Diego Sarmiento de Acuña (later Count Gondomar), who protested that such an expedition amounted to an invasion of Spanish territory. James's response was that if it was in Spain's effective possession and Ralegh consequently came into conflict with Spaniards he would suffer the penalty of death. He would permit him to go only on condition that he avoided any conflict with Spanish forces. James's position was entirely consistent with his general policy in respect of Spain's claims and possessions overseas and Ralegh accepted the condition. On arriving at Trinidad, Ralegh sent Keymis up the river to obtain gold and at San Thomé the inevitable conflict between English and Spanish forces occurred. Having captured the place, Keymis was unable to find the supposed mine, returned in despair to Trinidad and committed suicide. Ralegh came back to England and was executed without further trial. The motives and intentions of James and Ralegh are of course less easy to explain. Probably Ralegh hoped to demonstrate that the Spanish claim to

---

[43] V. T. Harlow (ed.), *Ralegh's Last Voyage* (London, 1932), a rather tortuous attempt to excuse Ralegh and blame James I, is typical of traditional prevarication on this question. Preferable is Williamson, *English Colonies in Guiana*, pp. 74–9. See also Quinn, *Ralegh and the British Empire*, pp. 240–67.

Guiana had little or no real basis and so, with proof of gold as an additional spur, to induce James to assert English sovereignty. If that increased the chances of war with Spain, well and good. James for his part permitted the expedition presumably with some small hope of gaining thereby if Ralegh should, against all odds, succeed; and if he failed James had nothing to lose, since he made it perfectly clear that he was no more prepared to fight for Guiana than to defend an irresponsible adventurer who had been warned as plainly as possible of the risk he ran.

For all his fraudulent claims and dangerous ambitions, Ralegh emerged the moral victor in the eyes of posterity, acclaimed alike by anti-Stuart Whigs and imperialist historians as a martyr in their respective causes. But to the cause of the English in Guiana his adventure contributed nothing but harm. In 1619 Roger North, one of his lieutenants in that last fiasco, formed a company, with the support of Robert Rich, earl of Warwick, and other members of the anti-Spanish faction at Court, for the exploitation of the Amazon. Gondomar objected that the Amazon Delta was actually in Portuguese possession and although in fact the most northerly Portuguese outpost, Pará, lay well to the south of the main estuary, the argument was sufficient to persuade the Privy Council to stay the venture pending further inquiry. North nevertheless defied the ban and sailed in 1620 to the Amazon, where he planted a hundred men, reinforcing the English and Irish settlers already there. Meanwhile the king, under strong Spanish pressure, suppressed the company. North went to the Tower on his return and was released only after pledging himself to abandon the enterprise. Thereafter things went badly for all the northerners in the Amazon area. Spain, once more at open war with the Dutch from 1621, moved the Portuguese in Brazil to launch a powerful campaign to clear the delta of foreigners. The assault, begun in 1623 and renewed in 1625, did not at once destroy the northern presence, for English efforts were resumed during the Spanish war of 1625–9 by the Guiana Company, founded by North and Harcourt in 1626. These efforts, however, were unavailing against the superior strength of the Portuguese, and the last of the struggling Amazon settlements appears to have perished in 1631. About the same time Harcourt himself came to grief in the Wiapoco along with a band of colonists whom the company had intended for the Amazon. Harcourt had diverted the expedition on his own initiative and so lost the company's support. The company itself soon afterwards went bankrupt.[44]

[44] Williamson, *English Colonies in Guiana*, pp. 91–132. V. T. Harlow (ed.), *English*

English enterprise on the Wild Coast was never strong. It owed its support largely to gentlemen who were unable to mobilize financial resources comparable to those provided by the City for the Virginia and East India companies. The focus of effort shifted from one area to another and the promoters had no common aim, some seeking gold and empire, some tobacco, while some apparently had no clear purpose in view. The different groups of interested parties failed to unite and the settlers in the country often had more dealings with Dutch traders than with their principals at home. Firm political support was conspicuously lacking, whereas Spain, once awakened to the threat to her South American empire, took the matter seriously. And these adverse circumstances counted all the more because Guiana was no easy country to colonize: the pioneers suffered heavily from fevers and dysentery and many were slaughtered by the Caribs. All these difficulties converged in the 1620s to ruin English enterprise in Guiana and to turn the attention of some of the pioneers to the Caribbean islands as potential sites for tobacco plantations.

The opening of the Thirty Years War in 1618 ended the uneasy lull which had prevailed in the Caribbean for some twelve years and by 1623 Dutch, French and English marauders had thoroughly demonstrated the vulnerability of all Spain's possessions beyond the immediate vicinity of her main bases. In the southeast, it is true, the men of Cumaná did well to fight off powerful Dutch attempts to take over the Araya salt pan, but in the islands the corsairs wrought havoc with the local trade, operating from bases in the Lesser Antilles – Nevis, Virgin Gorda and Santa Cruz, for example. Here, as the Spanish authorities were aware, they had their safe anchorages, watered, victualled and repaired their ships and frequently wintered. Parts of that great arc of islands were in fact falling under the maritime dominance of the northern intruders and the Spaniards were too busy elsewhere to do much about it. They had seriously contemplated creating a base at Guadalupe in 1606, but had abandoned the idea in 1608, when Florida suddenly seemed more important owing to the new English presence in Virginia. Now it was too late. The Windward Islands to the south were by no means inviting, possessed as they were by warlike and violently hostile Caribs: Leigh's colonists had been destroyed at Santa Lucia in 1605 and an English attempt to settle Grenada had been annihilated with the loss of many lives in 1609, while in 1614 a Spanish expedition failed to colonize Tobago. But the

Colonizing Expeditions to the West Indies and Guiana, 1623–1667 (London, 1925), pp. lxxvi–lxxxiii.

Leeward Islands, now much frequented by northern shipping, offered better prospects.[45]

Captain Thomas Warner, who established the first English colony in the Caribbean at St Kitts in 1624, had gone to the Amazon with North in 1620. Discouraged by his experience in that area, he had learned from another gentleman and soldier of the fertility of St Kitts, and on his way home from Guiana he reconnoitred the Leewards and selected that island as 'a very convenient place for the planting of tobaccoes, which ever was a rich commodetie'.[46] It offered safe anchorage, a good water supply and a healthy climate, and Warner found the ruling chief friendly. Back in London, he attracted the interest of a group of London merchants who, led by Ralph Merrifield, financed a colony consisting in the first instance of less than twenty men, described as 'gentlemen adventurers', under Warner's command. These arrived at St Kitts in January 1624 and proceeded to plant tobacco. The following year they were joined by a party of Frenchmen, with whom they agreed to divide the island in 1627, having by that time jointly massacred the majority of the Caribs and driven the rest off the island in what appears to have been a calculated campaign of genocide.[47] The advent of war with Spain in 1625 assisted Warner and his companions by removing for the time being any danger that they might be penalized for their initiative. Indeed he obtained a royal commission that same year appointing him governor of St Kitts, Nevis, Barbados and Montserrat, while the state of war also enabled him to carry letters of marque on his outward voyage in 1626 and to attack Trinidad, though without success.

The settlement of Barbados followed fast upon that of St Kitts. The conditions were more favourable in that Barbados was uninhabited and remote from any likely Spanish interference, lying as it did well to the east of the Windwards. Tobacco was again the object and again the moving spirit came from Guiana. In 1624 Sir William Courteen, member of a rich Anglo-Dutch firm formerly interested in a tobacco colony on the Essequibo, sent a ship called the Olive in the Dutch fleet which captured Bahia that year. Her captain, John Powell, touched at Barbados on his return voyage in 1625 and the result of this visit was the formation of a syndicate, including Sir William and his brother Sir Peter, their brother-in-law John Mounsey and John Powell and his brother Henry, to settle the island. In 1627 Henry Powell disembarked

[45] Andrews, *Spanish Caribbean*, pp. 234–42.

[46] Harlow, *Colonizing Expeditions*, pp. 1–4, 18. This is useful for source materials. For interpretation see J. A. Williamson, *The Caribbee Islands under the Proprietary Patents* (London, 1926).

[47] Harlow, *Colonizing Expeditions*, pp. 2–4; Williamson, *Caribbee Islands*, pp. 21–31.

eighty planters and some slaves taken in a prize and went on to Guiana to obtain roots and seeds from Amos van Groenewegen, an experienced tobacco planter whom he had known in the Essequibo. The colony grew rapidly thereafter. In 1629 it was estimated that over 1500 people had gone or were going to Barbados and that some £10,000 had been invested.[48]

In the years around 1630 the colonizing movement in the West Indies made considerable progress. Nevis was settled from St Kitts in 1628, Antigua and Montserrat in 1632. Nevis and St Kitts were very quickly re-colonized after the removal of their settlers by a Spanish fleet in 1629. In the late 1620s the Dutch were frequenting various islands for salt, notably San Martín, Saba and St Eustatius, where the French may have had a footing in 1627. By 1635 the French were established in Martinique and Guadalupe and the Dutch in Curacão. In 1630 the Providence Company was formed in England under the leadership of Robert Rich, earl of Warwick, Sir Nathaniel Rich and other gentlemen and merchants of the anti-Spanish faction, including the future leader of the Parliamentary cause, John Pym, for the colonization of the island of Santa Catalina towards the coast of Nicaragua. Thus the privateering of the war period was continued as piracy in the years of peace. From the beginning the colonies of the West Indies were directly associated with anti-Spanish operations. Captain Anthony Hilton, who first planted Nevis, went on to establish the English in Tortuga, linking the Providence Company and the tobacco plantations with the buccaneers of that island.[49] It is inconceivable that settlement in the islands could have advanced without such conflict and pervasive violence, for the Spanish Caribbean was not only vulnerable and attractive to predators, but also well able to resist and endure. Indeed the English settlements owed their survival largely to Dutch sea power, which came to be felt in the Caribbean from 1625, when Boudewijn Hendricksz invaded that sea with a formidable fleet. Thereafter the Dutch offensive developed unrelentingly so that by 1635 the maritime and commercial supremacy of the Hollanders in the West Indies could not be denied. Already by 1630 their shipping supplied the wants of St Kitts and Barbados and disposed of much of their produce.

In these early years the Caribbean colonies were nothing like the slave plantations of later times. They certainly contained some slaves: Maurice Thompson, a London merchant with a great interest in the West Indian and African trades, took out sixty Negroes to St Kitts in

[48] Williamson, *Caribbee Islands*, pp. 33–8; Harlow, *Colonizing Expeditions*, pp. 30–42.
[49] A. P. Newton, *The Colonizing Activities of the English Puritans* (London, 1914).

1626 and Dutch traders supplied the islands with many more over the years. Some Indians were also enslaved, including the Arawaks who had cheerfully volunteered to accompany Powell from the Essequibo to Barbados.[50] But the workforce consisted for the most part of white indentured servants shipped out from England, young men usually between fifteen and twenty-four, many of them Irish.[51] Tobacco planting was essentially a parcellated form of agriculture in which small groups worked plantations of anything from five to fifty acres – rarely more.[52] The settlements were production units within the orbit of commerce rather than colonial societies and their *raison d'être* was profit, principally for the merchants of the tobacco trade and secondarily for the few gentlemen planters among the emigrants. The rival groups of merchants engaged in colonizing could not, however, obtain proprietary rights for themselves, but could only hope, in the political climate of Charles I's rule, to secure or enhance their respective positions by finding at Court a protector, paying him handsomely for his patronage. The Courteens found one in William Herbert, earl of Pembroke, while Merrifield's syndicate found another in James Hay, earl of Carlisle. To these parasites Charles granted conflicting patents for colonization, which caused much legal wrangling in London and considerable harm in the colonies, particularly when Carlisle, having won his claim to Barbados, proceeded to neglect the island, which consequently suffered its starving time. When the earl of Warwick entered the arena with the Providence Company it came into conflict with Carlisle's interest and rivalry between the parties persisted for many years.[53] King Charles thus played a sorry hand in the West Indian game, and the best that can be said for his performance is that he hindered the overseas expansion movement less there than elsewhere.

[50] C. and R. Bridenbaugh, *No Peace Beyond the Line: the English in the Caribbean, 1624–1690* (New York, 1972), pp. 10, 30.

[51] *Ibid*. pp. 9–34.

[52] K. G. Davies, *The North Atlantic World in the Seventeenth Century* (London, 1974), pp. 144ff.

[53] Williamson, *Caribbee Islands*; Newton, *Colonizing Activities*, p. 48.

14

North America
1591–1630

The invasion of North America was a European movement. Throughout the sixteenth century Portuguese, Spanish, French and English explorers and fishermen reconnoitred the coasts from Florida to Baffin Island. For a long time among these early pioneers collaboration between men of different nationality was not uncommon – indeed it was normal in the Newfoundland fishery. Towards the end of the century, however, national rivalry intensified for economic as well as political reasons. The Anglo-Spanish war made the dominance of the coast from Florida to Chesapeake Bay a bone of contention. The war itself from 1588 to 1602 ironically prevented either side from doing anything effective about it, but once it became clear that the war was coming to an end Virginia re-emerged as a live issue and action to resolve it became the order of the day. Here national claims and pride heavily overlaid a great deal of rather vague talk about commercial and religious intents.

In the more northerly zone of European interest, comprising what became the New England coast, the Maritimes, the Gulf and River of St Lawrence, Newfoundland and Labrador, urgent economic interests came to the fore from the 1580s. As population pressure in southern Europe increased the demand for fish, competition in the cod trade grew fierce, particularly between the aggressive English sailors and the Basques: whether the latter came from San Sebastián in Spain or St Jean de Luz in France seemed to matter little to them and even less to their West Country foes. The Basques were especially dominant in whaling off Labrador and in the Gulf of St Lawrence, where they also hunted walrus, the main product of both whale and walrus being train-oil, widely used for lighting and lubrication and above all for the soap required by the cloth industry. Bretons were joining the Basques in the walrus business in the nineties and French ambitions in the Gulf and the River, deriving from Jacques Cartier's pioneering voyages sixty years before, were gaining shape and substance as the fur trade gradually evolved from casual contact to regular exchange, a transition first accomplished at Tadoussac at the mouth of the Saguenay within the great river. At the same time the French stretched their attention south from Cape Breton Island to Nova Scotia, the Bay of Fundy and even beyond. From the early eighties some Frenchmen seriously contemplated colonization, which became a definite objective in the last few years of the century, though at that time settlement was envisaged rather as a means of developing and protecting the fish and fur trades than as an end in itself.[1]

The English made their bid for a place in the Gulf in the 1590s.[2] In 1591 a Bristol privateer captured a Breton fishing vessel returning from the Magdalen Islands with the spoil of walrus-hunting: a rich cargo of train-oil, tusks and hides. In response to this stimulus Bristol merchants and others sent two ventures to the Gulf in 1593 and 1594. These managed to acquire cargoes by fair means and foul, but could not compete with the Basques in whaling or walrus-hunting. Now, however, interest was aroused, and in particular Burghley's interest. Always an advocate of the fisheries, Burghley lent a sympathetic ear to the schemes of Edward Hayes for English settlement in the northerly zone and was especially attracted to this northwest fishery, nursery of the formidable Basque marine. Meanwhile some of the many Separatists gaoled by Archbishop Whitgift (called then Brownists after Robert Browne, one of their former leaders) began to contemplate America as an alternative to banishment. While others died in prison or saved themselves by emigrating to Holland, these few, led by their pastor, Francis Johnson, decided to plead for freedom of worship as the queen's loyal subjects beyond the Atlantic. It was probably early in 1597 that they petitioned the Privy Council:

Whereas meanes is now offered for our beeing in a forraigne and farre Countrie which lieth in the West from hence in the Province of Canada where by the providence of the Almightie, and her Majestes most gratious favour, wee may not onlie worshippe god as wee are in conscience perswaded by his Word, but also doe unto her Majestie and our Country great good service, and in tyme also greatlie annoy that bloodie and persecuting Spaniard about the Baye of Mexico. Our most humble suite is . . . that with her most gracious favour and

---

[1] Ch.-A. Julien, *Les Voyages de Découverte et les Premiers Etablissements* (Paris, 1948), pp. 281–6; D. B. Quinn, 'The voyage of Etienne Bellenger to the Maritimes in 1583', *Canadian Historical Review*, 43 (1962), 328–43; D. B. Quinn, *North America from the Earliest Discovery to the First Settlements: the Norse Voyages to 1612* (New York, 1978), pp. 389–95; J. B. Brebner, *The Explorers of North America* (London, 1937), pp. 145–7.

[2] Quinn, *England and the Discovery of America*, pp. 311–63. The whole episode is documented in Quinn, *New American World*, IV, pp. 56–80.

protection wee may peaceablie Depart thither, and there remayning to bee accounted her Majestes faithfull and loving Subjectes.[3]

Burghley was more inclined than Whitgift to tolerate dissent and he almost certainly was responsible for the holy alliance between these first 'pilgrims'—the word had already been used by Separatist exiles in the Netherlands[4]— and the Londoners who proposed to use them to man an English base in the Magdalen Islands, specifically on 'Ramea' (later named Amherst Island). Charles Leigh, commander of the expedition, was of merchant stock and behind him stood Abraham van Harwick, a London merchant of Dutch extraction, John Watts the privateering magnate, who provided his ship the *Hopewell* and her fighting captain, William Craston, and possibly Peter Hills the ship-owner. The intention was to oust the Basques from the Magdalens and establish English control over the walrus fishery and presumably over much else besides. The first expedition would take Ramea, leaving the second ship, the *Chancewell*, and a party of four colonists to hold it over the winter; walrus-hunting, fishing and plundering the Basques were expected to provide the wherewithal to mount a further voyage, which would take out the main body of settlers and again pursue walrus, cod, Spanish prize and so on. Of course in practice this cheerful plan broke down. Leigh's attempt on the islands in 1597 was easily repulsed by the Basques and their Breton allies, the four dissenting pioneers dissented from each other and everyone else, the sailors showed interest in nothing but pillage, the *Chancewell* was wrecked and only the privateering aspect of the venture proved even moderately successful. As for the pilgrims, they quickly on their return to London collected other members of their sect and escaped to Amsterdam, where Francis Johnson with others formed what came in retrospect to be called the Ancient Church. Years of hardship followed, but a decade later other sectaries moved from England to Amsterdam and later to Leyden, where eventually the idea of migrating to North America reappeared. Thus, however indirectly and tenuously, the Pilgrim Fathers of Plymouth Plantation descended from Johnson and his forlorn flock.

Leigh's expedition had a significant influence upon the orientation of English enterprise in North America, for it helped to stimulate French activity in the Gulf and River of St Lawrence, which after 1597 advanced rapidly. The English had to look further south for a sphere of influence and were able to reconnoitre, to frequent and finally to settle

[3] Quinn, *New American World*, IV, p. 67.
[4] 'We are but strangers and pilgrims warring against many and mighty adversaries' – Henry Ainsworth, *A true confession of the faith* (Amsterdam, 1596).

the New England coast because the French were too occupied further north to interfere, though their claims extended as far south as the fortieth parallel and Champlain devoted his talents from 1604 to 1607 to the systematic exploration and charting of the coast from the Bay of Fundy to southern Massachusetts,[5] while Acadia (later Nova Scotia) lay in practice within the French domain in spite of the English refusal to accept the fact. Thus in the northerly zone English hopes came to rest upon Newfoundland and New England, in both of which the sea remained for a considerable time more interesting than the land. Colonization in the full sense seemed less attractive than the creation of bases to support or monopolize the fishery, to conduct trade with the Indians or to assist a northwest navigation to the Pacific. Fish, fur and the northwest passage all offered lucrative prospects, whereas settlement would prove far more troublesome in reality than projectors like Hayes were prepared to admit. Indeed it would be mistaken to suppose that Hayes and similar enthusiasts represented the main current of opinion about such matters. From 1586 to 1602 at least scepticism if not downright hostility prevailed, nor did the colonial schemes of the years that followed escape the ridicule of popular playwrights.[6]

Bartholomew Gosnold, a gentleman of Otley in Suffolk, made the first of the New England reconnaissance ventures in 1602, perhaps with some support from the earl of Southampton.[7] Deriving his ideas from Edward Hayes, Gosnold hoped to rediscover the bay Verrazzano had found so attractive nearly eighty years before, probably in fact Narragansett Bay. He sailed in the small bark *Concord* with several gentlemen companions and a certain Captain Bartholomew Gilbert, who managed the ship and crew (described as 'few, and they none of the best'), followed the Maine coast south into Cape Cod Bay and explored beyond that almost to Narragansett Bay, doing some trade with the Indians and collecting some sassafras roots and cedar to pay

[5] Cumming, Skelton and Quinn, *North America*, pp. 261–4.

[6] The play *Eastward Hoe* by Ben Jonson, George Chapman and John Marston satirized the Virginia propaganda. For a cool and sober view of the colonial prospects see the anonymous reply to Hayes's 1592 scheme for a northerly plantation: Quinn, *New American World*, III, pp. 172–5.

[7] W. F. Gookin, *Bartholomew Gosnold, Discoverer and Planter* (London, 1963). Original accounts of the voyage: J. Brereton, *A Briefe and true Relation of the Discoverie of the North part of Virginia* (1602); G. Archer, 'The Relation of Captaine Gosnols Voyage', in *Purchas*, XVIII, 302–13, and Gosnold's letter to his father, in *Purchas*, XVIII, 300–302. Gosnold was not financed by Ralegh, as is often stated. He had commanded the *Diamond* of Southampton in a privateering cruise in 1599, taking at least one prize: PRO, HCA, 13/35, 18 Feb. 1600/1; PRO, HCA, 24/67, no. 5/6. He planned to venture again with two ships in 1600: BL, Additional MSS, 15208, fos. 510–11.

expenses. Gosnold decided not to leave a holding party on the coast and so returned, but his modest achievement became important because it occurred at an opportune moment – the war was coming to an end, releasing private initiative and resources for new Atlantic ventures – and because it was speedily, widely and favourably advertised by the Reverend John Brereton's *Relation*. This was dedicated to Ralegh, who on hearing of this infringement of his patent confiscated the sassafras, but gave his 'permission' *ex post facto* for the voyage, since his interest lay in southern rather than northern 'Virginia'.[8]

Ralegh also permitted the next venture, conducted by the Bristol sailor Martin Pring 'upon many probable and reasonable inducements, used unto sundry of the chiefest Merchants of Bristoll, by Master Richard Hakluyt Prebendary of Saint Augustines the Cathedrall Church of the said Citie'.[9] The leading promoter was Robert Aldworth, 'aswell with his Purse as with his travell'. Accompanied by Robert Saltern, who had sailed with Gosnold, Pring took two barks of 50 and 26 tons laden with a variety of merchandise for trade with the Indians and resorted to the same coast in 1603. Again there was friendly contact with the native people, whom the English nevertheless regarded with manifest contempt, for they took mastiffs with them and 'when we would be rid of the Savages company wee would let loose the Mastives, and suddenly with out-cryes they would flee away'. Pring brought back a glowing report of the natural resources of the country and a cargo consisting mainly of sassafras, 'a plant of sovereigne vertue for the French Poxe, and as some of late have learnedly written good against the Plague and many other maladies'. The London plague of 1603 may thus conceivably have helped to advertise New England.

No further venture occurred, however, until 1605, when Sir Thomas Arundell, the earl of Southampton's brother-in-law, sent out the *Archangel* under Captain George Waymouth, who had conducted a northwest passage expedition in 1602. Arundell hoped to find a refuge for Catholics returning from the Continent after the end of the war and Waymouth succeeded in interesting certain Plymouth merchants in the prospect of rich fishing grounds. This was another fortunate and promising voyage – to Penobscot Bay, its neighbouring islands and the St George River. James Rosier, the reporter of the expedition, portrayed waters teeming with fish, a land 'whose pleasant fertility bewraieth it selfe to be the garden of nature' and 'a people of very good

---

[8] Quinn, *England and the Discovery of America*, pp. 413–14.
[9] *Purchas*, XVIII, 322–9.

invention, quick understanding, and ready capacity'.[10] It was for future use of these qualities in the colonial cause that Waymouth seized five of the local people and brought them to England. Unfortunately in his absence the Jesuit Robert Parsons had publicly warned English Catholics against such projects and Arundell had withdrawn from the venture to take up a post abroad. Waymouth then managed to interest Sir John Zouche and certain Plymouth merchants in a new scheme, but this in turn was superseded in the early months of 1606 by larger plans for a national enterprise.[11]

Meanwhile the English had resumed the initiative in the more southerly zone between 35° and 38°. As a note attached to Brereton's narrative of Gosnold's voyage of 1602 relates, in that year

Samuel Mace of Weimouth, a very sufficient Mariner, an honest sober man, who had beene at Virginia twice before, was employed thither by Sir Walter Raleigh, to finde those people which were left there in the yeere 1587. To whose succour he hath sent five severall times at his owne charges.[12]

Ralegh did send expeditions to Virginia in search of the lost colonists in 1588 and 1590, as we have seen, but we lack any evidence of the others. He had some interest in trying to prove or sustain belief in the survival of White's people, for his patent was hardly defensible if the colony no longer existed. It is not unlikely, therefore, that he had already dispatched two ventures for Virginia before 1602 (assuming Mace's voyage to be one of the alleged five), especially since opinion about the fate of the colony remained divided. It was only later, about 1610, that William Strachey, himself a reliable authority, acquired what he regarded as sufficient evidence that some of the colonists had lived for over twenty years with the Chesapeake tribe until, at or shortly before Christopher Newport's arrival in Chesapeake Bay in the spring of 1607, they were massacred along with all that tribe on the orders of the great Indian chief Powhatan.[13]

Mace had orders to seek 'the port of Hatarask' (just south of Roanoke), but after trading with the Indians further south he found the

---

[10] J. Rosier, *A true relation of the most prosperous voyage made in this present yeere 1605, by Captaine George Waymouth* (London, 1605). Another version, with variations, was printed in *Purchas*, xviii, 335–60. Quinn, *England and the Discovery of America*, pp. 388–91.

[11] On Zouche's project see Quinn, *England and the Discovery of America*, pp. 390–91, and Quinn, *New American World*, iii, pp. 391–5.

[12] *Purchas*, xviii, 321

[13] L. B. Wright and V. Freund (eds.), *The Historie of Travell into Virginia Britannia (1612) by William Strachey, gent.* (London, 1953), pp. 34, 91, 104–6. It is unlikely that Powhatan massacred the entire tribe: N. O. Lurie, 'Indian cultural adjustment to European civilization', in J. M. Smith (ed.), *Seventeenth Century America: Essays in Colonial History* (Chapel Hill, 1959).

weather too dangerous to reach his objective and returned home with some sassafras and other goods. The following year Ralegh sent Bartholomew Gilbert, captain of Gosnold's *Concord* in 1602, for Chesapeake Bay, but he too failed to reach his goal and met his death at the hands of Indians on some unspecified part of the North American coast.[14] In July 1603 Ralegh was imprisoned. Interest in Virginia continued to grow, for in September certain 'Virginians' appeared on the Thames in a canoe – brought back presumably by another expedition, perhaps one under Mace's command,[15] but in 1604 no further voyages appear to have occurred and in 1605 only an Anglo-French expedition, which had instructions to call at Croatoan in the course of reconnoitring the coast from Florida to the Bay of Fundy.[16]

All this suggests that the misfortunes of Mace, Gilbert and Ralegh caused a recession in Virginia venturing, but probably more important was the attitude of James I. It was to him that Ralegh's charter rights reverted in 1603 and it is quite clear that James was resolved to defend those rights in principle and that he supported Salisbury and Nottingham in their refusal to abandon England's North American claims during and after the peace negotiations. On the other hand his dislike of privateering, his hostility to Ralegh, his disapproval of Caribbean venturing and his eager pursuit of a Spanish marriage for his son were sufficiently well known to deter any individual from attempting to step into Ralegh's treacherous shoes. Initiative for the time being was suspended by uncertainty and when the game was resumed – probably late in 1605 – the key moves were made in high quarters in a mysterious manner characteristic of the earl of Salisbury. Moreover they were moves towards a kind of collective action which avoided both individual responsibility on the one hand and active leadership by the state on the other. In such political circumstances was the Virginia Council conceived.

The scrappy evidence available suggests that it was Waymouth's return to Plymouth in July 1605 which set the process in motion. The Plymouth merchants who had backed his voyage, including William Parker the shipowner and privateering captain, were now joined by Sir Ferdinando Gorges, the governor of Plymouth fort. Gorges was well placed to appreciate the dangerous scale of unemployment among soldiers and sailors created by the ending of the war and shared the feelings of those who 'rather chose to spend themselves in seeking

[14] *Purchas*, XVIII, 329–35.
[15] Quinn, *England and the Discovery of America*, pp. 419–31.
[16] Quinn, *New American World*, v, pp. 108–27. The two ships – the *Castor and Pollux* and the *Pollux and Castor* – were captured by Spanish forces on the Florida coast.

a new world, than servilely to be hired but as slaughterers in the quarrels of strangers'.[17] At Plymouth, too, the sons of Sir Humphrey Gilbert – Sir John and Raleigh – were fired by their father's old ambition, while Thomas Hanham, recorder of Plymouth, added his weight to the local movement. Hanham may well have been responsible for bringing his grandfather, Sir John Popham, Lord Chief Justice of the King's Bench, into the arena. Sir John, who had connections with Bristol, was to be the moving spirit of the West Country effort to colonize New England and his cousin George – another privateering captain – was to lead that attempt. In Bristol Richard Hakluyt and Robert Aldworth, the promoters of Pring's expedition, rallied support and Dr Matthew Sutcliffe, dean of Exeter, did the same there. Sir George Somers, who with Amyas Preston had sacked Caracas in 1595, was one of the most important figures in this gathering, for as M.P. for Lyme Regis he was already a prominent spokesman for West Country interests in the House of Commons.[18]

Popham and Salisbury, with the aid of Sir Walter Cope, Salisbury's friend and M.P. for Westminster, managed the marriage of these western gentlemen and merchants with the wealth of the capital on terms the crown could approve and institutionalize. On the City side Sir Thomas Smythe, son of Customer Smith, was the most influential man, the main link between the government and the merchants. He had been a governor of the Levant and East India Companies, an ambassador to Moscow, whence he returned to London in September 1605, and had already interested himself in Virginia in 1589. Seconded by Sir William Romney and John Eldred, he carried the City to the support of what became in the early months of 1606 a national enterprise. Salisbury was undoubtedly responsible for the shape of this organization, which combined two companies in one. The charter, dated 10 April 1606, was granted to Sir Thomas Gates, Somers, Hakluyt and Edward Maria Wingfield and others as 'Adventurers of and for our Cittie of London' and to Thomas Hanham, Raleigh Gilbert, William Parker and George Popham and others of Plymouth, Bristol and Exeter, each group constituting a distinct company. Together they would have the right to colonize, between the latitudes of 34° and 45°, parts of America 'not nowe actuallie possessed by anie Christian Prince or people', but the Plymouth company was given responsibility for planting northwards from 38° – in effect for New England – while the London company had the right to plant from 41° southwards, which meant essentially Chesapeake Bay. It did not matter that the grants

[17] Brown, *Genesis*, p. 50.
[18] Croft, 'Free trade'.

overlapped between New York and Washington, for neither party had designs on that region.[19]

This oddly double company may be considered joint-stock in the sense that it consisted of shareholders who expected a return on capital invested in the exploitation of certain lands on certain terms, but it differed from the chartered trading companies in its government. This was entrusted to a royal council of, in the first instance, fourteen royal nominees, eight of whom were officials or lawyers (Sir William Wade, Sir Walter Cope, Sir George Moore, Sir John Trevor, Sir Henry Montague, John Dodderidge, Thomas Warr and James Bagg: the last, a Plymouth merchant, and Trevor were notoriously corrupt admiralty men, creatures of the earl of Nottingham). Popham's son Francis, Gorges and Thomas James of Bristol represented the West Country and Smythe, Romney and Eldred represented the City.[20] What is surprising is the absence of any major political figure, such as Sir John Popham, Nottingham or Salisbury himself. Each of these had his own man on the council, but it is a measure of the relative unimportance of American matters that none of them saw fit to attend to them personally. On the other hand the people most seriously interested in the business were a minority, outnumbered by a body of government men of varied standing and reputation. Moreover this 'King's Councel of Virginia' was to nominate the members of two subordinate councils, one for each of the colonizing companies, these junior bodies having responsibility for running their respective colonies under the general guidance of the superior council. No wonder there was an outcry. Not only the merchants of Plymouth, but according to Gorges merchants of Exeter, Bristol and London disliked the royal council and were unwilling to proceed.[21] These protests were of course overruled, but in March 1607 the council was enlarged to include sixteen new members nominated by the London company and ten by that of Plymouth.[22]

James thus took the plunge in 1606, committing the crown to the colonial enterprise, but he did so in response to pressure from below and seemed more concerned to assert royal sovereignty over the colonies than to govern them – or even to create an effective form of

[19] P. L. Barbour (ed.), *The Jamestown Voyages under the First Charter, 1606–1609* (Cambridge, 1969), pp. 23–34 (the editorial commentary in this work is unreliable). On the constitution of the Virginia Company see W. F. Craven, *The Southern Colonies in the Seventeenth Century, 1607–1689* (Baton Rouge, La., 1949), pp. 61–3; C. M. Andrews, *The Colonial Period of American History* (4 vols., New Haven, 1934), I, pp. 80–88; Quinn, *North America*, pp. 440–45; Brown, *Genesis*, pp. 46–75.

[20] Brown, *Genesis*, p. 66; H. A. Lloyd, 'Corruption and Sir John Trevor', *Transactions of the Honourable Society of Cymmrodorion for 1974–5* (London, 1976), pp. 77–102.

[21] Andrews, *Colonial Period*, I, p. 85.

[22] Brown, *Genesis*, pp. 91–5.

government. For while the council advised, instructed and supervised the companies, it left the work of administration, justice, evangelization, exploitation, trade and so forth to them. The crown contributed nothing to the financing of the companies, though it claimed its share of the proceeds in the shape of a fifth of the precious metals produced. Neither the system of government nor the capitalization of the colonies proved at all adequate and failure forced the wholesale revision of both in 1609. Although it would be unfair to blame King James alone for the weakness of the initial organization of the Virginia enterprise, the crown signally failed to give a decisive lead and so far shrank from challenging Spain that during the year 1607, when Spanish threats and protests resounded from Madrid to London, Virginia was diplomatically explained as the private business of the king's subjects, conducted at their own risk. James refused to interfere with their activities, but he equally refused to acknowledge responsibility for them at this stage.

The energy which produced the Virginia enterprise came not from the state but from the nation. The desire to exploit American lands and waters was shared by all the interested parties and some were moved by zeal to convert the heathen or – like Sir John Popham – by fear of the idle poor and cashiered soldiers 'whose Encrease threateneth the state',[23] but the overriding thrust was nationalistic. Anti-Spanish feeling was still virulent among the seamen and merchants of the southwest, where complaints about maltreatment of Englishmen in Spanish ports had aroused fresh anger since 1603 and where men like Sir Richard Hawkins found it hard to accept the end of the privateering war. Gilbert, Parker, George Popham, Somers, Gosnold, Aldworth, Pring and Gorges, not to mention Ralegh and scores of other West Country undertakers of the Virginia project, had been prominent actors in the Atlantic war, and they had many allies in London, both among gentlemen of the court like Sir Thomas Roe and among the merchants. Eldred himself had good cause to resent Spain's monopoly of the New World: in 1603 he had lost two pinnaces trading in the West Indies, captured by Spaniards, their men being killed, wounded or taken prisoner and allegedly treated with sadistic cruelty in some cases, and in 1606 he lost another vessel, the *Aid*, in the Caribbean with with similar results.[24] In 1607 the Lord Mayor of London was Sir John Watts, whom the Spanish ambassador at that time, Pedro de Zúñiga, described as 'the greatest pirate that has ever been in this kingdom'.[25] Zúñiga was convinced that the English were interested in Virginia only

[23] Quinn, *New American World*, v, p. 166.
[24] Andrews, *Spanish Caribbean*, pp. 202, 206–7.
[25] Brown, *Genesis*, p. 99.

as a potential privateering base and in this he was certainly mistaken, but in the early years of the colony, when a renewal of the war with Spain seemed likely and even desirable to many of the Virginia promoters, the strategic advantage of such a base could not be a minor consideration. The prevailing mood was one of national assertiveness and resentment of the exclusive claims of Spain in the New World, a mood accurately indicated by Ferdinando Gorges in a letter of 2 May 1608 to Salisbury:

I beseeche God we repent not too late oure too soone concluding of peace: for (as now the case standeth) our Kinge is by them (as it seemeth) contemned, our people unjustly proceeded withall, and generally our Nation of all other, lyke to be debarred from the liberty of making use of the sea, or land; saving wher and how they list to dispose of us. These reports ar horrable to honeste Natures to beare; and occasions much to grive our people in generall to understand of, whose eares ar dayly filled with it by every common mariner, that comes from thence. Which what it hath bred amongest the multitude, I protest, I am affraied to write.[26]

The London company's first fleet, consisting of the *Susan Constant* (120 tons) under Christopher Newport as admiral, the *Godspeed* (40 tons) under Bartholomew Gosnold and the pinnace *Discovery* under John Ratcliffe, departed in December 1606, took the Caribbean route and entered Chesapeake Bay towards the end of April.[27] Captain John Smith's description of Newport as 'a Marriner well practised for the westerne parts of America'[28] scarcely does justice to that sailor, who probably knew the Caribbean better than any Englishman at that time and who may well have acquired some knowledge of the Virginia coast on his numerous return voyages by way of the Florida Channel or possibly on a deliberate reconnaissance since the end of the war.[29] Much impressed by the broad stream of the James River, Newport and his companions soon selected a site for settlement on a narrow-necked peninsula some fifty miles up river from the ocean, well placed to resist attack by land or surprise by sea and possessing an excellent anchorage. In these respects it was a great improvement on Roanoke, but low-

[26] Brown, *Genesis*, pp. 149–50.
[27] G. Percy, 'A Discourse of the Plantation of the Southerne Colonie in Virginia', in *Purchas*, XVIII, 403–19. Gabriel Archer's account is printed in Barbour, *Jamestown Voyages*, pp. 80–104.
[28] Barbour, *Jamestown Voyages*, p. 378.
[29] Andrews, 'Christopher Newport'. Since 1603 he had been to the West Indies in the *Peter* of London 'in trade' and in 1605 he presented King James with two live crocodiles and a wild boar from Española. The confidence with which he entered Chesapeake Bay in 1607 suggests either previous personal experience or the presence aboard of a pilot with such experience.

lying and marshy – an unhealthy place, which they called Jamestown.

The appalling tale of Jamestown's first three years cannot be related here in detail. It is a tale of confusion further confused by those who reported it, and above all by Captain John Smith, a notoriously subjective reporter as well as a born leader. His domineering personality may well have saved the colony from extinction, as his own accounts suggest,[30] but it has also exerted a hypnotic effect upon posterity, tending to obscure from his admirers and critics the root causes of the misfortunes and mistakes which almost overwhelmed the colony and necessitated what was virtually a new start in 1609–10. Sealed orders opened on arrival in Virginia revealed that Edward Maria Wingfield was to command the colony as its president. This was an unfortunate choice, for Wingfield lacked personal authority and could not depend on the loyal support of the councillors appointed to assist him. The colony needed strong government particularly because about a third of its members were gentlemen, many of whom were averse to discipline and hard work. Quarrels, intrigue and the death of the reliable Gosnold soon led to Wingfield's deposition, but the same troubles continued to bedevil the settlement's affairs until Smith took over the command in the summer of 1608.[31] Petty malice and factious feuding among the leaders (one of whom was executed for treason) did untold damage to the morale of the whole community, but the individuals were less to blame than the defective social constitution of the colony. In that respect Ralph Lane's expedition was better designed. Furthermore when Newport returned with reinforcements in January 1608, 28 of the 120 new people were gentlemen, and in the 'second supply', which arrived in April, 28 out of 70.[32] Too many of the rest were specialized craftsmen, sent out by the company in the expectation that Virginia would almost immediately begin to produce such goods as iron, copper, soap-ash, olive oil, silk, glass, pitch and tar. Those listed as 'labourers' in the first group of planters numbered only twelve and Smith complained that 'the labour of 30 of the best only preserved in Christianitie by their industrie the idle livers of neare 200 of the rest'.[33]

[30] Smith, *Works*. He wrote three accounts of Virginia: *A true relation of such occurrences and accidents of noate as hath hapned in Virginia* (London, 1608); *A map of Virginia* (Oxford, 1612), which is in two parts; and *The generall historie of Virginia, New England, and the Summer Isles* (London, 1624). *A map of Virginia* is reprinted in Barbour, *Jamestown Voyages*, pp. 327–464.

[31] Wingfield himself gave an account of these petty squabbles on his return to England: Barbour, *Jamestown Voyages*, pp. 213–34.

[32] E. S. Morgan, *American Freedom, American Slavery* (New York, 1975), p. 84. A list of the first settlers and their occupations is in Barbour, *Jamestown Voyages*, pp. 382–3.

[33] Barbour, *Jamestown Voyages*, p. 374.

While many of the pioneers were unprepared physically or mentally to cope with an environment which proved much more hostile than it seemed at first sight, the promoters at home looked for an early return on their investment. Their greatest hope, of course, was for gold or some other rich mineral. Newport took specimens of stones and ore home from his first trip and although these proved worthless his return to Virginia in January resulted in a treasure hunt which occupied much of the settlers' attention for many weeks, during which, to Smith's disgust, 'there was no talke, no hope, nor worke, but dig gold, wash gold, refine gold, load gold'.[34] Much time and attention were devoted also to attempting to grow vines, sugar cane, olive trees and other plants which might attract investors and to producing samples of pitch, glass, soap-ash and so on. All this had to be done at the expense of achieving elementary self-sufficiency, which the promoters and the planters alike seem to have regarded as a secondary matter. In practice the colony depended for its food partly on shipments from home and partly on what it could grow or forage for itself, but chiefly on corn acquired by way of trade with tribes both near at hand and further afield. From the start, therefore, the relations between the intruders and the natives were fundamental to the survival of the settlement and those relations were concerned essentially with food supplies. These stark realities emerged clearly in the months from August 1607 until Newport's return in January, during which time the planters suffered sorely by disease and famine, as George Percy relates:

Our men were destroyed with cruell diseases as Swellings, Fluxes, Burning Fevers, and by warres, and some departed suddenly, but for the most part they died of meere famine. There were never Englishmen left in a forreigne Countrey in such miserie as wee were in this new discovered Virginia. Wee watched every three nights lying on the bare cold ground what weather soever came warded all the next day, which brought our men to bee most feeble wretches, our food was but a small Can of barlie sod in water to five men a day, our drinke cold water taken out of the River, which was at floud verie salt, at a low tide full of slime and filth, which was the destruction of many of our men. Thus we lived for the space of five moneths in this miserable distresse, not having five able men to man our Bulwarkes upon any occasion.[35]

Scurvy, typhoid and dysentery probably accounted for the loss of half the planters in these terrible months. Raw, ill-fed, infected and badly led, the whole colony was in danger. Yet Percy here went on

---

[34] Smith, *Works*, I, p. 104. However, as Craven (*Southern Colonies*, pp. 67–9) shows, the notion that the Jamestown colony was essentially a misguided gold hunt is mistaken.
[35] *Purchas*, XVIII, 418.

with the bewildered and bewildering statement that 'it pleased God, after a while, to send those people which were our mortall enemies to releeve us with victuals, as Bread, Corne, Fish, and Flesh in great plentie, which was the setting up of our feeble men, otherwise wee had all perished'. Clearly the relationship between the Indians and the English was by no means a simple one. In fact the English had lodged themselves in the territory of the Paspahegh tribe, but over them and over the greater part of tidewater Virginia the great chief Powhatan held sway. Smith and his companions usually described Powhatan as a king and although this misrepresents the nature of his authority it indicates the respect in which he was held by the inferior chiefs and even by the English themselves. For Powhatan had already created and was continuing to build a considerable empire based upon a complex society well adjusted to the environment. While the invaders could not but admire the natives' skill in hunting, fishing and agri-culture, what most impressed them was Powhatan's power:

Although the countrie people be very barbarous, yet have they amongst them such government, as that their magistrats for good commanding, and their people for du subjection, and obeying, excell many places that would be counted very civill. . . . Yet when he listeth his will is a law and must bee obeyed: not only as a king but as halfe a God they esteeme him. His inferiour kings whom they cal werowances are tyed to rule by customes, and have power of life & death.[36]

On the other hand Powhatan had no very strong reason at this stage to admire or fear the English. The latter were few in number and pitifully unable to feed themselves, dying like flies of strange diseases. Their boasted Christianity and civility, which apparently meant so much to them, had neither meaning nor relevance for the Indian, but they did have some bits of technology which were worth borrowing: some of their tools and above all their weapons. These would make the newcomers useful allies for a chief who ruled an unstable empire of numerous tribes fringed by powerful nations who seemed to him far more dangerous than the tiny band of feeble white men.[37] In some ways of course those white men were unwelcome: they had squatted on the Paspahegh lands, they continually demanded corn, even when there was little or no surplus to trade, they caused offence by their arrogant behaviour and they showed themselves prepared to ally with Powhatan's enemies. Friction and conflict were therefore part of the pattern of Anglo–Indian relations throughout the early years of the Virginia colony, but for the time being each suffered the other's

[36] Barbour, *Jamestown Voyages*, pp. 369–71. [37] Lurie, 'Indian cultural adjustment'.

existence with a curious mixture of hostility, cordiality and wary suspicion. On the English side attitudes to the Indians in general and to Powhatan in particular varied considerably. Newport, who was in close touch with the council and promoters at home, did his best to forward their policy of inducting the Indian peacefully into acceptance of English sovereignty, law, religion and economic hegemony. As a step in this direction he brought out with the second supply a crown for Powhatan, who was duly invested as the rightful ruler (under King James) of his own people, a ceremony Smith frankly deplored: 'For we had his favour much better, onlie for a poore peece of Copper, till this stately kinde of soliciting made him so much overvalue himselfe, that he respected us as much as nothing at all.'[38] Smith was probably right and before long the company veered to the other extreme, deciding that the best course was to destroy Powhatan's influence and bring all the tribes under English rule as tributaries. Such was the policy Sir Thomas Gates was instructed to pursue in 1609.[39]

By this time the need for change and a great new effort was clear, for the first two years of bitter experience at Jamestown had disappointed the hopes of the promoters. The exploration of the Bay and the hinterland – chiefly by Smith and Newport – had indeed provided some basis in knowledge for a more ambitious venture, and Smith's leadership had eventually pulled the colony through in spite of further food-shortage during the second winter, but the English foothold on the continent still consisted of a mere two hundred people confined to a single location and continually menaced by a much more powerful and far from predictable neighbour. Above all, national prestige was at stake. In 1609 the structure was therefore re-organized and a new charter incorporated the Virginia Company, which now replaced the double company of 1606, since the Plymouth Company's attempt to settle New England had meanwhile failed. The council of the new company became the 'Royal Council for Virginia', responsible for colonizing lands up to 200 miles north and the same distance south of the entrance to the James River.

To mobilize support for this much enlarged enterprise the government lent its influence to an unprecedented propaganda campaign. Many officials, gentlemen of the court, West Country men and others were induced to subscribe in addition to the City companies and individual merchants who formed the core of the organization. The total amount raised is not known. It was certainly small in comparison with the kind of sum invested in an East India expedition at that time,[40]

---

[38] Barbour, *Jamestown Voyages*, p. 411.   [39] Craven, *Southern Colonies*, p. 81.
[40] The East India Company raised £70,000 for its first voyage, £60,000 for its second,

but the number of contributors was nevertheless impressive for a colonial project, particularly in view of the existing scepticism and resistance of a public so recently reminded of the very poor financial prospects of western planting. The pamphlets issued by or on behalf of the company and the sermons printed and circulated at its expense put the emphasis therefore on national objectives and national honour. Of course the clergy made much of the mission to the heathen and commended the enterprise as a pious work: since the company sought their help they took the opportunity to preach the furtherance of God's cause and the extension of the Church overseas. But the mission was invariably portrayed as a national undertaking for God and King. Robert Johnson's *Nova Britannia*, the first of these publications, set the tone:

So I wish and intreat all well affected subjects, some in their persons, others in their purses, cheerefully to adventure, and joyntly take in hand this high and acceptable worke, tending to advance and spread the kingdome of God, and the knowledge of the truth, among so many millions of men and women, Savage and blind, that never yet saw the true light shine before their eyes, to enlighten their minds and comfort their soules, as also for the honor of our King, and enlarging of his kingdome, and for preservation and defence of that small number of our friends and countrymen already planted, least for want of more supplies we become a scorne to the world subjecting our former adventures to apparent spoile and hazard, and our people (as a prey) to be sackt and puld out of possession.[41]

Johnson referred at some length to the Elizabethan ventures in glowing terms which suggest that a nationalistic legend was already in the making. He expressed envy of Spain's success in the New World and thundered against the Papists, but he also, like many another advocate of American plantation, acknowledged 'the blind diffidence of our English natures, which laugh to scorne the name of Virginia, and all other new projects, bee they never so probable'. Nothing is more remarkable (yet normally unremarked) in this literature than the common assumption that slanderers of Virginia and Doubting Thomases abounded, voicing objection after objection to which the writers felt obliged to reply – not always convincingly. Very often their

£53,000 for its third, and so forth. In 1613 Sir Thomas Smythe stated that £46,000 had been laid out for both the Virginia and the Somers Islands companies since the beginning, of which Virginia accounted for £36,000: Scott, *Joint-Stock Companies*, II, p. 253; Chaudhuri, *East India Company*, p. 209.

[41] R. Johnson, *Nova Britannia* (London, 1609), reprinted in Quinn, *New American World*, v, p. 236. The missionary aspect of the promotion literature is discussed in L. B. Wright, *Religion and Empire: the Alliance between Piety and Commerce in English Expansion, 1558– 1625* (Chapel Hill, 1943), and Parker, 'Religion and the Virginia colony'.

defence depended on moral condemnation of such backsliders as greedy, faint-hearted, unpatriotic, Papistical or simply evil.[42] Conversely their attack appealed to the nobler side of the Englishman's nature: 'This being the Religious and honourable intendment of the enterprise, what glory shall heereby redound unto God? What Honour to our Soveraigne? What comfort to those his Subjects, who shall be the meanes and furtherers of so happy a worke?'[43] Tract after tract made it clear that the English owed it to God, to the King and their own self-respect as a nation to undertake this task, which the promoters were at pains to justify. As Johnson in his specious way put it: 'And as for the supplanting of the savages, we have no such intent: Our intrusion into their possession shall tend to their great good, and no way to their hurt, unless as unbridled beastes, they procure it to themselves.' A certain impatience with the infidel is evident here and elsewhere in the Virginia propaganda. He would assuredly gain redemption, but might suffer in the process, whereas the bringer of the gospel would be rewarded on earth as in heaven: 'O all ye worthies, follow the ever-sounding trumpet of a blessed honour; let Religion be the first aim of your hopes. . . and other things shall be cast unto you: your names shall be registered to posterity with a glorious title; These are the men, whom God raised to augment the State of their countrey, and propagate the Gospell of Jesus Christ.'[44] The same hollow rhetoric embraced the common weal: the navy needed Virginia's timber; 'againe, whither shall wee transport our cloth, and how shall we sustaine our Artisans?'. As for the Council of Virginia, 'neither the imbracements of their wives, nor indulgence to their babes, nor the neglect of their domesticke fortunes, nor banishment from their native soile, nor any experimented dangers have broken their noble resolution'.

Difficult though it may be now to swallow such sanctimonious bombast, we can only assume that the leading preachers of the day knew well enough how to rouse the Christian conscience and national feeling of the Jacobean public. The campaign was apparently successful and in consequence the company was able to dispatch a fleet of nine vessels in June 1609 under the command of Sir George Somers, bearing a new lieutenant-governor for Virginia, Sir Thomas Gates, and about 500 planters. After seven weeks at sea the ships ran into a hurricane

---

[42] For example William Crashaw, *A sermon preached in London* (London, 1610): 'For how can they speake good things when themselves are evill?'

[43] Richard Crakanthorpe, *A sermon solemnizing the happie inauguration of our most gracious and religious soveraigne King James* (London, 1609), quoted in Parker, 'Religion and the Virginia colony'.

[44] *A true declaration of the estate of the colonie in Virginia* (London, 1610), reprinted in Quinn, *New American World*, v, p. 261.

and were scattered. With Somers, Gates and Newport aboard the flagship *Sea Adventure* sailed William Strachey, secretary to the colony, and it was his powerful description of the wreck of that ship on the Bermudas that inspired Shakespeare's *The Tempest*.[45] The company of 150 by good luck survived and with admirable resource salvaged what they needed from the wreck to winter over and build two pinnaces in which they made their way to Jamestown in May 1610. What they found there was the haggard and demoralized remnant of a settlement which had barely survived the most terrible of Virginia's disasters. The other ships of the 1609 fleet had arrived in August with some 350 colonists, many of them sick. Strife and disorder immediately became rampant, partly because the new contingent included 'many unruly gallants'[46] and partly because councillors formerly packed home by Smith now returned to challenge him. He was deposed and discipline collapsed. It would in any case have been difficult to assimilate so large a number of raw planters, whose health was already undermined, and probably the colony could not have escaped severe losses that winter. As it was, famine and pestilence destroyed the majority and left the rest too weak and wretched to maintain the site, which Gates and his people found in ruins. Since the newcomers had no supplies to spare, there was nothing for it but to abandon the colony. Early in June, therefore, Gates embarked the survivors and made down-river to head for Newfoundland and England. Before he reached the sea, however, he met three ships with fresh supplies and more colonists from England under the command of Lord De la Warr, with whom he thereupon turned back to re-establish the settlement.

Only this lucky encounter saved Virginia from total failure, for the promoters were then on the brink of giving up the enterprise altogether. De la Warr, who had been appointed governor in 1609, was to have followed Gates with a major expedition, but had been delayed by lack of funds because, having been rallied by political pressure to show their goodwill, many subscribers jibbed at putting down the cash they had promised. Renewed and desperate appeals proved necessary, and when De La Warr finally got away with his reduced force he had orders to report on the commercial prospects of the colony so that the company could decide whether or not to continue. Gates returned to England that summer (1610) and appears to have persuaded the company to persist, indicating forest products as the main hope, along

---

[45] L. B. Wright (ed.), *A Voyage to Virginia in 1609* (Charlottesville, 1964). *Purchas*, xix, 5–7: 'A true repertory of the wracke. . . by William Strachy, Esquire'.
[46] Smith, *Works*, i, p. 162.

with various other dubious possibilities. But the case for Virginia as a business venture had by now worn extremely thin. Once again the leaders of the company had to beat the patriotic drum to summon up subscriptions from old and new adventurers.[47] Once again they succeeded. In 1611 they were able to dispatch two relief expeditions to tide the colony over further difficulties and to begin its physical expansion under the draconian rule of Sir Thomas Dale. Dale imposed strict discipline upon the planters, who had to work set hours each day under supervision, to attend divine services twice daily and to suffer severe penalties not only for ordinary crime but for breaches of the Sabbath, evasion of labour duty and so forth.[48] Dale revealed much about his own attitude (shared by De la Warr, Gates and Strachey) as well as about the common colonists of those days in a letter to Salisbury:

Nor can I conceive how sutch people as we are inforced to bring over hither by peradventure, and gathering them up in sutch riotous, lasie and infected places can intertaine themselves with other thoughts or put on other behaviour then what accompanies sutch disordered persons, so prophane, so riotous, so full of Mutenie and treasonable Intendments, as I am well to witness in a parcell of 300 which I brought with me, of which well may I say not many give testimonie beside their names that they are Christians, besides of sutch diseased and crased bodies as the Sea hither and this Clime here but a little searching them, render them so unhable, fainte, and desperate of recoverie as of 300 not three score may be called forth or imploied upon any labour or service.[49]

Dale's methods kept the colony alive, but it did not begin to prosper until one of the settlers, John Rolfe, succeeded after some years of trial and error in producing a marketable tobacco. In 1616 the English in Virginia still numbered only 350 persons, among whom Dale discerned 'a generall desire in the best sort to returne for England'.[50] Gentlemen, including gentlemen of distinction such as George Sandys, poet and son of an archbishop, were prominent in the first generation of Virginians, but in the 1620s they virtually disappeared, to be replaced by a self-made plantocracy.[51] At home the company, though re-organized in 1612 by its third charter making the council responsible to the shareholders as in a normal joint-stock company,

---

[47] Craven, *Southern Colonies*, pp. 102–3.
[48] Dale's laws were published in 1611: W. Strachey, *For the colony in Virginia Britannia. Lawes divine, morall and martiall* (London, 1611).
[49] Dated 17 August 1611. Brown, *Genesis*, pp. 506–7.
[50] Craven, *Southern Colonies*, p. 116.
[51] B. Bailyn, 'Politics and social structure in Virginia', in Smith, *Seventeenth Century America*, pp. 90–115.

still found it difficult to raise funds even when the colony itself – from 1617 – was expanding and earning a living by 'smoke'. It therefore resorted to offering grants of land to individual adventurers as a form of dividend, which offers were increasingly taken up by groups of investors to create substantial private plantations. At the same time the company encouraged existing settlers to acquire a stake in the country by allowing them sizeable holdings at very low rents – a shilling a year for fifty acres – or rent free if they had settled at their own expense; and it encouraged emigration by land grants to anyone who paid his own (or another's) transportation costs. In 1618, under the influence of Sir Edwin Sandys, the leading critic of Smythe's conduct of the company's affairs, these and other economic reforms accompanied the partial suspension of Dale's laws and the institution of a general assembly at Jamestown with advisory and legislative powers. Sandys became Treasurer of the company early in 1619 and pushed on vigorously with a policy of expansion financed chiefly by lotteries. In the four years 1618 to 1621 over 4000 persons emigrated to Virginia, many of them at the company's expense, including batches of paupers, convicts and ragged children.[52]

It was an unhealthy boom, and shortlived. Disease destroyed most of the new emigrants, so that in March 1621 the population of Virginia remained at 843.[53] On the other hand the surviving settlers occupied more and more land, chiefly to produce tobacco, moving out from Jamestown to live cheek by jowl with the Indians. In spite of much talk in England about missionary work, little occurred in practice and the co-existence of the two peoples concealed a gradual growth of tension as the English progressively encroached on the living space and essential resources of the Indians. The marriage between John Rolfe and Powhatan's daughter Pocahontas in 1614 had certainly improved relations, but Powhatan died in 1618, to be succeeded by his less amenable brother, Opechancanough. Thereafter Indian tolerance of the intruders rapidly evaporated, though the latter failed to perceive what was happening and so exposed themselves to the surprise attack which came in March 1622. About 350 colonists were killed. This shock naturally precipitated a bitter war, in which the English desire for revenge was reinforced both by determination to destroy the Indian menace once and for all and by the prospect of an empty land ready for exploitation.

The so-called massacre of 1622 undoubtedly had a powerful effect upon English attitudes towards the natives, but it would be mistaken

[52] Craven, *Southern Colonies*, pp. 120–36.
[53] Andrews, *Colonial Period*, I, p. 136.

to suppose a complete transformation from general sweetness and light beforehand to blackest race hatred afterwards. It is also important to distinguish between the views of colonists, influenced more or less by observation and experience, and opinions expressed by clergymen and other publicists without knowledge of Virginia. Most of the surviving literature dealing with the Indians was in any case written to justify the enterprise, to defend the company's conduct of it and to attract support by representing the Indians as good or bad according to the situation and policy at the time of writing. Before 1622 the promotional literature sponsored by the Virginia Company gave a favourable impression of the Indians: rude and barbarous though they appeared, they were in fact loving and gentle, intelligent and industrious, apt for conversion to Christianity and harmonious collaboration with paternal Anglo-Saxon settlers. After 1622 the company's propagandists took the opposite line, describing them as bestial, cruel, treacherous and cowardly, and advocating the war of revenge and destruction which was in fact being pursued.[54] Such abstractions had little in common with the reactions of the pioneers themselves. The planters of this first generation were continually in contact with the Indians, trading, fighting, parleying and even working with them. Some, like John Smith and John Rolfe, knew them closely and others, like Henry Spelman and William White, lived with them. These and other early reporters – George Percy and William Strachey, for example – took a realistic interest in the Indians and described their way of life in considerable detail. The picture was not always flattering, but for the most part it showed respect for fact, recognizing the actuality of an elaborate culture. It contained little false sentiment and few illusions. Fear, distrust and hostility, present from the start, were continually reinforced by bitter experience. Edward Waterhouse, who wrote the official account of the 'barbarous massacre', strayed far from the truth in suggesting that the settlers were betrayed by their own faith in the Indians' goodwill and by 'their hopes of speedy winning the savages to civility and religion by kind usage and fair conversing among them'.[55] Of course after 1622 a hardening of hearts is much in evidence, but in 1623 and 1624 the Jamestown assembly still found it necessary to prohibit trade and intercourse with the natives, while Captain John Martin's arguments against genocide

[54] L. E. Pennington, 'The Amerindian in English promotional literature, 1575–1625', in Andrews, Canny and Hair, *Westward Enterprise*, pp. 175–94; H. C. Porter, *The Inconstant Savage: England and the North American Indian, 1500–1660* (London, 1979).

[55] Cited in Porter, *Inconstant Savage*, p. 462. The observant fairness of many early eyewitness reports is attested in Kupperman, *Settling with the Indians*.

suggest that some at least of the colonists recognized that the colony still needed the Indians.[56]

The Virginia Company, torn by faction and financially almost bankrupt, now approached its final collapse. In 1621 the king stopped the lotteries which had provided most of its funds recently. The industrial experiments in which Sandys and the leading group of the company invested great hopes as well as money were unsuccessful. In 1623 famine and disease once again afflicted the colony with heavy mortality. Sandys, moreover, had made enemies within the company by his hurtful attacks upon the former leaders and was disliked by some of the Privy Council as a noted trouble-maker in the House of Commons. Worst of all for Sandys and for the stability of the company was his quarrel with the earl of Warwick, who had backed him against Smythe in 1618–19. Powerful and shrewd, Warwick headed a group of adventurers deeply interested in commercial, privateering and colonizing projects, particularly at that time in the Bermudas. The Somers Islands Company, though closely associated with the Virginia Company, was incorporated as a separate body in 1615 and soon came to be dominated by Warwick and his cousin, Sir Nathaniel Rich. In 1622 and 1623 Warwick's supporters attacked Sandys for his conduct of the Virginia Company, while Sandys and his allies accused Warwick of aiming to take control of both organizations. The confused and disorderly disputes between factions in the Virginia Company's quarterly courts became a public scandal. Finally the Privy Council became directly concerned with the condition of both companies because they wished to arrange with the crown a contract giving them control of all tobacco imports, the crown being allotted its share of the proceeds. Sandys reached agreement with the government about this, but the Warwick party refused to accept it and took the matter back to the Privy Council, which in April 1623 cancelled the contract and ordered an official inquiry into the affairs of both companies and their plantations. At the same time the Privy Council took the management of the colony directly into its own hands.[57]

These measures, which American historians were wont to condemn as unjust interference actuated by hostility to Sandys and the 'democratic' as well as patriotic posture of the company, were in fact necessitated by the manifest failure of that body. During the subsequent inquiry the charges and counter-charges of the opposing parties exposed a hopeless state of discord, mismanagement and

[56] Porter, *Inconstant Savage*, pp. 470–73. See Porter, 'Reflections on ethnohistory', for a select bibliography of this voluminous *genre* of modern comment.

[57] Andrews, *Colonial Period*, I, pp. 150–73.

bankruptcy, which virtually forced the crown to dissolve the company in 1624. It thereby assumed direct rule, and in the following year Charles I's government clarified its position by proclaiming that no corporation could properly be entrusted with the running of that colony.[58] In practice, however, the crown did not effectively replace the company: it provided no funds for the settlement, nor did it attempt to organize private investment. In respect of policy it simply commissioned successive governors to rule with the advice of an appointed council in accordance with general instructions, leaving almost everything else to them. It was an arrangement the colonists themselves appear to have preferred to the restoration of company rule and it allowed them largely to make their own way so long as the weak and otherwise preoccupied régime of the early Stuarts lasted.[59]

Indeed in the later 1620s Virginia entered the long period of expansion and prosperity associated with the hey-day of the tobacco plantations. The Indians were in retreat and the tidewater was free for exploitation; the market for tobacco was expanding rapidly; the larger planters allied themselves to enterprising London merchants prepared to back them on easier terms; indentured servants and black slaves swelled the labour force. Virginia came through its anaemic and battered infancy to flourish in its youth.

Under the charter of 1606 the so-called Plymouth Company was quick to pursue Waymouth's promising lead and in August of that year dispatched Henry Challons in the *Richard* of Plymouth (55 tons) for 'Mawooshen' (the Penobscot Bay area) with twenty-nine Englishmen and two of Waymouth's Indians, intending to leave a party in the country. Challons – whether by choice or by mistake sailing too far south on the first leg – took the Caribbean route and was captured with ship and crew by a Spanish fleet in the Florida Strait. A few of the crew managed to get back to England via Bordeaux, but the rest were imprisoned in Spain.[60] The protests of the English ambassador, Sir Charles Cornwallis, met only with adamant assertions by the Spanish government that all such intruders were to be treated as enemies and that the English must abandon the Virginia enterprise altogether. Salisbury, himself a principal backer of that enterprise, was unable to take a strong line because James at this juncture was more eager than ever for friendship with Spain, while the Spaniards for their part

[58] Craven, *Southern Colonies*, p. 149. This declaration applied only to Virginia: the Bermuda Company was left to its own devices.
[59] Craven, *Southern Colonies*, pp. 150–54; W. F. Craven, *The Dissolution of the Virginia Company: the Failure of a Colonial Experiment* (Gloucester, Mass., 1964).
[60] *Purchas*, XIX, 284–96.

increased their pressure even to the point of sending some of the prisoners to the galleys. Although neither Salisbury nor James was prepared to sacrifice Virginia, until the international situation changed at the end of 1607 they seemed to equivocate, disavowing responsibility for the English initiatives in North America while in practice they encouraged them. Spain's treatment of these and other English prisoners at this time, however, had in the long run the opposite effect from that intended, for it aroused national anger and ensured that when the diplomatic advantage shifted from Spain to England in 1608 the crown at last swung firmly behind the Virginia Company.[61]

The total loss of its first expedition did nothing to help the prospects of the Plymouth Company, but the supporting vessel which followed Challons some two months later under Thomas Hanham and Martin Pring retrieved the setback by a highly successful and encouraging exploration of Mawooshen and its rivers, especially the Sagadahoc (modern Kennebec): 'Upon whose Relation the Lorde Chiefe Justice, and we all waxed so confident of the businesse, that the yeere following every man of any worth, formerly interested in it, was willing to joyne in the charge for the sending over a competent number of people to lay the ground of a hopefull Plantation.'[62] The Pophams were the backbone of this new venture. Sir John and his son Sir Francis shared the main burden with Sir Ferdinando Gorges, while George Popham took command of the expedition and of the colony as president thereof. Among a number of other West Country men interested Raleigh Gilbert (Sir Humphrey's son) stood prominent. Of the two ships – the *Gift* and the *Mary and John* – he commanded the latter and evidently had a considerable following among the hundred or so colonists. They reached the Sagadahoc in August 1607 and fortified themselves within the river, but when the *Mary and John* returned to Plymouth in December she carried the unpleasant news, immediately reported by Gorges to Salisbury, that 'the Childish factions, ignorant timerous, and ambitiouse persons, (for of that nature I founde the commposition to bee) hath bread an unstable resolution, and a generall confusion, in all theyr affayres'. Popham, though an honest and sensible man, was weak and Gilbert, whom Gorges described as 'humerouse, head stronge, and of small judgment and experiense' was 'desirous of supremasy', talking wildly about his father's patent.[63] When the *Gift* returned in February 1608 the news was worse. Factious squabbles had grown so far as to cause the

[61] Quinn, *New American World*, iii, pp. 403–19.
[62] *Purchas*, xix, 270; Quinn, *New American World*, iii, pp. 420–24.
[63] Quinn, *New American World*, iii, p. 438.

Indians, who had been remarkably friendly, to withhold their aid and trade and the venture was failing to realize the return of furs and other goods that had been expected. Sir John Popham, the moving spirit of the whole enterprise, had already died in the summer of 1607 and in the following February George Popham died in the colony, which was reduced to less than fifty by the return of some of the settlers and the death of others. It had been very cold, and although Gorges sent out fresh supplies in the summer the remainder had not the heart to face another winter, the more so because Raleigh Gilbert himself decided to go home on hearing that his elder brother Sir John was dead, leaving him the heir. Sagadahoc was thereupon abandoned and with that the Plymouth Company's attempt to colonize New England ended.[64]

But the coast of Maine was not abandoned. Its rich waters, frequented long before this by fishermen of various nationality, continued to attract the West Country men and in particular members of the Plymouth Company, notably Sir Francis Popham, who repeatedly sent ships there to fish and conduct trade with the Indians. In the years after 1608 fishing stages on the off-shore islands, at Pemaquid Point and elsewhere, became centres for the fur trade, where men got used to wintering, and as the coast became more familiar its reputation rose. The men of Virginia found it a welcome source of supply during their hardest times and in 1611 the earl of Southampton sent a ship to prospect the whole New England shore. Edward Harlow, the commander, drove off a French intruder and two years later Samuel Argall came north from the Chesapeake to attack the French settlements in Acadia, so preserving New England as an English sphere of influence. These developments had a significant effect upon the eventual choice of a New England site by the Pilgrim Fathers and gave them and later settlers there a better chance of survival.[65]

How the group of Separatists who later acquired that hallowed name came to make their way from Holland to Plymouth in Massachusetts is the theme of their leader William Bradford's epic, *Of Plimmoth Plantation*, which is the basis of all subsequent accounts.[66] The congregation had subsisted for some eleven or twelve years in Leyden, he tells us, before its leaders began to think seriously of moving the community as a whole to America. Then, in 1617, the drums of war were already sounding the approaching end of the Dutch-Spanish truce and in any

---

[64] Quinn, *New American World*, III, pp. 425–65.
[65] Andrews, *Colonial Period*, I, pp. 94–7; Quinn, *North America*, pp. 412–13.
[66] W. T. Davis (ed.), *Bradford's History of Plymouth Plantation* (New York, 1908). Some significant subsequent accounts and discussions are mentioned in J. E. Pomfret and F. M. Shumway, *Founding the American Colonies, 1583–1660* (New York, 1970), pp. 101–30. See also Andrews, *Colonial Period*, I, pp. 249–99.

case these displaced people, for the most part unskilled and illiterate, found themselves worn down by heavy labour and their children corrupted by temptation. 'The place they had thoughts on', he explains, 'was some of those vast and unpeopled countries of America, which are frutfull and fitt for habitation, being devoyd of civill inhabitants, wher ther are only salvage and brutish men, which range up and downe, litle otherwise then the wild beasts of the same.' Almost in the same breath, however, he spoke of 'propagating and advancing the gospell of the kingdom of Christ in those remote parts of the world' – a remarkable indication of the divided attitude of the godly towards those whose land they proposed to appropriate.[67] Having considered and rejected Guiana as a possible habitation, they opted for Virginia, and after prolonged negotiations reached agreement with a group of London merchants headed by one Thomas Weston to create a 'particular plantation' under a patent issued by the Virginia Company. That would mean operating as a private group of adventurers, with the merchants providing the funds and the Separatists the personnel, on land allotted by the company within its Jamestown jurisdiction. Both elements would have preferred New England: the Pilgrims, though emphatically loyal to their king and country, were not all happy at the prospect of dwelling in an Anglican colony, while the merchants looked askance at the parlous condition of the Virginia Company. The old Plymouth Company, moreover, was about to be replaced by a Council for New England, which body was expected to obtain a monopoly over the New England fisheries, giving any new colony there a commercial advantage of no small worth. Unfortunately the charter of the new council was delayed and the Pilgrims therefore failed to obtain a patent for settlement in New England, so that at the time of their departure they were ostensibly bound for Virginia, though they probably intended to establish themselves well north of Jamestown in the Hudson River.[68]

In the tortuous course of their dealings with Weston and his associates the Separatist leaders showed themselves by no means unworldly. Although they had little money to contribute, they bargained hard with the merchants and took great care to protect the

---

[67] Bradford, *Of Plimmoth Plantation*, pp. 46–7. The actual relations between the Plymouth colonists and the Indians are analysed in N. Salisbury, *Manitou and Providence: Indians, Europeans and the Making of New England, 1500–1643* (Oxford, 1982), pp. 110–47.

[68] Pomfret and Shumway, *American Colonies*, p. 113. Bradford says that at Cape Cod the *Mayflower* was bound for the Hudson: *Of Plimmoth Plantation*, p. 94, but Salisbury argues that before leaving England the Pilgrims already knew of and planned to use the depopulated site of Squanto's Patuxet – i.e. Plymouth: Salisbury, *Manitou and Providence*, p. 109.

interests of their flock as the prospective planters. Indeed it was precisely their corporate unity which enabled them to secure for the colonists better terms than those formerly available in Virginia. Each planter held a £10 share in the joint-stock simply by virtue of his labour contribution, which was equivalent to a merchant's single share. Planters who invested money or supplies would have merchant shares in addition to their basic holding. Furthermore the Pilgrims as a body stood equal to the body of merchants at home, whose advice they were not bound to accept. They chose their own governor before sailing, and on arriving at Cape Cod they concluded among themselves a formal compact to manage their own affairs, ensuring thus the supremacy of the close-knit Separatist group over the colony as a whole, which included a number of ordinary mortals.[69] It would be difficult to overstate the importance of the solidarity of this *élite* (using the term in its proper sense), which started on a footing altogether different from that of the Jamestown and Sagadahoc people and pursued the work of planting in quite a different spirit. Indeed the contrast was perhaps more important in the first ten years of hardship than it allegedly was in the long run of cultural evolution.

Of the 101 passengers who sailed in the *Mayflower* (180 tons) only thirty-five were from Leyden and the rest from London and Southampton. The latter included fourteen servants and artisans hired for wages as well as many people related to those from Leyden. Eighteen wives and thirty-one children accounted for half the complement and some planters left wives or children or both behind, 'who came afterwards'.[70] The voyage was long and hard, and rounding Cape Cod from the north proved so dangerous that they decided to seek safety in that bay and finally found Plymouth harbour. Here they settled, and as Bradford relates:

in 2. or 3. moneths time halfe of their company dyed, espetialy in Jan: and February, being the depth of winter, and wanting houses and other comforts; being infected with the scurvie and other diseases, which this long vioage and their inacomodate condition had brought upon them.[71]

A less well-disciplined community might have been unable to pull through, but the Pilgrims also owed an immense debt to the Indians from several tribes who occupied the area corresponding to the coastal part of modern Massachusetts. To one of these, the Patuxet, belonged a certain Squanto, who contacted the English in March 1621. He had

[69] Andrews, *Colonial Period*, I, pp. 264–6, 290–94.
[70] Bradford, *Of Plimmoth Plantation*, pp. 407–9.
[71] Bradford, *Of Plimmoth Plantation*, p. 108.

been kidnapped in 1615 and had somehow found his way to England, where he met Gorges and by him was sent back to Cape Cod. On his return Squanto found that his own tribe had been wiped out in the catastrophic pandemic – usually described as 'the plague' – which reduced the Massachusett to a fraction of their former numbers in the years 1616–18. It was a widowed land to which the Pilgrims came in 1620 and they echoed to each other that Christian sentiment uttered by Captain John Smith: 'that God had laid this country open for us'.[72] In fact the country had been laid waste by the Europeans who brought the disease and the result was that the local people, fearful of their now greatly superior neighbours and unable to compete with them in trade, welcomed the newcomers and readily concluded peace and friendship with them through the mediation of Squanto, whom Bradford described as 'a spetiall instrument sent of God'. Indeed he 'directed them how to set their corne, wher to take fish, and to procure other comodities, and was also their pilott to bring them to unknowne places for their profitt, and never left them till he dyed'.[73] With these advantages the little colony survived. Down to 1630 it grew slowly, reaching a population of barely 300, and evolved from a collective community dependent on the Indians to a family-based society providing for its own subsistence by corn-growing and livestock, by fishing and by trade in furs, ironware and wampum beads. Meanwhile the London adventurers, losing their money and their patience with the unco-operative Pilgrims, defected and Plymouth became a self-governing colony under the nominal rule of the Council for New England. The real ruler was Bradford, who became governor by vote of the congregation in 1621 and kept that office with only a few breaks until 1656, holding power by, with and for the members of the church.[74]

The unique character of the Plymouth colony accounts for its success at a time when many other attempts to settle New England proved abortive. It was not until 1629 that the Massachusetts Bay Company, a far more powerful and wealthy organization, finally emerged and created a settlement comparable in strength to that of the Pilgrims. In the meantime the existence of a colony served to attract interest to the area, as did also the continuing development of fishing. Gorges' Council for New England, chartered in 1621, consisted of courtiers and officials and was essentially a land company interested in apportioning territory on quasi-feudal terms to subordinate groups. Under its

[72] Smith, *Works*, II, p. 747. On the distribution of the Indians, Squanto and the plague see Salisbury, *Manitou and Providence*, pp. 15, 21, 101–9.
[73] Bradford, *Of Plimmoth Plantation*, p. 111.
[74] Andrews, *Colonial Period*, I, pp. 279–99.

patents several unsuccessful colonizing ventures occurred, including one in 1623–4 mounted by Gorges himself and led by his son Robert.[75] The most famous of these efforts, however, was the shortlived settlement called Ma-re Mount run by Thomas Morton, a gentleman of whose views and conduct Bradford vehemently disapproved. Morton appears to have taken over the remnant of a plantation begun in 1625 at Quincy and in 1628, according to Bradford, 'became lord of misrule, and maintained (as it were) a schoole of Athisme', presiding over licentious and profane bacchanalia in which the Indians freely joined. Bradford also accused him of selling guns to the Indians and soon managed to have him and his servants deported to England.[76] There is good reason to believe, however, that Bradford's charges were grossly exaggerated and that he had other reasons for wishing to get rid of Morton. The latter was certainly no atheist and his own account suggests that what he called his 'revels' were by no means the drunken orgies Bradford portrayed. Nor is it likely that he sold any considerable number of guns to the Indians. On the other hand his presence seemed to threaten the Pilgrims, for his free and easy ways with the Indians not only deprived them of trade but challenged their conception of the proper relationship between colonists and natives. Morton's tolerance and regard for the Indians did not carry far, for he believed they would have to make way for European colonization and the Christian religion, but the episode demonstrates the fact that not all English colonizers were domineering bigots.[77]

The failure of Morton, Gorges and other New England venturers did not seriously interrupt the steady growth of English activity on the Massachusetts coast in the 1620s. Competition in the fishery mounted, not only between fishermen but also between these and groups interested in settlement. All alike were concerned with rights ashore as well as off shore, since both were necessary for fishing and a shore base gave access to the fur trade. The charter of the Council for New England gave it a monopoly of all trade and fishing within the land and waters between latitudes 40° and 48° N. Although this monopoly was challenged and somewhat unreal in practice, the council could issue licences and in 1622 did so to Richard Bushrod, a Dorchester merchant, and his associates, for a venture of fishing and exploration. This voyage led to the formation in 1624 of the Dorchester Company, consisting of 119 West Country gentry and others as well as merchants, led by the Reverend John White of Dorchester, the object of which

[75] Andrews, *Colonial Period*, I, pp. 320–43.
[76] Bradford, *Of Plimmoth Plantation*, pp. 236–42.
[77] Salisbury, *Manitou and Providence*, pp. 154–62.

enterprise was to create a fishing plantation at Cape Ann in the north of Massachusetts and to preach the Gospel among the heathen and the fishermen of England. Bradford's men, who had a fishing stage at Cape Ann, tried to prevent the Dorchester people establishing themselves there, and the Separatists and the Anglican newcomers nearly came to blows, but the latter eventually were allowed to proceed. The Cape Ann colony, however, was yet another failure and what was left of it moved south in 1627 to struggle on at the place which later became Beverly. It was at this stage that White and the treasurer of the Dorchester Company, John Humfry, sought wider and more powerful support to form the New England Company, which combined the resources of certain gentlemen and merchants of Devon and Dorset with those of some wealthy Londoners, notably Samuel Whetcome, Mathew Cradock, Sir Richard Saltonstall and John Venn. The Puritan influence in the new organization was strong, if not overwhelming.[78]

In 1628 this company sent out a party of colonists under John Endecott, who was related to Cradock by marriage, to take over the remnant of the Dorchester colony and prepare the way for new settlers. In the following year the New England Company was transformed by royal charter into the Massachusetts Bay Company, which had still wider and more powerful support, especially from the earl of Warwick, Lord Saye and Sele and Nathaniel Rich, who were political patrons of the Puritan cause, and from London merchants with Puritan sympathies or a taste for commercial adventure. The Massachusetts Bay Company was a trading organization designed to make a profit out of settling Massachusetts and exploiting its natural wealth. The 110 shareholders included conforming members of the Church of England as well as radical Puritans and although religious objectives were acknowledged as important from the start, it was not formed for the purpose of creating a new church in the New World in defiance of Church and King at home. This, however, was what happened under the driving pressure of John Winthrop and the radical Puritans, who conspired to take over the company and transferred its seat to New England. By this revolutionary action they set the stage for the great Puritan migration which followed in the 1630s and gave the Bay Colony its peculiar character.[79]

The conditions which affected Newfoundland enterprise in the early seventeenth century were in certain major respects different from those we have seen at work in Virginia and New England. The island

[78] Andrews, *Colonial Period*, I, pp. 344–60.
[79] Andrews, *Colonial Period*, I, pp. 361–99.

had long been familiar to generations of fishermen from Portugal, Spain, France and England. The fishery was important to substantial merchant groups of all these nations and it served a growing market in southern Europe. It was strategically significant as a victualling base for shipping and because it employed ships and seamen – the raw material of naval power – on a large scale. For all these reasons national control over this international field of enterprise was a prize much to be coveted. It was, however, the English who coveted it most: not English fishermen, who were content to work amicably with the rest as was customary, but English colonial projectors, inspired by anti-Iberian nationalism and hopes of a lucrative monopoly of the fishery, precious metals, a northwest passage and a maritime base for raids upon Spain's treasure fleets and colonies. Denying the Banks to Spain and monopolizing them for England would change the naval balance of power and give a welcome boost to the West Country fishing ports. The idea of colonizing the island in order to control the fishery appealed particularly to the English not only for such nationalistic, commercial and predatory reasons, but also because no other nation was so closely identified with the shore fishery. Most of the others salted their catch at the Banks and made little use of the shore except for watering or repairs, but the English worked from the shore in small boats and dried the cod on land, economizing on salt and leaving their gear, including huts, stages, flakes and boats, over from season to season. Thus a good deal of reasoning (well expressed by Anthony Parkhurst, the leading Elizabethan specialist on Newfoundland) lay behind the somewhat impulsive annexation of the island by Sir Humphrey Gilbert on the queen's behalf in 1583.[80]

Bernard Drake's raid on the Iberian fishing fleet in 1585 was an indication of the strategic interest in Newfoundland, but nothing was done to follow it up during the war, though Edward Hayes kept alive the idea of an English settlement by his writings.[81] It was the Bristol merchant John Guy who took the first practical steps towards colonizing the island. After visiting it in 1608 he gathered support from merchants of Bristol and London and from courtiers and gentlemen to form the Newfoundland Company, which was chartered in 1610. The bulk of the capital came from the Londoners, notably John and Humphrey Slany, Spanish traders with shipowning and other overseas interests, and Ralph and William Freeman, who were leading men

---

[80] G. T. Cell, *Newfoundland Discovered: English Attempts at Colonisation, 1610–1630* (London, 1982), pp. 1–3. Parkhurst's letters are in *PN*, VIII, 9–16, and Taylor, *Writings of the Hakluyts*, pp. 123–34.
[81] Quinn, *England and the Discovery of America*, pp. 227–45.

in the City, cloth exporters on a large scale, dominant in northern whaling, active in the East India, Virginia and Northwest Passage Companies: Ralph Freeman was unquestionably the greatest Muscovy merchant of his day. Prominent men at court also took part: Henry Howard, earl of Northampton, Sir Francis Bacon, Sir John Dodderidge and Sir Walter Cope (the last two had been members of the King's Council of Virginia in 1606) among others. Sir Percival Willoughby of Wollaton, Nottinghamshire, noted for his ambitious and unsuccessful speculations, was the most committed of the gentleman subscribers. The company had a council of twelve and forty-eight shareholders, but its starting capital was small – probably not much over £1200.[82] The promoters' motives were as usual mixed. Some, like Willoughby, hoped to find mineral wealth and there was much talk about forest products and other commodities: Parkhurst, Hayes and Guy had been at pains to argue, as others would in their turn, that Newfoundland was not really cold and barren. But the main purpose of the company was undoubtedly to develop a hold on the fishery.

Unfortunately for the colonial projectors, the vested interest of English merchants and fishermen in the Newfoundland fishery was by this time too powerful to be ignored. Some 200 ships annually used that trade, which was closely integrated with the Iberian and Mediterranean trades and had become a major source of the prosperity of the West Country. Any attempt to create a monopoly was bound to run up against this formidable opposition, which could and did not only raise the popular cry against monopoly but also present itself as defending a valuable national asset. So strong was the case for the *status quo* that the projectors carefully avoided any suggestion of interference and placed great emphasis in the charter upon their determination to leave the fishery open to all and sundry.[83] Apart from the practical problems of colonizing Newfoundland, which proved difficult enough, these and later promoters of settlement had always the special problem of justifying their initiative in the face of well-grounded suspicions and powerful arguments. The result was that Newfoundland colonial projectors produced an extraordinary quantity of tedious literature attempting to show that the settlement of the island would serve the national interest. The authors of these indigestible tracts, like Sir William Vaughan and Richard Whitbourne, were enthusiasts to whom any argument in favour of their cause doubtless appeared unanswerable, but there is no reason to suppose either that their arguments were

---

[82] Cell, *English Enterprise*, pp. 53–61; Quinn, *New American World*, IV, pp. 131–43.
[83] Cell, *English Enterprise*, pp. 55–7; Quinn, *New American World*, IV, pp. 131–9.

widely accepted or that they represented the actual motives of men like
the Freemans, the Slanys and Willoughby.[84]

John Guy set out in July 1610 with thirty-nine colonists to found his
colony in Conception Bay on the Avalon Peninsula, where English
fishing was already heavily concentrated and where the native population of Beothuk was very small. Profiting by the mistakes of the
Virginia Company, of which his promoters were clearly aware, and by
relatively mild weather, Guy made a promising start at Cupids Cove,
but in 1612 the plunder of the fishery by Peter Easton and his pirates
stopped the intended development of the colony, which then began to
decline as the initial hopes of furs, crops, metals and other products
faded and even the returns in fish proved disappointing. In 1613 Guy
went home, never to return. His successor Captain John Mason, a
naval man, held office from 1615 to 1621, during which time pirate
raids continued and disputes between the colonists and the fishermen
worsened. Mason concentrated on mapping the coasts of the island
and published *A briefe discourse of the New-found-land* (Edinburgh, 1620),
but the company's colony failed to recover. By 1630 it had withered to a
handful of settlers and two years later the death of the company's
treasurer, John Slany, apparently extinguished its last spark of life.[85]

Meanwhile other attempts at settlement had occurred. In 1616 in
order to raise funds and avoid a possible revocation of its charter under
pressure from the hostile fishing interest, the company had begun to
make grants of land to individuals or groups who would undertake to
promote settlement. At this time John Guy quarrelled with Slany and
led the Bristol contingent out of the company, after which the Bristol
Society of Merchants Adventurers promoted its own colony, on terms
arranged with the Newfoundland Company, at Harbour Grace on
Conception Bay. Although little is known of its history, this settlement
appears to have prospered, probably because the Bristol men concentrated on the fishery, a business they knew how to manage in
conjunction with their southward trades.[86] Sir William Vaughan also
took advantage of the company's arrangements to acquire a large tract
of land in the south of the Avalon Peninsula and sent out a group of
Welsh settlers in 1617. This Carmarthenshire gentleman pictured
Newfoundland in his voluminous and faintly absurd poetic works as
'our *Colchos*, where the *Golden Fleece* flourishethe on the backes of

---

[84] On Vaughan, Whitbourne and other propagandists see Cell, *Newfoundland Discovered*,
passim.

[85] Cell, *English Enterprise*, pp. 61–79.

[86] Cell, *English Enterprise*, pp. 87–8. Robert Hayman, its first governor, immortalized the
Bristol colony in his doggerel *Quodlibets, Lately Come Over from New Britaniola, Old Newfoundland* (1628), of which the less quoted the better.

Neptunes sheepe, continually to be shorne. . . . *Great Britaines Indies*, never to be exhausted dry', a new and more prosperous Wales beyond the ocean.[87] Richard Whitbourne, a sea captain long acquainted with the Newfoundland trade and by far the most knowledgeable and persuasive of the island's propagandists, went out as Vaughan's governor in 1618, but he found the settlers in poor shape. Indeed they were, like so many of the first generation of English planters in North America, ill-fitted for the pioneering life. Whitbourne sent most of them home and before long returned himself, discouraged by the experience and leaving but six of Vaughan's men to carry on as best they could at Renews. Whitbourne then acquired a patron in the person of Henry Cary, Lord Falkland, lord deputy of Ireland, who in 1620 obtained a huge slice of the island from the company and took over at the same time a narrow band of Vaughan's territory, where he began a colony in 1623. His aim was to create a feudal estate populated by emigrants from Ireland. In spite of having Whitbourne's practical experience and wise advice, however, the experiment did not progress, and after Whitbourne broke with Falkland in 1626 it appears to have failed.[88]

Perhaps the most interesting of the various Newfoundland projects of this period was that promoted by Sir George Calvert, who was secretary of state from 1619 to 1625, when he resigned, declared himself a Catholic and was created Lord Baltimore. Most famous as the founder of Maryland as a refuge for Catholics, he was already interested in planting in Ireland, where he was closely associated with Falkland, and even more than Falkland he was a colonial projector of the old-fashioned sort, concerned with creating a great feudal estate. His colonial ideas dovetailed with his socially conservative outlook, his Catholicism and his pro-Spanish political stance. He acquired land in Newfoundland from Vaughan in 1620 and began a colony at Ferryland the following year, though whether he intended it as a Catholic refuge from the start is doubtful. Under Captain Edward Winne, Ferryland fared well for a year or two, but after 1622 it failed to grow. From 1625 Baltimore planned to open the settlement to Catholics and to instal Carmelite priests and finally, after a preliminary visit, he went out himself in 1628 'to builde and sett, and sowe', accompanied by his wife, most of his children, a priest and about forty settlers. This was a time of war, however, and Baltimore found himself fully engaged in organizing the defence of the fishery against the French. Before winter set in he had already turned his thoughts southwards and applied to

[87] Cell, *English Enterprise*, p. 83.
[88] Cell, *English Enterprise*, pp. 88–91.

King Charles for land in Virginia. The experience of the winter of 1628–9 in Ferryland, where he and his people suffered severely from cold and scurvy, precipitated his removal to Jamestown and in 1632 the Maryland charter was granted. Some of the Ferryland settlers stayed on and the Calvert family retained an interest in the island, but Baltimore's attempt to colonize Newfoundland was defeated.[89]

The record of English colonial achievement in North America down to 1630 is far from impressive. Only at great cost in human and financial terms was Virginia, after two decades of sustained muddle, established. In New England, where conditions were in certain respects easier, the only successful group among many was that of the Pilgrim Fathers and in Newfoundland the story was again one of repeated failure, the only significant exception being the Bristol colony, which was not much more than a fishing station. This poor performance cannot be attributed to Indian resistance. In Virginia it was the presence of the Indians and their surplus food which enabled the colonists to survive, nor did the natives turn decisively against the intruders until 1622. In Massachusetts the Indians were already sadly wasted by disease and they with other New England tribes provided by way of trade the main livelihood of the planters. In Newfoundland the Indians were too few to affect the fortunes of the abortive colonies.

What, then, was wrong? In the first place the settlers were wrong: the wrong people. As pioneers most of them were useless. The good husbandmen were successful enough in England and so were the good artisans. Most of the gentlemen who opted to emigrate were, according to Smith, Gorges and other authorities, idle, feckless and quarrelsome gallants like Raleigh Gilbert. Nearly all, irrespective of class, were debilitated by bad diet, overcrowding and disease on the voyage and in the early months of settlement. But much more important than all these faults was their inability to adapt, to learn how to survive, to live off the country, to cope with a hostile environment. And they found it so hard to adapt because they began with false ideas both about America itself and about the kind of life they could lead there. Such false ideas were in part the results of deliberately deceptive promotional propaganda, much of it naïve and pernicious nonsense, and in part the natural assumptions of men who had almost no means of imagining a world different from their own. To minds filled with these misconceptions the grim reality came as a demoralizing shock, from which many of them never recovered, while others came voluntarily or were sent home as soon as possible, there to denounce the

[89] Cell, *English Enterprise*, pp. 92–5.

projectors and all their works: hence the 'slanders' so often mentioned by the apologists.

But the poor devils who went out to die like flies were less to blame than those who so blithely dispatched them: merchants who aspired to run a colony like a trading company, thinking in terms of such commodities as they normally acquired from Russia or from Spain and expecting the colonists to buckle to and produce them in order to show a profit; or noble and gentle courtiers desirous of building landed estates on a scale more ambitious than that of the Irish plantations, tenanted by their unfortunate, Welsh, Irish or English dependants. Again the ideas were false, based on inappropriate preconceptions of North America and of colonization as a process. In a sense the most determined promoters, such as Sir Edwin Sandys, were the worst because they persisted so energetically with unworkable projects. The collapse of the Virginia Company in 1624 did Virginia itself more good than anything the company had done since its foundation. It took a long time for experience to modify the original motives and images and bring them nearer to reality, and the process was both costly and painful. Great expectations were reduced to modest hopes and colonization became less and less a means to definite ends, more and more an end in itself.

The Stuart kings did little to help: so much is obvious from the foregoing. Virginia, which was undertaken in the king's name, got rather erratic support from behind; the Pilgrims, for all their loyalty, could count at best on a blind eye turned grudgingly in their direction; and the Bay Colony was openly a colony of the opposition. The monarchy and North America were like oil and water from the start. Yet it may be doubted whether the colonies would have done any better with more positive royal participation, bearing in mind the corruption and mismanagement displayed in the Cadiz expedition of 1625 and in similar enterprises of the previous Anglo-Spanish war. It is conceivable that the crown's contribution would have consisted in the provision of thousands of sickly convicts and half-starved vagrants victualled by Bagg, Trevor and their ilk and led by swaggering army captains interested chiefly in their own pockets. There is no reason to suppose that a Jacobean expedition for the conquest of Virginia or New England would have fared any better than Cromwell's disastrous assault on the West Indies in 1655. As it was, the colonial projectors could not reasonably blame their failures upon royal interference. For the most part they obtained the charters and the licences they requested and were left to do their usually honourable if frequently inglorious best.

In the end it was neither projectors nor promoters nor kings nor courtiers nor clergy but the colonists themselves who found ways to make a living in this continent. They did so by painful trial and error, by dogged persistence and with the aid of some improvement in the economic climate from the close of the 1620s, that dismal decade. By that time Virginia was on the road to fortune and New England was beginning its vigorous growth.

15

North and Northwest
1602–32

In the early seventeenth century the European invasion of the North got under way in earnest. As men probed north for passages from the Atlantic to the Pacific they found waters rich in whale, the promise of which helped explorers to gain support for their projects. At the same time whaling gave seamen greater familiarity with the Arctic, its geography and perils, and so assisted the work of discovery. English sailors were much to the fore in both aspects of this northern movement and behind them London merchants were the chief promoters, above all some leading members of the Muscovy and East India companies. It would be difficult to exaggerate the danger and hardship faced by this generation of explorers from George Waymouth to Luke Foxe and Thomas James, just as it is easy to understate their achievement. The opening and mapping of Hudson Bay and Baffin Bay with vessels puny and defective, crews unreliable and mutinous, victuals scant and poor, and navigation halfway between a medieval craft and a modern science must stand among the greatest feats of seamanship in any age, made possible only by the courage of the explorers and their collaboration with the best scientists of their time.[1]

The main growth-point of whaling was Spitzbergen, discovered by Willem Barentszoon in his third voyage to the northeast in 1596. By this time English and Dutch were already fishing north from Vardø, Kola and Pechenga in Finnmark, and in 1603 Stephen Bennet, set forth by the great Muscovy merchant Francis Cherry, put north from that coast to find Bear Island (Björnöya) in 74°. He named it Cherry Island and regularly thenceforth Cherry's ships (and some interlopers from Hull and elsewhere) hunted the walrus there, killing thousands each year. Finally in 1609 the Muscovy Company formally took possession of the island.[2] Meanwhile in 1607 Henry Hudson, attempting on behalf of the

[1] Waters, *Art of Navigation*, pp. 257–83.
[2] *Purchas*, XIII, 265–93.

Muscovy Company to reach the South Sea by way of the North Pole, sighted the western shores of Spitzbergen between 76° and 81°N. and reported the presence of numerous whale and walrus.[3] The company's next move was to send Jonas Poole, one of their most experienced masters in the Cherry Island trade, 'for a further discoverie to be made towards the North-Pole, for the likelihood of a Trade or a passage that way' in 1610.[4] This expedition, which was probably intended to combine walrus-hunting with the approach to the Pole, turned into a valuable reconnaissance of Spitzbergen and was followed in 1611 by the dispatch of two company ships – one under Poole for piloting and further discovery, the other for whaling with Bennet as master and Thomas Edge as factor. With the latter sailed six men of St Jean de Luz, Biscayners without whom neither the English nor the Dutch could undertake whaling at this stage. Edge carried authority from the Privy Council to warn off interlopers in defence of the company's charter.[5]

This voyage was not a success, for Edge's ship was cast away and he and his men owed their survival to the help of a Hull interloper called Thomas Marmaduke, but the company was not to be deterred by such a reverse, for the wealth of Spitzbergen was now no secret and the boom was on. In 1612 a Dutch ship, a Spaniard from San Sebastián and two English interlopers joined the company's two ships there, and the following year at least seven came from the Netherlands, eight from San Sebastián, several from France and two from Dunkirk, while the Muscovy Company, determined to secure a monopoly, obtained a royal charter authorizing them to exclude all rivals, alien or English, and fitted out a fleet of seven ships led by the *Tiger*, a small man-of-war (260 tons) carrying 21 guns. They thus forced their competitors to submit or leave the area.[6] This, however, was by no means the end of the matter. In 1614 the Dutch were back in strength and soon, united under the *Noordsche Compagnie*, they outnumbered the English and were able to rebuff the pretensions of the Muscovy men with superior force, leaving them in their turn aggrieved and protesting. In the late 1620s the Dutch were sending about 4000 tons of shipping a year to Spitzbergen, comprising some twenty or more vessels, and the English held a comparable share of the fishery, in which the Danes and Basques also took part. Thus the Muscovy Company failed to impose a monopoly and furthermore was unable to exclude English interlopers, especially the men of Hull who supplied the soapers of York with train-oil. In fact its efforts to suppress its English competitors only led to

---

[3] *Purchas*, XIII, 294–313.   [4] *Purchas*, XIV, 1–23.   [5] *Purchas*, XIV, 24–33.
[6] W. M. Conway (ed.), *Early Dutch and English Voyages to Spitzbergen* (London, 1904), pp. 3–38. An account of this voyage was written by William Baffin: *Purchas*, XIV, 47–60.

destructive reprisals and counter-reprisals in the fishery and weakened English whaling there, which declined and finally petered out in the 1650s.[7]

The search for a northwest passage to Cathay was resumed in 1602 by George Waymouth under the auspices of the East India Company. The company had already dispatched Lancaster by the Cape route to the Indian Ocean, but the directors and others were worried (rightly, as time would show) by the length and difficulty of that route and by indications of official and public 'mislike of the transportacion of treasure out of the land'. A shorter route was much to be desired and one which also made it possible to export cloth instead of treasure would be ideal, since it would render the East India trade not only more profitable but more acceptable *pro bono publico*. The proposed northwest route, they hoped, would serve both purposes and they were all the more receptive to Waymouth's approach for fear 'that private men shall deale therein, geaving them the benefite of the said discovery'.[8] The Muscovy Company of course objected to such an infringement of its monopoly rights, but the East India Company appealed successfully to the Privy Council and the Muscovy men were overruled. In April 1602 the company entered into a formal agreement with Waymouth to finance a voyage northwest in the *Discovery*, a flyboat of 70 tons and the *Godspeed* (60 tons), also a flyboat.[9] Although Waymouth was unable to advance substantially upon the achievements of earlier explorers, his voyage was important. He evidently hoped to find a passage between 57° and 64° and finally in 61°40' located what he called an inlet, 'where the great Current setteth to the West', but by this time his crew, egged on by that 'great travailer and learned Minister one Master John Cartwright', had taken it upon themselves to decide the course of the voyage and Waymouth was obliged to return before he could probe very far into what was probably Hudson Strait.[10]

He had done enough, however, to point the way. The company was sufficiently encouraged by his report to plan a further expedition, but when a dispute arose from the captain's financial claims in connection

[7] Conway, *Spitzbergen*, pp. 39–65, 73, 173–5. Thomas Edge wrote a survey of these developments from an English point of view, including an account of whaling methods and a description of 'Greenland' (as the English then called Spitzbergen) by Robert Fotherby: *Purchas*, xiii, 4–34.

[8] Stevens, *Dawn*, pp. 182, 198–9.

[9] Stevens, *Dawn*, pp. 211–14.

[10] *Purchas*, xiv, 306–18. Foxe's conclusion was that 'these two, Davis and he, did, I conceive, light Hudson into his Straights': Christy, *Voyages of Foxe and James*, pp. 80–85. John Cartwright, *The Preachers Travels* (London, 1611), is an account of his journey through Turkey and Persia, begun in 1599: see Chew, *Crescent and Rose*, pp. 49–51, etc.

with the first venture they dropped the matter.[11] The incentives to further effort nevertheless persisted and Waymouth's report gave grounds for optimism. Consequently in 1606 a syndicate composed of the East India and Muscovy companies calling itself the Society of English Merchants for the Discovery of New Trades dispatched one John Knight in a bark of 40 tons for the Labrador coast.[12] Knight had accompanied James Hall the previous year on the first of a series of three voyages (1605–7) to Greenland in the king of Denmark's service, the first two of which notably advanced knowledge of the western coast.[13] Knight's venture for the English syndicate was, however, a failure. With three of his companions he was apparently killed by Eskimo on the Labrador coast, where he had been driven aground by ice and storm and was salvaging what he could from his badly damaged ship. The survivors were brought before the Admiralty Court on suspicion of mutiny or desertion, but the story they told was convincing enough to clear them.

This renewed and mounting effort to penetrate the northern seas culminated in the work of Henry Hudson. Although we know little or nothing of Hudson's background and early life (apart from the fact that he had a son old enough to sail with him in 1607 but still a boy at that time), even the defective and obscure records of his four known voyages sufficiently indicate in him that quality to be found in most of the great explorers – an obsession with the task of discovery. In the first of these expeditions he pursued Robert Thorne's concept of a polar route to the Orient, sailing for the Muscovy Company in 1607 with ten men apart from himself and the boy. His course took them north up the eastern shore of Greenland to about 73° and thence northeast and along the ice barrier to reach the western side of Spitzbergen in 77° or thereabouts. He then explored the northern coast of Spitzbergen and returned with the conviction that no passage was possible that way.[14] The negative result of this voyage has led to a certain neglect of its geographical importance and of its nautical interest as a feat of intrepid seamanship, related albeit in the most laconic terms. In the following year the Muscovy Company again employed Hudson, this time in search of a passage northeast between Spitzbergen and Novaya

[11] Stevens, *Dawn*, pp. xxi, 233–40.

[12] *Purchas*, xiv, 353–65 (Knight's own journal, completed by one of his company); Quinn, *New American World*, iv, pp. 269–76, where additional material from the Admiralty Court appears.

[13] *Purchas*, xiii, 318–53; C. C. A. Gosch (ed.), *The Danish Arctic Expeditions, 1605–1620* (2 vols., London, 1897), i, *passim*. Hall was almost certainly a native of Hull.

[14] *Purchas*, xiii, 294–313. This journal was evidently written up by one of the crew from Hudson's notes: G. M. Asher (ed.), *Henry Hudson the Navigator* (London, 1860), pp. v–vii, clxxxiv–cxc, 1–22.

Zemlya, hoping to round the latter leaving it to starboard, and so to follow through Barentszoon's efforts rather than thrust once more past Vaygach Island into the ice of the Kara Sea in the wake of earlier English pioneers. Ice, however, prevented him from reaching as far as his Dutch predecessor had done and he therefore turned south to investigate a possible strait through the island and, failing to penetrate there, seriously considered putting west past Greenland

to make triall of that place called Lumleys Inlet, and the furious over-fall by Captayne Davis, hoping to run into it an hundred leagues, and to returne as God should enable mee.[15]

He thus had clear in his mind already the purpose of his final venture, and it seems likely that he was only deterred from undertaking it there and then by some excusable resistance on the part of his men, for they took the trouble, as he relates, to secure from him a signed certificate 'of my free and willing returne, without perswasion or force of any one or more of them'. Before embarking on this discovery, however, Hudson made a voyage for the Dutch East India Company, who summoned him, on the recommendation of Emanuel Van Meteren, to discuss another northeast passage search, for which he duly set forth in the *Halve Maen* from Amsterdam in the spring of 1609, apparently making for Novaya Zemlya. But either before or after reaching it, in circumstances that are shrouded in mystery, he turned back, probably because the crew, consisting of Dutch and English sailors, refused to go further in that direction. Hudson thereupon persuaded them to make for the coast of America in 40°, where his friend Captain John Smith had informed him of 'a sea leading into the western ocean' to the north of Virginia.[16] The result of this extraordinary change of course was the discovery of New York harbour and the Hudson River in September 1609, after which Hudson sailed for England.

By 1610 Hudson was recognized as an explorer of outstanding experience and authority. He had certainly exchanged thoughts with Peter Plancius, the leading geographer and adviser of the VOC, and very possibly with cartographers such as Jodocus Hondius and Hessel Gerritsz, who was to convey Hudson's last achievement to the world. In 1609 he was negotiating with Isaac le Maire and French officials to undertake a passage search for Henry IV.[17] But he was also well known

---

[15] *Purchas*, XIII, p. 332, from Hudson's journal, pp. 313–32. Purchas also possessed but failed to print a journal of this voyage by Robert Juet.

[16] Asher, *Hudson*, p. 148. Asher also gives Robert Juet's journal (pp. 45–93, from *Purchas*, XIII, 333–74) and translated Dutch accounts by Van Meteren and others, pp. 147–72.

[17] Asher, *Hudson*, pp. 181–94 (Hessel Gerritz), pp. 244–54 (Jeannin to Henry IV).

to the Muscovy Company magnates and other Englishmen interested in discovery. Between the three countries the interchange of ideas and men in the oceanic reconnaissance over the past generation had been accompanied by increasing rivalry as the prizes came within their grasp, and Hudson, who seems to have put the cause of discovery above national loyalty in his scale of values, found himself criticized both by the Dutch for allegedly having missed the western passage on purpose in his third voyage, and by the English for having opened part of their Virginia to the encroachment of foreigners.[18] In the event the English authorities refused to let him leave for Holland and his fourth voyage took place under English auspices.

Hudson's principal promoters in this enterprise were Sir Thomas Smythe, Sir Dudley Digges and John Wolstenholme. Smythe was of course interested as a great East India and Muscovy merchant and leader of the Virginia Company. Wolstenholme was another London merchant, who as a customs official (like Smythe's father, 'Customer Smith', and Sir Thomas Myddelton, who managed Walsingham's farm of the outports) successfully combined private and public business, acquiring a share in the great farm of the customs in 1608. Already at this time a member of the East India and Virginia companies, Wolstenholme became increasingly concerned in the affairs of both during the next two decades, but chiefly distinguished himself in the overseas movement as a patron of the search for a northwest passage. As for Digges, son of Thomas Digges the mathematician and authority on navigation, he was at this time a young man of 27 who had yet to make his mark. His support for Hudson's venture was one of the first signs of the passionate interest he was to take in overseas affairs, especially in Virginia and East Indian enterprise and above all in the northwest passage. Such was his enthusiasm for this last quest that John Chamberlain in one of his letters to Sir Dudley Carleton in 1611 remarked that the project would not 'give him leave to thincke of anything els, for yt possesseth him wholly'.[19] These prime movers of the venture were supported, moreover, by the earls of Northampton, Nottingham, Southampton, Salisbury (William, the second earl) and Suffolk, Theophilus Lord Walden, Sir Walter Cope, Sir Robert Mansell (treasurer of the navy), twelve of the most eminent London magnates and, corporately, the East India and Muscovy companies.[20]

These secondary contributors were running no great risk, since this

---

[18] Asher, *Hudson*, p. 192.
[19] N. E. McClure (ed.), *The Letters of John Chamberlain* (2 vols., Philadelphia, 1939), I, pp. 321–2; Brown, *Genesis*, pp. 878–9, 1057–8; Ashton, *Crown and Money Market*, pp. 93–5.
[20] Christy, *Voyages of Foxe and James*, pp. 642–3.

was hardly an expensive expedition, consisting as it did of a single 55-ton ship, the *Discovery*, carrying about 22 men and two boys victualled for eight months.[21] The crew at first included a certain Master Cole-burne, whom Hudson sent back to London before leaving the Thames for reasons he disclosed only to the adventurers. Luke Foxe later alleged that Hudson was jealous of the man's reputation, since he was 'held to be a better man than himselfe', but Hudson may well have had other and better reasons for ridding himself of this man.[22] Coleburne was presumably the mate and was replaced in that capacity by Robert Juet, who had been Hudson's mate in 1608 and one of his crew in 1609. He in turn was displaced during the voyage by Robert Bylot. One of the crew was described as 'student in the mathematickes' and another was 'a land man put in by the adventurers': Abacuk Pricket, a former servant to Sir Dudley Digges. Pricket produced the only extensive account of the voyage, which remains in major respects obscure because he was neither a sailor nor a convincing witness.[23] Hudson's own journal covers only the first part of the voyage, ending more than ten months before he was set adrift, but some further record of events appears to have been available to the officials of the Trinity House, who held an inquiry and took brief statements from the survivors.[24] Hessel Gerritz also somehow acquired information which enabled him to publish in 1612 a map of the discovery and a short account of the voyage.[25] A High Court of Admiralty inquiry produced some further evidence in 1617.[26]

These materials provide few firm points on which to build an account of the voyage. Hudson set out in April 1610 and made the coast of Greenland in 65° early in June. According to his reckoning he approached the strait in 62°29' and on 24 and 25 June ran into it in 62°17', sighting land to the north and continuing west on that latitude. On 3 August he entered Hudson Bay through a narrow passage, naming the land to larboard Cape Wolstenholme and that to starboard Cape Digges, head of the small island of the same name. Gerritz's map

[21] Christy, *Voyages of Foxe and James*, pp. 629–30.
[22] Christy suggests that he may have been the William Cabreth (or Cobreth) of Ratcliffe who had sailed as master with Waymouth in 1602: Christy, *Voyages of Foxe and James*, p. 115. This guess seems the more plausible now that we know that Cabreth had formerly gone captain of the *Flying Hope* to the West Indies in 1599 and had been charged afterwards with the murder of one of his shipmates in that voyage: Andrews, 'Annotated list', p. 248. If Hudson knew this, he had good reason to dismiss him.
[23] *Purchas*, XIII, 377–410 (Pricket); 411–12 (note by Wydowse, the mathematician).
[24] Christy, *Voyages of Foxe and James*, pp. 629–34.
[25] Asher, *Hudson*, pp. 181–94, 236–43; Hessel Gerritz, *Descriptio et delineatio geographica detectionis freti ab H. Hudsono inventi* (Amsterdam, 1612). Other versions in Dutch and Latin appeared in 1612 and 1613.
[26] Quinn, *New American World*, IV, pp. 294–6.

shows that in the course of these forty days Hudson obtained a fairly good general impression of the dimensions and shape of the strait, apart from its southeastern shore, even though his observations of the height of the Pole were quite unreliable and he was much troubled by ice. We know from Pricket that Hudson was roughing out a chart as he went, but his journal, which is extremely vague as to courses and distances (by comparison with Stephen Borough, Davis or Baffin, for example) gives little indication of his methods as an explorer. He undoubtedly kept more detailed records, leaving his crew in ignorance, since he also forbade them to make their own.[27]

Having entered the great bay, Hudson followed the near coast south to reach the bottom of James Bay (located by Gerritz in 50°, though actually in 51°) around the beginning of September and it was shortly after this that he assembled the company to examine the conduct of Juet, against whom various members of the crew bore witness, the conclusion being that 'hee had used words tending to mutinie, discouragement, and slander of the action, which easily tooke effect in those which were timorous; and had not the Master in time prevented, it might easily have overthrowne the Voyage'.[28] Bylot therefore replaced Juet as mate. For nearly two months after this Hudson continued exploring, but it is impossible to trace his movements, which resulted eventually in the grossly erroneous view of James Bay and the western side of Hudson Bay formulated by Gerritz. Early in November he laid up for the winter deep in James Bay. Quickly frozen in, they subsisted on what was left of their original victuals supplemented by sea birds and fish. When they came out of their wintering port in June their victuals were nearly exhausted and some of the men were sick, presumably from starvation and scurvy. It has often been said that a mutiny occurred because Hudson wished to proceed further with the discovery, but the only authority for this is Gerritz and it is striking that none of the survivors chose to mention this as an excuse. In fact Pricket and other witnesses make it sufficiently clear that, as the Trinity House inquiry concluded: 'to save some from Starving, they were content to put away so many', and that when the mutiny occurred Hudson was making ready to return to England. Indeed it seems that he was himself in so feeble a condition that he was 'past caring to goe one way

---

[27] *Purchas*, XIII, 396. For the return the survivors used Hudson's chart, but had difficulty in determining their course, probably because they could not make sense of Hudson's notes. Pricket says that he took charge of the chart and journals after the mutiny: *Purchas*, XIII, 400. See also E. C. Abbe and F. J. Gillis, 'Henry Hudson and the early exploration and mapping of Hudson Bay, 1610 to 1631', in J. Parker (ed.), *Merchants and Scholars: Essays in the History of Exploration and Trade* (Minneapolis, 1965).
[28] *Purchas*, XIII, 411–12 (Wydowse).

or other' and did not expect to reach home.[29] Thus it was that Hudson, his son and seven others were set adrift in a shallop on 23 June 1611, never to be seen again.

Towards the end of July the *Discovery* came again to Digges Island, where four of their number were killed in a fight with Eskimo. The remainder struggled back through the strait and across the ocean, too weak to stand at the helm. Juet died of starvation near the coast of Ireland. At the Trinity House inquiry in October the survivors put the main blame for the mutiny on two of those killed by the Eskimo and on Juet. Pricket, Bylot and the rest had on their own admission acquiesced and were not cleared officially until 1618, but the first two at least were far too valuable now to be cast aside, for it was assumed they could lead the way to the Pacific. In spite of the cautious and essentially correct conclusions of the Trinity House officials concerning the relationship between the bay and the two oceans, the fever of optimism which almost carried away Sir Dudley Digges infected many others. Some 160 individuals now subscribed for a new expedition under the naval captain Thomas Button and in 1612 the Northwest Passage Company was incorporated under the personal patronage of Prince Henry. Of its 288 members many were courtiers and officials, but it is noteworthy that all the 24 directors except Sir Robert Mansell were London merchants and that their full title was 'the Governor and Company of the Merchaunts of London, Discoverers of the Northwest passage'.[30] Among the non-merchant members were Pricket, Bylot and Edward Wilson (another survivor), as well as Richard Hakluyt and Henry Briggs the mathematician. Briggs, who was to be closely associated with Luke Foxe, published in 1622 'A Treatise of the North-West Passage to the South Sea' and about the same time compiled the map which accompanied Purchas's reprint of the treatise in 1625.[31] This map, based on materials derived from a series of expeditions, illustrated its author's continuing faith in the existence of a passage and was a significant landmark in the cartography of North America.[32]

Button sailed from London in April 1612 with two ships, the *Resolution* and the *Discovery*. His instructions, drawn up by Edward Wright in the name of Prince Henry, were to check the course through the strait and then,

remembring that your end is West, we would have you stand over to the

---

[29] *Purchas*, XIII, 392–4; Christy, *Voyages of Foxe and James*, p. 631.
[30] Christy, *Voyages of Foxe and James*, pp. 642–64.
[31] *Purchas*, XIV, 422–6. The treatise was appended to Edward Waterhouse, *A Declaration of the State of the Colony and Affaires in Virginia* (London, 1622).
[32] Abbe and Gillis, 'Mapping of Hudson Bay'.

opposite Maine, in the Latitude of some 58 degrees, where, riding at some Headland, observe well the flood; if it come in Southwest, then you maie be sure the passage is that waie; yf from the North or Northwest, your course must be to stand upp into it. . . . if it should fall out that the Winter growe uppon you before your finding a thoroughe fare into the South Sea, we thincke your safest waie wilbe to seeke Southward for some place to winter in; for we assure our self by Gods grace you will not returne, without either the good Newes of a passage, or sufficient assurance of an impossibility.[33]

He was also instructed to observe compass dip and variation, an expected eclipse, conjunctions of the planets and the angular distance between the moon and various stars as a means to calculating longitude. With Button sailed Pricket and Bylot as well as the leaders of two future expeditions, William Gibbons and William Hawkridge. This expedition of course failed to achieve what was expected, namely the discovery of the passage, but it appears to have been well conducted even though Button, being obliged to winter at Port Nelson in the bay, lost many men there. The voyage established in outline the greater part of the western shore. Not surprisingly, however, the promoters kept the details to themselves until Luke Foxe was able to piece together information supplied by Pricket, Hawkridge and Sir Thomas Roe, his patron, who got access to Button's own journal and gave Foxe an abstract of it.[34]

The company's next voyage, in 1614, was a total failure, for the captain, Gibbons, was unable to enter the strait and, as Foxe drily relates, was 'with the Ice, driven into a Bay, called by his Company Gibbons his hole', from which he escaped only after some ten weeks and returned home.[35] The *Discovery*, used in this as in both the previous expeditions, was yet again employed for the 1615 voyage under Bylot as master, accompanied by William Baffin, 'the greatest of the Jacobean navigators'.[36] Baffin had sailed with James Hall as mate in the last of the latter's Greenland ventures in 1612;[37] the following year he was chief pilot of the Muscovy Company's Spitzbergen fleet and supplied Purchas with a journal of that voyage;[38] and in 1614 he sailed once more to Spitzbergen for that company.[39] The 1615 expedition to Hudson Bay did not significantly extend the area so far explored but is

[33] Christy, *Voyages of Foxe and James*, p. 637.
[34] Christy, *Voyages of Foxe and James*, pp. 162–200.
[35] Christy, *Voyages of Foxe and James*, pp. 201–2.
[36] Waters, *Art of Navigation*, p. 272; C. R. Markham (ed.), *The Voyages of William Baffin, 1612–1622* (London, 1881).
[37] See *Purchas*, xiv, 365–78, for a fragment of Baffin's journal of this voyage, in which Hall was killed.
[38] *Purchas*, xiv, 47–60.
[39] *Purchas*, xiv, 61–81.

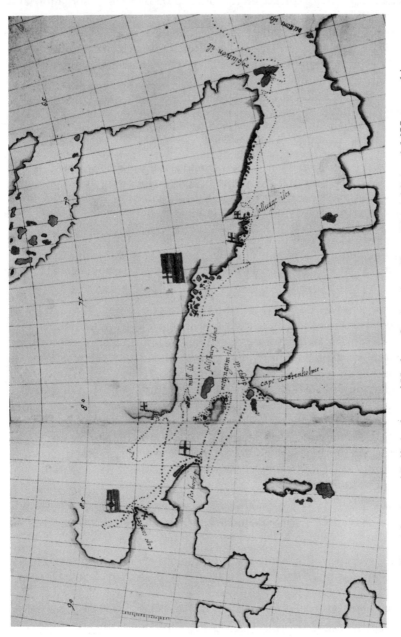

Fig. 6 Section of Baffin's chart of Hudson Strait, 1615. (From BL, Additional MSS, 12, 206.)

notable rather for the scientific quality of Baffin's observation and recording. His course – along the northern side of the strait and covering in some detail the islands at its western end and the eastern shore of Southampton Island – is outlined on a chart drawn in colour for the special benefit of Smythe, Digges and Wolstenholme, the chief adventurers. His magnetic and astronomical observations were meticulously executed and recorded and his tidal observations in the neighbourhood of Southampton Island were especially accurate and valuable.[40] His conclusion as to the likelihood of a passage, however, must have damped considerably the spirits of those worthies:

And now it may be that som expect I should give my opynion conserninge the passadge. To those my answere must be, that doubtless theare is a passadge. But within this strayte, whome is called Hudsons Straytes, I am doubtfull, supposinge the contrarye. But whether there be, or no, I will not affirme. But this I will affirme, that we have not beene in any tyde then that from Resolutyon Iland, and that the greatest indraft of that commeth from Davis Straytes; and my judgment is, if [there be] any passadge within Resolution Iland, it is but som creeke or in lett, but the mayne will be upp fretum Davis.[41]

   In 1616, therefore, Bylot and Baffin departed once more in the *Discovery* for the northwest, this time to seek a passage through Davis Strait, backed again by Smythe, Digges and Wolstenholme with others, among whom Alderman Francis Jones, one of the leading customs farmers, alone is named. Unfortunately Samuel Purchas decided not to print Baffin's 'mappes and tables' of this important voyage, but the navigator's brief journal records Smith Sound running north from 78° and Sir James Lancaster's Sound in 74°20′, named after that steady supporter of the enterprise, and Foxe's circumpolar chart of 1635, which incorporated Baffin's results, shows that in this voyage he performed a remarkable feat of patient exploration and accurate mapping.[42] On his return, however, he wrote to Wolstenholme in uncompromising terms:

there is no passage nor hope of passage in the north of Davis Straights. We having coasted all, or neere all the circumference thereof, and finde it to be no other then a great bay, as the voyage doth truely shew.[43]

Baffin went on to console his promoters with encouraging remarks upon the wealth of whale and walrus in that great bay, but the effect of

---

[40] Markham, *Baffin*, pp. 103–37, with the map. For a technical appreciation see Waters, *Art of Navigation*, pp. 272–82.
[41] Markham, *Baffin*, p. 137. I have supplied the words in square brackets.
[42] Markham, *Baffin*, pp. liv, 138–55; Christy, *Voyages of Foxe and James*, map opposite p. 1.
[43] Markham, *Baffin*, p. 150.

his rather over-confident report was to postpone the further exploration of it for a great many years. Indeed, the combined effect of his two
expeditions to the northwest was virtually to kill the Northwest
Passage Company. One more voyage, promoted by Wolstenholme
principally, was undertaken in 1619 – William Hawkridge's fruitless
venture into Hudson Bay – but the company was not mentioned in
connection with it.[44]

Twelve years elapsed before Luke Foxe of Hull and Thomas James of
Bristol made the last two attempts of this series upon the northwest
passage. The Hull man was a tough seaman of long experience in the
coasting trade and had been thinking about his venture for no less than
twenty-five years before he finally set out, at the age of 45, for Hudson
Bay. He had in those years learned not only patience but also – from
John Tapp the publisher and Henry Briggs the mathematician –
something of the new nautical science. He had acquired a high opinion
of himself, too, and a certain caustic wit which endeared him less to
some of his collaborators than to readers of his famous book, *North-
West Fox*.[45] It was Briggs who interested Sir John Brooke in Foxe's
project and Brooke brought in others. A petition for royal support
resulted after much delay in the loan of the 80-ton naval pinnace, the
Charles, to the adventurers, among whom Sir Thomas Roe and both the
Wolstenholmes (Sir John and his son John) were the main contributors. In the meantime, as Foxe relates,

one Captaine James, of Bristow, had so wrought with the Marchants of the said
Citie for to set forth one Ship for the same designe, as they were willing to
adventure, so as they might share with London in equall honour and profit
whether Ship soever found the same.[46]

The Bristol Society of Merchants Adventurers, in reacting thus
promptly to Foxe's initiative, made no secret of its motive for launching
a rival venture, namely 'that wee may enjoy such priviledges and
Immunities (yf the passage bee discovered) as are graunted to any
others',[47] but Roe and Wolstenholme nevertheless generously
encouraged their efforts and it was agreed that neither group should
obtain a patent at least until the discovery of a passage. James was thus
able to prepare his ship, the *Maria* of 70 tons (named after the queen),

[44] Christy, *Voyages of Foxe and James*, pp. xlviii–liii, 248–58. The tragic and unproductive
voyage of the Dane, Jens Munk, to Hudson Bay took place also in 1619–20: Gosch,
Danish Arctic Expeditions, ii, *passim*.
[45] Luke Foxe, *North-West Fox; or, Fox from the North-west passage* (London, 1635); Christy,
Voyages of Foxe and James.
[46] Christy, *Voyages of Foxe and James*, p. 263.
[47] Christy, *Voyages of Foxe and James*, p. cxlv.

quickly and got away on 2 May 1631, three days before Foxe. The contrast between the two commanders was dramatic, for James was young, well educated, born into a respectable merchant family and distinguished as a seaman by a remarkable mixture of incompetence and proneness to accident. His account of the voyage was entitled *The Strange and Dangerous Voyage of Captaine Thomas James. . .wherein the Miseries Indured, both Going, Wintering, Returning; & the Rarities observed, both Philosphicall and Mathematicall, are related in this Journall of it.*[48] This did not suffer from understatement of the perils and misfortunes that befell James and his hapless companions, for it was (unlike that of the uncouth Foxe) a literary work which included poems admired by no less a judge than that other Bristolian, Robert Southey. Foxe, who accepted James's hospitality with bad grace when they met in the bay, regarded his rival with unconcealed contempt:

> For it is not enough to be a Sea-man, but to be a painefull Sea-man; for a Sea-bred man of reasonable Capacity may attaine to so much Art as may serve to Circle the Earths Globe about; but the other, wanting the experimentall part, cannot; for I do not allow any to be a good Sea-man that hath not undergone the most Offices about a Ship and that hath not in his youth bin both taught and inured to all labours.[49]

James, he said, 'was no Sea-man' and it is true that the Bristol voyage achieved little more than literary success. Following his instructions, James pursued the western shore of the bay down to the southern bay which now bears his name and spent a harrowing winter there, after which – and the loss of several men – he completed the circumnavigation of the main bay and returned to announce, 'most probable it is that there is no passage'.[50] Foxe did better. He passed first to the southwest of Southampton Island and named Sir Thomas Roe's Welcome Island at the mouth of the strait which came to be called by that name, and having taken the same southward course as James (their instructions being similar), he stood north without wintering and ran up Foxe Channel to reach a point of land he called Foxe's Farthest, just north of the Arctic Circle. He thus pointed a way north and west for many a future explorer.[51] Moreover he reached home without the loss of a single man or boy. The few years left to him he devoted to producing not merely (as did James) a narrative of his own voyage, but a full study of the quest for the northwest passage, including some material not

---

[48] London, 1633.
[49] Christy, *Voyages of Foxe and James*, p. 11.
[50] Christy, *Voyages of Foxe and James*, p. 589.
[51] Christy, *Voyages of Foxe and James*, pp. xcviii–cviii, 261–445.

otherwise available and much interesting comment in addition to a chart which expressed the most advanced knowledge of that region.

Yet Foxe, despite his friendship with Henry Briggs, after whom, in his own quaint way, he named certain islands in the bay 'Brigges his Mathematickes', was not the most sophisticated of sailors. He scorned to take books on his voyage, on the grounds that 'there would be no leisure, nor was there, for I found worke enough; and, if the matter it selfe had not been in another place when sodaine occasion was present, it had bin too late for me (like the Holland Skipper to runne to his chest) to looke upon his Waggoner booke'.[52] As for instruments, he carried no more than those customary for an ordinary voyage. Of James he remarked:

The Gentleman could discourse of Arte (as observations, calculations, and the like), and he shewed me many Instruments, so that I did perceive him to bee a practitioner in the Mathematicks.[53]

Indeed James appended to his narrative a list of the many and elaborate instruments he provided for his voyage, including two watches (one of six inches diameter), six meridian compasses, two quadrants carefully corrected and 'a Table, every day calculated, correspondent to the latitude, according to Master Gunters directions in his booke; the better to keepe our Time and our Compasse, to judge of our Course'. Along with these went 'A Chest full of the best and choicest Mathematicall bookes'.[54] He arranged with Henry Gellibrand the mathematician that they should both observe the same eclipse of the moon in order to determine James's longitude, which they succeeded in doing to within 15' – an impressive exercise of the latest scientific methods.[55] Foxe and James were like chalk and cheese, yet together they represent the condition of English seamanship in their time and the uncomfortable but improving alliance between sailor and scientist.

[52] Christy, *Voyages of Foxe and James*, p. 265.
[53] Christy, *Voyages of Foxe and James*, p. 359.
[54] Christy, *Voyages of Foxe and James*, pp. 604–6.
[55] Waters, *Art of Navigation*, pp. 499–500.

⤐ 16 ⤐

Reflections

In the course of English overseas expansion trade, plunder and settlement were closely interwoven. Often indistinguishable in practice, they may be seen historically as aspects of the same process. Yet one reason why the British Empire took such an unconscionable time getting born is that the English put colonization well below trade and plunder in their priorities. Their primary objective from about 1508 down to 1630 was oriental trade. It was the northeast voyage of 1553 which finally launched the country's overseas expansion and the only substantial and lasting achievements of the next fifty years were the founding of the Turkey trade in 1580 and of the East India trade in 1600. Moreover the Muscovy and East India companies or their leading members were responsible for most of the work of northern exploration which constituted England's main contribution to discovery in this period and which was undertaken to promote eastern trade. Second only to this commercial campaign was the predatory drive of armed traders and marauders to win by fair means or foul a share of the Atlantic wealth of the Iberian nations. Plunder and the pursuit of treasure loomed large in this western offensive, but the captains and factors of the East India Company were also no strangers to maritime warfare, reprisals and piracy.

We have seen how the campaign of western plunder fathered the abortive colonial schemes of Grenville and Drake, how Ralegh's golden dream of Manoa evolved into a tobacco trade and how colonies grew out of that as continual raiding eroded Spain's control of the outer Caribbean. In these and other ways the seeds of colonies were sown in the course of trade, plunder or harvesting the sea. Both Gilbert and the elder Hakluyt envisaged colonial way-stations in northern passages and the younger Hakluyt conceived of a colony of pirates, ex-convicts and liberated black slaves strategically placed in Magellan's Strait. Such bases, they hoped, would develop as centres of trade and settlement, and so in fact did the Cape stations later, as did logwood-

356

cutting or fur-trade bases elsewhere, while out of the East India Company's factories did eventually grow an empire. But those factories existed in the first place only to serve trade – they were no more colonies than were the English rope-walks at Kholmogory and Vologda. The line is hard to trace between such trading stations and the transient so-called colonies for the management of tobacco planting in early seventeenth-century Guiana or the Newfoundland fishing colony known as Bristol's Hope. Sagadahoc was only one step further up the ladder of colonial evolution, as were the West Indian plantations: artificial creations of merchant syndicates, maintained with labour, capital and everything else necessary for the sole purpose of producing a marketable commodity. Virginia came to have much in common with the Caribbean plantations, though it also had from the start the character of a full-scale settlement. Indeed the troubles of Jamestown arose partly from its hybrid nature and the tendency of its founders to confuse the strictly commercial function of a colony of exploitation with the broader purposes of a colony of settlement. Such was the upshot of the collaboration of London merchants and landed gentry.

The desire to create a society beyond the sea, whether to fulfil the landowning ambitions of gentlemen or to provide a haven for recusants or dissenters, inspired a variety of projectors in this period, but in few actual enterprises was it the dominant motive and among those only one – that of the Pilgrim Fathers – succeeded. They were in this as in various other respects an exceptional group of people. Colonization in the full sense of the term was a concept which attracted much attention and discussion before 1630, but in practice it was not central to the development of English overseas enterprise and only became one of the leading themes in the Jacobean period. Some correction of the usual perspective is necessary here, for history always distorts what it describes and modern views of the expansion tend for obvious reasons to magnify the importance of North America. In fact that continent did not become a major field of English activity overseas until the seventeenth century. After discovering it in 1497 the English soon lost interest in the country and between 1505 and 1578, with the exception of Rastell and his associates, noticed it chiefly as an obstacle on the way to Cathay. Gilbert and Ralegh in the eighties brought it back to public attention, but neither could win enough public or private support to begin effective settlement, and in the end their efforts probably produced more scepticism than faith in the plantation of the mainland. In the subsequent discussion even an advocate of the cause had to admit:

Yt being a very noble action to enlarge a dominion . . . the most vertuous mindes are easly taken with falsest hopes; ambesion makinge a quick sence of the good & casting and conferminge the mind againste all difficulties. . . . I finde little foundation for hope of trafficke into thes partts untell Longe tyme have made us masters. . . . our able men are in the same trade at home allreddy, & Love ease and securitie and the poore men wantts welthe to disburse any thinge.[1]

As for the Jacobean promoters of North American colonies, they found it very hard to overcome public resistance. This accounts for the absence of any attempt to colonize New England between 1608 and 1620. Jamestown was saved from a similar humiliating collapse only by desperate and repeated appeals to national sentiment, while the Newfoundland projectors fought a losing battle against the fishing interest.

It was only slowly that active concern and engagement in extra-European enterprise developed over the fifteen decades here surveyed. The movement may appear to have gathered momentum gradually, but closer analysis suggests rather a series of spurts and relatively sluggish intervals. National interest was first awakened by the flurry of activity associated with the discovery of North America in the years around 1500. The blaze of the great European discoveries thus lit up new vistas for English venturers, but for the next fifty years their efforts to pursue the work they had so well begun were remarkably tentative, intermittent and feeble. At length in the early fifties a new surge of energy came with the Willoughby-Chancellor expedition northeast and the Guinea voyages. Although Sebastian Cabot played a vital part in this renewal of initiative, native forces were mainly responsible this time: the government of the duke of Northumberland and the merchants of the City of London. The combination of the political and economic motives of these two powerful bodies produced a thrust strong enough to set the expansion in motion and to prevent it slumping back into inertia. But the Guinea and Caribbean enterprises failed, the northeast search lapsed after 1556 and Persia after that raised hopes only to dash them repeatedly.

It was not until the later seventies that the movement picked up again under the spur of nationalistic hostility to Spain. In the years of rising tension from 1577 to 1585 Walsingham used his influence to encourage, to assist and to some extent to direct a new wave of expansionist projects of exploration, plunder, colonization and trade. Few of these were implemented and fewer still achieved anything of

---

[1] Quinn, *New American World*, III, pp. 172–5: an undated paper of the mid 1590s commenting on Edward Hayes's colonizing proposals.

note, the Turkey trade being the most valuable result in both political and commercial terms, but this extraordinary outburst of maritime enterprise, infused with nationalistic feeling and culminating in the naval drama of 1588, had an intellectual and emotional dimension which in the long run more than compensated for its disappointing practical returns. The later eighties and nineties mark another falling off in enterprise: Roanoke and Davis's fine work were abandoned, attempts to establish eastern trade by sea failed disastrously one after another and generally the human, nautical and financial resources applicable to overseas expansion went into privateering. This in turn, however, fostered both the will and the means to resume the advance later.

The fourth spurt occurred in the 1600s, when a British empire overseas may be seen to emerge, even though it was a sickly child and all but still-born. It began with the creation of the East India Company in 1600, the stimulus to which came not so much from within as from without, in the sense that the Dutch merchants set the pace and the Londoners could not afford to be left behind. But in the years 1602–4 the English took the initiative on several fronts at once: in the West Indies they moved into the contraband trade on a large scale; in Guiana Leigh, after reconnoitring the coast in 1602, set up his Wiapoco colony in 1604; in 1602 began the two series of voyages – to southern and northern Virginia respectively – which led on to the birth of that two-headed monster the Virginia Company in 1606; and in 1602 also Waymouth pointed the way into the strait which Hudson finally traversed eight years later. There can be little doubt now that Sir Robert Cecil, who became earl of Salisbury in May 1605, was the *éminence grise* behind much of this activity, to which the transition from war to peace lent a sense of urgency. In this delicate political situation Cecil had to play his cards with a subtlety and discretion of which he alone was capable, so that his influence is less easy to trace than that of Walsingham a generation before, but it was probably just as important, particularly because Cecil's two allies at the centre of power – Nottingham and Ralegh (until the summer of 1603) – stood strongly for overseas expansion.

To sustain this advance or even to consolidate it proved extremely difficult, but in spite of strong Spanish and Portuguese resistance and the superior commercial and maritime resources of the Dutch, the English struggled on through the adversities of the 1610s and the misfortunes of the 1620s, when Europe entered the Thirty Years War and a harsh economic winter, when the Dutch launched their global onslaught upon the Iberian empires, and when England's chief minister was no Walsingham nor Cecil, but the duke of Buckingham. Nor was any new thrust possible in the next two decades, chiefly for political reasons. Some revival of the overseas fortunes of the nation was foreshadowed in the fifties under Cromwell, but the main offensive came with the Restoration, when at last the British Empire began to flourish as the commercial revolution triumphed, naval power and maritime science came of age and the Court and the City combined to devise and carry out a more coherent colonial policy.

To argue from this pattern of fluctuating progress that certain statesmen, by administering a dynamic push at critical moments, played a decisive part in the emergence of the British Empire would be to overstate the case, for the evidence we have hardly ever shows the crown – or ministers on its behalf – taking the initiative, but rather responding more or less helpfully to private projects. Northumberland, Walsingham and Cecil deserve credit for forwarding the movement, but none of them gave a lead that can be called decisive and in each case the movement ebbed after a few years. This tendency to relapse of course indicates the fundamental weakness of the drive to expand overseas, and the diminished scale of the relapse in the early seventeenth century, even in the face of unprecedented adversity, is a sign of the growing strength of the movement.

Before the seventeenth century the supply of funds for new or young ventures in trade, discovery or colonization was almost always inadequate. England was not a poor country, but promoters found it hard to mobilize capital for this kind of enterprise. In the first place the country possessed no banks, nor had it great merchant houses comparable to those that had backed the Iberian expansion; its credit system lagged behind that of various other parts of Europe. The City of London, consisting of a few middle-sized fish and shoals of small fry, was conservative and shy of high-risk or long-term investment such as eastern trade or western colonization required. Its answer was the joint-stock system, which spread the burden and the risk so that, for example, the initial shares in the Muscovy Company were issued for £25 only and those in the 1609 Virginia Company for £12 10s. Even so, it fell to relatively few big merchants to provide most of the continuing funds for the Russia trade and the various new ventures undertaken by the Muscovy Company, while even the East India Company found its rank-and-file members reluctant to respond to calls for the fresh subscriptions frequently required to extend the scope of the trade or to finance special expeditions such as those to the northwest. Discovery had to depend largely on devotees like Lok, Sanderson, Digges and Wolstenholme, who would often try to attract other investors by promises of cod, whale or walrus. Colonial projectors had much the same problem, and failure caused by under-funding only made it still more difficult to capitalize the next attempt.

It was in the Jacobean period that a considerable money market developed in connection with government borrowing, with syndicates for customs farms and sales of crown lands, with increased use of mortgages by landowners as a normal means of creating cash-flow, and with commercial expansion generally.[2] In the 1620s the pool of capital accessible in London was much larger than it had been in Elizabeth's time. But as the experience of the East India Company in that decade showed, it was still difficult to raise sufficient capital to finance eastern trade in competition with the VOC, which had far greater funds at its disposal. These problems would not be solved until the later seventeenth century, when the great leap forward of commerce, banking and the money market was registered by the fall in the rate of interest. Likewise the comparatively primitive structure of England's overseas trading system hindered the development of her extra-European enterprise. In the sixteenth century English merchants conducted simple bilateral trade with the Baltic ports, the Netherlands, France, Spain and so forth, with some multilateral exchange developing in connection with the Mediterranean and Levant trades in the last quarter. Such a structure, which was associated with heavy reliance upon cloth exports, gave little scope either for acquiring the specie needed in eastern trade or for marketing the proceeds thereof, and the East India Company was obliged painfully to construct a multilateral system to suit its purposes[3] while the Dutch had only to adapt their already sophisticated and wide-ranging commercial network. In his great compendium on international trade published in 1638,[4] Lewes Roberts shows that England's overseas trade was already in the 1630s far more complex than it had been before 1600, but the commercial revolution which made London into a great international entrepôt was not finally accomplished until after 1660.[5]

These economic factors are particularly relevant to the changing pace of the expansion and although it is a mistake to suppose that economic fluctuations and overseas expansion were precisely synchronous or moved together like the spheres in some calculable rhythm,[6] there can be little doubt that the growth of wealth and luxury

---

[2] Ashton, *Crown and Money Market*.
[3] Chaudhuri, *East India Company*, pp. 114, 136, 140–50, etc.
[4] Lewes Roberts, *The Merchants Mappe of Commerce*.
[5] R. Davis, *A Commercial Revolution* (London, 1967); R. Davis, 'English foreign trade, 1660–1700', *EconHR*, 2nd series, 7 (1954), 150–66.
[6] It is nevertheless interesting that the years from 1570 to 1620, the critical phase

in Europe throughout this period provided the steady undertow which ensured the continuance of the movement from phase to phase despite hindrances and reverses. It is true that at the same time population pressure caused an obverse and equally conspicuous growth of poverty, pauperism, vagabondage, beggary and crime, and that large numbers of such uprooted people drifted to the towns, increasing the element of mobility in the population, but although all this certainly swelled the pool of unskilled labour for sea-service it cannot be shown to have promoted the formation of colonies or colonial emigration to any significant extent. Well-meaning intellectuals worried the problem of the idle poor as much then as ever since and many others, including colonial projectors, picked up and turned the common coin of such discourse to their own convenience, but in reality colonization, like all the other forms of overseas expansion, was a response to affluence, not to poverty.[7]

It was in the nautical sphere that the English achieved their most impressive advance. Between 1550 and 1630 the tonnage of the merchant marine more than doubled, largely owing to an increase in the number of substantial vessels, and the special strength of the nation's shipping lay in its aptitude for warfare and predation. This was both a cause and an effect of the success of privateering in the Elizabethan war with Spain, and after that private shipping continued to form the main body of the nation's effective sea power. This became evident in the wars of the later twenties against France and Spain, when the maritime war was conducted in much the same fashion as before. Small-scale privateering predominated but prize goods of great quantity and value were brought in,[8] while strategic operations were left to semi-official expeditions of royal and private ships and were conducted with a degree of inefficiency and corruption exceeding anything the Elizabethans had achieved. Thus the quantitative growth of England's sea-forces was not matched by the development of the navy as an instrument of war, and the ability of the state to wield power at sea for

---

of increasing vitality and effective power in English overseas expansion, marked also a phase of intense economic activity and commercial development within England.

[7] The thesis that poverty in England was the main cause of colonial development in the early seventeenth century is argued – in my opinion unconvincingly – in what is nevertheless a valuable work: C. Bridenbaugh, *Vexed and Troubled Englishmen, 1590–1642* (Oxford, 1968). G. R. Elton, 'Contentment and discontent on the eve of colonization', in Quinn, *Early Maryland*, pp. 105–18, argues that emigration 'testified to an energetic contentment with things English'.

[8] J. C. Appleby, 'English privateering during the Spanish and French wars.' This demonstrates striking similarities to Elizabethan privateering and estimates the total return of prize goods at between £800,000 and £900,000.

strategic purposes remained very limited.[9] Here again the vital advance was yet to come in the 1650s and the age of Pepys, just as scientific navigation, still in 1630 the skill of a select minority, had yet to establish its supremacy and be accepted as a necessary part of any sea-going master's equipment.[10]

The involvement of England in the process of European overseas expansion was a natural consequence of her integral rôle in the commercial, political and cultural life of Europe, but it did not come about easily. Entering late upon the imperial scene, the English found themselves in the position of intruders challenging the entrenched interests of Spain and Portugal, which tended to unite to resist any invasion of their respective spheres of influence by upstart competitors and which in 1580 fell under the rule of a single monarch until the Portuguese revolt of 1640. These circumstances alone would have given English maritime enterprise an aggressive edge, while the political and religious conflict within Europe, in which England and Spain emerged as the champions of opposing camps, allied it increasingly with a militant and popular nationalism. In the maritime struggle which ensued the English, with no great traffic of their own to defend and with the riches of Iberian commerce exposed to their attack, predictably adopted the usual tactics of have-nots at war with possessors and developed a pervasive campaign of plunder. Although they fell far short of 'beating that great empire in pieces', they caused serious damage to Spain's maritime strength and so enhanced their own that by the end of the war they had the upper hand in the Atlantic and were consequently able in the early years of the seventeenth century to mount the general advance we have noted, moving forward to claim the coveted prizes. For a few years, moreover, they had the advantage of peace with Spain while the Dutch had to bear the brunt of a renewed Spanish offensive.

With the conclusion of the Dutch-Spanish truce in 1609, however, the weakness of England's maritime capacity was at last exposed. The general superiority of Dutch shipping to English, both in volume and in efficiency, was evident long before 1600, but for some three decades – from the sixties to the eighties – English owners had been cushioned against Dutch competition by the adverse effects of the troubles upon their rivals. Then in the nineties the Dutch embarked upon a commercial offensive of formidable power reaching from South America to

---

[9] Mismanagement and corruption in the navy became notorious under the régime of Sir Robert Mansell, treasurer from 1604 to 1618: Oppenheim, *Administration*, pp. 189–96; A. P. McGowan (ed.), *The Jacobean Commissions of Enquiry, 1608 and 1618* (London, 1971).

[10] Waters, *Art of Navigation*, p. 498.

the Far East and sustained by resources of capital, shipping and organization unmatched in the world at that time. In 1609 this offensive moved into top gear and the English found their progress in one trade after another, from the North Sea to Japan, inhibited, checked or reversed by enterprise to which their merchants and shipowners could offer no effective reply. Their unspecialized, over-manned ships were too expensive and their freight-rates too high; their strong, 'defensible' ships performed well enough in the Mediterranean and some other trades which required such strength, but elsewhere the Hollanders carried all before them. The onset of economic depression and general war in Europe in the twenties did nothing to lighten this gloomy prospect. Fed by frustration and jealousy, nationalistic feeling in the early Stuart period turned against the Dutch, finding expression in, for example, numerous offensive remarks in *Purchas his Pilgrimes* and tirades of abuse in the naval tracts of Sir William Monson.[11] The Hollanders, admired and envied for their commercial success, were equally reviled for their ruthless greed and churlish ingratitude. Above all national pride demanded that they should strike their flags to acknowledge the king of England's sovereignty in the Narrow Seas, and eventually the quarrel over this matter of national prestige precipitated the first of the Dutch wars in 1652.[12] In these wars, which were essentially a struggle for maritime supremacy and control of the rich trades, English nationalism identified itself more firmly than ever with the cause long since espoused by the Hakluyts.

[11] *Monson's Tracts*, IV, pp. 421–3, etc.
[12] *Monson's Tracts*, III, pp. 45–55 (on the issue of the salute).

Bibliography

The following is not intended to be a comprehensive bibliography of the subject but is a list of the printed sources and secondary works mentioned in the text and footnotes of this book. See also the list of abbreviations.

A. Printed Sources

Ainsworth, H., *A true confession of the faith* (Amsterdam, 1596).
Andrews, K. R. (ed.), *English Privateering Voyages to the West Indies, 1588–1595* (Cambridge, 1959).
  The Last Voyage of Drake and Hawkins (Cambridge, 1972).
Anon., *A true declaration of the estate of the colonie in Virginia* (London, 1610).
Arber, E. (ed.), *Capt. John Smith, President of Virginia, and Admiral of New England. Works, 1608–1631* (2 vols., Birmingham, 1884).
  The First Three English Books on America (Westminster, 1895).
Armstrong, T. (ed.), *Yermak's Campaign in Siberia* (London, 1975).
Asher, G. M. (ed.), *Henry Hudson the Navigator* (London, 1860).
Barbour, P. L. (ed.), *The Jamestown Voyages under the First Charter, 1606–1609* (Cambridge, 1969).
Barrey, Ph. (ed.), 'Le Havre transatlantique de 1571 à 1610', in J. Hayem (ed.), *Mémoires et Documents pour Servir à l'Histoire du Commerce et l'Industrie en France* (Paris, 1911, etc.), v, pp. 47–209.
Benzoni, G., *La Historia del Nuovo Mondo* (Venice, 1572).
Beste, G., *A True Discourse of the late voyage of discoverie* (London, 1578).
Biggar, H. P. (ed.), *The Precursors of Jacques Cartier 1497–1534* (Ottawa, 1911).
Birdwood, G. and Foster, W. (eds.), *The Register of the Letters etc. of the Governor and Company of Merchants of London Trading into the East Indies, 1600–1619* (London, 1893).
Blake, J. W. (ed.), *Europeans in West Africa, 1450–1560* (London, 1942).
Bond, E. A. (ed.), *Russia at the Close of the Sixteenth Century* (London, 1856).
Boxer, C. R. (ed.), *The Tragic History of the Sea, 1589–1622* (Cambridge, 1959).
Bréard, C. et P. (eds.), *Documents rélatifs à la Marine Normande* (Rouen, 1889).
Brereton, J., *A Briefe and true Relation of the Discoverie of the North part of Virginia* (London, 1602).

Bruce, J. (ed.), *The Correspondence of Robert Dudley, earl of Leicester* (London, 1844).

Bry, T. de (ed.), *America* (parts I–XIII, Frankfurt, 1590–1634).

Burnell, A. C. and Tiele, P. A. (eds.), *The Voyage of Jan Huyghen van Linschoten to the East Indies* (2 vols., London, 1885).

Camden, W., *The History of . . . Princess Elizabeth* (London, 1688).

Cartwright, J., *The Preachers Travels* (London, 1611).

Cell, G. T. (ed.), *Newfoundland Discovered: English Attempts at Colonisation, 1610–1630* (London, 1982).

Christy, M. (ed.), *The Voyages of Captain Luke Foxe . . . and Captain Thomas James* (London, 1894).

Churchyard, T., *A generall rehearsall of warres, called Churchyardes choise* (London, 1579).

Collinson, R. (ed.), *The Three Voyages of Martin Frobisher* (London, 1867).

Conway, W. M. (ed.), *Early Dutch and English Voyages to Spitzbergen* (London, 1904).

Corbett, J. S. (ed.), *Papers relating to the Navy during the Spanish War, 1585–1587* (London, 1898).

Cortés, M., *The Arte of Navigation* (London, 1561).

Cortesão, A. and Teixeira da Mota, A. C. (eds.), *Portugaliae Monumenta Cartographica* (6 vols., Lisbon, 1960–63).

Crakanthorpe, R., *A sermon solemnizing a happie inauguration of our most gracious and religious soveraigne King James* (London, 1609).

Crashaw, W., *A sermon preached in London* (London, 1610).

Croft, P. (ed.), *The Spanish Company* (London, 1973).

Davenport, F. (ed.), *European Treaties bearing upon the History of the United States and its Dependencies* (4 vols., Washington, 1917–37).

Davis, W. T. (ed.), *Bradford's History of Plymouth Plantation* (New York, 1908).

Debus, A. G. (ed.), *John Dee, The Mathematicall Praeface* (New York, 1975).

Dee, J., *General and Rare Memorials pertayning to the Perfect Arte of Navigation* (London, 1577).

Domínguez, L. L. (ed.), *The Conquest of the River Plate (1535–1555)* (London, 1891).

Donno, E. S. (ed.), *An Elizabethan in 1582: the Diary of Richard Madox* (London, 1976).

Drake, F., *Sir Francis Drake Revived* (London, 1626).

Eden, R., *A treatyse of the newe India* (London, 1553).

The decades of the newe world or west India (London, 1555).

Ercilla y Zúñiga, A. de, *La Araucana* (Madrid, 1569).

Fernández Duro, C. (ed.), *La Armada Invencible* (2 vols., Madrid, 1884–5).

Fisher, F. J. (ed.), 'The State of England Anno Dom. 1600, by Thomas Wilson', in *The Camden Miscellany*, vol. XVI (London, 1936).

Foster, W. (ed.), *The Embassy of Sir Thomas Roe to the Court of the Great Mogul, 1615–1619* (2 vols., London, 1899).

The English Factories in India, 1618–1621 (Oxford, 1926).

The Travels of John Sanderson in the Levant, 1584–1602 (London, 1931).

The Voyage of Thomas Best to the East Indies, 1612–1614 (London, 1934).

The Voyage of Nicholas Downton to the East Indies (London, 1939).

The Voyages of Sir James Lancaster to Brazil and the East Indies, 1591–1603 (London, 1940).

The Voyage of Sir Henry Middleton to the Moluccas, 1604–1606 (London, 1943).

Fox, F. F. (ed.), *Adams's Chronicle of Bristol* (Bristol, 1910).

Foxe, L., *North-West Fox; or, Fox from the North-west passage* (London, 1635).

Frampton, J., *A briefe description of the portes, creekes, bayes, and havens, of the Weast India* (London, 1578).

Gerritz, H., *Descriptio et delineatio geographica detectionis freti ab H. Hudsono inventi* (Amsterdam, 1612).

Gosch, C. C. A. (ed.), *The Danish Arctic Expeditions, 1605–1620* (2 vols., London, 1897).

Hakluyt, R. (ed.), *Divers voyages touching the discouerie of America* (London, 1582), ed. D. B. Quinn (Amsterdam, 1967).

The Principall Navigations, Voiages and Discoveries of the English Nation (London, 1589).

The Principal Navigations, Voiages, Traffiques and Discoveries of the English Nation (3 vols., London, 1598–1600; 12 vols., Glasgow, 1903–5).

Hampden, J. (ed.), *Francis Drake Privateer* (London, 1972).

Harlow, V. T. (ed.), *English Colonizing Expeditions to the West Indies and Guiana, 1623–1667* (London, 1925).

The Discoverie of the large and bewtiful Empire of Guiana, by Sir Walter Ralegh (London, 1928).

Ralegh's Last Voyage (London, 1932).

Harris, C. A. (ed.), *A Relation of a Voyage to Guiana, by Robert Harcourt* (London, 1928).

Harte, W. J. (ed.), *Gleanings from the Common Place Book of John Hooker, relating to the City of Exeter, 1485–1590* (Exeter, 1926).

Harvey, J. H. (ed.), *William Worcestre, 'Itineraria'* (Oxford, 1969).

Hayem, J. (ed.), *Mémoires et Documents pour Servir à l'Histoire du Commerce et l'Industrie en France* (Paris, 1911, etc.).

Hayman, R., *Quodlibets, Lately Come Over From New Britaniola, Old Newfoundland* (London, 1628).

Herberstein, S. von, *Rerum Moscoviticarum commentarii* (Vienna, 1549).

Herrera Oria, E. (ed.), *La Armada Invencible* (Valladolid, 1929).

Hulton, P. and Quinn, D. B. (eds.), *The American Drawings of John White* (2 vols., London and Chapel Hill, 1964).

Jobson, R., *The Golden Trade* (London, 1623; reprint, 1968).

Johnson, R., *Nova Britannia* (London, 1609).

Keeler, M. F. (ed.), *Sir Francis Drake's West Indian Voyage, 1585–86* (London, 1981).

Las Casas, B. de, *The Spanish Colonie* (London, 1583).

Laughton, J. K. (ed.), *State Papers relating to the Defeat of the Spanish Armada* (2 vols., London, 1895).

Letts, M. (ed), *Hans Staden: the Story of his Captivity* (London, 1928; originally published Marburg, 1557).

López de Velasco, J., *Geografía y Descripción Universal de las Indias*, ed. M. Jiménez de la Espada (Madrid, 1971).

Lyte, H., *A niewe herball* (London, 1578).

McClure, N. E. (ed.), *The Letters of John Chamberlain* (2 vols., Philadelphia, 1939).

McGowan, A. P. (ed.), *The Jacobean Commissions of Enquiry, 1608 and 1618* (London, 1971).

Major, R. H. (ed.), *Notes upon Russia* (2 vols., London, 1851–2).

Manwaring, G. E. and Perrin, W. G. (eds.), *The Life and Works of Sir Henry Mainwaring* (2 vols., London, 1922).

Markham, A. H. (ed.), *The Voyages and Works of John Davis the Navigator* (London, 1880).

Markham, C. R. (ed.), *The Voyages of William Baffin, 1612–1622* (London, 1881). *Narratives of the Voyages of Pedro Sarmiento de Gamboa* (London, 1895).

Marsden, R. G. (ed.), 'Voyage of the Barbara to Brazil, A.D. 1540', in *Naval Miscellany*, 2 (London, 1912), 3–66. *Documents relating to the Law and Custom of the Sea* (2 vols., London, 1915–1916).

Maura Gamazo, G. (ed.), *El Designio de Felipe II y el Episodio de la Armada Invencible* (Madrid, 1957).

Medina, P. de, *Arte de Navegar* (Valladolid, 1545).

Morgan, E. D. and Coote, C. H. (eds.), *Early Voyages and Travels to Russia and Persia* (London, 1886).

Mun, T., *A discourse of trade, from England unto the East Indies* (London, 1621; reprinted in McCulloch, J. R. (ed.), *Early English Tracts on Commerce* (London, 1856)).

Murdin, W. (ed.), *Collection of State Papers . . . in the Reign of Queen Elizabeth* (London, 1759).

Naish, G. P. B. (ed.), 'Documents illustrating the history of the Spanish armada', in C. C. Lloyd (ed.), *Naval Miscellany*, vol. IV (London, 1952), pp. 1–84.

Norman, R., *The Newe Attractive* (London, 1581).

Nuttall, Z. (ed.), *New Light on Drake* (London, 1914).

Oppenheim, M. (ed.), *The Naval Tracts of Sir William Monson* (5 vols., London, 1902–14).

Park, T. (ed.), *The Harleian Miscellany* (10 vols., London, 1808–13).

Penzer, N. M. (ed.), *The World Encompassed and Analogous Contemporary Documents* (London, 1926).

Purchas, S. (ed.), *Hakluytus Posthumus or Purchas his Pilgrimes* (4 vols., London, 1625; 20 vols., Glasgow, 1905–7).

Quinn, D. B. (ed.), *The Voyages and Colonising Enterprises of Sir Humphrey Gilbert* (London, 1940). *The Roanoke Voyages, 1584–1590* (London, 1955). *The last Voyage of Thomas Cavendish, 1591–1592* (Chicago, 1975).

New American World: a Documentary History of North America to 1612 (5 vols.,
    London, 1979).

Quinn, D. B. and Cheshire, N. M. (eds.), *The New Found Land of Stephen
    Parmenius* (Toronto, 1972).

Ralegh, W., *A Report of the Truth of the Fight about the Iles of the Açores, this last
    Sommer* (London, 1591).

Recorde, R., *The Castle of Knowledge* (London, 1556).

Ribault, J., *The whole and true discoverye of Terra Florida* (London, 1563).

Roberts, L., *The Merchants Mappe of Commerce* (London, 1638).

Rodríguez Demorizi, E. (ed.), *Relaciones Históricas de Santo Domingo* (Ciudad
    Trujillo, Dominican Republic, 1945).

Rosier, J., *A true relation of the most prosperous voyage made in this present yeere
    1605, by Captaine George Waymouth* (London, 1605).

Sainsbury, W. N. (ed.), *Calendar of State Papers Colonial, East Indies, China and
    Japan, 1513–1616* (London, 1862).

Schmidt, A. J. (ed.), *Of the Rus Commonwealth by Giles Fletcher* (Ithaca, N.Y.,
    1966).

Skilliter, S. (ed.), *William Harborne and the Trade with Turkey, 1578–1582* (Oxford,
    1977).

Steane, J. B. (ed.), *The Unfortunate Traveller and Other Works, by Thomas Nashe*
    (London, 1972).

Stefansson, V. and McCaskill, E. (eds.), *The Three Voyages of Martin Frobisher*
    (2 vols., London, 1938).

Stevens, H. (ed.), *The Dawn of British Trade to the East Indies* (London, 1886).

Strachey, W., *For the colony in Virginia Britannia. Lawes divine, morall and martiall*
    (London, 1611).

Tawney, R. H. and Power, E. (eds.), *Tudor Economic Documents* (3 vols.,
    London, 1924).

Taylor, E. G. R. (ed.), *A Brief Summe of Geographie, by Roger Barlow* (London,
    1932).

    The Original Writings and Correspondence of the Two Richard Hakluyts (London,
    1935).

    The Troublesome Voyage of Captain Edward Fenton, 1582–1583 (Cambridge,
    1959).

    A Regiment for the Sea, by William Bourne (Cambridge, 1963).

Thevet, A., *Les Singularitez de la France Antarctique* (Paris, 1557), translated by
    by T. Hacket as *The new found worlde, or Antarctique* (London, 1568).

Vaux, W. S. W. (ed.), *The World Encompassed by Sir Francis Drake* (London,
    1854).

Warner, G. F. (ed.), *The Voyage of Robert Dudley to the West Indies, 1594–1595*
    (London, 1899).

Waterhouse, E., *A Declaration of the State of the Colony and Affaires in Virginia*
    (London, 1622).

Willes, R., *The History of Travayle into the West and East Indies* (London, 1577).

Williamson, J. A. (ed.), *The Voyages of the Cabots and the English Discovery of North
    America under Henry VII and Henry VIII* (London, 1929).

The Observations *of Sir Richard Hawkins* (London, 1933).

The Cabot Voyages and Bristol Discovery under Henry VII (Cambridge, 1962).

Wright, I. A. (ed.), *Spanish Documents concerning English Voyages to the Caribbean, 1527–1568* (London, 1929).

Documents concerning English Voyages to the Spanish Main, 1569–1580 (London, 1932).

Further English Voyages to Spanish America, 1583–1594 (London, 1951).

Wright, L. B. (ed.), *A Voyage to Virginia in 1609* (Charlottesville, 1964).

Wright, L. B. and Freund, V. (eds.), *The Historie of Travell into Virginia Britannia (1612) by William Strachey, gent.* (London, 1953).

B. Secondary Works

Abbe, E. C. and Gillis, F. J., 'Henry Hudson and the early exploration and mapping of Hudson Bay, 1610 to 1631', in J. Parker (ed.), *Merchants and Scholars: Essays in the History of Exploration and Trade* (Minneapolis, 1965).

Anderson, M. S., *Britain's Discovery of Russia, 1553–1815* (London, 1958).

Andrews, C. M., *The Colonial Period of American History* (4 vols., New Haven, 1934).

Andrews, K. R., 'New light on Hakluyt', *Mariner's Mirror*, 37 (1951), 303–8.

'Thomas Fenner and the Guinea trade, 1564', *Mariner's Mirror*, 38 (1952), 312–14.

'Christopher Newport of Limehouse, mariner', *William and Mary Quarterly*, 11 (1954), 28–41.

Elizabethan Privateering: English Privateering during the Spanish War, 1585–1603 (Cambridge, 1964).

'The aims of Drake's expedition of 1577–1580', *American Historical Review*, 73 (1968), 724–41.

'Sir Robert Cecil and Mediterranean plunder', *EHR*, 87 (1972), 513–32.

'The voyage of the *Jaquet* of Falmouth to the West Indies and Newfoundland, 1585–86', *Mariner's Mirror*, 59 (1973), 101–3.

'Caribbean rivalry and the Anglo-Spanish peace of 1604', *History*, 59 (1974), 1–17.

'English voyages to the Caribbean, 1596–1604: an annotated list', *William and Mary Quarterly*, 31 (1974), 243–54.

The Spanish Caribbean: Trade and Plunder, 1530–1630 (London, 1978).

'Beyond the equinoctial: England and South America in the sixteenth century', *Journal of Imperial and Commonwealth History*, 10 (1981), 4–24.

'The Elizabethan seaman', *Mariner's Mirror*, 68 (1982), 245–62.

'On the way to Peru: Elizabethan ambitions in America south of Capricorn', *Terrae Incognitae*, 14 (1982), 61–75.

Andrews, K. R., Canny, N. P. and Hair, P. E. H. (eds.), *The Westward Enterprise* (Liverpool, 1978).

Appleby, J. C., 'English privateering during the Spanish and French wars, 1625–1630' (unpublished Ph.D thesis, University of Hull, 1984).

Ashton, R., *The Crown and the Money Market, 1603–1640* (Oxford, 1960).

Bailyn, B., 'Politics and social structure in Virginia', in J. M. Smith (ed.), *Seventeenth Century America: Essays in Colonial History* (Chapel Hill, 1959).

Ballesteros-Gabrois, M., 'Juan Caboto en España', *Revista de Indias*, 4 (1943), 607–27.

Barbour, V., 'Dutch and English merchant shipping in the seventeenth century', *EconHR*, 2 (1929–30), 261–90.

Bassett, D. K., 'Early English trade and settlement in Asia, 1602–1690', in J. S. Bromley and E. H. Kossmann (eds.), *Britain and the Netherlands* (London, 1968), pp. 83–109.

Beer, G. L., *The Origins of the British Colonial System, 1578–1660* (New York, 1922).

Bindoff, S. T., Hurstfield, J. and Williams, C. H. (eds.), *Elizabethan Government and Society* (London, 1961).

Blake, J. W., 'The farm of the Guinea trade', in H. A. Cronne, T. W. Moody and D. B. Quinn, (eds.), *Essays in British and Irish History in Honour of James Eadie Todd* (London, 1949).

West Africa: Quest for God and Gold, 1454–1578 (London, 1977).

Boxer, C. R., *The Dutch Seaborne Empire, 1600–1800* (London, 1965).

The Portuguese Seaborne Empire, 1415–1825 (London, 1969).

Brebner, J. B., *The Explorers of North America* (London, 1937).

Brenner, R., 'The social basis of English commercial expansion, 1550–1650', *Journal of Economic History*, 32 (1972), 361–84.

Bridenbaugh, C., *Vexed and Troubled Englishmen, 1590–1642* (Oxford, 1968).

Bridenbaugh, C. and R., *No Peace beyond the Line: the English in the Caribbean, 1624–1690* (New York, 1972).

Brown, A., *The Genesis of the United States* (Boston, 1891).

Brulez, W., 'L'exportation des Pays-Bas vers l'Italie par voie de terre au milieu du XVIe siècle', *Annales ESC*, 14 (1959), 461–91.

'Les routes commerciales d'Angleterre en Italie au XVIe siècle', in *Studi in onore di Amintore Fanfani* (Milan, 1962), IV, pp. 121–84.

Canny, N. P., *The Elizabethan Conquest of Ireland: a Pattern Established, 1565–1576* (London, 1976).

Carus-Wilson, E. M., *Medieval Merchant Venturers* (London, 1967).

Cell, G. T., *English Enterprise in Newfoundland, 1577–1660* (Toronto, 1969).

Chaudhuri, K. N., *The East India Company: a Study of an Early Joint-Stock Company, 1600–1640* (London, 1965).

Chaunu, P., *Conquête et Exploitation des Nouveaux Mondes, XVIe Siècle* (Paris, 1969).

Chaunu, H. and P., *Séville et l'Atlantique, 1504–1650* (11 vols., Paris, 1956–9).

Chew, S. C., *The Crescent and the Rose* (Oxford, 1937).

Cheyney, E. P., *A History of England from the Defeat of the Armada to the Death of Elizabeth* (2 vols., New York, 1914, 1926).

Chope, R. P., 'New light on Sir Richard Grenville', *Transactions of the Devonshire Association*, 49 (1917), 210–82.

Christy, M., *The Silver Map of the World* (London, 1900).

Clark, G. N., *The Colonial Conferences between England and the Netherlands in 1613 and 1615* (2 vols., Leyden, 1952).

Connell-Smith, G., *Forerunners of Drake* (London, 1954).

Corbett, J. S., *Drake and the Tudor Navy* (2 vols., London, 1898).

The Successors of Drake (London, 1900).

Craven, W. F., *The Southern Colonies in the Seventeenth Century, 1607–1689* (Baton Rouge, La., 1949).

The Dissolution of the Virginia Company: The Failure of a Colonial Experiment (Gloucester, Mass., 1964).

Croft, J. P., 'English trade with peninsular Spain, 1558–1625' (unpublished Oxford University D.Phil. thesis, 1970).

Croft, P., 'Free trade and the House of Commons, 1605–6', *EconHR*, 2nd series, 28 (1975), 17–27.

Cruickshank, C. G., *Elizabeth's Army* (Oxford, 1966).

Cumming, W. P., Skelton, R. A. and Quinn, D. B., *The Discovery of North America* (London, 1971).

Davies, K. G., *The Royal African Company* (London, 1957).

The North Atlantic World in the Seventeenth Century (London, 1974).

Davis, R., 'English foreign trade, 1660–1700', *EconHR*, 2nd series, 7 (1954), 150–66.

'England and the Mediterranean, 1570–1670', in F. J. Fisher, (ed.), *Essays in the Economic and Social History of Tudor and Stuart England* (Cambridge, 1961).

The Rise of the English Shipping Industry (London, 1962).

A Commercial Revolution (London, 1967).

English Overseas Trade, 1500–1700 (London, 1973).

The Rise of the Atlantic Economies (London, 1973).

Dietz, F. C., *English Public Finance, 1559–1641* (New York, 1932).

Earle, P., 'The commercial development of Ancona, 1479–1551', *EconHR*, 2nd series, 22 (1969), 28–44.

Edler, F., 'Winchcomb kerseys in Antwerp (1538–44)', *EconHR*, 7 (1936), 57–62.

Edmundson, G., 'The Dutch on the Amazon and the Negro in the seventeenth century: part 1', *EHR*, 18 (1903), 642–63.

Edwards, E., *The Life of Sir Walter Raleigh and his Letters* (2 vols., London, 1868).

Eliot, K. M., 'The first voyages of Martin Frobisher', *EHR*, 32 (1917), 89–92.

Elliott, J. H., *The Old World and the New, 1492–1650* (Cambridge, 1970).

Elton, G. R., 'Contentment and discontent on the eve of colonization', in D. B. Quinn (ed.), *Early Maryland in a Wider World* (Detroit, 1982).

Epstein, M., *The Early History of the Levant Company* (London, 1908).

Ewen, C. H. L., *The Golden Chalice: a Documented Narrative of an Elizabethan Pirate* (Paignton, 1939).

Falconer, A. F., *Shakespeare and the Sea* (London, 1964).

Foster, W., *England's Quest of Eastern Trade* (London, 1933).

French, P., *John Dee, the World of an Elizabethan Magus* (London, 1972).

Froude, J. A., *Short Studies in Great Subjects* (4 vols., London, 1891).

Glasgow, T., 'H.M.S. Tiger', *North Carolina Historical Review*, 43 (1966), 115–21.
'List of ships in the Royal Navy from 1539 to 1588', *Mariner's Mirror*, 56 (1970), 299–307.
Gokhale, B. G., *Surat in the Seventeenth Century* (London, 1979).
Gookin, W. F., *Bartholomew Gosnold, Discoverer and Planter* (London, 1963).
Gosling, W. G., *The Life of Sir Humphrey Gilbert* (London, 1911).
Gunther, R. T., 'The great astrolabe and other scientific instruments of Humphrey Cole', *Archaeologia*, 75 (1926), 273–317.
Hair, P. E. H., 'Protestants as pirates, slavers and proto-missionaries: Sierra Leone 1568 and 1582', *Journal of Ecclesiastical History*, 21 (1970), 203–24.
Hamel, J., *England and Russia* (London, 1854).
Hamy, E.-T., 'Francisque at André d'Albaigne, cosmographes lucquois au service de la France', *Bulletin de Géographie Historique et Descriptive* (Paris, 1894), pp. 405–33.
'Nouveaux documents sur les frères d'Albaigne', *Bulletin de Géographie Historique et Descriptive* (Paris, 1899), pp. 101–10.
'Documents rélatifs à un projet d'expeditions lointaines', *Bulletin de Géographie Historique et Descriptive* (Paris, 1903), pp. 266–73.
Hanna, W. L., *Lost Harbor: the Controversy over Drake's California Anchorage* (Berkeley, 1979).
Henry, L. W., 'The earl of Essex as strategist and military organizer (1596–7)', *EHR*, 68 (1953), 363–93.
Hill, C., *Intellectual Origins of the English Revolution* (Oxford, 1965).
Hussey, R. D., 'America in European diplomacy, 1597–1604', *Revista de Historia de América*, 41 (1956), 1–30.
Jennings, F., *The Invasion of America* (Chapel Hill, 1975).
Julien, Ch.-A., *Les Voyages de Découverte et les Premiers Établissements* (Paris, 1948).
History of North Africa from the Arab Conquest to 1830 (London, 1970).
Kraus, H. P., *Sir Francis Drake, a Pictorial Biography* (Amsterdam, 1970).
Kupperman, K. O., *Settling with the Indians: the Meeting of English and Indian Cultures in America, 1580–1640* (London, 1980).
Lang, R. G., 'The greater merchants of London in the early seventeenth century' (unpublished Oxford University D.Phil. thesis, 1963).
Lefranc, P., *Sir Walter Ralegh, Ecrivain: l'Oeuvre et les Idées* (Paris, 1968).
Lessa, W. A., *Drake's Island of Thieves* (Honolulu, 1975).
Lloyd, H. A., 'Corruption and Sir John Trevor', *Transactions of the Honourable Society of Cymmrodorion for 1974–5* (London, 1976), pp. 77–102.
Lorimer, J., 'Ralegh's first reconnaissance of Guiana? An English survey of the Orinoco in 1587', *Terrae Incognitae*, 9 (1977), 7–21.
'The English contraband tobacco trade in Trinidad and Guiana, 1590–1617', in K. R. Andrews, N. P. Canny and P. E. H. Hair (eds.), *The Westward Enterprise* (Liverpool, 1978), pp. 124–50.
Lurie, N. O., 'Indian cultural adjustment to European civilization', in J. M. Smith (ed.), *Seventeenth Century America: Essays in Colonial History* (Chapel Hill, 1959).

MacCaffrey, W. T., *Queen Elizabeth and the Making of Policy, 1572–1588* (Princeton, 1981).

McGrath, P., 'Bristol and America, 1480–1631', in K. R. Andrews, N. P. Canny and P. E. H. Hair (eds.), *The Westward Enterprise* (Liverpool, 1978).

McIntyre, R., 'William Sanderson: Elizabethan financier of discovery', *William and Mary Quarterly*, 13 (1956), 184–201.

Marsden, R. G., 'The early career of Sir Martin Frobisher', *EHR*, 21 (1906), 538–44.

'The vice-admirals of the coast', *EHR*, 22 (1907), 468–77 and 23 (1908), 736–57.

Mattingly, G., *The Defeat of the Spanish Armada* (London, 1959).

Meilink-Roelofsz, M. A. P., *Asian Trade and European Influence in the Indonesian Archipelago between 1500 and about 1630* (The Hague, 1962).

Millard, A. M., 'The import trade of London, 1600–1640' (unpublished Ph.D. thesis, University of London, 1956).

Morgan, E. S., *American Freedom, American Slavery* (New York, 1975).

Morison, S. E., *The European Discovery of America: the Northern Voyages, A.D. 500–1600* (New York and Oxford, 1971).

Newton, A. P., *The Colonizing Activities of the English Puritans* (London, 1914). *The European Nations in the West Indies, 1493–1688* (London, 1933).

Nicoll, A. (ed.), *Shakespeare in his own Age* (Cambridge, 1964).

Nowell, C. E., 'Aleixo Garcia and the White King', *HAHR*, 26 (1946), 450–66.

Ohberg, A., 'Russia and the world market in the seventeenth century', *Scandinavian Economic History Review*, 3 (1955), 123–62.

Ojer, P., *La Formación del Oriente Venezolano* (Caracas, 1966).

Oppenheim, M., *A History of the Administration of the Royal Navy and of Merchant Shipping in relation to the Navy* (London, 1896).

The Maritime History of Devon (ed. W. E. Minchinton, Exeter, 1968).

Parker, J., *Books to Build an Empire* (Amsterdam, 1965).

(ed.), *Merchants and Scholars: Essays in the History of Exploration and Trade* (Minneapolis, 1965).

'Religion and the Virginia colony, 1609–1610', in K. R. Andrews, N. P. Canny, and P. E. H. Hair (eds.), *The Westward Enterprise* (Liverpool, 1978).

Parks, G. B., *Richard Hakluyt and the English Voyages* (New York, 1928).

Parry, J. H., *The Spanish Seaborne Empire* (London, 1966). *The Discovery of South America* (London, 1979).

Pennington, L. E., 'The Amerindian in English promotional literature, 1575–1625', in K. R. Andrews, N. P. Canny and P. E. H. Hair (eds.), *The Westward Enterprise* (Liverpool, 1978).

Pomfret, J. E. and Shumway, F. M., *Founding the American Colonies, 1583–1660* (New York, 1970).

Porter, H. C., *The Inconstant Savage: England and the North American Indian, 1500–1660* (London, 1979).

'Reflections on the ethnohistory of early colonial North America', *Journal of American Studies*, 16 (1982), 243–54.

Porter, R., 'The Crispe family and the Africa trade in the seventeenth century', *Journal of African History*, 9 (1968), 57–77.

Quinn, D. B., 'Sir Thomas Smith (1513–1577) and the beginnings of English colonial theory', *Proceedings of the American Philosophical Society*, 89 (1945), 543–60.

Raleigh and the British Empire (London, 1947).

'The voyage of Etienne Bellenger to the Maritimes in 1583', *Canadian Historical Review*, 43 (1962), 328–43.

'Sailors and the sea', in Nicoll, A. (ed.), *Shakespeare in his own Age* (Cambridge, 1964).

The Elizabethans and the Irish (Ithaca, N.Y., 1966).

Richard Hakluyt, Editor (Amsterdam, 1967).

England and the Discovery of America, 1481–1620 (New York, 1974).

(ed.), *The Hakluyt Handbook* (London, 1974).

North America from the Earliest Discovery to the First Settlements: the Norse Voyages to 1612 (New York, 1978).

(ed.), *Early Maryland in a Wider World* (Detroit, 1982).

Rabb, T. K., *Enterprise and Empire* (Cambridge, Mass., 1967).

Ramsay, G. D., *The City of London in International Politics at the Accession of Elizabeth Tudor* (Manchester, 1975).

P. Ramsey, 'Overseas trade in the reign of Henry VII: the evidence of the customs accounts', *EconHR*, 2nd series, 6 (1953), 173–82.

Read, C., *Mr Secretary Walsingham and the Policy of Queen Elizabeth* (3 vols., Oxford, 1925).

Reddaway, T. F. and Ruddock, A. A., 'The accounts of John Balsall, purser of the *Trinity* of Bristol, 1480–1', *Camden Miscellany*, 23 (1969), 1–27.

Ross, E. D., *Sir Anthony Sherley and his Persian Adventure* (London, 1933).

Rowe, J. H., 'Ethnography and ethnology in the sixteenth century', *Kroeber Anthropological Society Papers*, 30 (1964).

Rowse, A. L., *Tudor Cornwall: Portrait of a Society* (London, 1941).

Ruddock, A. A., 'John Day of Bristol and the English voyages across the Atlantic before 1497', *Geographical Journal*, 132 (1966), 225–33.

'The reputation of Sebastian Cabot', *Bulletin of the Institute of Historical Research*, 47 (1974), 95–8.

Ruffman, K.-H., *Das Russlandbild im England Shakespeares* (Göttingen, 1952).

Salisbury, N., *Manitou and Providence: Indians, Europeans and the Making of New England, 1500–1643* (Oxford, 1982).

Salisbury, W., 'Early tonnage measurement in England', *Mariner's Mirror*, 52 (1966), 41–51.

Salyer, J. C., 'Algunos aspectos del tratado de paz entre Inglaterra y España del año 1604', *Simancas*, 1 (1950), 371–82.

Scammell, G. V., 'Manning the English merchant service in the sixteenth century', *Mariner's Mirror*, 56 (1970), 131–54.

The World Encompassed: the First European Maritime Empires, c. 800–1650 (London, 1981).

'European seamanship in the great age of discovery', *Mariner's Mirror*, 68 (1982), 357–76.

Scott, W. R., *The Constitution and Finance of English, Scottish and Irish Joint-Stock Companies to 1720* (3 vols., Cambridge, 1912).

Shammas, C., 'English commercial development and American colonization, 1560–1620', in K. R. Andrews, N. P. Canny, and P. E. H. Hair (eds.), *The Westward Enterprise* (Liverpool, 1978).

Sheehan, B., *Savagism and Civility: Indians and Englishmen in Colonial Virginia* (Cambridge, 1980).

Shillington, V. M. and Chapman, A. B. W., *The Commercial Relations of England and Portugal* (London, n.d.).

Shirley, J. W. (ed.), *Thomas Harriot, Renaissance Scientist* (Oxford, 1974).

Skelton, R. A., *Explorers' Maps* (London, 1958).

Skilliter, S. A., 'The Hispano-Ottoman armistice of 1581', in C. E. Bosworth (ed.), *Iran and Islam* (Edinburgh, 1971), pp. 491–515.

Sluiter, E., 'Dutch-Spanish rivalry in the Caribbean area, 1594–1609', *HAHR*, 28 (1948), 165–96.

Smith, C. F., *John Dee* (London, 1909).

Spate, O. H. K., *The Spanish Lake* (London, 1979).

Stanford, M. J. G., 'The Raleghs take to the sea', *Mariner's Mirror*, 48 (1962), 18–35.

Steensgaard, N., *The Asian Trade Revolution of the Seventeenth Century* (Chicago, 1974).

Stone, L., 'Elizabethan overseas trade', *EconHR*, 2nd series, 2 (1949), 31–58.
An Elizabethan: Sir Horatio Palavicino (Oxford, 1956).

Taylor, E. G. R., 'More light on Drake', *Mariner's Mirror*, 16 (1930), 134–51.
Tudor Geography, 1485–1583 (London, 1930).
Late Tudor and Early Stuart Geography, 1583–1650 (London, 1934).
'The voyages of Martin Frobisher', *Geographical Journal*, 91 (1938), 360–63.
'John Dee and the map of northeast Asia', *Imago Mundi*, 12 (1955), 103–6.
'A letter dated 1577 from Mercator to John Dee', *Imago Mundi*, 13 (1956), 56–68.

Thompson, I. A. A., 'The Armada and administrative reform: the Spanish council of war in the reign of Philip II', *EHR*, 82 (1967), 698–725.
'Spanish Armada guns', *Mariner's Mirror*, 61 (1975), 355–71.
War and Government in Habsburg Spain, 1560–1620 (London, 1976).

Tong, R., 'Captain Thomas Wyndham', *History Today*, 7 (1957), 221–8.

Vigneras, L. A., 'New light on the 1497 Cabot voyage to America', *HAHR*, 36 (1956), 503–9.

Wagner, H. R., *Sir Francis Drake's Voyage around the World* (San Francisco, 1926).
'A map of Sancho Gutiérrez of 1551', *Imago Mundi*, 8 (1951), 47–9.

Wake, C. H. H., 'The changing pattern of Europe's pepper and spice imports, ca. 1400–1700', *Journal of European Economic History*, 8 (1979), 361–403.

Wallis, H., 'The first English globe: a recent discovery', *Geographical Journal*, 117 (1951), 277–90.
'Further light on the Molyneux globes', *Geographical Journal*, 121 (1955), 304–11.

Waters, D. W., *The Art of Navigation in England in Elizabethan and Early Stuart Times* (London, 1958).

(ed.), *The Elizabethan Navy and the Armada of Spain* (London, 1974).

Webb, J., 'Apprenticeship in the maritime occupations at Ipswich, 1596–1651', *Mariner's Mirror*, 46 (1960), 29–34.

Wernham, R. B., 'Queen Elizabeth and the Portugal expedition of 1589', *EHR*, 66 (1951), 1–26 and 194–218.

'Elizabethan war aims and strategy', in S. T. Bindoff, J. Hurstfield and C. H. Williams (eds.), *Elizabethan Government and Society* (London, 1961).

Willan, T. S., 'Some aspects of English trade with the Levant in the sixteenth century', *EHR*, 70 (1955), 399–410.

The Muscovy Merchants of 1555 (Manchester, 1953).

The Early History of the Russia Company, 1553–1603 (Manchester, 1956).

Studies in Elizabethan Foreign Trade (Manchester, 1959).

Williams, P., 'The ownership of Drake's *Golden Hind*', *Mariner's Mirror*, 67 (1981), 185–6.

Williamson, J. A., *Maritime Enterprise, 1485–1558* (Oxford, 1913).

English Colonies in Guiana and on the Amazon, 1604–1668 (Oxford, 1923).

The Caribbee Islands under the Proprietary Patents (London, 1926).

Sir John Hawkins, the Time and the Man (Oxford, 1927).

A Short History of British Expansion. The Old Colonial Empire (3rd (revised) edition, London, 1945).

Hawkins of Plymouth (London, 1949).

Wood, A. C., *A History of the Levant Company* (Oxford, 1935).

Wright, L. B., *Middle Class Culture in Elizabethan England* (Chapel Hill, 1935).

Religion and Empire: the Alliance between Piety and Commerce in English Expansion, 1558–1625 (Chapel Hill, 1943).

C. Late Items

The following were received too late to be used in this work:

D. B. Quinn and A. M. Quinn (eds.), *The English New England Voyages, 1602–1608* (London, 1983).

D. B. Quinn and A. N. Ryan, *England's Sea Empire, 1550–1642* (London, 1983).

R. B. Wernham, *After the Armada: Elizabethan England and the Struggle for Western Europe, 1588–1595* (London, 1984).

Index

Index